英汉文体翻译教程

A Guide to English—Chinese
Translation of Stylistic Varieties

陈 新　　　　主编

陈　新　王丹阳　杨蕙娴　　编著
丁建宁　李　霞

北京大学出版社
·北京·

图书在版编目(CIP)数据

英汉文体翻译教程/陈新主编. —北京：北京大学出版社，1999.4
ISBN 978-7-301-03638-9
Ⅰ. 英… Ⅱ. 陈… Ⅲ. 英语–翻译–教材 Ⅳ. H315.9

书　　　　名：	英汉文体翻译教程
著作责任者：	陈　新　主编
责 任 编 辑：	汪晓丹
标 准 书 号：	ISBN 978-7-301-03638-9/H·0387
出 版 发 行：	北京大学出版社
地　　　　址：	北京市海淀区成府路205号　100871
网　　　　址：	http://www.pup.cn　新浪官方微博:@北京大学出版社
电　　　　话：	邮购部 62752015　发行部 62750672　编辑部 62759634　出版部 62754962
电 子 信 箱：	zpup@pup.pku.edu.cn
印　刷　者：	河北涿县鑫华书刊印刷厂
经　销　者：	新华书店
	850×1168毫米　大32开本　16.5印张　420千字
	1999年4月第1版　2020年9月第17次印刷
定　　　　价：	32.00元

未经许可，不得以任何方式复制或抄袭本书之部分或全部内容。
版权所有，侵权必究　　举报电话：010-62752024
　　　　　　　　　　　　电子信箱：fd@pup.pku.edu.cn

内容提要

本书完全不同于以往教材以词、语、句翻译为探讨对象的做法。作者从全新的角度——文体的角度,以文体为内容,以文体为对象,分别详述了应用文、新闻、广告、科技和文学这五大类文体的语言文字特点及其翻译方法,具有很强的针对性和实用性。对提高实用翻译能力大有裨益。

目 录

- 前 言 1
- 第一章 翻译绪论 1
  - 第一节 我国翻译简史 1
  - 第二节 翻译的基本原理 4
  - 第三节 翻译理论的主要流派 11
  - 第四节 翻译的方法与技巧 17
- 第二章 应用文文体的翻译 27
  - 第一节 应用文文体的特点与翻译 27
  - 第二节 信函 30
  - 第三节 电报 87
  - 第四节 便条、通知、启事、海报 91
  - 第五节 合同、协议 106
  - 第六节 规则、指南、说明 115
  - 第七节 演讲 123
- 第三章 新闻文体的翻译 142
  - 第一节 新闻文体的语言特点与翻译 142
  - 第二节 各类体裁新闻的翻译 165
- 第四章 广告文体的翻译 208
  - 第一节 广告文体的语言特点与翻译 208
  - 第二节 不同类型广告的翻译 216
- 第五章 科技文体的翻译 230
  - 第一节 科技英语的特点与翻译 230
  - 第二节 科技报道 246
  - 第三节 科技论文 261
  - 第四节 专利文献 276

第五节　科普读物……………………………………　294
　　第六节　科幻小说……………………………………　303
第六章　文学文体的翻译……………………………………　315
　　第一节　文学文体的语言特点与翻译………………　315
　　第二节　散文…………………………………………　323
　　第三节　小说…………………………………………　383
　　第四节　戏剧…………………………………………　400
　　第五节　诗歌…………………………………………　426
翻译练习参考译文……………………………………………　443

前　言

目前国内各高等院校英语专业的翻译课所使用的英汉翻译教材大都沿用传统模式,将重点放在词语和句子的翻译方法与技巧上。然而在实践中翻译者所面对的翻译材料一般均为较完整的篇章。撇开篇章而孤立地探讨词句的翻译是不科学的,因为同样的词句在不同的上下文中,由于情景、环境的不同,以及说话人或写作者的目的、意图、语气、心境等方面的差异,可以有不尽相同的意思,因而也有不同的译法。不言而喻,词句的翻译必须放在篇章的大环境中来斟酌。

决定篇章语言应用特征的首要因素是文体。不同文体的文字其语言表达的方式十分不同。例如应用文强调实用,而文学作品的语言则偏重于创造性、形象性和象征性。即便在应用文类中,信函和电报文字也差别极大,而私人信件与正式公文行文又大不相同。至于文学作品中的诗歌、散文、戏剧、小说四大体裁,又各有独自的语言特点。在翻译这些不同体裁的文字时必须牢牢把握住各种不同特点,才能使译文在内容与形式两个方面尽可能充分地达到与原文等值。

为了改进翻译教学的现状,使教学与研究和翻译实践紧密结合起来,做到有的放矢,本书将重点转移到篇章的分析与研究上,从文体的角度来探讨各类文字的不同特点与翻译方法,将词句的翻译置于篇章总的文体要求统帅之下。这种编写思路与方法是一个新的尝试。新就新在:第一,观念新,更贴近于翻译教学的实用性与实践性;第二,角度新,从篇章的角度入手,将词句的翻译结合其中;第三,体系新,按不同文体文字的分类来划分章节,分别论述;第四,内容新,涉及翻译实践中可能遇到的各类文字的翻译;第五,方法新,强调精讲多练,讲练结合,以练为主,理论联系实际。

全书共分六章：第一章为翻译绪论，简要地阐述了我国翻译史，翻译的基本原理，各种翻译理论和常用的翻译方法和技巧，使学生对翻译这一学科有一较系统全面的认识；第二章至第六章分别介绍了应用文、新闻、广告、科技、文学这五大门类的文体，论述了各类文体的语言特点和翻译方法。各章又分成若干小节，分别论述各类文体的各种不同类别。如第五章科技文字的翻译就包括了科技报道、科技论文、专利文献、科普读物、科幻小说等不同的类别。在每一类别总的论述后，都附有一、两篇典型范文及其译文，并作深入分析与评论，以帮助学生通过实例，具体掌握这一类别文字和作品的语言特征与翻译方法。每一小类中均有三至五篇英语短文翻译练习，练习的答案按章节顺序集中附于书后。由于翻译是一种再创作，同样的原文，不同的译者可能有不同的译法。其中确有对错之分，但在更多的情况下只具好差或文野之别。练习答案所提供的译文绝非唯一或模范的版本，仅供参考。文学作品的译文若引自名译者的译本，均注上名字。其余大多为本书作者所译。

本书可用作英汉翻译教材，也可供自学或爱好翻译者参考使用。由于内容涉及面较广，量较大，在使用本书时不必拘泥于每章每节的顺序，可根据学生的需要与教学的要求突出某些章节，略过某些关系不大的内容，或浅尝即止。练习亦不一定全做，可根据学生实际适当选择。

本书由王丹阳编写第一章和第六章的第三节；杨慧娴编写第二章；丁建宁编写第三和第四章；李霞编写第五章；陈新编写第六章的第一、二、四、五节。

编　者

1998.8 于金陵

第一章　翻译绪论

第一节　我国翻译简史

关于我国翻译历史的分期问题,至今尚无定论。为了清楚明了起见,现按照不同历史时期的次序,分别介绍各时期的概况。

我国古代的翻译活动主要是佛经的翻译。在东汉桓帝建和二年时(公元148年),安世高已开始较大规模地从事译经活动,到魏晋南北朝时代译经活动有了进一步的发展。我国的佛经翻译在唐代达到鼎盛,到北宋时开始走向衰落。这期间,出现了我国历史上著名的佛经三大翻译家:鸠摩罗什、真谛和玄奘。

鸠摩罗什,祖籍天竺(印度),十几岁时便因精通佛经而出名。后秦弘始三年(公元401年)罗什来长安开始译经,共译七十四部三百八十四卷。罗什译经的质量,在当时和后来都有极高的评价。梁启超曾盛赞道:"鸠摩罗什者,译界第一流宗匠也。"罗什对翻译方法及理论有深入的研究,可以说他最早提出了如何表现原文的文体与语趣的重要问题,对后世的翻译影响很大。同时,他还提倡译者署名以负文责。

真谛,西印度优禅尼人,在南北朝时(公元546年),应梁武帝之聘来到中国,译了四十九部经论,其中尤以《摄大乘论》的翻译,对中国佛教思想有较大影响。

玄奘,唐代名僧,我国古代杰出翻译家。唐太宗贞观三年(公元629年),他从长安出发去印度求经,往返十七年,行程五万里,带回梵文经典六百五十余部。他在二十年间共主持译出经论七十五部,一千三百三十五卷。他不但把佛经由梵文译成汉文,而且还把老子著作的一部分译成梵文,是第一个向国外介绍汉文著作的中国人。玄奘主持的译场,比以前要严密和健全得多,译经质量也很高。玄奘提出的"五种不翻"的翻译观在当时已很见功力。他所谓的"不翻",指的是译音不译意。这五种情况指神秘语、多义词、中国没有的物名、久已通行的音译以及宣扬佛教的用语。

当然,除了上述佛经三大翻译家外,还有其他一些翻译家也取得了令人瞩目的成就。例如,公元三世纪三国时的支廉提出翻译要"因循本旨,不加文饰";公元四世纪东晋时的道安提出了"五失本""三不易"之说,即翻译佛经在五种情况下会失去本来面目,有三件事决定了译事是很不容易的。所谓"五失本"是:①经文的词序在汉译时被改从汉语语法;②经文的译文较原文有了一定的修饰;③经文的反复论述在汉译时被删简;④经文的偈颂复述在汉译时被删去;⑤经文中联接上下文的话语在汉译时被删除。所谓"三不易"是:①译文要改古以适今,很不容易;②要把千年前古代圣哲的微言大义传达给后世的浅俗之众,很不容易;③要由平凡人来传译古代圣贤的精心之作,更是不容易。东晋高僧慧远认为翻译应"简繁理秽,以详其中"。六世纪末隋初的彦琮在《辩证论》中提出了"八备说",即一个合格的佛经翻译者必须具备八条,如要忠于佛法,立志帮人;要宽和谦虚不武断;要埋头研究道术,自甘寂寞;要博览佛教诸典,加强文学修养等等。

十七世纪西方的科学技术有了很大的发展,因此从明末清初起,我国的翻译事业已从佛教翻译转入对西方科技的译介。其中主要的代表人物有徐光启、冯桂芬、林纾、严复等。徐光启与意大利人利玛窦合作翻译了欧几里得的《几何原本》、《测量法义》等书。林纾(琴南)则对外国文艺作品的译介作出了巨大的贡献。他虽不懂任何外语,但他与人合作,一生翻译的西洋小说约有一百八十余种,共一千数百万字,是其他译者无可企及的。其主要译作有《巴黎茶花女遗事》(La Dame auc Camelias),《黑奴吁天录》(Uncle Tom's

Cabin)、《块肉余生述》(Dalid Copperfield)等。

严复(1854—1921),字又陵,又字几道,福建侯官人,是我国清末新兴资产阶级的启蒙思想家。他在戊戌变法到辛亥革命的十三年中译书十余种,著名的有《天演论》(Evolution and Ethics and Other Essays)、《原富》(Inquiry into the Nature and Cause of the Wealth of Nations)、《群学肆言》(Study of Sociology),以及《群己权界论》(On Liberty)等。他不断介绍西方资产阶级的哲学、政治著作,并发表自己的见解,堪称向西方寻找真理的先进的中国人的代表。

严复还在《天演论》卷首的《译例言》中提出了著名的"信达雅"的翻译标准。他说:"译事三难:信、达、雅。求其信,已大难矣。顾信矣不达,虽译犹不译也,则达尚焉。海通以来,象寄之才,随地多有;而任取一书,责其能与于斯二者,则已寡矣。其故在浅尝,一也;偏至,二也;辨之者少,三也。"严复对"信"和"达"的论述清楚明晰,即便是现在的译界也与之有同感。但其对"雅"的解释在今天看来是有疑问的,因为他所说的"雅"是指"汉以前字法句法",这在今天的翻译中已不能作为标准之一。但总的来说,严复作为我国翻译史上明确提出翻译标准的第一人,对译界的影响是深远的,意义是重大的。

"五四"以后,我国翻译事业的重点开始转向介绍马列主义经典著作和无产阶级文学作品。这一时期的翻译家可以从社团与流派角度来区分,而且有关译学的争论也越来越多。

这一时期的代表人物及其译作主要有:陈望道所译的我国第一个《共产党宣言》(Communist Manifesto)汉译本,李达翻译了马克思的《政治经济学批判》(Critique of Political Economy)和其他多部马列主义经典著作。鲁迅、瞿秋白等译介了俄苏文学。同时,这一时期的文学大家往往也是翻译名家,他们大多对翻译理论的发展作出了很大的贡献。例如,茅盾论述了"直译"与"神韵"的概念;朱自清论述了"译诗"的问题;郭沫若创造性地提出了翻译的"媒婆"论及"风韵译"的说法;鲁迅在三十年代发表了几乎涉及翻译问题的各个重要方面的译论;瞿秋白强调翻译必须"非常忠实",追求"精确",他还指出了"语言"和"言语"两个概念的异同之处。

这之后,我国还出现了不少杰出的翻译家,他们不断译介先进的科技知识、优秀的文艺作品以及各民族的文化,使中国不断走向世界,也使世界更加了解中国,为促进国际间的文化交流做出了重大贡献。

第二节　翻译的基本原理

一、性质

翻译是一种语言活动,而人们进行语言活动的目的是为了进行思想交流。奈达将翻译定义为:"翻译是指用接受语(receptor language)复制原语(source language)信息的最近似的自然等值,首先在意义方面,其次在文体方面。"

翻译不同于创作,它是一个再创造的过程。译者所要表达的不是自己的思想,而是原作者的思想。如果是创作,作者当然可以用自己喜欢的表达方式来表达自己的观点。但翻译则完全不同了。译者只起到一个传声筒的作用。他不能根据自己的喜好来选择观点或表现手法,内容和文体都已固定,不能作任意改动。

由于翻译牵涉到两种语言,因此译者对原语的掌握和理解程度与其对译入语的驾驭能力将决定其译文的质量。众所周知,理解和表达是翻译活动的两个重要环节,在任何一个环节上出了问题都将影响译文的质量。

二、标准

自从严复提出"信达雅"这一翻译标准以来,我国翻译界曾先后出现几种不同的翻译标准的主张。例如,有人强调翻译应讲求"通顺、易懂";有人则认为"流畅、通顺"最重要,还有人提出翻译的标准应是"准确、流畅"。

事实上,衡量一篇译文好坏的唯一尺度应该以原文本身为准,译文的通顺与否、流畅与否、易懂与否,都应取决于能否准确全面地反映原作。因此,我们的翻译标准应该只有一个,那就是忠实。

好的译文应该忠实于原文,即在尽可能保持原文语言形式的基础上努力做到译文与原文的信息等值与艺术上的等同效果。

从内容上来说,应求信息等值。

由于两种语言在思维方式和表达方式上都存在着很大的区别,因此,要在译语中找到一个与原语完全对应的词、短语或句子常常是很困难的事。以中文的"学校"一词为例,表面看似乎译为"school"就可以了,其实"school"在英语中既可指"primary school",又可指"high school",还可以指"college"或"university";再如,英语中的"cousin"一词在汉语中有多个意思,既指"堂兄弟姐妹",也指"表兄弟姐妹",甚至还可指不同辈份的亲戚。那么,到底应该用哪一个汉语词来翻译呢,这就要看上下文了。要做到信息等值,就不能只顾表面的相似,否则译文就不再是对原文忠实的反映,而是译者的随意杜撰。

有人把"lazy Susan"译为"懒惰的苏珊"(应为"转动大餐盘"),把"leave somebody cold"译为"让某人着凉"(应为"没有打动某人"),把"walk a Virginia fence"译为"走过一个维多利亚式的篱笆"(应为"摇摇晃晃地走"),把"What is done by night appears by day."译为"夜晚做的事白天就看见了。"(应为"要想人不知,除非己莫为。")所有以上这些错误译文都没有能够正确传达原文的信息,都是译者想当然的结果。可见,翻译不能只追求形式上的一致,而忽视意义上的差别。既然不能做到既使两种语言形式保持完全一致,同时又准确地再现原文的信息,那么就应该舍形式而求信息。下面是朱生豪翻译的《汉姆雷特》(Hamlet)中的一段话:

"… I have of late — but wherefore I know not — lost all my mirth, forgone all custom of exercises; and indeed it goes so heavily with my disposition that his goodly frame, the earth, seems to me a sterile promontory, this most excellent canopy, the air, look you, this brave o'erhanging firmament, this majestical root fretted with golden fire, why, it appeareth nothing to me but a foul and pestilent congregation of vapours."……我近来不知为了什么缘故,一点兴致都提不起来,什么游乐的事都懒得过问;在这一种抑郁的心境之下,仿佛负载万物的大地,这一座美好的框架,只是一个不毛的荒岬;这个覆盖众生的苍穹,这一顶壮丽的帐幕,这个点缀着金黄色的火球的庄严的屋宇,只是一大堆污浊的瘴气的集合。

　　译者在翻译这段话时,没有拘泥于原文的形式,更没有只顾追求字面的对应。译文省略了原文的两个破折号,句式简洁对称,用词准确,充分传达了原文所包含的信息,是一篇忠实的译文。

　　当然,追求信息的等值,也只能相对而言,没有绝对意义上的、完全的等值。

　　从风格上来说,还应追求同等的艺术效果。

　　一篇译文要忠实于原文,不单单是内容上的忠实,而且包括风格上的忠实。也就是说,译文应当具有与原文同等的艺术感染力,应当体现原文的写作方法与技巧。由于两种语言存在着很多差异,译者与原作者之间的思维方式、艺术修养、驾驭语言的能力等各方面也存在着一定的距离,以及两种语言所反映的文化各具有一定的民族性和地域性,这都给风格的传译带来了困难。

尽管如此，译者仍应努力揣摩原文的风格，再现原文的意境。以王佐良翻译的《温泉胜地》(A Watering Place)中的两段为例：

The Warwickshire Avon falls into the Severn here, and on the sides of both, for many miles back, there are the finest meadows that ever were seen. In looking over them, and beholding the endless flocks and herds, one wonders what can become of all the meat! 华立克厦的爱望河在此处流入色纹河，两河沿岸若干哩水草丰美，前所未见。草地上牛羊成群，沿途不断。看着这景色，这牛羊，心想这些好肉可作多少用途，不禁感到神奇。

These things are notorious; and, Sir William Scott, in his speech of 1802, in favour of the non—residence of the Clergy, expressly said, that they and their families ought to appear at Watering places, and that this was amongst the means of making them respected by their flocks! 这等丑事，尽人皆知。然而威廉·司各特爵士在1802年演讲，明白主张牧师不必定居教区，而应携眷到温泉游览，据说这样反而能得到他的教区子民的尊敬云云。

这篇《温泉胜地》的作者是被王佐良称为"未忘本的平民政治活动家"的威廉·科贝特(William Cobbett)。他的散文风格质朴，语言精练，在英国文学史上占有重要的一页。人们评价他的这篇散文"成功地将山水的美丽同时代的苦难融合在一起，既有随笔小品的情致，又有政论文的锋利……"。王的译文深得原文的写作风格，语言简洁明了，结构匀称，无斧凿痕迹，给人一气呵成之感。尤其第二段译文放得开收得拢，言语之间满含嘲讽，准确再现了原文"朴实中见雄奇"的文风。

再如卞之琳翻译的《英国人民歌》(A Song: "Men of England")中的一小节：

Sow seed — but let no tyrant reap:
Find wealth — let no imposter heap:

Weave robes — let not the idle wear;
Forge arms — in your defence to bear.

你们播种子,别人来收获;
你们找财富,别人来收罗;
你们织衣裳,别人来穿用;
你们造兵器,别人来搬弄。

这是雪莱(shelly)的一首政治抒情诗,诗的形式、音调与内容紧密结合,充分反映出诗人的革命思想。下的译文形式整齐,韵律工巧,从内容到形式都逼肖原诗,是再现原文风格的一个好例证。

三、过程

一般说来,翻译活动包括三个步骤,即理解、表达和审核。

1. 理解

理解是整个翻译活动的开始,也是最关键的一步。在这一阶段当中,译者要从各方面做好对原文的分析工作,包括分析原文的语言形式,分析原文的深层含义以及分析原文的总体风格等。译者一旦在这个步骤出现错误,那么译文必不可能做到准确无误,有时甚至会与原文大相径庭。有些人认为理解原文不是难事,大概看懂就匆匆动笔,结果译文质量低劣。从下面的具体例子中可看出理解过程中容易出现的问题。

The great streets were wall-lined mysteries to her; the vast offices, strange mazes which concerned far-off individuals of importance. She could only think of people connected with them as counting money, dressing magnificently, and riding in carriages.
在她看来,大街是些两边围着高墙的神秘的地方。宽大的写字楼是和可望而不可及的大人物有关的奇异的迷宫。她想到的那些人只是和数钱、穿着华丽和坐马车有关。

这个译文反映出译者对第二句的语法结构分析得不正确。原文中的"connected with them"是修饰"people"一词的,"them"指的是"streets"和"offices",意为"在大街和办公楼里来往和工作的人",因此第二句的译文应改为:"她觉得这里的人们只想着赚钱,穿华贵的衣服,坐着马车来来去去。"再如:

① This is a mere apology for soup.

② It seems to me what is sauce for the goose is sauce for the gander.

这两个句子都有表层含义和深层含义之分。从表面上看,似乎应分别译为(1)"这只是汤的粗劣的代用品。"(2)"我觉得煮母鹅用什么酱油,煮公鹅也要用什么酱油。"这样的译文说明译者并没有把握原文的真正含义,其实应译为:

①这实在不成其为汤。

②我认为应该一视同仁。

彻底理解原文还包括理解原文中的谚语、成语及其他具有民族特色的语言现象。例如:

①John can be relied on. He eats no fish and plays the game. 约翰为人可靠,他既忠诚又正直。

②Last night I heard him driving his pigs to market. 昨夜我听见他鼾声如雷。

③His retort was delivered with a strong note of vinegar. 他用非常不快的口气作了反驳。

2. 表达

当对原文有了一个完全彻底的理解之后,译者始可着手用地道的译入语将原文的信息准确传达出来,即翻译活动进入第二个阶段——表达阶段。

理解是表达的前提和基础,理解有误,表达必定不准确,但即使在理解完全正确的情况下,表达也不一定十分完美。译者表达得如何,不仅取决于他对原文的理解程度,而且取决于他运用译入语的熟练程度。

以下列两句为例:

①Some people say fear and caution are now a part of their daily routine. 有些人说害怕和小心现在已经成了他们日常生活的一部分。

②When Smith was drunk, he used to beat his wife and daughter; and the next morning, with a headache, he would rail at the world for its neglect of his genius, and abuse, with a good deal of cleverness, and sometimes with perfect reason, the fools, his brother painters. 史密斯喝醉之后常常打老婆和女儿;第二天就头痛,发牢骚,抱怨世人不能赏识他的才华。他用很多的聪明才智痛骂同行的画家们都是傻瓜,有时理由也很完美。

这两个译文在理解上应该说都没有什么问题,但在表达上却不尽如人意。比如第一句译文,汉语中很少说类似于"害怕已经成为日常生活的一部分了"这样的话;第二个译文的结尾部分把"With a good deal of cleverness"直接翻译为"用很多的聪明才智",也不符合中文的表达习惯。可改译为:(1)"有人说,现在总是提心吊胆地过日子。"(2)"……他痛骂同行的画家们都是傻瓜,话很尖刻,有时也很有道理。"

再以下列句子为例:

①Ruth was upsetting the other children, so I showed her the door. 露丝一直在扰乱别的孩子,我就把她撵了出去。

②Not too much can or should be read into the percentage. 这些百分比不能说明太多的问题,也不应该用它们来说明太多的问题。

③His weariness and the increasing heat determined him to

sit down in the first convenient shade. 他疲惫不堪,天气也越来越热。他于是下了决心,一碰到舒适的阴凉处就坐下休息。

④But his wife kept dinning in his ears about his idleness, his carelessness, and the ruin he was bringing on his family. 可是他妻子不断地在他耳边唠叨个没完,说他懒惰,说他粗心,并且说他的一家人都要毁在他的身上。

3. 审核

审核阶段可分三个步骤进行。第一步着重检查内容方面,包括译文有无漏译和错译现象,以及译文在字、词、句等各个语言层面上是否全部准确地传达了原文的信息。当确信译文在内容上没有问题之后,译者还应进行第二步的检查,即核查译文在总体效果上是否已做到与原文风格尽量贴近。如果原文文笔轻松幽默,而译文沉重呆板,那么它显然就不是原文的忠实反映。审核阶段的最后一步着重于译文的润色与美化工作。译者应在现有的基础上用尽可能找到的更好的表达方法来增加译文的美感,使译文的表达效果更上一层楼。

译者只有在圆满完成了以上三个阶段的任务以后,才能算是完成了翻译工作。

第三节 翻译理论的主要流派

翻译是一门艺术,同时它也是一门科学。翻译牵涉到诸多的领域,比如语言学、文艺学、符号学、逻辑学、美学、文体学等等。翻译工作者不仅要了解翻译活动本身的各个方面,而且还要掌握有关翻译活动的各种不同的理论观点。下面将着重从翻译的文艺学理论、语言学理论、美学理论及文体学理论几个方面加以介绍。

一、翻译的文艺学理论

　　一般来说,翻译的文艺学理论是与翻译的语言学理论相对而言的,前者强调翻译是一门艺术,而后者则更多地把翻译看成是一门科学。

　　翻译的文艺学派普遍认为翻译活动不是单纯的语言间的转换,语言只起到一个媒介作用,否则翻译活动很可能成为一种"技术过程",而不再是一种创作过程。他们所着重研究的是作为艺术实体的原作,是译者如何借助语言达到跨越时空的心灵契合。正像翻译家弗洛利(Florey)在其《翻译的艺术》中所说的那样:"只有演员和剧中人物双方思想感情融合时,才能演出个性、风格和精神世界。同样,只有译者和作者双方思想感情融为一体时,译文与原文才能风格一致,进入化境。"要想抓住作者的感情,透视其精神活动,如实译出原文的风貌,必须经过判断、推理、演译、归纳、抽象、升华等一系列再创作的过程,这就是翻译活动的艺术再创造。莫里逊(Morrison)在其《翻译的艺术观》中对翻译的艺术性作了精辟的论述:"翻译是艺术的高级形式。绘画必须栩栩如生,跃然纸上;音乐必须抑扬顿挫,富有旋律;雕塑必须精镂细刻,曲尽其妙。而翻译既需要绘画之真实,又需要音乐之谐律,更需要雕塑之匠心。这不是技术,而是艺术,而且是精湛的综合性艺术。"

　　翻译的文艺学派强调翻译活动中译者的主动性与创造性,这固然有其正确的一面;但与此同时我们也不能忽略语言因素在翻译过程中的重要地位。因为语言是信息的载体,译者与作者能否达到心灵的契合毕竟要取决于语言这个媒介。如果一味强调译者主观能动性,很可能会导致译文偏离原作,无法达到忠实的标准。

二、翻译的语言学理论

　　由于翻译活动是在两种语言之间进行的,因此研究翻译必定要研究语言。卡特福德在翻译的语言学理论研究方面做出过突出贡献。他把自己研究语言学的成果应用于翻译理论的研究,推动了翻译研究走上科学发展的道路。与他同时的一些著名翻译理论家也从语言学的角度对翻译理论进行了深入细致的探讨与研究,为丰富和发展翻译的语言学理论做出了卓越的贡献,如苏联的巴尔胡达罗夫,英国的纽马克,美国的奈达和法国的穆南等。

卡特福德于1965年写成了《翻译的语言学理论》(A Linguistic Theory of Translation)一书,书中将现代英国描写语言学的框架用于翻译的分析之中,指出了一条翻译理论研究的新途径。该书首先介绍了普通语言学理论,接着详细阐述了翻译的定义和基本类型、翻译等值、形式对应、意译、完全翻译、转移、翻译等值的条件、音位翻译、字形翻译、音译、词汇翻译、翻译转换、翻译中的语言变体以及可译性限度等问题。全书的中心论点是翻译的"等值"(equivalence)。作者详细论述了确立等值关系的性质和条件,以及分别从"形式"(morphological)对等和"转移"(shift)及按语言的不同层次(如音位、字形、语法、词汇)进行翻译的特点。

苏联的翻译理论家费道罗夫认为翻译理论是语言学的一个分支,任何一种形式的翻译,无论是应用文、新闻报道、科技、历史还是文学翻译都是两种语言的转换。他认为翻译与其他学科如文艺学的相关性并不能改变它作为语言学科的特点。

语言学派强调翻译是一门科学,认为翻译过程中原文的语言和译文的语言具有客观性这一事实是不容忽视的。他们十分重视翻译过程中的语言现象的研究与分析,借助于语言学、符号学、信息论等具体学科中的术语、概念、定理、实证方法和技术处理手段,从语音、语法、词汇等不同角度探寻翻译活动的普遍规律。

但语言学派的观点忽略了翻译的文艺学特点及其主观性。译者作为翻译活动的主体必然带有主观能动性,而译文与原文的总体效果是否贴近也是衡量译文质量的标准之一。因此应当倡导的是将文艺学派与语言学派的观点结合起来,建立一个既有主观因素主导,又有客观规律制约的完整的理论体系。

三、翻译的美学理论

翻译的过程也是一个审美的过程。一般说来,翻译美包括内容美、形式美、和意境美这几个方面。如果是文学翻译,还应再现原文的音韵美、结构美、修辞美等其他的美学品质。下面举例说明。

1. 内容美

请看由吕叔湘翻译的《伊坦·弗洛美》(Ethan Frome)片段:

The village lay under two feet of snow, with drifts at the windy corners. In a sky of iron the points of the Dipper hung like icicles and Orion flashed his cold fires. The moon had set, but the night was so transparent that the white housefronts between the elms looked gray against the snow. Clumps of bushes made black stains on it, and the basement windows of the church sent shafts of yellow light far across the endless undulations. 整个的乡镇埋在两尺深的雪的底下,迎风的墙角有更深的雪堆。在铁色的天空,北斗的星点像冰柱,南天的猎户星射出寒冷的光芒。月亮已经下去,但是夜色清朗,榆树中间的一所所白色的房子让积雪衬托着变成灰色,灌木丛在那上面造成一些黑的斑点。教堂的地下室的窗户送出一条条黄的灯光,远远地横在无穷的雪浪之上。

在这个译例中,原文对夜色的描写是细致入微的,译文则不仅理解正确,而且表达也顺畅传神。读者通过阅读译文,能够对原文的内容有一个全面正确的了解。

2. 形式美

But one hundred years later, we must face the tragic fact

that the Negro is still not free. One hundred years later, the life of the Negro is still sadly crippled by the manacles of segregation and the chains of discrimination. One hundred years later, the Negro lives on a lonely island of poverty in the midst of a vast ocean of material prosperity. One hundred years later, the Negro is still languishing in the corners of American society and finds himself an exile in his own land. 然而一百年后的今天,我们却不得不面对黑人依然没有自由这一可悲的事实。一百年后的今天,黑人的生活依然悲惨地套着种族隔离和歧视的枷锁。一百年后的今天,在物质富裕的汪洋大海中,黑人依然生活在贫乏的孤岛上。一百年后的今天,黑人依然在美国社会的阴暗角落里艰难挣扎,在自己的国土上受到放逐。

这是马丁·路德·金(Martin Luther King)的一段演说词。原文句子结构和谐,语言铿锵有力,具有较强的音韵美。译文忠实地再现了原文的形式美。

3. 意境美

我国宋朝诗人宋祈有一名句"红杏枝头春意闹"。一个"闹"字成为全句的点睛之笔。下面是黄宏荃的译文:

Among the apricot's sprays

spring riots in her play.

黄译用"riot"一词来体现原文的意境可谓贴切之至。透过"riot",人们不仅看到了红杏的"繁多"和"欢闹",而且感觉到春天盎然的生机。

四、翻译的文体学理论

语言是为人们交际服务的,在不同的场合人们所使用的语言的特点也各不相同。这样一来,便形成了各种类型的文体,如科技文体、广告文体、新闻文体、文学文体等等。

从六十年代开始,英国的韩礼德(Halliday)等人就从文体学角度探讨文体与翻译理论的关系及翻译教学问题。到了七十年代,欧美翻译理论研究工作者已开始深入研究文体学。这一研究对翻译工作和它的社会功能具有重大的实践意义,并为翻译理论的探讨开辟了新的途径。文体学对语域的研究以及对句与句之间、段与段之间的逻辑发展关系的探讨(也称"篇章分析"),对翻译理论与实践都具有不可忽视的意义。

不同的文体具有不同的语言特点,在词汇、句式、修辞、结构等方面都表现出很大的差异。例如,广告文体注意语言的感召力,句子比较简短,讲求凝练,大量使用省略句和祈使句,并注重修辞手法的运用;而文学文体由于涉及的题材、体裁很广,因此词汇丰富,语言形象生动,句法变化多端,风格多样。

翻译必须随文体之异,随原文风格之异而调整译文,必须保证译文和原文的文体与风格相适应。著名的美国翻译理论家布鲁姆菲尔德(Bloomfield)曾说过:"从文体学的观点来看,原文和译文在语言和体裁的风格方面必须保持一致。"翻译家欧内斯特·格兰瑟姆(Earnest Grantham)也曾明确指出:"决不能把中世纪的莎士比亚译成现代的法国荒诞派剧作家尤金·尤奈斯,也不能把现代的拉丁美洲魔幻现实主义作家阿斯图里亚斯译成古代的荷马。"

《飘》(Gone with the Wind)是一部文学作品,注重对人物形象的塑造,描写细腻生动,收放自如。译文也应当具有与原文贴近的总体效果,反映原文的文体特征。例如:

Scarlett O'Hara was not beautiful, but men seldom realized it when caught by her charm as the Tarleton twins were. In her face were too sharply blended the delicate features of her mother, a Coast aristocrat of French descent, and the heavy ones of her florid Irish father. 那郝恩嘉小姐长得并不美,可是极富于魅

力,男人见了她,往往要着迷,就像汤家那一对双胞胎兄弟似的。原来这位小姐脸上显然混杂着两种特质:一种是母亲给她的娇柔,一种是父亲给她的豪爽。因为她母亲是个法兰西血统的海滨贵族,父亲是个肤色深浓的爱尔兰人,所以遗传给她的质地难免不调和。

与文学文体不一样,科技文体主要说明社会和自然现象,揭示客观事物的发展规律,因此用词必须清楚明了,且多用专业术语。例如:

Scientists thought that regular orbits of such faint particles were pratically nonexistent. The idea has now been rejected by facts. 科学家原来以为这样微弱的粒子实际上不存在有规则的轨道。这种看法现在已被事实所否定。

综上所述,不同的文体在翻译时对语言有着不同的要求,本书正是从文体出发对各类文字的翻译作具体论述的。

第四节 翻译的方法与技巧

对于一个译者来说,掌握一定的翻译理论固然是必不可少的,然而要真正提高翻译的技能与质量,还必须讲究一些方法和技巧。本节将从以下几个方面介绍一些切实可行的翻译方法与技巧。

一、直译与意译

直译和意译作为翻译的两种不同表达方法,各有其优缺点。前者是指在尽量保持原文语言形式不变的基础上,用地道的译入语准确再现原作的内容与风格。后者则是舍形式而取内容,用贴切的译入语准确传达原作的意义,至于原文的句法手段、修辞特点、选词用字等方面已无法兼顾。例如:

①There was no possibility of taking a walk that day. We had been wandering, indeed, in the leafless shrubbery an hour in the morning; but since dinner (Mrs. Reed, when there was no company, dined early) the cold winter wind had brought with it clouds so sombre, and rain so penetrating, that further outdoor exercise was now out of the question. 那一天是没有散步的可能了。不错,早晨我们已经在无叶的丛林中漫游过一点钟了,但是午饭之后——在没有客人的时候,里德夫人是早早吃饭的——寒冷的冬风刮来这样阴沉的云,和这样侵人的雨,再做户外运动是不可能的了。

②My rest might have been blissful enough, only a sad heart broke it. It plained of its gaping wounds, its inward bleeding, its riven chords. It trembled for Mr. Rochester and his doom; it bemoaned him with bitter pity; it demanded him with ceaseless longing; and, impotent as a bird with both wings broken, it still quivered its shattered pinions in vain attempts to seek him. 我本来可以休息得十分安详自在,只是一颗悲伤的心把它给搅了。由于受到了严重的创伤,我的心在流血,在撕裂。它为罗切斯特先生,为他的厄运颤抖;怀着强烈的怜悯为他悲叹;怀着无休止的渴望要求知道他的情况。我的心,好像折断了双翅的小鸟,已经无能为力;但还在拍打着残翅,为了寻找他去作徒劳的尝试。

从以上两个译例当中,可以看出直译和意译的异同及各自的优势和劣势。例1是直译,译文在保持原文句法基本不变的情况下传达了原文的柔美的意境。由于内容正确无误,译语的表达也顺畅自然,因此直译的方法在这里的运用是成功的。而例2的译文在句法上比起原文有较大改变,并没有逐字逐句地翻译原文,而是采用了读者所能接受的汉语表达方式来传译原文的意义。

直译从内容到形式都贴近原文,自然是最好的方法,然而事实上,它在许多场合并不适用。当原文的表达形式在译语中难以再现时,我们应当求助于意译。虽然意译在表面上看似离原文远了些,但它可以保证译文内容正确，顺畅，易懂。比如，英语成语"to be born with a silver spoon in one's mouth"，若直译成"含着银勺子出生"，中国读者必不解其意。这时只有舍弃原文的修辞手法，意译为"出生于富贵人家"。

需要说明的是直译并不等于死译、硬译、照搬照抄；意译也不等于乱译、胡译、离题万里。直译和意译虽是两种不同的翻译方法，但它们所要达到的翻译标准却都是一样的，那就是译文必须在各方面尽量忠实于原文。译者应当从这一点出发，选择较好的译法。例如：

①For Kino and Juana this was the morning of mornings of their lives, comparable only to the day when the baby had been born. 在基诺和胡安娜看来，这是他们一生中最了不起的早晨，只有宝宝出生的那一天，才可以与之媲美。

②He was deprived of his liberty in a manner as unexpected as it was extraordinary. 他被剥夺了自由，其经过情形之出人意料，不亚于其情形之古怪蹊跷。"

第一句译文采用了直译的方法，保留了原文的表达方式，既忠实又传神。如果意译为"基诺和胡安娜认为，这一天非常重要。"那么译文就损失了很多的东西，效果也较原文大为逊色。而第二句话如果采用直译的方法译为"……在一种意料不到的情形如同非常的一样"，读者会感到不知所云。因此译文舍形而取义，使原文的内容得到了正确的传达。

二、几种技巧

1. 词类转换法

在翻译的过程中，经常要用到词类转换法。即原文中某些词的词性在译文中要根据上下文作相应的变化，以便使译文读起来更加顺畅，更加符合译语的表达习惯。例如，

①A glance through his office window offers a panoramic view of the Washington Monument and the Lincoln Memorial。从他的办公室窗口可以一眼看到华盛顿纪念碑和林肯纪念馆的全景。(名词转译成动词)

②"Coming!" Away she skimmed over the lawn, up the path, up the steps, across the veranda, and into the porch. "来啦!"她转身蹦着跳着地跑了,越过草地,跑上小径,跨上台阶,穿过凉台,进了门廊。(介词转译为动词)

③Yachtmen vying for the America's Cup practised their maneuvers in dead earnest. 争夺美洲杯的赛艇运动员都拼命认真地演习技巧。(形容词转译为副词)

④The poet had an ardent yearning for the supernatural. 诗人憧憬超自然的东西。(形容词转译为名词)

2. 增删法

由于两种语言的用法各有其特点,因此在翻译的过程中,原文当中的某些词、词组、甚至句子在译文当中需要省去,否则将影响译文的效果。而有些时候却相反,译文中需要增加一些原文所没有的词、词组以及句子,以便使译文在内容上更加忠实于原文,在表达上更加符合译语的习惯。例如:

①Life is indeed a tragedy at times and a comedy very often, but as a rule it is what we choose to make it. 生活有时确实是一场悲剧,但也时常是一出喜剧,一般来说,这取决于我们自己。(原文中"a comedy"之前省略了动词"is",但在译文中必须加上动词"是"。)

②The first of these is the application of the machines, products and systems of applied knowledge that scientists and technologists develop. 第一方面是使用科学家和技术专家研制的机器

和产品,以及<u>建立起来</u>的应用知识体系。

(虽然原文只用了"develop"一个动词,但由于汉语中的搭配不一样,因此在译后一短语时必须加一个不同的动词来跟相应的名词搭配。)

③University applicants who had worked at a job would receive preference <u>over those who had not</u>. 在报考大学的人中,有工作经验者优先录取。

(如果不省略"比那些没有工作经验的"一语,译文将失之简洁。)

3. 句式转换法

句式转换法是指由于两种语言各有其句式特点的缘故,译者在翻译时不可照搬原文句式,以防译文读来晦涩难懂,不自然。比如,英语多用被动句,而汉语则更强调动作的施行者;英语句子结构多具"形合"特点,而汉语句子结构则注重"意合"。因此我们在把英语译成汉语的时候,要注意使用汉语惯用的句法,从而使译文做到地道、畅达。以下列句子为例:

①Business took me to town. 我因事进城去了。

②A bit of knowledge kept me from making a big mistake when an important question was to be decided. 我因稍具知识,所以在决定重要问题的时候,还没有犯过大的错误。

这两句原文的主语分别为"business"和"a bit of knowledge",如果译文不改变其句式,直接译为"公事把我带进了城里,""一点知识使得我在决定重大问题的时候不犯错误",那么效果就很差,使人产生翻译腔很浓的感觉。再如:

①By the end of the war 800 people had been saved by the organization. 大战结束时,这个组织拯救了八百人。

②Nothing was gained by all the overcaution. 尽管已是处处小心,结果还是一无所获。

以上两个例子体现了英语常用被动句式,而汉语则多用主动句式这一特点。

另外,在翻译的过程中,英语复杂的句子结构经常被转换成简单的汉语句子结构,体现各自"形合"与"意合"的特点。例如:

①He had to stay at home because he was ill. 他病了,不得不呆在家里。

②Chilly gusts with a taste of rain in them had well nigh dispeopled the streets. 阵阵寒风,带着雨意,街上冷冷清清,几乎没有什么行人了。

翻译过程中句式的转换是很常见的现象,但这并不意味着译者可以随心所欲地改变原文的表达方式。只有当发现原文的表达方式在译文中行不通时,译者才能运用合适的惯用表达法将原文的意思准确地传达出来。

4. 正反表达法

英汉两种语言思维方式的异同决定了其表达方式各具特点。英语可能从这一角度来思考问题,而汉语则往往着眼于相反的角度。如英语说"Wet Paint",而汉语说"油漆未干";英语说"No Smoking",而汉语说"禁止吸烟"。这里有一个正反表达的问题。所谓正反表达,是指两种语言是否使用否定词或者是否带有含否定意义的词。例如:

①His illness prevented him from attending the class. 由于生病,他没能来上课。

②Suddenly he heard a sound behind him, and realized he was not alone in the garage. 他突然听见背后有声响,便立刻意识到车库里还有别人。

第一个例子的原文没有用否定词,是从正面表达的,而译文却从反面表达;第二个例子中的原文里有否定词"not",译文却正面表达。

由于汉语中往往正面表达较多,故英语如果也从正面表达,理解起来就相对容易一些,翻译时出差错的可能性也就小一些。如:

①They went there on foot instead of by bus. 他们是步行到那儿去的,没乘公共汽车。

② The war clamor of imperialism, far from showing its "strength", only indicates its weakness. 帝国主义的战争叫嚣并不表示它有"力量",相反却只表明它的虚弱。

③Both sides thought that the peace proposed was one they could accept with dignity. 双方认为他们可以不失体面地接受这一和平建议。

但是英语如果从反面表面,理解上的难度就要大一些,尤其是英语否定句的某些惯用表达法,常常成为翻译时的陷井,因此要格外小心。例如:

①He manifested a strong dislike for his father's business. 他对他父亲的行业表示强烈的厌恶。

②Such flights couldn't long escape notice. 这类飞行迟早会被人发觉的。

③A whale is no less a mammal than a horse is. 鲸和马一样都是哺乳动物。

④It is a long lane that has no turning. 路必有弯,事必有变。

⑤The examination left no doubt that he was the right person for the position. 调查结果清清楚楚显示他是这个职位的合适人选。

以上例子的译文都是从正面表达了原文从反面表达的意思。当然,这里介绍的正反表达法,并不意味着任何时候都要采用与原文不同的表达方法,而是表明两种语言各有其表达习惯,译语的表达应力求地道、自然。有时也许采用与原文不同的表达方式为好,有时则用相同的表达方法更恰当。

5. 长句拆译法

英语句式重"形合"的特点使长句的翻译产生了一定的难度。经常是一句话中使用很多的联结性词语，引出一个又一个的修饰成分，从而使句子结构变得错综复杂，给翻译带来困难。

一般情况下，翻译长句时需要采用拆译法。英语句式中叠床架屋的情况在汉语中是不行的，因此译者需要对原文作深入分析，弄清主次，为着手翻译作好准备。分析主要包括两个方面，一个是对原文进行语法结构的分析，另一个是对原文所要表达的意思加以分析。只有做好分析工作，译者才能保证自己对原文理解的正确性，否则译文势必会出现差错。

词语的组织是长句翻译的另一个重要环节。汉语的句式特点是联结性词语用得少，注重句与句之间的内在联系，译者如何选词构句、如何安排译文的语序，都将直接影响到译文的效果。例如：

I never questioned that this ambitious, intelligent woman, who had had a career before I was born and would eventually return to a career, would spend almost every lunch hour throughout my elementary school years just with me. 母亲在生我之前有过一份工作，而且以后还会再找一份工作。而我从来没有想过：像我母亲这样一个既有抱负又聪明的女人居然会在我上小学的那几年，几乎每天都只和我一起度过午餐时的每一分钟。

这一长句中的中心词"woman"前后有好几个修饰成分，如果翻译时不进行适当的拆分，而把所有的定语全部堆到中心词的前面，那么译文必将给人以沉重、累赘之感。

在翻译英语长句时，还可以用一些辅助手段来进一步表现汉语句式灵活多变的特点。例如可以在译文中增加破折号、括号，增删一些词语，改变原文的顺序等等。例如：

What seemed to concern many people as much as the squandered money and the deaths of young men for a cause in which they did not believe was the feeling that the war was doing something terrible to the fabric of society, forcing the nation and its sons to betray the very ideals upon which the country had been founded. 许多人觉得这场战争正在使社会的结构受到可怕的损害,强迫国家和它的子孙背叛构成立国基础的理想。这种情况似乎同花钱如流水、青年人为了自己并不信仰的事业白白送命一样使他们感到不安。

需要指出的是拆句法并不仅仅适用于长句的翻译,当某些修饰成分在译文中不能直接起到修饰作用时,可以把它们拆开来翻译,成为一个相对独立的单位。

6. 翻译中的一些变通手段

两种语言之间的差异决定了翻译活动的复杂性。通常情况下,仅仅依靠某种翻译方法是很难完成翻译活动的。因此在翻译过程中,经常需要采取一些必要的、切实可行的变通手段。这些手段包括解释翻译法、借译法、音译法、形译法等等。例如:

It is just like carrying coal to Newcastle. 这简直是运煤炭到纽卡索,多此一举。

译文加上了"多此一举"能更好地帮助读者理解原文的比喻。由于译语中没有原语中的某些表达方式,因此在译文中增加一些解释说明性的词语是很必要的。如:

The May-day dance, for instance, was to be discerned on the afternoon under notice, in the disguise of the club revel, or 'club-walking' as it was there called. 比如在通知里所讲的那个下午,就可以看到五朔节舞①,它以狂欢(或者本地称之为游行会)的形式出现。

①五朔节舞:英国风俗,五月一日在草地上竖起五朔柱,围柱跳舞。

加了这一注解,译者不仅向读者传达了原文的含义,也介绍了文化背景。

形译和音译的例子也有很多,如:

T-shirt	T恤衫
Cross	十字架
Coca Cola	可口可乐
shilling	先令

有时,一些特殊词语的翻译也需要使用一些变通或补偿的手段,像成语、拟声词、外来词等。英语有个成语"the sword of Damocles",若直接译为"达摩克利斯头上的剑",读者必难解其意,后面最好加注"比喻随时可能降临的危险",这样读者既了解了原文丰富的语汇,又领会了这一表达方式的确切含义。外来词的翻译可借助于解释法、音译法等手段,如:

hippy	嬉皮士
rifle	来复枪
White House	白宫
coffee	咖啡

第二章 应用文文体的翻译

第一节 应用文文体的特点与翻译方法

应用文体是一个很广泛的范畴,运用的语言也不是一成不变。不同类别的应用文,其语言的差别也十分悬殊。它们根据不同的内容与目的有不同的要求。例如,公函、书信与合同、协议所使用的语言和格式互不相同,而通知、电报、演讲等也各有其特点。因此应用文从内容到形式都很驳杂。但尽管如此,各类应用文体还是有其语言和格式上的相同点和共性的,所以应用文的翻译也有其相应的共同原则和方法。

1. 语言简练,直接了当,条理清晰

应用文的内容有很强的针对性,与实际的工作、学习、生活联系紧密,具有"实用"的特点,因此,应用文必须语言简洁,直接了当,条理清晰。例如公函,主要在记实,文体较为正式,不求虚饰,不容自由挥洒。必须使对方一目了然,不存疑问。下面举一索赔的商业函件为例:

Dear Sir,

We wish to draw your attention to the result of inspection made by CCIB Shanghai of the consignment of sulphur under Contract No. OXHJ73091 MC Shipped per s. s. "Sanming" and discharged at Shanghai:

purity: 99.81% which is 0.09% lower than 99.9% as stipulated in the contract;

acidity: 0.066% which is 0.056% higher than the contracted

0.01%;

hydrocarbon: 0.101% which is higher by 0.031% than 0.07% as stipulated in the contract.

On the strength of the Inspection Certificate No. 221003 in one original and the Freight Account enclosed herewith we file a claim against you for the following amounts:

    1. goods value on FOB basis: US$ 2046.00
    2. freight: 805.78
    3. insurance premium: 9.15
    4. inspection fee: 2720.60

    total   US$ 5,581.53

If you do not challenge the claim after your verification please credit by remittance the said total amount in compensation to our account at the Bank of China, Beijing.

                              Yours faithfully
                              (signature)

先生：

OXHJ73091 MC 合同项目下的硫磺由 SANMING 轮运卸上海，希望贵方能对中国上海进出口商品检验局检验的结果予以重视。检验发现该批货物的

    纯度：99.81%，比合同规定的 99.9% 低 0.09%；
    酸度：0.066%，比合同规定的 0.01% 高 0.056%；
    碳水化合物：0.101%，比合同规定的 0.07% 高 0.031%。

随函寄去商检证书第 221003 号正本一份和运费帐单，现向贵方提出如下索赔：

    1. FOB 货值   2046.00 美元
    2. 运费   805.78 美元

3. 保险费　　　　　　　　　　　　9.15美元
4. 商检费　　　　　　　　　　　　2720.60美元

　　总计　　　　　　　　　　　　5581.53美元
若审核无误,请将索赔款项汇付北京中国银行我公司帐户上。

　　　　　　　　　　　　　　您忠实的
　　　　　　　　　　　　　　（签名）

这是一封常见的索赔信。此函件篇幅不长,但目的明确,内容具有很强的针对性,从头至尾没有多余的客套话和无关的字句,直接了当,简洁明了,条理清晰,层次分明,充分体现了应用文语言上的第一个特点。

2. 表达准确,用词恰当,明白易懂

应用文的第二个特点就是表达准确,用词恰当,明白易懂。

下面举一封外交公文为例。外交公文表达必须明白、准确,力戒晦涩,用词也必须恰当、讲究、轻重适宜。

May 10, 1983

Your Excellency,

　　The various subjects we discussed yesterday were all matters of very great importance. To avoid possible misunderstanding in our talk, I have composed a memorandum of the subjects we covered. I beg to send it herewith to Your Excellency and to ask you to examine it and to see if there are any mistakes therein. I hope you will favour me with a reply at your earliest convenience.

　　I avail myself of this opportunity to express to you my best wishes.

(Signed, in full name)

> Charged Affaires ad.
> Interim of the Embassy
> of the U. S. A.

外交大臣阁下：

  昨日与阁下所谈各项事务都极为重要。为避免言语之间可能有误会之处，兹将所商各事拟成备忘录一份呈上。请阁下查阅其间有无错误，并希早日答复为盼。顺致
敬意

> 美利坚合众国大使馆临时代办
> （签署全名）
> 1983年5月10日

此信行文虽寥寥数语，但表达准确明了，不仅把写信者的观点和请求表达得一清二楚，而且此信的文体风格也十分正式，语言庄重，用词讲究。例如信函中的第一句话：The various subjects we discussed yesterday were all matters of very great importance."在这儿写信者不用"very important matters"，而是用"matters of very importance"来表达"极为重要的事务"。再比如：信函中作者在表达"早日答复"此意时用的是"favour me with a reply at your earliest convenience"，十分彬彬有礼，而不是口语中的"answer me as soon as possible"。从这两个例子不难看出写信者在用词上颇下功夫。也正因为用词恰当讲究，才使此函不仅内容清晰，而且文体得当。

  这是应用文语言上的共同特点，也是译文所应具备的特点。当然，应用文的种类繁多，除了共性外，每一种类还有其各自的特点。在以后的各节中将分门别类加以阐述。

第二节 信　函

  虽然现代科技一日千里，通讯手段越来越先进，信函这一古老

而普通的通讯方式,始终为人们使用着,因为信函具有精确、长久、正式的特点。信函的种类繁多,但就其内容而言,大致可分为社交信函、事务信函和商业信函三大类。

一、英语信函的特点与翻译方法

1. 英语信函的组成部分

(1)信端(Heading),即信头。即寄信人的地址和日期,写在信笺的右上角。

(2)信内地址(Inside Address),即收信人的姓名和地址,写在左上角,比右上角的日期约低两行。

(3)称呼(Salutation),即对收信人的敬称或称谓,其位置在信内地址的下两行处,并与之平头。

(4)正文(Body),即信函的内容。

(5)结束语(Complimentary Close),即写信人表示自己对收信人的一种谦称。

(6)签名(Signature),即写信人的姓名。

(7)附件(Enclosure),缩写成 Encl。

(8)再启或又及(Postscript),缩写成 P.S.,用于补叙信的正文中遗漏的话。

以上八项内容中,第一项至第六项是英语信函的主要组成部分,一般不可缺少。第七项和第八项是否需要,则视具体情况而定。

下面举一英语信函实例,以便能更清楚地展示英语信函的结构以及以上各项在信内的排列位置。

(1)信端(Heading)
Physics Department
Zhejiang University
Hangzhou, China
Sept. 20, 1980

(2)信内地址(Inside Address)
Chairman
Department of Physics and Astronomy
Northwestern University
Evanston, Illinois
U.S.A.
(3)称呼(Salutation)
Dear Chairman,
(4)正文(Body)

  I am at present applying for admission and financial aid to your Department of Physics and Astronomy. I am now a student in the Physics Department of Zhejiang University, Hangzhou, China. I expect to graduate at the end of this academic year with a speciality in low-temperature physics.

  I am interested in pursuing graduate studies in the United States toward a Ph.D. degree. It has been suggested to me that your Department has an excellent program in experimental solid and liquid state physics. Could you send me some general information about your University catalogue? Also, please send me application forms for graduate admissions as well as for financial aid.

  I am looking forward to hearing from you soon.

(5)结束语(Complimentary Close)
Sincerely yours,
(6)签名(Singnature)
Liu Dawei
(7)附件(Enclosure)
(8)又及(Postscript)

P. S. Please send all material by mail.

2. 英语信函的语言特点

不管哪一类书信,语言的明了、简洁、准确乃是首要的要求。明了(Clearness)指的是一封信一般着重说明一两件事,段落分明,层次清楚,主题突出,使对方一目了然。简洁(Conciseness)指言简意赅,避免陈词滥调,必要的事项皆说清楚,不提无关之事。准确(Correctness)主要指语言准确达意,语法正确,避免使用过多的修饰词。此外,还应注意礼貌(Courtesy)。书信语言应文雅有礼貌,掌握分寸,不亢不卑,既不迎合恭维,也不吹嘘浮夸。

这四个特点可以归结为 Four Cs 原则。此乃一般英语信函语言的共同特点。此外,还可以再补充三个 Cs,即:个性(Character)、完整性(Completeness)和坦诚性(Candor)。这三个特点对于一些信函的内容表达,也十分必要的。譬如对于推销信函(Sales letter),个性(Character)就很重要,因为只有使自己的宣传性信件充满特色,与众不同,才能吸引客户。磋商信(Negotiation Letter)则应特别注意坦诚(Candor),这才能使磋商有良好的开端并获得期望的结果。完整性(Completeness)对于陈述式的书信(Letter of Representation)来说则是必不可少的。

3. 英语信函的翻译

鉴于英语信函格式和语言上的特点,翻译时也需有相应的要求。一般也有四个方面,或称 ABCD 四字诀。

(1)A 代表准确(Accuracy)

信函以结构固定,语言简洁,表达清楚,通俗易懂为其主要特征。译文也同样要准确体现这些特征。譬如:翻译留学申请信时,要准确地译出申请者姓名、入学时间、学习科目、经济担保等。

(2)B 代表简洁(Brevity)

翻译英文信件时,还要注意语言的简洁。以下面短信为例:

Dear Frank,

  I repeatedly tried to telephone you yesterday, but your line was busy all the time and I was unable to make contact with you, and therefore, I am writing this letter, to which I wish you would give me a prompt reply.

Love
Maria

若将此信译成:
  亲爱的福兰克:
  昨日尽管我曾一直不断地尝试着给你打电话,然而你的电话线路始终是很忙,所以我没有能够和你联系得上。我现在写这封信给你,希望你能立即给我一个及时的答复。

爱你的
玛丽亚

  虽然译文把原信件的意思一丝不苟地表达出来了,但语言不够简洁,给人造成一种啰啰嗦嗦、拖泥带水的感觉。可改译为:
  亲爱的福兰克:
  昨日我一再试拨电话给你,而电话始终占线,无法和你取得联络。故写此信,望你能立刻给我答复。

爱你的
玛丽亚

  这样的译文简洁明快得多,读上去流畅通顺,一目了然。
  (3)C 代表清楚(Clarity)
  翻译英语书信除了要做到达意准确、语言简洁外,还要注意表达清楚,用词要简易,忌用大词或生僻词。若用词不当的话,会造成表达上的晦涩与不清楚,使人难以理解。例如:

July 7, 1995

My dear Dorothy,

Congratulations upon the birth of your daughter. May the good fairies shower upon her the gifts of goodness, wisdom, and beauty.

Very sincerely yours
Charlotte Trent

若将此信译成：

亲爱的多萝茜：

敬贺你弄瓦之喜。愿天使赐与她善良，聪明和美丽的福祉。

忠诚于你的
夏洛蒂·特伦特
1995年7月7日

译文虽十分简练，但出现了"弄瓦之喜"、"福祉"这类古旧而生僻的词，结果反而弄巧成拙，使一般人难解其意。可改译为：

亲爱的多萝茜：

恭贺你喜得千金。祝她善良、聪明、美丽。

夏洛蒂·特伦特敬贺
1995年7月7日

同时还需注意要尽量使用短句，若原文句子太长，可分成几个短句来译。例如：

Dear Mr. Li,

We very much regret that because of long standing arangements it will not be possible for me to attend, but we do appreciate the opportunity to have met the visiting study group, and sincerely hope that their stay in this country has been both pleasant and profitable.

Yours faithfully
Bob Adams

李先生：

由于早已有了别的安排，恕本人届时不能参加，不胜抱歉之至。有幸会见来访小组的成员，感到十分高兴。衷心希望他们在我国的逗留既愉快，又有所裨益。此致

敬礼！

你忠实的
鲍勃·亚当斯

Dear Mr. Wang,

I acknowledge receipt of your invitation for the 15th November and regret to inform you that I shall be unable to attend due to a projected trip to Australia and the Far East.

Yours sincerely
Alden Ade

王先生：

参加十一月十五日活动的邀请已经收到。由于我已预定前往澳大利亚和远东地区一行，恕届时不能前往，谨表歉意。此致

敬礼！

你诚挚的
奥尔登·艾德

以上两封原信中都只含一个长句。译文却有意识地把长句分成二至三个短句，这样不仅清楚，易懂，也更符合汉语的表达习惯。

(4) D 代表不同点(Difference)

英语正式信函的信头均写上地址，次序为从小到大：门牌，街道，城市，州或省，国家；而中文信函一般没有信端和信内地址。若要告诉对方写信人的地址的话，一般附在信的正文后，或在信笺底部注上。次序为由大至小：国家，州或省，城市，街道，门牌。英语信函中日期通常写在信右上角，次序一般为月、日、年，或日、月、年，而中国人习惯把日期写在信结尾处署名的下端，次序为年、月、日。

翻译时要注意各自的习惯,在格式上作必要的调整。

除了上述四点外,还要注意英汉书信的不同文体。一般可分为正式文体(formal style)、非正式文体(informal style)和介于两者之间的半正式文体(semi-formal style)这三种。私人之间的信件多数属于非正式文体,语言通俗,口语化,很少用大词,读起来轻松活泼,翻译时,也应用通俗的口语。而推荐信则属比较正规的文体,用词讲究,行文端庄,句子较长,结构严谨,翻译时相应地也使用书面语,词句规范,这样才能体现彬彬有礼的正式文体的特色。值得注意的是,千万不要在同一篇译文中混杂不同的文体特征,否则就会显得不伦不类,读起来令人啼笑皆非。

二、社交信函(Social Letters)

社交信函亦称礼节性书信。

社交信函包括的范围很广,按内容与功能来分,有祝贺、慰问、感谢、介绍、吊唁、邀请、道歉、询问和通知等等。

社交信函在英文书信中所占比例较大,使用人数较多,应用范围较广。每一封社交书信都有一个特定而明确的目的。此类书信一般都开门见山,中肯切题,不涉及与该目的无关之事。在翻译英语社交书信时,行文要审慎,遣词造句应真挚恳切,并根据不同类型书信的各自风格,采用灵活多样的翻译方法,使译文在语言和风格上尽可能地忠实于原信。此外还需遵循其应有的格式。

1. 邀请信

在社交书信中,邀请信或请柬是比较重要的一种,一般有正式和非正式两种。正式请柬格式严谨,有固定程式,用第三人称书写;非正式邀请信格式要求不如请柬那么严格,用第一人称书写,称呼也较自由。

Mr. and Mrs. Charles Robert Oldname

request the honour of your presence

at the marriage of their daughter
Pauline Marie
to
Mr. John Frederick Hamilton
Saturday, the twenty-ninth of April
at four o'clock
church of the Heavenly Rest
New York

兹定于四月廿九日(星期六)下午四时在纽约天安教堂为小女玻琳·玛丽与约翰·弗雷德里克·汉密尔顿先生举行婚礼,恭请光临。

查尔斯·罗伯特·奥德内姆夫妇谨订

这是一张正式的英文结婚请贴,格式采用固定的分行式。在内容安排上按照邀请者──▶被邀请者──▶邀请之意──▶活动内容──▶时间──▶地点这样的先后顺序。汉语的顺序是活动时间、地点,活动内容,然后再表达邀请之意,最后才出现邀请者的姓名,邀请者的姓名应写在右下角,与正文分开。无论是英语请柬还是汉语请柬,在语言上的要求是一致的,都需简洁明了,措词庄重,文雅。比如:原柬中表达邀请之意用的是"Request the honour of your presence",翻译时用"恭请光临"与之对应。此外,译文的开头用了"兹定于",结尾处用"谨订",这样的用词都充分体现了请柬正规文体的风格。但有两点不同:第一,英文请柬从头至尾都采用第三人称,译成中文时,一般应改用第一人称。如:"the marriage of their daughter"译成"为小女"。第二,英文请柬中星期应写在日期之前;译成汉语时,星期则需写在日期后面的括号内。

Mr and Mrs Roger Clark present their compliments to Mr and Mrs Peter Kenway and request the pleasure of their company at dinner on Saturday evening, August the tenth, at seven o'clock, 45 The Maple Street.

罗杰·克拉克先生和夫人谨订于八月十日(星期六)晚七时在枫树街四十五号设宴,敬请彼得·肯威先生和夫人光临为盼。

此译文和例1的译文相比,在格式上稍有不同,它把邀请者的名字按原文次序仍旧置于开头处,这虽然和汉语的习惯有所出入,但更忠实于原柬,这种形式也是可取的。

除了正式的请柬外,还有一类非正式的邀请信,例如:

Dear Ruth:

Next Friday, September the fifth, is Tom's birthday and I thought it would be pleasant to have some of his friends here to help him celebrate. Will you and Bill come? We'll have dancing from nine until midnight, and then cut the birthday cake!

Tom and I are both very eager to have you here, so don't disappoint us!

Affectionately yours,
Maria

亲爱的露丝,

下周五(9月5日)是汤姆的生日。我想邀请他的几位朋友来庆祝一番。你和比尔能来吗?我们从晚上九点钟开始跳舞,直到午夜,然后切生日蛋糕。

我和汤姆希望你能来,千万别让我们失望呀!

爱你的
玛丽亚

在翻译此类非正式邀请信时,最值得注意的不是格式问题,而是措词问题。此类信件通常是写给亲朋好友的,所用的语言往往不很正式,非常口语化,在翻译时就要体现这一大特点。比如在表达邀请之意时,原文"Will you and Bill come?""Tom and I are both very eager to have you here, so don't disappoint us!"在翻译时就不能再用"敬请光临"这类文绉绉的客套语了,而是译成"你和比尔会来吗?""我和汤姆希望你能来,千万别让我们失望呀!"这种非常亲切自然的口语化句子来体现相互间的亲密关系。

附：练习

将下列邀请信译成中文。

①   Mr. and Mrs. Thomas Matthew Benton
at home
Friday, June the eighth
from four until six o'clock
250 Park Avenue

Cocktails

②   Mr and Mrs Alfred Kent
request the pleasure of your company
at the marriage of their daughter
Jane
to
Mr John Atwater
on Monday, the tenth of June
at five o'clock
14 William Street
New York

③   Dr. and Mrs. Thomas Matthew Benton
request the pleasure of your company
at a small dance
Thursday, the eighth of November
at ten o'clock
The Savoy Plaza

Please reply to

250 Park Avenue

④

Dear Julie,

　　I learn from today's paper that an exhibition of fine arts will be opened in the Park on the 10th this month, and that there are many excellent pictures on show. Besides I hear the peonies in the park are now at their best. I intend to take a walk there to have a look at them next Sunday, should the weather be fine.

　　To have a brief respite from work in this lovely season, please join me if you have not yet promised to go elsewhere that day.

　　What do you say about going to see them with me next Sunday? Shall we meet at the entrance of the Park at 10 a.m.?

　　　　　　　　　　　　　　　　　　With love,
　　　　　　　　　　　　　　　　　　　Anita

⑤

Dear Mrs. Harris,

　　Frank Peters and I are to be married at my home on Tuesday, October the fourth, at eight o'clock in the evening.

　　Frank has been so long and so happily associated with Mr. Harris, that the wedding just wouldn't be complete without him! We hope you can both come, and that you will stay on for the small reception following the ceremony.

　　　　　　　　　　　　　　　　　　Sincerely yours
　　　　　　　　　　　　　　　　　　Catherine Miller

⑥

Dear Jack,

　　Haven't seen you for a long time. How have you been? I am

missing you all the time. As the weather is splendid now, Alice, Bob and myself plan to have an outing in the suburban countryside. Zhang Ping suggests that we all go by bike. Each of us may take something for the picnic, which we will have at the hillside. The countryside must be very lovely, with grass and trees growing flourishingly, flowers in full bloom and the earth covered with green plants and bright sunshine. We can enjoy the scenery to our hearts' content. We hope that you will take along your new camera so that we can have some pictures taken of nature and ourselves in memory of this occasion. Is it possible for us to meet at the ferry service at 7 a.m.? I am sure we will have a good time. Do come and join us.

Yours always,
Bill

2. 祝贺信

根据英美人的习俗,当收到自己的朋友结婚、添子、毕业、晋升、过生日、过新年、事业成功和创造发明等喜讯时,应当写信表示祝贺。信中主要应表示出为对方的喜事而高兴的心情。因此,翻译此类信时,用词要亲切,热情,字里行间充满美好而真诚的祝贺,但切勿过分夸张,言过其实。

Dear Mr Harper,

I have learned with delight that you and your wife are the proud parents of a new baby boy. My hearty congratulations! You must be overjoyed at having become a father.

Kindly let me know when I may come over to see the mother and baby.

I wish you both all possible joy and happiness with your

son.

Yours most sincerely,
Nellie Martin

亲爱的哈普先生：

我高兴地获悉你们夫妇新生一子，你们定会为此感到自豪。我向你表示衷心的祝贺！你一定会为自己做了父亲而极感愉快。请告诉我，什么时候可以前去看望你的夫人和小宝贝。

祝愿你们俩和爱子快乐、幸福。

你最真诚的
内莉叶·马丁

这是一封写给好友得子的贺信，属于非正式文体。在表达其高兴的心情和良好祝愿时，写信者用了"learn with delight"，"hearty congratulations!"，"Wish you both all possible joy and happiness with your son."这样一些普通的词句。翻译时，也采用了与之相对应的语言，如，"高兴地获悉"，"衷心的祝贺"，"祝愿你们俩和爱子快乐，幸福"等。原文"I have learned with delight that you and your wife are the proud parents of a new baby boy."是一个典型的英语宾语从句，若按原句的语序译成"我高兴地获悉你们夫妇已成为一个新生孩子的骄傲的父母了"不符合汉语的表达习惯。译者把这个句子分成两个单句来译，这样表达更为准确、通顺。再比如："Kindly let me know when I may come over to see the mother and baby."句中"kindly"一词原意为"好心地，仁慈地"，但在此句中若按字面意思直译成"好心地让我知道"，显然词不达意。改译成"请告诉我"，用了"请"字就将写信者既想去看望母子，又不想给朋友添麻烦的心意清楚地表达出来了。另外，最后一句中的"all possible joy and happiness"，译者有意将"all possible"这两个词在译文中省略了，这种省略使译文更简洁明了。

Dear Dr. Harmon,

  From today's paper I have learned with much delight that you were recently appointed editor-in-chief of *the Morning Post*. I would like to add my congratulations to the many you must be receiving on your promotions.

  Your speedy advancement at such a young age is quite rare. This is surely owing to your untiring industry, coupled with your extraordinary ability.

  With your qualifications and unyielding will, the position will surely prove to be a pleasant one. *The Morning Post* at last has an editor-in-chief who can make it the dominant, outstanding daily of the country.

  With my best wishes for your further success.

Cordially yours,
Bert Fellows

亲爱的哈蒙博士：

  从今天的报纸上，我非常高兴地获悉，你最近被任命为《晨报》的主编。你这次晋升想必收到许多贺信，而我还是要给你添上一封，以表贺意。

  你年纪很轻就迅速得到晋升，是极其难得的。这肯定是由于你工作勤奋、坚持不懈、才能非凡的缘故。

  凭你的坚强意志和所具备的种种好条件，你对这一职务肯定会愉快胜任的。《晨报》终于有了一位能使该报成为风靡全国的出色日报的主编。

  衷心地预祝你取得更大的成就。

您真诚的
伯特·费罗斯

  这是一封祝贺朋友或同事晋升的信，此信的行文比第一封信要正规。信中使用了祝贺的套语,如:"I would like to add my congratulations to the many you must be receiving on your promotions","With my best wishes for your further success"等,翻译时用词也要庄重、正式,这样才能和原文的文体相符。又如:在翻译"This is surely owing to your untiring industry, coupled with your extraordinary ability."这句话时,译者用了"工作勤奋、坚持不懈、才能非凡"的四字结构,以体现原信端庄典雅的语言风格。

附:练习

将下列贺信译成中文。

①
Dear Mrs Taylor,

  We hear that your son Paul has graduated from the notable M. I. T. with honors. You must be quite happy with his splendid accomplishment. He is doubtlessly a pride of your family.

  We are very happy for you and wish to extend to you our utmost congratulations. I believe that the knowledge he has acquired will enable him to be successful in whatever calling in life he may enter.

  With best wishes for his success and happiness.

Sincerely yours,
Myra T. Clark

②
Dear Anne and Jerry,

  A merry Christmas and a happy New Year to you! Allow me to offer you Season's Greetings on the advent of what will surely be a bright and prosperous New Year. I trust that you and your family are enjoying this holiday season in excellent health.

My family, who are well and happy, join me in my good wishes. May every year unite our hearts more closely.

Yours very sincerely,
Barbara

③
My Dear Carter,

What big news! You are going to be married to Miss Greenwood next Saturday. Let me offer you my warmest congratulations on the happy occasion.

Tom and I send you both our love and best wishes for every happiness that life can bring. As a small token of our good wishes, we take pleasure in sending you a small present. It will arrive separately.

May lasting happiness and joy be yours forever.

Yours sincerely,
Myra Phillips

3. 感谢信

感谢信是社交书信中极常见的一种,翻译时措词要热情真诚,语气应恭谦有礼。

Dear Laura,

I was truly enraptured beyond expression to receive your flowers which turned our living room into a garden. How considerate and wonderful of you to remember my birthday. You just couldn't have selected anything I'd have liked more ! You have a positive genius for selecting the right gift!

The four years I spent with you at the college have been the pleasantest period in my life. I will cherish this memory forever.

How nice it would be to see you again.

You have been more than kind, and I won't ever forget it. My love and deepest gratitude, now and always!

        Sincerely yours,
         Jane

亲爱的劳拉:

  你送给我的鲜花使我的欣喜之心真是难以言表。这些鲜花把我们的起居室点缀得如同花园一般。承蒙你如此关注,记住了我的生日。你所选择的礼物是我最喜爱的了。你真有眼力,选择了这样恰当的礼物。

  我们在大学同学四年,那是我一生中最快活的时光。我将永远珍视这一美好的记忆。我们如能再次相见将该多好啊!

  你一向对我格外好,我也决不忘怀。永远祝福你,并致深切谢意。

         你真诚的
          简

  这是一封感谢老同学赠送鲜花的信件。译文体现了原信措词热情诚恳、行文活泼流畅的特征,对有些句子的翻译,译者处理得十分得当。比如:第一句"I was truly enraptured beyond expression to receive your flowers which turned our living room into a garden."这句中有一个由"Which"引导的定语从句。译者把原句分成两个句子来译,译成"你送给我的鲜花使我的欣喜之情真是难以言表。这些鲜花把我们的起居室点缀得如同花园一般。"这样的译法既达意准确,又轻重得当。再如:"You just couldn't have selected anything I'd have liked more!"这是一个否定形式的比较级的句型。译者采用了意译的方法,把它译成"你所选择的礼物是我最喜爱的了。"用最高级来代替比较级不仅准确表达了原意,也符合中国人的思维方式和语言习惯。

Dear Dan and Laura,

　　Jim and I want to thank you for the beautiful salad bowl set. We're looking forward to getting lots of use out of your thoughtful and practical wedding gift.

　　We're having fun getting organized in our little apartment. Soon we'll be ready for company, and we'll be giving you a call. After all the times you've had us over for dinner, we'll get to play host for a change.

　　Thanks again for the lovely gift.

Fondly,
Minnie

亲爱的唐和劳拉：

　　我和吉姆非常感谢你们送的这一套漂亮的色拉盘。你们送的结婚礼物既周到又实惠，会有很多用处的。

　　我们正在高兴地布置我们的小天地，很快就可以接待朋友了，到时会给你们打电话的。一直是你们请我们吃饭，现在该轮到我们做东道主了。

　　再次感谢你们送的好礼物。

爱你的
明妮

　　这是一封亲密朋友之间的信函，行文自由、活泼。译文所用的轻快的、口语化的语言，体现了这封感谢信原文的特点。

附：练习

　　将下列感谢信译成中文。

①
Dear Muriel,

　　You are incredible. The set of bath towels you personally

monogrammed for us is beautiful. Thank you very much for this precious gift. Hand-made presents are always special because they are created with time, talent, and more than anything else-love.

Ted was thrilled to finally see something with "HIS" name on it. He said to be sure to say thanks from him, too.

With love,
Laura

②

Dear Mr Peterson,

I was thrilled and excited when I received the book "Modern English" you sent me. It's indeed an invaluable book and a real help to the study of the English language. What a precious book! Thank you ever so much for your generosity and thoughtfulness.

Many of my colleagues have constantly mentioned its merits and I should say that it is the only book of its kind which suggests to the Chinese students ways to read, write and speak English to their great benefit. It is, in fact, a key to the mastery of idiomatic English.

I repeat my thanks, in which my wife joins me.

Sincerely yours,
Anthony Stewart

③

My Dear Anne,

Yesterday afternoon I arrived home safely and well I'm now writing these few lines to express my sincere thanks, not only to yourself but to your mamma and papa for the hospitality and kindness shown me. I shall ever remember the visit I have just paid you as one of the most pleasant weeks in my life.

I am afraid that my stay there has given you a great deal of trouble, but I know your kind parents will forgive me for being a burden upon them.

My father and mother deeply appreciate your courtesy and we hope to have the opportunity of reciprocating when you come to see me.

With many thanks to you for entertaining me so generously and please give my kind regards to your parents.

Yours truly,
Carol

4. 慰问信和吊唁信

在社交信中,此类信函属于比较难写的一种。翻译此类信函自然也非易事。既需表示悲伤同情,语气又不宜低沉灰暗,而应给收信人以勇气和慰藉。因此,用词要含蓄、慎重、恰当。

Dear Mrs. Cordin:

I was sorry to learn of your illness. You must hurry and get well! Everybody in the neighborhood misses you and we're all hoping you'll be back soon.

Mr. Burke joins me in sending best wishes for your speedy recovery.

Sincerely yours,
Barbara Aveling

亲爱的卡迪夫人:

得悉你身体欠佳,我非常难过。你一定会很快好起来的!邻居们都很想念你,盼望你早日康复出院。

我和布克先生都祝你尽快恢复健康。

您真诚的
芭芭拉·艾夫林

此封慰问信的译文体现了用词得体的特点。例如：第一句话中的"your illness"不直译成"你生病了"，而译成"身体欠佳"，这样显得更为含蓄。此外，将两个祝愿康复的词组"hurry and get well"和"speed recovery"分别译成"很快好起来"和"尽快恢复健康"，这就和原文一样避免了语言的重复和单调。

Dear Gloria,

I am most grieved to hear the news of the passing away of your beloved husband. Heartfelt sympathy and much love to you, dear friend, as you go through this time of grief.

Stan was one of those extraordinary people who will never be forgotten. His life was like a sunbeam that lit up the world around him. Now we can bask in the rainbow of the memories that we'll nurture in the years ahead.

No, it won't be the same without him by any means, but we will go on as best as we can and look forward to the day we will meet again in eternity.

Love,
Bonnie

亲爱的格劳莉亚：

获悉你深爱的丈夫去世的消息，我万分难过。在你历经悲痛的时刻，亲爱的朋友，请接受我深切的慰问。

斯坦是个了不起的人，我们永远不会忘记他。他的一生就像一束阳光，照亮了他周围的世界。在未来岁月里，让我们在记忆的彩虹里永远珍藏着对他的怀念。

确实，没有他生活无论如何都不再会是原样，但我们一定要尽可能努力地生活下去,并期望在天国有重逢的一天。

邦尼

此封吊唁信较上一封正式,充满感情,用美好的词汇表达了对逝者的赞扬与思念。有些地方用词含蓄,如文中提到死亡一词时,不用"death"而用"passing away",译文也体现了这一特色,译成"去世"。整篇译文较好地体现了原文的风格,用词美而不浮,充满真挚的情感。

附:练习

将下列慰问信译成中文。

①
Dear Mr Thompson,

I just can't tell you how sorry I was to learn of the fire which broke out in your neighbourhood and destroyed your beautiful house. What a misfortune! How frightful it was and how distressed you and your family must be! I hasten to offer my sympathy. I hope you all managed to escape without injury.

If the sender can be of service in any way, you have only to employ him. I hope to hear of your safety and to see you soon.

Sincerely yours,
Roger Whitney

②
Dear Tom,

We were shocked and saddened beyond words by news of the car crash. But we were grateful, too, that your injuries were not too serious.

Your family tells us that you are progressing nicely, and that you'll be out of the hospital in about ten days. We are certainly relieved to know that!

We are sending some books we think you'll enjoy. I hope to hear very soon that you are well.

Faithfully yours,
Bob

③

Dear Bill,

I certainly was sorry to hear that you had to go to the hospital. The only good thing about it is that you picked a hospital near us so that we can drop in to see you during the noon hour. While you're away from the office we will send your salary to Mrs. Jackson. If there is anything you want and don't let us know about it, you will be fired on the spot. Take warning.

All my best wishes.

Sincerely,
Anselm

④

Dear Bob and Julie,

Words seem so useless at a time like this, but I had to let you know how much I care and how much I hurt with you.

Mike was the kind of son any parent would be proud of. His self-confidence and charming way were evidence of the fact that he was very much loved at home.

Be sure of my availability and eagerness to help in any way I can. Call on me, please.

Sincerely,
Dexter

⑤
Dear Jerry,

The news of Evelyn's death came as a shock. There isn't much one can say to ease your sense of loss, but I want you to know my thoughts are with you in this time of sorrow.

When Alice died four years ago, I felt the bottom had dropped out of my world, too. But there's nowhere to go but up from the depths of despair, and little by little, you'll find that time begins to heal your grief.

Please accept my deepest sympathy.

Your friend,
Dean

⑥
Dear Edward,

The painful news of the passing away of your beloved father reached us this morning, and we were so shocked that we could not at first believe it.

How great the sorrow of your family must be and I know of no words to console you in this sad hour. I wish to offer my sincerest condolences upon this sad event. I'll call on you immediately in person to pay the last mark of respect to the spirit of the deceased.

My wife joins with me in sending our kindest condolences and sympathy.

Yours sincerely,
Conrad Ellis

5. 道歉信

翻译道歉信时要注意用词的谦恭和诚恳。

Dear Mr. Harkness,

　　Much to my regret I was unable to keep my engagement to meet you at the park gate. I fear you are displeased at my failing to keep my promise, but I trust you will forgive me. Let me explain. My mother suddenly fell sick early yesterday morning, and I had to send her to hospital.

　　I shall be obliged if you will kindly write and tell me when and where we may meet again. I hope to see you soon.

Yours sincerely
Evelyn McCormack

亲爱的哈克尼斯先生

　　非常抱歉我未能践约去公园门口与你相会。我怕我的失约令你不快，但相信你会原谅我的。让我来解释一下。昨天清晨，由于我母亲突然患病，我只好送她去医院。

　　如蒙来信告诉我下次见面的时间、地点，我将不胜感激。希望很快见到你。

您的真诚的
伊夫琳·麦科马克

Dear Mr Russell,

　　I am excessively sorry to say that I am just now using the dictionary you mentioned in my teaching work. So I can't lend you this copy. And I tried to buy you another copy of the dictionary from the bookshop but failed to get it. Therefore it's not in my power to comply with your request.

　　Hoping you may be successful in some other quarter and with feelings of deep regret at my inability to render you a service.

     I remain

       Yours ever,

       Duncan Livesey

亲爱的拉塞尔先生：

  非常抱歉，我在教学中正在使用你提及的那本词典，故不能借给你。我曾到书店去想另买一本给你，但未能买到。因此，我力不从心，未能满足你的要求。

  希望你能从别的什么地方借到这本词典。我为未能帮你的忙，深感歉疚。

       你永远的

       邓肯·利文瑟

  从这两篇译文中，不难看出译好道歉信的关键在于措词要朴实委婉，语气要诚恳真挚，解释要详细明了。例如原文中"much to my regret"、"I'm excessively sorry"、"feelings of deep regret"皆为致歉之词，分别译为"十分抱歉"、"抱歉之至"和"深感歉疚"，这就恰如其分地表达了写信人的真诚歉意！

附：练习

将下列道歉信译成中文。

①

Dear Mr Wood,

  Pardon me for my long delay in replying to your kind letter of the 20th last month. The reason for my delay was that I was out of town about a month on an urgent business tour when your letter arrived. It had been lying on my desk during my absence. Now the first thing I hasten to do is to write you these few lines, to express my deep regret.

Next week, I'll call on you and we'll discuss our academic thesis which you mentioned in your letter.

With kind regards,

Yours truly,
Edward David

②

Dear Mrs Benton,

Please excuse me for my brief delay in returning your book, which I read through with great interest. I had finished reading it and was about to return it, when an intimate of mine came to see me. He was so interested in the nature of the book that he begged me to allow him to read it. So I ventured to keep it from you longer than I promised.

I trust you will overlook my negligence. We both are grateful to you and are ready to return the favour,

Faithfully yours,
Marta Lang

③

Dear Joan,

Let's not let a little misunderstanding come between us. I was sure you had said you would pick up a gift for Holly, and you thought that I was taking care of it. When we both arrived at the bridal shower separately, each without the present, it was embarrassing for both of us.

I'm sorry I didn't check with you before the shower. Holly was very understanding, but I'm eager to get her a gift soon. I suggest we each get our own gift this time so there won't be any more confusion.

Sincerely,
Kitty

三、事务信函

事务信函包括私人事务信函和公务信函两种。

不管私人事务信函还是公务信函大都按固定程式行文,使用套语,讲求规范。语言正式简洁,用词准确庄重,表达婉转含蓄,避免空泛,讲求实效。鉴于事务信函的这些特征,翻译时要注意以下要点:第一,译文不求虚饰,但求简明、严谨、准确,特别是事实细节(如:日期、数字、代号等等)。第二,尽量保留英语正式书信程式,不必套用我国传统格式。第三,掌握分寸,体现原文文体,尽力保持"公事公办"的慎重态度。第四,酌情使用一些常用文言词语,如:收悉、承蒙、乞谅、为盼、赐复等。

1. 私人事务信函
(1)索要信与申请信

Post Office Box 2418
Department of Mechanical
Engineering
Nanjing University
Nanjing, China
4 Aug, 1996

The Registrar of Admission
The Graduate School
The Pennsylvania State University
University Park, Pennsylvania 16802
U.S.A

Dear Sir

  Having graduated from the Department of Mechanical Engineering at Nanjing University in June, 1996, I am deeply interested in your graduate school in the Department of Mechanical Engineering. I would now like to apply for admission and a tuition scholarship at your university for the spring semester of 1997. I would appreciate your sending me catalog and application forms.

  As soon as I receive your letter, I shall forward you all my supporting documents. I am looking forward to your response at your earliest convenience.

Respectfully yours
Huang Peng
2418 信箱
机械工程系
南京大学
南京,中国
1996年8月4日

招生办公室
研究生院
宾夕法尼亚州立大学
大学公园,宾夕法尼亚16802
美国

亲爱的先生：

  我于1996年6月毕业于南京大学机械工程系,久慕贵校研究生院机械工程系之大名,现拟申请贵校1997年春季入学许可及奖学金,如蒙惠寄有关的简章和申请表,则不胜感谢。

收到贵校的复信后，我会立即寄上所有证明材料。急盼早复。

您真诚的

黄鹏

这是一封索取简章和申请表的信函。全信格式规范，语言庄重，表达严谨。译文在格式上完全忠实于原文，在表达上同样采用了正式的书面语。如原文第一句"I am deeply interested in your graduate school in the Dept. of M. E…"若直译成"我对贵校研究生院机械工程系非常感兴趣。"，虽然意思表达完全正确，但这种通俗的句子不仅和全信的正规文体相悖，也显得不够礼貌。改译成"久慕"或"久仰"则更能体现出写信者谦虚和敬仰之情。原信中用了一些礼貌的套语，如："I would like to …"，"I would appreciate your sending …"、"I am looking forward to your response at your earliest convenience"，翻译时，也应采用相应的汉语礼貌套语，如："现拟"、"蒙惠"、"盼早复"等。此外，情态动词的频繁使用也是此类信函的特征之一，为的是使表达更婉转、更礼貌。

Dear Sir：

  I am writing this letter in the hope that you will admit me into your Intensive English class starting in January. I have heard a lot about your institute, and I hope I could study with you.

  I have enclosed a copy of the I-20 form issued by the University of Montana. As soon as I finish your course I plan to work for my M. A. degree in the University of Montana. I am sure that if I attend your Intensive Englsih class, I can get much more out of my graduate work.

  If you can send me the I-20 form indicating my acceptance, I can prepare to leave at once. I hope that you will allow me to come and study with you. I hope to hear from you soon.

Sincerely yours,
John Smith

亲爱的先生：

久闻贵校大名，盼能来贵校学习。今特写此信，希望获准入学参加贵校一月份的英语强化班。

随信寄上一份蒙大拿大学发的I-20表格。我打算学完贵校的课程以后，去蒙大拿大学读硕士学位。我相信你们的强化班对我将来的研究生课程的学习一定会大有帮助。

如果能收到你们寄来的I-20表格，确认我已被录取，我随即启程前往。我希望能同意我来贵校学习。

请及早赐复。

您真诚的
约翰·史密斯

这是一封申请参加英语强化班的信函。此信的最大特色是语言比较平易，但又不失正式的风格。译者在翻译此信函时充分注意到了此特色，尽可能地把书面语、套语以及口语有机地结合起来，使译文既通俗易懂，又严谨正规。此外，译者在处理有些句子的翻译时，采用了句子移位，省略或意译的方法，使译文的表达更简洁明了，逻辑性更强。譬如信的第一段，若直译成："我写此信是希望你们能答应让我参加一月份开始的英语强化班。我已知道了许多有关你们学院的情况，所以我希望能到你们学院学习。"这虽"忠实"于原文，但太口语化，不够正规，语言啰嗦，逻辑性不强。因此译者浓缩了语言，使用礼貌性词汇，并打破了原来的句序，采用移位的方法，将第一段的第二句移前，变成第一句，第一句推后，反成第二句。译文改成："久闻贵校大名，盼能来贵校学习。今特写此信，希望获准入学，参加贵校一月份的英语强化班。"这种变动使译文更加简洁正式，彬彬有礼，也更符合汉语的表达习惯。

附：练习

将下列申请书译成中文。

①
Dear Sir,

　　I am planning to apply for admission to Smith College in the fall of 1995. Please send me a catalog, application form, and information about your entrance requirements.

Very truly yours
Thomas Eduard

②
Gentlemen,

　　I should like to obtain application forms for your school.

　　I am presently in the second grade of Senior High school of No. Four Middle School in Beijing. Will you please inform me your entrance requirements and examination dates.

Very truly yours,
Yang hua

③
Dear Sir,

　　I am currently a graduate student pursuing an MBA degree at the University of Florida in Gainesville, Florida, and wish to transfer to your MBA program in Fall 1990. I have completed 12 semester credits now and shall have completed 8 more by the end of June. My grades are all above B.

　　Before coming to the University of Florida, I had earned a BBA degree from Wuhan University and had worked with a state-run factory for one year. Transcripts of my undergraduate and graduate records can be arranged.

I would greatly appreciate it if you would send me the application forms as soon as possible.

Sincerely yours,
Li Lin
Department of Electrical Engineering
Hunan Polytechnical University
Changsha City, Hunan Province
People's Republic of China
April 2, 1984

④

Admission Officer
Graduate School of Engineering
Massachusetts Institute of Technology
Cambridge, Massachusetts 02139
United States of America

Dear Sir,

I left ××University as a graduate in electrical engineering in Aug. 1981. Now I am an assistant and experimenter, working in the Department of Electrical Engineering of the Hunan Polytechnical University. To pursue further studies I wish to enter the Graduate School of Engineering of the Massachusetts Institute of Technology to read for the degree of Master of Science. Your institute has a long history and a fine tradition of scholarship. It is well staffed and equipped, enjoying world-wide fame. To find a place in such an ideal school of higher learning is indeed a matter of the greatest honour. It is my long-cherished hope that I will be fortunate enough to be admitted into it.

I should be grateful to know the conditions under which the applicants are accepted. Would you please send me an application form and some related information?

I am looking forward to your early reply.

Respectfully yours,
Li Fengsheng

⑤

Dear Sir:

As I have gladly heard that your society has done excellent work ever since its foundation and enjoys high prestige both at home and abroad, I deem it a great honour to become one of its members.

I graduated from the Physics Department of ×× University in 1958, when I was engaged as an assistant by ×× Laboratory. In 1964, I joined the ×× High - Energy Physics Society, working as a research member. Now I still belong to it. In the past 25 years since my graduation, I have written two books on high-energy physics and five papers on atomic physics and other subjects. I always feel that on many occasions my individual efforts were not adequate to overcome the difficulties in research work. More often than not I had to ask for help and support from others. In order to learn from senior colleaues, to obtain their guidance, cooperation and coordination, to keep up with the rapidly developing situation in physics, I hope to join your association if I am eligible for membership.

I shall be much obliged if you will be so kind as to let me have by return mail a copy of your regulations together with an application form for me to fill in.

Your prompt attention to my request will be highly appreciated.

           Sincerely yours,
           Blair Arden

(2)推荐信与谋职信

推荐信对被推荐人能否成功地获得某职位或某机会起着举足轻重的作用。推荐人的身分和地位决定了推荐信的文体。语言需端正文雅,措词需考究恰当,以体现写信人的修养和学识。例如:
Dear Mr Gilbert,

I have the honour to recommend to you Mr North, the bearer of this letter. The other day you spoke of the vacancy in your accounting section, and now he wishes to offer his service. He is trustworthy, industrious and a very enjoyable sort of man. Here I recommend him to you with all my heart. You won't be so wrong by hiring him. Enclosed is his personal history.

Any attention you may extend to him will be gratefully appreciated.

           Sincerely yours,
           Walter Hanley

[译文1]

亲爱的盖伯特先生:

  我荣幸地向你推荐持信人诺思先生。他愿意谋求你不久前提过的会计部门空缺的职位。他为人可靠,工作勤奋,且饶有风趣。因而我至诚推荐。你可以完全放心地雇用他。兹附上他的简历。

  若承照顾,感激不尽。

           你真诚的
           沃尔特·汉雷

[译文 2]

亲爱的盖伯特先生：

向你推荐持信人诺思先生我感到很荣幸。前几天你提到了会计室有一空缺，现在诺思先生愿意担任此职。他忠实可靠，工作勤奋，是一个很风趣的人。在此，我衷心地推荐他。你雇用他肯定没错。随信附上他的简历。

你给他的任何照顾都将使我非常感激。

你真诚的

沃称特·汉雷

试比较以上两译文。显然译文 1 较之译文 2 更能体现出原信的语言特色。

如信件开头用的一个套语："I have the honour to recommend to you……"，译者译成"我荣幸地向您推荐……"释意准确，用词恰当。而在结尾处译者用了类似文言文的四字结构"若承照顾，感激不尽"，这正是此类汉语函件的常用套语。译文 2 虽然行文通顺正确，但语言太口语化，不正规，因而不足取。

谋职信类似自我推荐信，属于较正式文体，但又不如推荐信那样严肃正式。例如：

Dear Mr. Williams,

Someday in the future you may have need for a new private secretary.

Here is why I should like to offer myself for the job, and here is why I am so much interested in obtaining it. For one thing, I know that you do an enormous variety of work very fast and well. This offers a real challenge to whoever works for you. It is the kind of challenge I like to meet because, with all due modesty, I have so trained myself in secretarial work that only exacting problems are interesting to me.

As to my mechanical abilities, I can take dictation at the rate of 180 words a minute, and transcribe at the rate of 100 words per minute, a speed which won me the Junior Transcribing Championship in Ohio. I taught at the Hooper Business School in Toledo, covering the subjects of book-keeping, filing, and elementary accounting.

I am familiar with your type of work because my father ran a small printing business in Toledo and for some time before I left home at the age of 22, I was acting secretary and the treasurer of his company.

I cannot think of any job in which I would be so useful as that of private secretary to you, since, in addition to my business training and experience, I could put to work for you and your organization the knowhow of practical everyday business handling that I acquired in growing up in the printing industry.

Sincerely yours
Jane Kent

亲爱的威廉姆先生：

您将来或许需要一位新的私人秘书。

我之所以毛遂自荐，极感兴趣的原因为：首先，我听说您日理万机，迅速妥贴，这对在您手下工作的人无疑是一种挑战。这种挑战正是我所企盼的，因为毫不夸张地说，我在文秘方面受过严格的训练，只对高难度的工作感兴趣。

至于机械性工作能力，我可以每分钟笔录180个词，誊写100个字，这个速度使我赢得了俄亥俄州初级誊写竞赛第一名。我在托利多市胡珀商业学校教过书，教过薄记、档案和基础会计。

我对您那里的业务很熟悉，因为家父曾在托市开过一家小印刷厂。在我22岁离开家以前，曾在那里当过一段时间的秘书并管理过公司的财务。

我想不出还有什么工作能比当您的私人秘书更能发挥我的特长的了,因为我不但受过职业训练,有工作经验,我还在印刷业的环境中长大,学到了处理日常具体事务的方法,可以为您和您的企业效劳。

您真诚的
简·肯特

原文中的"I"若译成"敝人",则显迂腐,译成"本人"或"我"更为自然。但若将"my father"译成"我爸爸"又太随便,译成"家父"则较妥贴。此外,信的最后一句话太长,如直译会显得复杂沉重,译文分成三句,读上去则清晰自然得多。

附:练习

将下列推荐信或求职信译成中文。

①

Dear Mr. Cotton,

It affords me much pleasure to recommend Miss House, one of my former classmates to you. She is a lady of integrity and ability. She has received some special training in typewriting. Her moral character and habits are praise-worthy. She has always been punctual in attendance, diligent in the discharge of her duties and careful and practical in dealing with everything. In a word, she is specially qualified to act as a secretary.

Should you favour her with a situation in your company, I am sure that her future conduct will prove worthy of your confidence.

Sincerely yours,
Roy Fowler

②

Dear Mr. Reid:

In reply to your letter of June 27, I am pleased to inform you that I can recommend Miss Kao in the highest terms as a governess for your son. My wife and I found her very intelligent, sincere, and always jovial, and both my girl and boy liked her very much. During all the three years of our engagement of her, we never saw her in indisposed mood. If there is anything that I may comment on her, she appeared just a little too masculine, but it would do rather good to your boy.

While she was with us she mastered almost perfect English. As to her mother tongue, I understand she speaks good Chinese and is well versed in the Chinese literature. We released her only because our children got grown up. Anyway I believe you won't go wrong by hiring her.

Yours sincerely,
J. P. Houser

③

Dear Professor ···,

I am writing to introduce to you Dr. ··· , who is a doctor at the Institute of Infectious Diseases,··· Medical College.

He graduated from ... Medical College in 1983 and continued his postgraduate work in infectious diseases, receiving the Master Degree in 1986.

Dr. ... was an excellent student, and has boundless prospects as a doctor. I am confident that he could be one of the best students in your department if he were accepted. His English is good, and he has passed an official English examination given by our government. He now qualifies for government sponsorship to do research and studies abroad. That is, the Chinese government will provide him with a stipend and round trip airfare. I would be grateful if you could accept him as a visiting scholar in your department.

   I look forward to hearing from you at the earliest possible moment.

Sincerely yours
(Signature)

④
Gentlemen,

   It's my pleasure to make application for the position of interpreter in your firm, which you have advertised for in the Morning Post.

   I was born in 1952 in Japan and graduated from a foreign language institute in 1977. Served the office of the International Travel Service from 1977—1981 as an interpreter. Was married in 1980. Resigned from the service in 1981 and came to America. I can speak English fluently and understand Japanese and Russian. So I trust I am competent at the job.

   As for my moral character and habits, I wish to refer you to your friend Mr George Black.

   I hope that you accord me an opportunity of interview and give a favourable reply.

I am, Gentlemen,
Harry Greenwood

⑤
Dear Sir:

I have learned from a friend that there is a vacancy in the Willow Street Grammar School, and I wish to apply for the position.

I am a graduate of the Lincoln High School and of the State Normal College, class of 1986. For the last two years I have been teaching chemistry at Watton High School, in this city.

Inclosed you will find testimonials from Principal R. B. West of Watton High School, and from Dr. C. K. Lyons of the State Normal College. I am also permitted to refer to Professor Raymond Powell of the Education Department at the Normal College.

I should welcome a personal interview at your convenience.

Yours sincerely
Bert Miller

⑥

Dear Sir.

Having known that your office needs a typist and stenographer, I hasten to apply for the post.

I was born in 1944 and graduated from a Commercial School in Chicago in 1963, Took one year's special training in shorthand and typewriting, served at a ship company in San Francisco from 1964 to 1972 as private secretary to the manager. Was married in 1971. Resigned from the Company due to severe illness.

My husband teaches at Illinois University and we have a son of six years and a daughter of four years of age. As they are now old enough and also naive enough to be nursed by my mother-in-law while I am out, I feel I would like very much to work again in an office.

My speeds were:shorthand 100 words per minute and typewriting 60. I was often entrusted to compose the manager's letters and in most cases they were approved as they were. Of course, I am out of practice now, but confident I can regain my abilities in a short time.

I shall be much obliged if you will accord me an opportunity for an interview.

           Yours sincerely,
           Helen Perking

 2. 公务信函：
 公务信函可分为普通公函和外交公函。普通公函指机关团体之间的来往信函。而外交公函是国家间涉及外交事务的公文。

        187 Peacock Avenue
        ×× District, Shanghai
        Sept. 16, 1997

Reception Office
Exhibition Palace, Shanghai
Gentlemen,

 We were very pleased to learn from the local newspaper that many important and valuable inventions of science and technology made since the Second World War are now on display in your exhibition hall. We all know that there have been a large number of scientific and technical achievements, the application of which has been greatly changing our total view of the world. The past four decades in particular have witnessed the birth of many new theories of epoch-making significance. They deal with almost everything in all spheres of human activities. Thanks to the selfless efforts of scientists, Chinese and overseas, man's life has been daily improving. Today, science and technology are advancing in our country much more rapidly than at any time in the past. They are being applied to the needs of production and life. We, young science workers, intend in all eagerness to make in-depth studies of national and international trends of science and technology developments and keep in pace with the rapid progress of sciences in various fields. To do this, it is necessary for us to get well informed of the latest results of scientific researches.

We hereby write to ask for a chance to visit your exhibition. We will very much appreciate it if you can arrange for us to come on Sept. 25, 1997, next Saturday.

Thank you in advance for a favourable reply at your earliest convenience.

Yours sincerely
(Signature)

上海市××区
孔雀大街187号
1997年9月16日

上海市展览馆接待室
先生们：

　　我们高兴地从本地报纸上得知，贵馆展览大厅目前正展出第二次世界大战以来科技方面有价值的重大发明。众所周知，许多科技成果的运用大大改变了我们对世界的整个看法。特别是在过去四十年中，出现了许多具有划时代意义的新理论，涉及人类活动的各个领域。由于中外科学家们的无私劳动，人类的生活日益改善。今天，我国在科技方面取得的进步比过去任何时候都要快得多。这些成果正被应用来满足生产和生活的需要。我们年轻的科学工作者极欲深入地研究国内外的科技发展趋势,以便在各方面跟上科学的迅速发展。为了达到这一目的,我们就必须充分了解科学研究的最新成果。

今特写此函,请求准予我们参观贵馆的展览,并希望能安排在 1997 年 9 月 25 日(星期六)这一天。

敬请早日赐复,不胜感激。

您真诚的
(签名)

这是一封要求参观科技发明展览的普通公务信函,较之私人事务信函在格式上更规范。译文采用书面语,语气和措词非常客气庄重。比如:在提及对方单位时都用"贵"字开头,结束语采用了中文的套语"敬请早日赐复,不胜感激"来对应原文的"Thank you in advance for a favourable reply at your earliest convenience"。

May 18, 1993

Excellency,

I have the honour to inform Your Excellency that I have today presented my credentials (or: my Letter of Credence, the Letter) to His Excellency Mr. ×××, Chairman of the Standing Committee of the National People's Congress of the People's Republic of China as Ambassador Extraordinary and Plenipotentiary of ×× Country to the People's Republic of China.

On assuming my duties, I wish to assure Your Excellency of my best efforts to maintain, strengthen and promote the friendship and cooperation which have all along existed between our two countries, and I am looking forward to closer cordial relations, both official and personal, between our two Missions.

I avail myself of this opportunity to convey to Your Excellency the assurances of my highest consideration.

　　　　　　　　　　　(Signed, in full name)
　　　　　　　　　　　Ambassador Extraordinary and
　　　　　　　　　　　Plenipotentiary of ×× to China

His Excellency Mr. ×××,
Minister Extraordinary and
Plenipotentiary of ×× to China
Beijing

北京
××国驻中华人民共和国特命全权公使×××先生阁下：
　　兹特荣幸地通知阁下，我于今天向中华人民共和国全国人民代表大会常务委员会委员长×××先生阁下递交了我任××国驻中华人民共和国特命全权大使的国书。
　　在我就任本职期间，我愿向阁下保证，我将尽力维护、巩固和促进我们两国之间的传统友谊和合作。我盼望我们两国使团之间的公务和私人友好关系日益亲密。顺致
　　崇高敬意
　　　　　　　　　　　××国驻华特命全权大使
　　　　　　　　　　　（签署全名）
　　　　　　　　　　　1993年5月18日

　　外交公函一般要求有信端。在信端内要求写上发文机关名称、地址和日期。如果收文单位知道其名称和地址，可免写，仅在信端上写上发文日期。其次注意称呼用语。外交公函的称呼与其他信函不同，有其固定的用语，视对象而定。常用的有"Excellency(Excellencies)"、"Your Excellency (Excellencies)"、"Your Excellency Mr President"、"Your Excellencies Messrs. (Ministers)"等。这一类称呼一般用于总统、总理、大使、部长、公使、特别代表等重要人物，以表示尊敬。翻译时可相应地译成"阁下"、"总统先生阁下"、

"部长先生阁下们"等。而对于国王、王后的称呼则为"Your Majesty King"、"Your Majesties King and Queen",译成"国王陛下"、"国王和王后陛下"。"Your Highness Prince"、"Your Highness Princesses"是对亲王、王子、公主等的称呼,相对应的译语为"亲王殿下"、"公主殿下们"。翻译时必须仔细,切不可张冠李戴。外交公函中收信人的姓名、头衔、地址不像其他信函放在信的左上角,而是写在信的左下角,比签名一项的末行低一至二行。因此,在翻译外交公函时,在格式上也要相应地作些变动。把信右上角的日期移至签名的下端,而把原函左下角收信人的姓名、头衔和称呼用语合并在一起,放在信端,不需分行,如上例所示,译成"××国驻中华人民共和国特命全权公使××先生阁下"。外交公函属非常正式的文体,为了体现正规文体的特征,翻译时用词需非常谨慎、考究,如原公函的开头语和结束句句式都很正规:"I have the honour to inform Your Excellency……"、"I avail myself……"译成汉语时,也需使用正式的外交语言:"兹特荣幸地通知阁下"、"顺致,崇高敬意"。此外,外交公函句式均较复杂冗长。在翻译这样的长句时,应根据汉语的表达习惯,把长句译成几个短句。译文甚至将原句中"which have all along existed between our two countries"这个定语从句概括成"传统"两字。再如译"I am looking forward to closer cordial relations……"这一句时,译者有意识作了词性上的变动,把原来的名词词组改为动词词组,译成"我盼望我们……的友好关系日益亲善,这样的译文不仅通顺,语言也简洁庄重得多。

附:练习

将下列公函译成中文。

①   Sept. 2, 1989

Dean

Dental Department

University of Penn.

Philadelphia, PA 19104

Dear Mr Perkins,

　　We have received your completed application form and all the necessary documents and materials from other sources.

　　A preliminary check of the materials indicates that you are academically eligible for admission. We wish to inform you that you will be admitted into the graduate course of ... Medieal College for the fall term 1989 to work towards the degree of medicine.

　　We heartily welcome you to join us on our campus.

　　　　　　　　　　　　　　　　　　　　Yours truly,

　　　　　　　　　　　　　　　　　　　　(Signature)

②

Professor & Chairman

Department of Anaesthesia

The Univ. of Western Ontario

London, Canada N6A 5A5

January 29, 1995

Dear Dr. Taylor,

Dr. Cortland has discussed your correspondence with me and I am completely supportive of your plans to encourage an exchange of faculty between ... Medical College and the University of Western Ontario.

　　Certainly we will be very pleased to welcome exchange visitors from your University to our College and provide assistance to cover their living expenses while here. I will also encourage members of our College to accept your invitation to visit London. I am particularly grateful for your kind invitation to me to visit your university as diplomatic liaison between our two institutions.

With very best regards and kind wishes,

Sincerely yours,

(Signature)

③

His Excellency Mr. ×××,
Ambassador Extraordinary and
Plenipotentiary of ××Country to China,
Beijing

May 19, 1983

Your Excellency,

I have the honour to acknowledge receipt of your letter dated May 18, 1983, in which you were kind enough to inform me that you presented yesterday your Letter of Credence, accrediting you as Ambassador Extraordinary and Plenipotentiary of the Republic of ×× Country to the People's Republic of China, to His Excellency Mr. ×××, Chairman of the Standing Committee of the National People's Congress of the People's Republic of China.

In thanking you for the courtesy of this message, I have the great pleasure to enter into both official and personal relations with Your Excellency and to assure you of my constant endeavour to maintain and further develop the close cooperation between our two Missions, which happily reflects the growing bonds of friendship between our two countries.

Please accept, Your Excellency, the assurances of my highest consideration.

(Signature, name in full)
Minister Extraordinary and
Plenipotentiary of ×× to China

④
His Excellency Mr. ×××,
Minister of Foreign Affair,
People's Republic of China,
Beijing

Feb. 24, 1988

Your Excellency,

I have the honour to inform Your Excellency that I have returned to Beijing on Feb. 20, 1988 and have resumed charge of the Embassy since that date.

I avail myself of this opportunity to renew to your Excellency the assurances of my highest consideration

(Signed, name in full)
Ambassador Extraordinary and
Plenipotentiary of ××

⑤
His Excellency,
Chief of the Protocol Department,
Foreign Ministry of the P. R. C.,
Beijing

Feb. 16, 1984

Your Excellency,

I beg to inform Your Excellency that a member of our Embassy formerly asked for a passport to be issued to him for the purpose of travelling in Tibet. Three days ago he returned to Beijing and handed back his passport. He said he had received satisfactory attention from the local authorities wherever he went, for which he is deeply grateful. I beg to return the passport originally received and hope that Your Excellency will take note thereof and cancel the name. I avail myself of this opportunity to extend to you my best regards.

(Signed, name in full)
Cultural Counsellor of the
Embassy of the U.S.A

四、商务信函

当代国际贸易竞争激烈,这就必然带来商务信函风格和语言上的变化。过去千篇一律、陈词滥调的文字正在逐渐消失。当前各国商界人士在互通书信时都强调内容简明扼要,说明问题,因为收信人无暇欣赏舞文弄墨、深奥难懂、客套连篇的书信。现代商务书信的特点可以概括为:直截了当,开门见山,层次分明,语言简洁,态度礼貌。在翻译此类信函时也要力求体现这些特点。

1. 商务信函的语言风格

Dear Sirs,

We thank you for your enquiry of April 2 and are pleased to offer as follows, subject to our final confirmation:
Commodity: Torch Brand Men's Shirts
Specifications: White, long sleeves, made of 80% Dacron
    Polyester and 20% Cotton
Sizes: Large 20%, Medium 50%, Small 30%
Packing: Each in a polybag, half dozen to a carton and 10 dozen

to a wooden case
Quantity: 1,500 dozen
Price: £... each dozen CIF ...
Shipment: May/June 1981
Payment: By confirmed irrevocable L/C payable at sight

  Although we have too many commitments at present to allow us to take on new orders, we are glad to make you the above special offer to show our good will in order to establish business relations with you. If you think our offer meets your requirements, please let us have your order at an early date.

           Yours faithfully,
           (Signature)

亲爱的先生们：

  收到了贵方四月二日的询价信,谢谢。兹报盘如下,以我方最后确认为准：

  品名：火炬牌男衬衫

  规格：白色,长袖,涤纶80%,棉20%

  尺码：大号20%,中号50%,小号30%

  包装：每件用塑料薄膜袋装,每六件一纸盒,二十盒一木箱

  数量：1,500打

  价格：到岸价格,每打……英镑

  装运：一九八一年五月或六月

  付款：需保兑,不可撤销的即期汇票信用证

  目前,合同量虽然很大,难以再接受新定单,但我方仍高兴地特向贵方提出上述报盘,以示同贵方建立业务关系的良好愿望。如贵方认为我方的报盘适合要求,请及早订购为盼。 顺致

  敬礼

           （签名）

这是一封商业书信中常见的报价信。短短一句起始语像一个联络信号,既让阅信人立刻想起上封信的时间和内容,又直接点出此封信要涉及的报价正题,起到了承上启下的作用。接着立即提出报价,层次清楚,内容扼要,结束语直接了当地提出愿望和要求,避免了不必要的客套。译者在翻译时注意到了这种语言和格式的特征,一条一款,条理分明,译文同样简洁、明确、自由、通俗、易懂、贴近口语。

商业书信还要避免语气生硬。例如:

Dear Sirs,

It is in November, 1996 that we signed our contract. As every businessman knows, in international trade price naturally fluctuates at different time. Under the present circumstances that goods are in short supply while many enquiries keep coming in, we can not accept your request for a reduction of price. We would appreciate it very much if you could immediately establish the covering L/C at the contracted price. Otherwise, we must cancel the contract.

Yours sinlerely
(Signatrue)

亲爱的先生们:

我们的合同是1996年11月份鉴订的。众所周知,在国际贸易中,时间不同,价格自然有变动。在目前货源紧张,询盘较多的情况下,我们难以接受贵方的降价要求。盼望贵方立即按合同价开证。否则,我们不得不撤销合同。　　　　致

礼

(签名)

这是一封拒绝减价,要求对方履行合同的信函。译者在翻译过

程中十分注意语气的婉转和礼貌。如"As every businessman knows"若译成"每一个商人都知晓",语气则显得生硬,不够礼貌,看了令人反感。译成"众所周知",则语气就缓和有礼得多。再如:"We cannot accept…""We must cancel…"若直译成"我们不能接受……","我们必须……"也不如"我们难以接受……","我们不得不……"显得婉转客气一些。

2. 商务信函和翻译技巧

商务书信的语法和句式比较复杂,在翻译时需经常使用一些翻译技巧,常见的有:重复省略、否定、转换等。

现举一例来说明这些技巧在实际翻译中的应用。

Dear Sirs,

We thank you very much for the warm hospitality accorded to Mr. Garcia during his visit to your country and for your close cooperation in the business discussions.

Mr. Garcia was invited to visit China in 1986 for the first time. He stayed in Beijing for about two weeks for technical presentations on oil exploration. During his stay in China he also visited Shengli Oil Field. He spared the last two days for discussion with SINOCHEM on the possibility of importing China's crude oil.

Aiming at the promotion of the bilateral trade, SINOCHEM and our company have, through friendly consultations, come to the following agreement: (omitted)

亲爱的先生们:

非常感谢你们在加西亚先生访问贵国期间给予的盛情款待,感谢你们在业务洽谈中的密切合作。

加西亚先生于1986年第一次应邀访华,在北京逗留了大约两星期,进行石油勘探技术的座谈。在华期间他还参观了胜利油田,并在最后两天和中国化工进出口总公司商讨了进口中国原油的可能性。

为促进双方的贸易,中国化工进出口总公司和我公司经友好协商达成如下协议:(略)

英语的特点之一是尽可能地避免重复,而在译成汉语时,有时却必需重复以表达得更加清楚。例如:原信的第一段只用了一个谓语词组"Thank you",而译文却重复了"感谢你们"这一短语。整句译成"非常感谢你们在加西亚先生访问贵国期间给予的盛情款待,感谢你们在业务洽谈中的密切合作。"这样的重复起了承上启下的作用,并不累赘,反更符合汉语的习惯。

省略的技巧也经常运用于商务书信的翻译中。如:英语中人称代词,物主代词的使用频率高于汉语。原信第二段中出现了三次"he"和二次"his",译文根据汉语习惯酌情省略了人称代词。

英汉这两种语言在表达否定意思时,差异比较明显,有时会给翻译工作带来一些困难,尤其在翻译商业英语信函时,常会碰到此类问题。例如:

Dear Sirs,

The New York Port Authority stipulates that barium carbonate should be packed in fibre drums instead of in bags. The leakage was attributed to your failure to effect shipment according to the packing terms as stipulated in the contract.

We find difficulty in entertaining your claim.

In the absence of a settlement through negotiation, the case under dispute can be submitted to arbitration.

Yours sincerely

亲爱的先生们:

纽约港务局规定碳酸钡应用纤维板制成的桶装,而不应袋装。

泄漏是由于贵方未按合同规定的包装发货所致。

我方难以受理贵方的索赔。

如谈判无法解决，争执之事可提交仲裁。

此致

敬礼

原信中并没有出现英语否定句中常用的 no 或 not，而是用了"instead of"、"failure to"、"in the absence of"这几个包含否定意思的词组。翻译时若不了解这点，仅按字面意思直译成"失败"、"代替"、"空缺"，译文不仅极不通顺，读者也难明其意。因此应译成"不应"、"未"、"无法"，这样译文才简明扼要，通顺达意。

3. 商务信函中的缩写与简称

商务书信中经常出现缩写和简称，通用于外贸业务中。若不熟悉，翻译时则会出现困难。现列出商务信函中常见的一些缩写、简称及其译语。

(1) 职称

  MD——总经理　　　　　EVP——执行副总裁

  CEO——首席执行官

(2) 度量衡

  kg——公斤　　　　　　in——英寸

  MT——公吨　　　　　　yd——码

  Ib——磅　　　　　　　min——最小(少)

  gal——加仑　　　　　　max——最大(多)

  ft——英尺

(3) 付款方式

  L/C——信用证　　　　　D/A——承兑交单

  B/L——提单　　　　　　COD——交货付款

  T/T——电汇　　　　　　L/G——保函

D/P——付款交单

(4)运输业务

ETA——预抵期　　　CIF——到岸价
ETD——预离期　　　C&F——成本加运费价
ETFD——预计卸毕时间　AFRA——平均运费率指数
FOB——离岸价

附：练习

将下列商务信函译成中文。

①

Dear Sirs,

We are very glad to have your letter of July 23 and to hear that you are interested in our building nails.

In reply, we regret that we are not in a position to meet your requirements at present because heavy orders have nearly cleared our stocks. However, we are now working at replenishment, which is expected to arrive in a month or two.

We assure you that we will keep your enquiry in mind and will make you an offer as soon as new supplies are available.

Yours faithfully,

Harry Sinith

②

Dear Sirs,

In our last letter, we asked you about the shipment of the goods we ordered but regret that we have, so far, received no news from you.

As we have pointed out in our first enquiry, we are in urgent need of these goods. You will well remember it was your promise of early shipment that brought us to book this order with you. As we have already extended the L/C, we are afraid we cannot do it again. You will note that the L/C expires on May 31.

We hope that you will give this matter your immediate attention and that we'll have your shipping advice without further delay.

Yours faithfully,
John Clark

③
Dear Sirs,

We have your letter of December 14 and note with regret that the case we sent you did not contain the pens you ordered.

On investigation, we find that mistake was indeed made in the packing, through the confusion of numbers. We have arranged for the right goods to be dispatched to you at once and shall be obliged if you will send back the wrong case. We will pay all charges for this purpose.

We apologize for the trouble caused to you by the error, and will make every effort not to let such a mistake happen again.

Yours faithfully,
Catherine Harris

第三节 电 报

一、英文电报的特点

电报是一种常用的应用文体，亦属书信范畴。如：

THANK INVITATION SORRY UNEXPECTEDLY PREVENTED STOP CONVEY CHAIRMAN QUOTE APOLOGIZE SUDDEN ABSENCE AUTHORIZE YOU MY PROXY ALL RESOLUTIONS UNQUOTE WISH SUCCESS

对于不熟悉英文电报的人来说,这封普通电文如同天书,极难理解,更谈不上准确翻译。所以要译好英文电报应先熟悉电文的简化规则和标点的使用方法。

1. 为了减少字数,英文电文中常把几个专有名词或人名、地名连结起来。如将 United States of America 写成 UNITEDSTATESOFAMERICA, Rosy Mary 写成 ROSYMARY, Manchester England 连结并缩写成 MANCHESTERENG。

2. 只要不影响意思,冠词、介词、连词均可省略。

3. 第一人称主语 I、We 一般可以省略。

4. 现在分词代替动词原形或将来时,如将 I will accept your idea 写成 ACCEPTING YOUR IDEA。

5. 形容词或分词前面的 be 和主语一并省略,如:We are willing 和 It is reported 可省略写成 WILLING 和 REPORTED。

6. 主动句式常改为被动,如 I solicit you assistance. 电文为 YOUR ASSISTANCE SOLLCTTED。

7. 否定词用字首冠以 UN, MIS, DIS 等表示,如:We cannot accept his explanation. 电文为:HIS EXPLANATION UNACCEPTABLE。

8. 以单词代替短语。如以 DESPITE 代替 IN SPITE OF,以 BECAUSE 代替 ON ACCOUNT OF。

9. 多使用缩略字。如:YOU = U, YOUR = YR/UR, PLEASE=PLS, FOR YOUR REFERENCE=FYR。

10. 标点的使用也有特殊规律。一般结尾不用标点,句中的标点多用文字代替。如:STOP 等于句号,QUOTE 和 UNQUOTE

为前后引号。

了解了这些英文电报的规则后,就不难理解上封电报的内容为:

I thank you for the invitation to the meeting but I am sorry that I have unexpectedly been prevented from attending. Please convey the following message to the Chairman:

"I apologize for my sudden absence. I hereby authorize you with my proxy on all resolutions."

I wish success for the meeting.

二、英文电报的翻译

翻译英文电报时同样也应尽量简洁。例如:
CONGRATULATIONS TO GROOM AND BEST WISHES TO BRIDE STOP THROUGH ALL THE YEARS A HAPPY LIFE AND LOTS OF LUCK BESIDES

如译成:"祝贺新郎新娘有生之年生活幸福,幸运之神时刻相伴。"译文虽通顺达意,但不够简洁,若译成:"祝新郎新娘终身幸福,事事如意。"则更符合汉语电报的习惯。

又如:AWAITING YR INSTCTN SOONEST 译成"我们正等着您的指示,尽快告知。"显然过长,若译成:"急待指示。"则更可取,因为将人称省略,又将"SOONEST"译成"急"一词,电文显得更为简练准确。

现举一些实例,盼有助于了解各种类型的英语电报的翻译。

1. 新年贺电

BEST WISHES FOR A HAPPY AND PROSPEROUS NEW YEAR 谨祝新年快乐,事事如意。

2. 诞辰贺电

MANY HAPPY RETURNS OF THE DAY 生日快乐!(健康长寿!)

3. 添子贺电

CONGRATULATIONS TO BOTH OF YOU AND HAPPI-NESS HEALTH TO THE NEW ARRIVAL 谨致贺并祝婴儿康乐。

4. 毕业贺电

MAY YR GRADUATION DAY BE THE COMMENCE-MENT OF A CONTINUED SERIES OF UPWARD STEPS TO SUCCESS 祝毕业之日即不断取得成就之始。

5. 祝旅途平安电

BON VOYAGE AND THE HAPPIEST JOURNEY TO U 一路平安,旅途愉快。

6. 吊唁电:

HEARTFELT SYMPATHY IN YR GREAT SORROW 对于你的悲痛谨致深切同情。

7. 接送电

ARRIVE BEIJING TOMORROW 214 TRAIN MEET STATION 明214车到京接站。

8. 商业电

(1) 询价电报

PLS QUOTE LOWEST AND SOONEST 500 MENS MSIZE RAINCOATS CIF HONGKONG 中号男式雨衣五百件,请报香港到岸最低价和最早装船期。

(2) 报价电报

500 MENS MEDIUM RAINCOATS 1900 CIF HONGKONG DELIVERY END FEBRUARY 兹报中号男式雨衣五百件香港到岸价1,900英镑,二月底交货。

(3) 订货电报:

OFFER ACCEPTED AIRMAILING ORDERS 接收报价,订

单航邮中。

(4)感谢电报

TKS FOR YR PROMPT REPLY 蒙迅速回电,谨此致谢。

(5)致歉电报:

CANCELED LAST FEB DUE … BUT REGRET HAVE FAILED TO REPORT YOU ……已于二月到期取消,未能及时通知,殊感歉疚。

附:练习

将下列电报译成中文。

① CONGRATULATIONS AND GOOD WISHES ON YR BIRTHDAY
② GOOD WISHES FOR A SAFE AND DELIGHTFUL VOYAGE
③ SORRY TO KNOW YR ILLNESS STOP BEST WISHES FOR SPEEDY RECOVERY
④ TANG ARRIVING BEIJING JL471 NOV/11 PLS ASK LIN MEET AIRPORT
⑤ PLS TELEX IF ABV QUTN ACPABLE
⑥ YR 222 AND 333 WL BE REVERTING NEXT MON
⑦ WL CONTACT U AGAIN WHEN READY TO OFFER
⑧ REGRET UNABLE ACCEPT FURTHER ORDERS UNTIL END OCTOBER

第四节 便条、通知、启事、海报

在日常生活中,便条、通知、启事和海报属于最常见的一种通告性的应用文。中英文的便条、通知、启事、海报在格式和表达方式上既有相似处又有不同点。翻译时需特别注意。

一、便条

便条是一种简便的书信。常见的有请假条和留言条两种。不论哪种便条都格式简单，内容简短，用词通俗。

1. 请假条

请假条一般采用书信格式，并使用信封，比较正式。如：

Class 3, Grade 2
Oct. 14

To Department Office
Secretary Wang
Dear Sir,

  I beg to apply for one week's leave of absence from the 4th to the 10th instant, both days inclusive, in order to return home to see my father, who is now dangerously ill.

  To support my application, I herewith submit a telegram to that effect received from my elder sister.

  I should be very much obliged if you will grant me my application. As regards the lessons to be missed during my absence, I will do my best to make them up as soon as I get back from leave.

Yours respectfully,
Peng Zhi

  请假条的开头需写明日期，称呼中"Dear"一词不可省略。正文中需说明请假时期和理由，段落分明，层次清楚。结尾时加上结束语，署名用全名。而汉语请假条的写法与英语稍有区别，日期写在右下角，比署名低一行。汉语请假条一般不分段，一层一层意思用句号分开即可。请假条的文体一般比较正式,语言也比较礼貌。如上例中用"I beg to apply for ……"这样正式的句式来代替口语的表达方式"I want to ask for……"。因此翻译时也需相应地用正式礼貌的汉语。

上面的请假条可译为:

系办公室王秘书:

　　因父亲病重,欲回家探望,请假一周,从本月四日起至十日止。现附上姐姐发来的电报,以资证明,敬请批准为盼。请假期间所缺功课,返校后定努力补上。　　此致

敬礼

二年级三班学生彭志
10月14日

2. 留言条

留言条的内容皆为一两天内的事,简明扼要,一两句话而已,格式不如请假条那么正规。称呼直用其名,结束语可省略,署名一般只具姓或名。用词也随便通俗,接近口语。例如:

Friday

Bruce,

　　I shall be very glad if you can find time to call on me at your convenience. I need your advice and suggestions about my preparation for the lectures to be given next week.

Lucy

布鲁斯:

　　有空来我处一叙,想请你对我下周课的讲稿提意见和建议。

露西
星期五
April 13

Barrie,

　　I wonder if you can lend me your COD for a couple of days. I am translating an important article and must consult it now and then. I would, of course, be very careful of it, and see that no damage is done to it.

　　With many thanks from

Aubrey

巴里：

　　想借你的《简明牛津词典》用几天。我正在翻译一篇重要文章，常要查阅。我一定小心爱护，决不损坏。

　　非常感谢！

奥布里
4月13日

　　以上两例，不论是原文还是译文都体现了留言条的特色，格式随便，内容扼要，语言通俗。

附：练习

将下列请假条和留言条译成中文。

Monday

①

Dear Sir,

　　I am very sorry that I can not come to the meeting this afternoon. Enclosed please find a certificate from my doctor stating that I must remain in bed for a few days before returning to my office.

　　I trust my absence will not cause you any serious inconvenience.

Yours faithfully,

②   (Signature)
                                                May 12, 1996

Dear Mr. Smith,

    I beg to inform you that I shall be unable to attend classes today owing to an important business in the family.

    I shall be very much obliged if you will grant me my application.

                                                        Yours truly,

                                                        (Signature)

③

Dr. Brown.

    Upon receipt of this note, please go to Room 202, Foreign Guest House, where David Becker is seriously ill and in urgent need of your service. Immediate treatment is absolutely necessary.

    Be quick, and many thanks.

                                                                       Jack

④

Linda,

    Will you please tell me what time will be convenient for us to get together this week to discuss the teaching and research work for this year? I remind you that you will be in charge of the meeting.

                                                                       Alice

二、通知

    一般来说，如果通知对象较少或内容不便公开，则采用书信形式为宜。因直接写给被通知的对象，故使用第二人称。翻译通知信时，同样也要采用正规的书信格式。如：

Dear Neighbour,

  I am pleased to announce the June 15 opening of CHARLIE'S FIX-IT SHOP. If the name suggests to you that Charlie can repair just about anything, you are right.

  Lawn mowers, snow blowers, small appliances, bicycles, even light welding. I'll tell you in advance how much it will cost and when the job will be completed.

  So the next time something breaks down, don't throw it away. Bring it in a free estimate to:

Charlie's Fix-It Shop
416 Frontage Road
Phone:876—2144
Hours:8:00 AM—5:00 PM Monday through Saturday

Yours sincerely,
Charlie

亲爱的邻居：

  敬告7月15日查理修理店开业。如果你觉得这店名说明查理无所不修，那就对了。

  割草机，扫雪机，小型器具，自行车，甚至小型焊接，均在服务之列。还将事先告知修理费多少及何时修好。

  下次东西坏了，请别扔掉，可把它拿来免费检查一下。

地址：弗郎堤路416号查理修理店
电话：876—2144
时间：周一至周六上午8：00—下午5：00

此致

敬礼

查理

通告和通知信在格式上大不相同,现举一例:

Notice

Notice is hereby given that the water supply is not available from 7:00 am to 11:00 pm tomorrow, owing to the repairs of the water pipes.

General Affair Service

Feb. 2 1996

首先,通知需写上 Notice 或 Notification 字样作为标题置于正上方,翻译时也需在正上方写上"通知"或"通告"的标题。其次,发出通知的单位或负责人名字一般写在正文的右下方,有时也写在标题之上,作为标题一部分。译成中文时,则均写在正文的右下方。第三,出通知的日期在英文通知中一般写在左下方,单位具名的下一行,而译成中文时,则要把时间移到右下角,署名的下一行。最后,英文通知的开头常用一些套语,如:"Notice is hereby given that …"或"This is to announce that …"译成中文时可用"特此通告"或"特此公告"的相应套语。但这样的套语一般不放在开头,而是放在最后。不论是英文通知还是中文通知,语言都要简洁清晰,条理分明,使人一目了然。

根据汉英通知的同异之处,上面的英文通知可译为:

通　　知

由于自来水管检修,明天从早晨7点至晚上11点停水,特此通知。

总务处
1996年2月2日

附:练习

将下列通告和通知信译成中文。

①   Hong Kong, April 23, 1995

Dear Mr. and Mrs. Ellis,

    It is with the greatest grief and regret that I have to inform you of the sudden death of my wife, Mary Ann on the evening of April, 16th due to heart failure. It was a blow like a thunderbolt from the blue sky, as she had never complained of heart trouble before, although her blood-pressure was slightly on the high side.

    The farewell service was held yesterday at St. Peter's Church, Hong Kong.

    Having been bereaved all of a sudden of my life partner, I don't know what to do right now, but I suppose time will gradually cure my pain and make me used to the solitary life.

    I hope this will find you in good health and spirits.

                                              Sincerely yours,

                                              Ed. R. Smith

②   NOTICE OF DISMISSAL

    It is hereby proclaimed that the Board of Directors has unanimously voted to dismiss Mr. ... from the post of Director of the President's Office.

                                          The Director's Office

May 20, 1988

③   NOTICE

    The Foreign Affairs Office has informed us that Dr. Joseph Gonnella, Dean & Vice President of Thomas Jefferson Medical College, Thomas Jefferson University will be unable to travel to

China as planned. His report on medical education has been rescheduled for next Thursday, April 22, 1994, at 2:00 p. m. in the school auditorium.

Teaching Affairs Department

April 10,1994

三、启事

启事是一种公告性的通知。其特点为：

第一，一般需在启事的上方正中写上标题，标题要根据启事的具体内容而定。翻译时，标题必须确切。常见的有 Lost（遗失启事），Found（招领启事），Needed（征求启事），For Sale（出售启事），Contribution Wanted（征稿启事），Removal（迁移启事），Acknowledgements（鸣谢启事），Corrections（更正启事）。

第二，英文启事日期写在右上方，简单的启事也可不署日期。而译成中文时，日期应写在右下角启事者署名的下方。

第三，不论是英文启事还是中文启事，启事者署名都在右下方，若在文中已讲明启事者姓名，就不必再具名。

第四，不论是英文还是中文启事，一般都不用称呼语。

第五，英汉文字均需简洁，通俗，条理清晰。例如：

LOST

Aug. 18, 1996

I was careless and lost a copy of Longman Modern English Dictionary when studying in the reading room yesterday. Will the finder please send it to the office of the Foreign Languages Department or ring me up to fetch it back.

Profound thanks from

Loser,
Euphemia

Address:Room 404, Student Dormitory 3
Tel No:3275

遗失启事

本人不慎于昨日在阅览室遗失《朗曼现代英语词典》一本,拾者请送交外文系办公室,或电话通知失者去取,不胜感激。

失者　尤菲米娅
1996年8月18日

失者地址:学生宿舍三舍404室
电话号码:3275

又如:

CONTRIBUTIONS WANTED

(1) The magazine is mainly intended for teachers and students of middle schools. It is published on the tenth of every month in Changsha, Hunan Province.

(2) Contributions in all forms or styles are warmly welcome, e.g.

a) Revolutionary stories, fables, poems, skits, folksongs;

b) Technical and scientific writings and essays;

c) Essays in phonetics, grammar and language;

d) Speeches, dialogues and lectures;

e) Articles about sports and recreational activities, riddles and games, humour and jokes, and cartoons;

f) Background knowledge about history and geography, travel notes and biographies;

g) Translated articles, bilingual readings, theories and techniques of translation;

h) Study notes and teaching plans;

3) Contributions are expected to be within a 4000-word lim-

it. They should be written clearly and legibly on one side of the paper, double-spaced, with a wide margin. Manuscripts in English must be typewritten or printed in ink.

4) Translated articles should be accompanied with the original. Quotations must be noted with their sources.

5) Manuscripts, if not accepted for publication will be returned to the sender within three months.

6) Contributors will be paid after their manuscripts are published.

7) Manuscripts may be published in the authors' real names or in their pen names as they wish.

8) Contributions should be sent directly to the editorial board, not to individuals. Our address is: Editorial board of the monthly magazine English Teaching and Learning in Middle Schools, the Foreign Languages Department, Hunan Normal University, Changsha, Hunan Province.

    Editorial Board of Monthly Magazine

   English Teaching and Learning in Middle Schools

征稿启事

1. 本刊的主要对象是中学教师和学生,每月10号于湖南省长沙市出版。

2. 热烈欢迎下列各种形式和体裁的稿件：

  ①革命故事、寓言、诗歌、短剧、民谣；

  ②科技作品和文章；

  ③有关语音、语法和语言方面的文章；

  ④演说、对话、讲解；

  ⑤关于文体活动的短文、谜语、游戏、幽默、笑话和漫画；

  ⑥历史和地理的背景知识、游记、人物传记；

⑦翻译作品、双语读物、翻译理论和技巧；

⑧读书笔记和教案。

3. 来稿请勿超过 4000 字，用单面稿纸，隔行书写，字迹清晰，稿纸左右应多留空边。英语稿需打字或用印刷体书写。

4. 凡翻译文章，需附原文，引文必须注明出处。

5. 来稿如不采用，三个月内退还。

6. 来稿一经发表，即付稿酬。

7. 可用真名或笔名发表，由作者自定。

8. 来稿请直接寄本刊编辑部，勿寄私人。

本刊地址：湖南省长沙市湖南师范大学外语系《中学英语教学》月刊编辑部。

《中学英语教学》月刊编辑部

附：练习

将下列启事译成中文。

① Lost   July 10, 1996

Money lost. Whoever found it, please inform us about it. Tel. 577577 Ext. 2202

Chemistry Department Office

② NOTICE OF ENGAGEMENT

Mr. and Mrs. Holand Walshman have the pleasure to announce the engagement of their daughter, Miss Lucy, to Mr. Samual Russell on Saturday, August 17, 1996.

Dec. 6, 1995

③ A Briefcase Found

A briefcase was found, inside of which are money and other

things. Loser is expected to come to identify it. Please apply at the Lost Property Office, Room 107, the Office Building. Open from 8.00 to 11.00 a.m. and 2.00 to 5.00 p.m.

四、海报

　　海报是具有宣传广告性质的大幅张贴通告,英文海报的写法和中文海报有所不同。在中文海报中,活动组织者或主办单位的名称一般都放在海报后面或右下角,而在英文海报里,这项内容往往出现在最前面。在多数情况下,中英文海报均可以不署日期。如果出现日期,在中文海报里则写在右下角,在英文海报中需写在具名的下一行左下角。中文海报的格式比较规范化,变化不大,语言也比较拘谨。而英文海报的格式则多种多样,语言也比较生动活泼,一个突出的特点是常有一句口号或警句。另外,简单句、省略句、缩写形式、俗语在英文海报中也常见。例如:人们常用 tonite 代替 tonight,用 thru 代替 through,用 X-mas 代替 Christmas 等等。

　　鉴于英汉海报各自的特点,将英文海报译成汉语时,要取长补短,即既要考虑到中文海报的格式和语言特征,又要最大可能使原英文海报的风格在译文里得以体现。如:

①

```
              CECF Presents
               FILM SHOW
             THE SWORD SOCIETY
          A Classical Chinese Dance Drama
          ─────────────────────────────
   1½ HOUR        May 9th, Monday
   COLOUR           CECF CINEMA
                Doors open 7:15 p.m.
                  Starts 7:30 p.m.
                      FREE!
```

②

> ┌─────────────┐
> │ 彩色影片 │
> └─────────────┘
>
> ## 小刀会
> （中国古典舞剧）
>
> ———
>
> 五月九日（星期一）
> 交易会电影厅
> 下午七时十五分开始入场，七时半开映。
> **免费入场！**
> 中国出口商品交易会主办

这是一则电影海报。英文海报中主办者的名称写在海报最上方，并用了缩写的形式。在译文中，译者把此项移至海报最下方，并使用了全称。这样的格式和语言比较符合中文的表达习惯。该英文海报的形式自由活泼，别具一格，比如在 1½ HOUR COLOUR 周围框上了一个带花边的图案，目的是引人注目。而中文海报的形式比较规范拘谨，不能照搬，但又要在译文中加以体现，因此译者采取了折衷的办法，把"1½ HOUR COLOUR"译成"彩色影片"，用一个规则的方框套在此译语上，并把此项挪至海报的左上角。这样的变动既传达了原文的内容，在形式上也更能让中国的读者接受。原海报中使用黑体字、大写体或画横线的地方，译文中也分别采用了黑体字、括号或横线与之相对应。

附：练习

将下列海报译成中文。

①

Surgical Operations
under
ACCUPUNCTURE ANAESTHESIA
A truly Chinese miracle!
Time: May 5, Fri. at 8 : 30 a. m.
Place: The No. 2 Hospital Affiliated
with the Guangzhou Zhongshan
Medical College
TO AVOID DISAPPOINTMENT, GET YOUR
TICKET NOW!

②

INTERNATIONAL FOOTBALL MATCH
"United Kingdom"

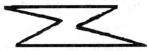

"Germany"
Venne: Zhongshan University Ground
K. O. : 3. 30 p. m. , April 28, 1995

Buses with seating available for about
30 people leave at 4/14. 30 from the
Dongfang. Taxis are available for others.
Come and Cheer for them!

③

```
CECF presents
  ACROBATICS
      by
The Shanghai Acrobatics Troupe

50 of the finest acrobats
EXCITING AND THRILLING FEATS
BREATHTAKING COLOUR & BEAUTY
   April 16 at 7:30 p.m.
   in the Friendship Theatre

Tickets from Rm. 406 NOW!
```

第五节 合 同

合同是为了搞好协作而拟订的一种凭证,涉及当事人经济、技术、法律等问题,因此在语言上形成了正式严格、详尽准确、迂腐陈旧、复杂艰深的特点。

一、合同的文体特点

1. 内容上的针对性

合同不像文章、书籍那样有广泛的读者,它是针对特定的事物、内容、项目、场合而拟订的,只与双方当事人和相关人员有关。

2. 格式上的规范性

合同的格式结构由前言(写明当事人的名称及缔约目的和原则等内容)、正文(明确规定当事人的具体权利和义务、违约赔偿、争议解决、适用法律等条款)和最后条款(包括合同的法定地址、效力范围、有效条件、双方代表签字等)。

3. 句式结构的复杂性

为了严密地表达各部分之间的关系,避免疏漏,合同的句子均较长,中间插入成分较多。一个句子就是一个段落的情形随处可见。例如:

Technical Documentation means the technical literatures, drawings, pictures, tapes, etc, that Party B possesses and has applied or developed for its own production as well as in its current manufacture during the validity term of the contract for designing, calculating, manufaturing, quality control, assembling installations, maintaining and testing of the Contract Products (hereinafter referred to as Documentation)... 技术文件指的是乙方所持有的并在生产中加以应用和开发的技术文献、图纸、照片、磁带等,在合同有效期内仍在当前的制作过程中,用于对合同的产品进行设计、计算、制造、质量控制、安装、维护、测试等(以下称文件)……

4. 指称上的间接性

为了表明条款内容对各方一视同仁,合同通篇使用间接指称的代词。例如:

Both Party A and Party B agree that a technology transfer agreement shall be signed between the joint venture company and Party × (or a third party) 甲、乙双方同意,由合营公司与×方(或第三方)签订技术转让协议……

上例中的 Party A、Party B、Party X、a third party 都是间接指称,指合同当事的一方。

这类间接指称还有 the Seller(卖方)、the Buyer(买方)、the Recipient Party(受方)、the Supplying(供方)、the Transferer(转

让方)、the Transferee(受让方)等。

5. 表达上的条理性

合同一般包括纲目、条款和细则。表达时必须条理分明,不仅在逻辑上,而且在语言上都必须条理分明。合同不同于论述文,不求铺陈,但求明晰;也不同于描述文,不求修饰,但求达意。

6. 措词上的法律性

合同规定了各方的权利和义务具有法律约束力。为了避免产生任何误解和歧义,必须行文严谨,措词准确,具有法律文字特有的稳重性。例如:there of, aforesaid, herein 等这些古词、旧词常见于合同之中。Shall 一词在文中也不是一般用语,而是特定的法律词汇,表示下面的情况属法定范围。并且广泛应用非人称句式。

二、翻译合同的步骤及注意事项

翻译合同除了要了解有关合同本身的专业知识外,还要涉及到国际贸易、国际汇兑、会计学、运输学、保险学、法学等方面知识。译者在翻译过程中应遵循以下步骤及注意事项:

首先,要通读全文,以求全面理解,掌握内涵。通读全文的目的在于从宏观上了解契约的总体概貌和篇章结构。

第二,细研章节。这是在通读全文的基础上进行的。由于契约的章节条款具有相对的独立性,可逐字、逐句、逐条、逐段、逐节、逐章地仔细研读,反复推敲,以求达到细致深入的理解。

第三,准确表达。在翻译过程中,关键是要求译文内容与原文内容保持等值,避免出现差错和误解。

最后,在准确表达的前提下,力求使译文的格式和文体符合合同的规范和要求。例如:

TRADE CONTRACT BETWEEN THE
GOVERNMENT OF THE PEOPLE'S REPUBLIC OF CHINA
AND THE GOVERNMENT OF THE

REPUBLIC OF ××

The Government of the People's Republic of China (hereinafter referred to as China) and the Government of the Republic of × × (hereinafter referred to as × ×), in pursuance of the Trade and Payments Agreement signed between the two governments on 14th September, 1995, have, through friendly negotiations on the trade for the first agreement year (1996) between China and × ×, entered into the following agreement:

Article 1

The People's Republic of China shall, according to its requirements, import from × × commodities enumerated in List "A" for a total amount of $... (U.S. dollars)

Article 2

The Republic of × × shall, according to its requirements, import from China commodities enumerated in List "B" for a total amount of $... (U.S. dollars)

Article 3

The quality and prices of the commodities to be exchanged between the importers and exporters in the two countries shall be acceptable to both sides and the prices shall be fixed in accordance with world market prices.

Article 4

In accordance with the stipulation mentioned in Article 16 of the Trade and Payments Agreement referred to above, the credit line shall be $... (U.S. dollars).

This Contract shall become operative from the date on which the Trade and Payments Agreement comes into force and shall be valid for one year.

Done in duplicate in Beijing on the 14th day of September, 1995 in the English and Chinese languages, both texts being equally authentic.

For the Government	For the Government
of the People's	of the Republic
Republic of China	of ××
…	…
(signiture)	(signiture)

从标题看,这是中华人民共和国政府和××共和国政府的贸易合同。整个合同由前言、五条具体贸易条款及包括时间、地点、有效范围、双方代表签字等项内容在内的最后条款三部分组成。本合同的前言段落只由一个长句构成,按正常的语序该句应写成:"In pursuance of the Trade and Payments Agreement signed between the two governments on 14th September, 1995, the Government of the People's Republic of China (hereinafter referred to as China) and the Government of the Republic of ×× (hereinafter referred to as ××) have entered into the following agreement through friendly negotiations on the trade for the first agreement year (1996) between China and ××."但为符合合同的规范和要求,必须首先提出合同的签署者,故将主语放在句首,状语"In pursuance of…"移至主语之后。同时考虑到宾语 agreement 后面宜紧跟一连串有关协议的内容,故最好放在句末,加上冒号,以起承上启下的作用。因此,在助动词"have"后插入了第二个状语短语

"through…"。通过仔细的语法分析,对句子的结构有了清楚的了解,理解与翻译也就不难了。

在理解的基础上,下一步该考虑如何翻译。上面所举的长句句式太长,结构复杂,应采用断句法,译成几个短句,这样才能清晰通顺。此外,有的英语介词短语如"through…negotiations…"译成汉语时,应转变成动词短语为好,可译为:"进行……商谈,"这样更符合汉语的表达习惯。

在翻译时,还需注意合同的文体特征。例如:此合同中多次提及"Trade and Payments Agreement"。日常生活中,"payment"可译为"付款"而"agreement"可译为"同意",但此处却应译成"支付协定",才符合合同的措词。又如:在前言中出现了一个旧体词"hereinafter",此处应译成"下文",若译成"以下",则显得不够正规文雅。再如:"Shall"一词的译法可根据内容而定,但应记住,这是一个法律用语而非一般的助动词。现附该合同的译文如下:

中华人民共和国政府和××共和国政府

贸易合同

中华人民共和国政府(下文简称中国)和××共和国政府(下文简称××),根据1995年9月14日签订的两国政府贸易和支付协定,就第一个协定年度(1996年)的贸易进行了友好商谈,达成如下协议:

第一条

中国根据需要从××进口附表"甲"所列的商品,总值为××美元。

第二条

××根据需要从中国进口附表"乙"所列的商品,总值为××美元。

第三条

本合同的附表"甲"和附表"乙"为本合同的组成部分。对未列入上述附表内的商品的交换,并无限制之意。
第四条
两国进出口公司所交换的商品的质量和价格应是双方都能接受的,价格应按照国际市场的价格确定。
第五条
根据上述的贸易和支付协定第16条规定,透支额为××××美元。

本合同将于贸易和支付协定生效之日起施行,有效期为一年。

本合同于1995年9月14日在北京签订,一式两份,用中文和英文写成,两种文本具有同等效力。

中华人民共和国政府代表　　　××共和国政府代表
×××(签字)　　　　　　　×××(签字)

附:练习

将下列合同译成中文。

①   CONTRACT OF EMPLOYMENT

The Pharmacology Department of ... Medical College (the engaging party) has engaged Dr. ... (the engaged party) as a teacher of pharmacology. The two parties, in the spirit of friendship and cooperation, have agreed to sign and comply with the below stated conditions:

1. The term of service is one year, beginning September 1, 1988 through August 31, 1989.

2. The duties of the engaged party is mutually agreed to be:

a. Training teachers of pharmacology and students taking refresher courses.

b. Conducting pharmacology classes and advising students

and teachers on pharmacological activities.

c. Compiling pharmacology textbooks and supplementary teaching material, undertaking other work connected with the pharmacology.

d. Having 18 up to 20 teaching periods in a week.

e. The engaged party works five days a week and eight hours a day. The engaged party will have legal holidays as prescribed by the Chinese Government. The vacation is fixed by the school callendar.

3. The engaging party agrees to pay the engaged party a monthly salary of nine hundred yuan (Chinese currency) and provide him with various benefits.

4. The engaged party must observe the regulations of the Chinese Government concerning residence, wages and benefits, and travel for foreigners when entering, leaving and passing through the PRC territories, and must follow the work schedules of the engaging party.

5. The engaging party will welcome any suggestion put forward by the engaged party and will render favourable consideration when circumstances permit. The engaged party will abide by the decisions of the engaging party and work in the spirit of active cooperation to accomplish assigned tasks.

6. Neither party shall, without sufficient cause or reason, cancel the contract.

If the engaging party finds it imperative to terminate the contract, then, in addition to bearing the corresponding expenses for wages and benefits, it must pay the engaged party one month's extra salary as compensation allowance, and arrange for him and his family's return to their own country within a month.

If the engaged party submit his/her resignation within the contract period, the engaging party will be relieved of the responsibility for wages and benefits as of the date the engaged's resignation is accepted and approved by the engaging party. In addition, the engaged party must provide for his and his family's return to the country of origin without expense to the engaging institution.

7. The present contract becomes effective on the first day of service herein stipulated and ceases to be effective on the last day of service. If either party wishes to renew the contract, negotiations must be entered prior to the expiration of the original contract. Upon agreement by both parties through consultation a new contract may be signed.

8. Should any matter, not provided for in this contract, arise during the course of performance, it will be settled through consultation by the two parties.

9. The Chinese translation of this contract will faithfully represent the spirit of the English version and shall be binding on both parties.

....
(the engaging party) (the engaged party)

②   Contract of Business
 NO. ······················
 Date ······················
 Buyers ······················

Sellers ················

This CONTRACT is made by and between the Buyers and the Sellers; whereby the Buyers agree to buy and the Sellers agree to sell the under mentioned goods on the terms and conditions stated below:

Name of Commodity:
Specifications:
Quantity:
Price:
Packing:
Shipment:
Port of Destination:
Terms of Payment:

······   ······

(the Buyers)   (the Sellers)

第六节 规则、指南、说明

从工业装置说明书,到一般机械或家用器具的操作简介,以及规章、守则、旅游指南、交通手册、医药说明和服务须知等均属此范围。这类文字的文体特点为简略性、描述性和技术性。

一、简略性

这类文字大都明了通俗,句子结构简单,避免使用不必要的修辞手段。其特点为:第一,广泛使用祈使句;第二,广泛使用复合名词词组,以代替后置定语;第三,尽量省略冠词、介词及无关重要的形容词、副词、连词等。例如:

A Notice to Consumers (U.S. Postal Service)

Packing and Mailing Parcels Failure to pack and mark packages adequately is a major source of parcel damage and loss. You should use a container strong enough to prevent damage from handling, transportation, and compression. Cushion the content to make sure it does not move within the container, and use pressure sensitive filament or reinforcement of flaps and seams. Avoid using paper wrappers on fiberboard containers.

Be sure the address is clear and shown on one side only. Repeat address information inside the package.

邮寄须知　　（美国邮局）

打包不当以及标识不详是导致包裹损坏和遗失的主要原因。应使用坚固的容器，以防止邮件因处理、运输或受压而受损。在邮寄的物品上下周围加上衬垫，以防止其在容器中移动，使用耐压包装带或强力胶带密封加固包裹。纤维板容器外请勿用纸包扎。

在包裹的一侧写清地址，在包裹内也应写上相同地址。

这段须知多处使用祈使句，使句子结构简略。复合名词的使用如：parcel damage and loss 和 address information 等，使语言更简洁明了。译文也体现了原文的这一特点。

二、描述性

一切指南、规则（Instructions）都是为了要求读者遵循而编写的，因此都具有直观效果，使读者见文如见物。然而直观效果的产生只能凭借有效的、生动的描述才能办到。好的指南、规则都是对某一客体的完满描述。所谓"完满描述"指描述中要包含科学的思维逻辑，即使文字具有层次感、程序性和说服力。以下是一则超车程序：

Passing Procedures

When you decide there is sufficient clear road ahead to permit safe passing, you should do the following:

• Look for signs and pavement markings. Many roads have signs and lane markings that tell you when you can or cannot pass safely under normal driving conditions.

• Look ahead carefully before you start to pass. Check for any hazards in the passing area.

• Look in your side and rear-view mirrors. Make sure there are no vehicles about to pass you when you start your move left to pass.

• Before passing, give the proper turn signal to show you're going to move into another lane. Signal early enough so others will know your intentions in advance.

• After passing, signal that you intend to return to your lane.

• Return to the proper lane as soon as possible after passing.

• Make sure you can see the front of the vehicle you passed in your rear-view mirror before cutting back into the lane.

超车程序

在确认前方道路通畅,有足够距离便于你安全超车后,你必须按下列步骤操作

• 看清路标和人行道标志。许多道路都设有路标和车道标志,提醒你何时可以、何时不可以在正常行驶情况下安全超车。

• 超车前看清前方道路,仔细检查超车路段有无障碍。

• 细看侧镜和反光镜,确保左移准备超车时没有其他车辆超越自己的车。

- 超车前,打开正确的方向灯,标明你准备进入另一车道。方向灯要及早打开,以便预先告知他人你要超车的意图。
- 超车后,打开方向灯,表明你将返回原车道。
- 超车后,尽快返回原车道。
- 必须在反光镜中看到被超车辆的车头后方能折回原车道。

三、技术性:

此类文字大多涉及某方面专业知识,即便是一般家用电器的使用说明书也颇带技术性,工用机械说明书则技术性就更强。现举一个医药说明书来说明翻译中应注意的事项:

ISOKET

For long-term and/or emergency treatment of angina pectoris.

Composition:

Isosorbide dinitrate 20 mg per tablet, with prolonged action.

Indications:

Angina pectoris, especially the so-called "effort angina"; prevention and subsequent treatment of myocardial infarction. Angina pectoris vasomotorica, a form induecd by central nervous disorder, is not affected.

Contra-indication:

Glaucoma.

Dosage:

One tablet of Isoket retard to be taken with water and without chewing in the morning after breakfast, and one in the evening before retiring; this will protect the patient from attacks of angina pectoris during both the day and the night. If an attack does occur, half a tablet should be chewed and then swallowed, whereby an immediate action is produced.

Note:

No side-effects are to be expected, but some patients may develop the well-known "nitrate headache" which in itself is harmless. In such instances, it is recommended that the dosage be reduced. Because this nitrate effect is subject to tachyphylaxis, the lsoket retard medication need not be interrupted. Security for angina pectoris patients for 8-10 hours. In cases of extreme severity, immediate relief can be obtained by chewing Isoket retard.

Packings of 60 tablets.

Made in Germany

异速凯他(山梨糖醇硝酸盐)
供心绞痛长期或急救使用
[成分] 每片含二硝酸异山梨醇脂20毫克。长效。
[适应症] 专治心绞痛,特别是"一累就犯"这种类型的心绞痛。预防和治疗心肌梗塞。但对由中枢神经紊乱而引起的血管舒缩性心绞痛不起作用。
[禁忌症] 青光眼。
[剂量] 早饭后用开水服1片,不用咀嚼。晚间睡前服1片,这样可以避免患者在白天和晚间心绞痛发作。如心绞痛已发作,应咀嚼半片,咽下后即可立刻发挥作用。
[注意事项] 一般不会发生副作用。有些患者可能出现常见的,并无大害的"硝酸盐性头痛"。如遇此种情况,可酌减剂量。因为患者对这种硝酸盐作用易产生快速耐受性,所以不必停药。本品可在8—10小时内保护心绞痛患安全。严重患者咀嚼本品可立即缓解。
[包装] 60片包装

德国制造

在翻译技术性文章或含有许多技术术语的文章时,要求准确,如有差错,会引起严重后果。在翻译药品说明书时,更要特别注意,尤其是对一些术语的翻译,如:Composition(成分),Description(性状),Action(作用),Indication(适应症),Contra-indications(禁忌症),Precaution(注意事项),Side Effects(副作用),Dosage and Administration(剂量和用法),Packing(包装),Expiry Date(失效日期),Manufacturing Date(出厂日期)等等。其次,对药品名称的翻译也要慎重,一般有四种译法:第一,音译:如上文的例子,按音译将"Isoket"译为"异速凯他";第二,意译:为了使中国读者更明白药品的化学性质,也可将"Isoket"译为"山梨糖醇硝酸盐";第三,音意兼译:如将 kanamycin 译为"卡那霉素";第四,谐音意译:如 Miltown 译为"眠尔通",Reserpine 译为"利血平",使服药者一望便知它们的功能和作用。

此外,在翻译这类技术性的文字时,切忌望文生义,意思模棱两可,含糊不清,让使用者无所适从。如在"Angina pectoris vasomotorica, a form induced by central nevous disouder, is not affected."一句中,a form 作为 angina pectoris vasomotorica 的同位语,说的其实是一回事,那么在译时,就不一定按原样译为"血管舒缩性心绞痛,一种由中枢神经紊乱而引起的病"。按汉语习惯也不宜把"is affected"再用被动语态译出。将这句译为"但对中枢神经紊乱而引起的血管舒缩性心绞痛不起作用。"则译文更简练明白,更通俗易懂。

附:练习

将下列规则或说明书译成中文。

① RULES OF THE READING ROOM

1. Read and study seriously and be concerned about world affairs.

2. Keep quiet and pay attention to cleanliness.

3. Do not talk or laugh loudly; do not smoke or eat; do not litter the floor with waste paper.

4. Spit only in the places designated.

5. Produce your student card or identity card when borrowing books. Borrow only one book at a time.

6. Protect public property. Do not scribble on the pages of books or tear them out. Pay the cost price for any damage done.

7. Do not move the desks or chairs about. Close the windows when leaving.

8. Let the readers and librarians help each other and jointly run the reading room well.

② DIRECTIONS FOR TV MAINTENANCE

1. The set is highly sensitive and should be handled with care.

2. Don't install the set in a location near heat sorces, such as radiators and stoves, or in a place subject to excessive dust, mechanical vibration or shock.

3. Avoid placement and operation in direct sunlight or in very humid places.

4. Take care to allow adequate air circulation on all sides to prevent internal heat build-up.

5. Don't place the set on soft surfaces (rugs, blankets, etc.) or near curtains or draperies, as they may block the venti-

lation holes.

6. Don't open the cabinet, inside which are present dangerously high voltages.

7. Save the shipping carton and packing material for the set, which will come handy if it has to be repacked and reshipped. Repack the set as it was originally done at the factory.

8. Clean the set periodically with a soft cloth so as to keep it looking always new.

9. Stubborn stains may be removed with a cloth slightly dampened with a little mild detergent solution. Never use strong solvents, such as thinner or benzine, or abrasive cleaners, as they will damage the cabinet.

10. Unplug the set from the wall outlet if it is not to be used for a long period of time. Pull the mains lead-in by the plug when disconnecting it. Never pull the mains lead-in itself.

③ ANTISTINE: DIRECTIONS FOR USE

Antihistine for the Treatment of Allergic Affections

[Properties]

Antistine either attenuates or suppresses the effects of histamine, which plays a major role in provoking allergic disorders. It is upon this experimentally confirmed ability to antagonize histamine that the indications for Antistine are based.

[Indications]

Urticaria; food allergies; hay fever; vasomotor rhinitis; itching due to skin diseases, including eczema; pruritus; and serum sickness.

[Adminstration and dosage]

Tablets

Adults: 1 tablet, 3—4 times daily.

Small children: 1/2 tablet, once daily.

Children of school age: 1/2 tablet, 2—3 times daily.

The tablets should be taken during meals and swallowed whole with a little fluid.

Ampoules

1 ampoule is given each time by intramuscular or slow intravenous injection, 2—3 times daily. For children the doses should be correspondingly reduced.

[Note]

Since Antistine may cause temporary drowsiness, caution is indicated when it is employed, for example, to treat drivers of vehicles. Like other antihistamines, Antistine, too, may give rise to allergic reactions. In such cases the preparation should be withdrawn.

[Composition and forms of issue]

2—(phenyl—benzyl—aminomethyl)—imidazoline(=antazolin): tablets of 100 mg. and ampoules of 2 ml containing 100 mg.

Made in Switzerland

第七节 演 讲

演讲主要有三种:外事演讲、科坛演讲和政治演讲。

一篇好的演说词。在语言上具有用词精确、言简意赅、深入浅出、通俗易懂、扣人心弦等特点。

一、外事演讲

在外事活动中经常有迎送、宴请、聚会的场合，主宾双方都要发表讲话，如欢迎词、欢送词、答词、献词、贺词、祝酒词等。这一类的讲话一般称为外事演讲。

根据场合的不同，外事演讲可分为正式和非正式两大类。政府高级代表团的讲话比较正式。在这类讲话中，讲话人不仅颂扬双方的友谊，而且也表明各自对国内、国际重大问题的看法。这种讲话稿的结构比较严谨，语言也比较规范。一般性的代表团和个人的讲话则较多属于非正式性的。这类讲话稿以颂扬双方之间的友谊为主，语言比较随和，基调也比较轻松。现举两例：

A Visiting Professor's Answering Speech
at a Welcome Meeting

Dear Prof. Hobar, President of ×× University,

Ladies and gentlemen,

　　Thank you, Mr. President, for your warm and friendly remarks, and you all, ladies and gentlemen, for your hearty welcome. It is a great pleasure for me to be able to visit your university, a university of world fame and unique achievements.

　　In the magnificent and glorious history of American science and culture, your university has fostered and trained many outstanding scientists and men of letters, who have made immense contributions to the advancement of science and culture of your country, and in many respects, of the world.

　　The U.S. is a great country and the American people are a great people. The past hundred years have witnessed a speedy development of your science and technology. Here there is much for me to see and much for me to learn. Of course, I will avail myself of this visit to swap experience with American friends and colleagues.

As a scientist, I heartily welcome the great strides made in the past few years in the scientific, scholarly and cultural exchanges between your country and mine, many of which have yielded fruitful results. This is conducive to the furtherance of mutual understanding, friendship and cooperation of our two countries. I am sure all of you would gladly agree when I say that we, scientists and scholars, must join our minds and hands to explore the secret of science and open new realms of civilization for the common progress of mankind.

I feel really overwhelmed by your kindness and hospitality with which you have received me. Allow me once again to express my sincere thanks to you all for everything you have done on my account.

客座教授在欢迎会上的答词

亲爱的××大学校长霍巴特教授,

女士们,先生们:

校长先生,感谢您刚才说的一些热情友好的话,感谢女士们和先生们的诚挚欢迎。你们的学校誉满全球,取得了卓越的成就。我有幸能来访问,感到非常高兴。

在美国辉煌灿烂的科学文化史上,你们学校培养和造就了许多杰出的科学家和文学家,他们为你们国家,在许多方面也为世界科学文化的发展作出了巨大的贡献。

美国是一个伟大的国家,美国人民是伟大的人民。过去一百年中,你们的科学和技术取得了迅速的发展。这里有许多东西值得我参观学习。当然,我还将利用此次访问的机会与美国朋友和同行交流经验。

  作为一名科学家,我衷心欢迎过去几年中我们两国之间在科学、学术和文化交流方面取得的巨大进展。这些交流有许多已产生丰硕的成果。这有助于增进两国之间相互了解、友谊与合作。我们两国的科学家和学者,为了人类的共同进步,应同心协力探索科学的奥秘,开拓新的文明领域。我想大家会欣然同意我这一见解的。

  承蒙你们热情款待,使我感激不已。请允许我对各位为我所做的一切再次表示真诚的感谢。

U. S. Commerce Secretary's Toast at a Welcome Banquet

Mr. Li Qiang, the Minister of Foreign Trade,

Ladies and Gentlemen,

 Your hospitality is extraordinary.

 For myself and for our entire delegation, I thank you for your warm welcome.

 Our two countries have embarked on a new adventure — an adventure as exciting in its prospects as it is important in its implications. It is a venture that will bring together two great nations. As I visited the Great Wall and the Summer Palace, I glimpsed something of the sweep of your history, and sensed the pride and the dignity which that legacy bestows upon your people.

 We meet today as we have in the past — yours a great and ancient civilization; ours derived from many great and ancient civilizations. It is a privilege to be a part of the process that brings our peoples closer together.

 The ties between our two countries are developing rapidly.

 Chinese and American students are now studying in each

other's universities. American tourists are visiting China in increasing numbers. Our trade is expanding. In recent months, at least eleven Chinese and American cabinet level officials have traveled between our countries; more visits are planned. Four U. S. Congressional Delegations visited Beijing during the spring. Forty official Chinese delegations are in the United States at this moment. American teachers of English are in many Chinese cities. American petroleum engineers will be off your shores working with you in the exploration of your oil reserves. These developments are but the beginning of a flourishing Sino-American relationship.

Normalization has opened new vistas among our two peoples.

Our goal now is to derive the economic benefits that normalization makes possible. We must build an enduring relationship.

To this end, my visit has three purposes:

— first, to advance our economic relations, particularly in the pursuit of trade, maritime and aviation agreements.

— second, to expand our cooperation in science and technology, on the basis of reciprocity and in the interest of our common progress.

— and third, to establish contact between your management specialists and ours, so that we can share our knowledge in this important aspect of economic development.

Our shared interests bring us together. President Carter has noted that the United States has an interest in a strong, secure and peaceful China. You have an interest in a strong, confident and globally engaged United States. These considerations alone impel us to expand our economic relations. But there is a sentimental dimension to our relationship as well. President Carter frequently speaks of the friendship which the American people traditionally have felt for the Chinese people, and I cannot help but note the special warmth of this evening.

The opportunities before us in the next several days are historic. Despite our differences we approach this work with a shared belief that from cooperation will come important benefits for both your country and ours. The words and details over which we must labour are important steps toward a more peaceful and prosperous world. We take them with great hope and confidence. I propose a toast

  to the health of Mr. Li Qiang, the Minister of Foreign Trade

  to the health of the Chinese people, and

  to our growing friendly as well as commercial ties!

美国商业部长在欢迎宴会上的答词

外贸部长李强先生,

女士们,先生们:

你们的款待是非同寻常的。

我谨以我个人和整个代表团的名义感谢你们的热情欢迎。

我们两国正在着手一个崭新的事业——一个意义重大而又前景光明的事业。这个事业将把我们两个伟大的国家联结在一起。我在长城和颐和园游览的时候,领略了贵国悠久的历史,感受到了贵国的历史遗产给贵国人民带来的自豪和尊严。

今天我们又像往常一样地会面了。贵国是一个伟大的历史悠久的文明古国,我国则是一个从许多伟大的古老文明发展出来的国家。此行能够成为把我们两国人民更紧密联结在一起的整个纽带的一部分,我感到莫大荣幸。

我们两国之间的联系正在迅速发展。

中美两国互派的留学生正在彼此的大学中学习。到中国来旅游的美国人愈来愈多。我们之间的贸易正在扩大。在最近的几个月中,中美至少有十一位部长级的官员对彼此的国家进行了互访,而且更多的互访已经列入计划之中。今春已经有四个美国国会议员代表团访问了北京。目前,有四十个中国官方代表团正在美国访问。许多来自美国的英语教师正在中国各大城市教授英语。美国的石油工程师将在贵国的沿海与你们一起勘探贵国的石油资源。这些仅仅是不断发展的中美两国关系的一个开端。

两国关系正常化为两国人民开拓了新的前景。

我们现在的目标是取得经济的成果,两国关系正常化使这一点成为可能。我们一定要建立一个持久的关系。

正因为此,我的这次访问有三个目的:

第一是发展我们的经济关系,特别是商谈签订两国间的贸易、海运和航空协定。

第二是在互利的基础上为了共同的进步扩大我们之间的科学技术合作。

第三是建立两国管理专家之间的联系,以便我们能在这一经济发展的重要方面共享彼此的学识。

我们之间的共同利益把我们结合在一起。卡特总统说过,美国愿意看到一个强大、安定、和平的中国。你们愿意看到一个强大、自信、负有全球义务的美国。仅这些考虑就足以促使人们要扩大我们的经济关系。在我们的关系中还有感情上的一面。卡特总统经常谈及美国人民对中国人民的传统友谊。今晚我亲自体会到了这种特殊的温暖。

在今后几天中展示在我们面前的机会是具有历史意义的。尽管我们之间存在着一些分歧,但我们都怀着只有通过合作彼此才能获得重大利益的共同信念在进行工作。我们将要花费精力去讨论的一些措词和细节是向着一个更加和平和繁荣的世界所迈出的重要步骤。我们对此充满了希望和信心。

现在我提议：

为外贸部长李强先生的健康，

为中国人民的健康，

为我们日益增强的贸易上的和友谊上的联系干杯！

以上两篇范例都为欢迎会上的答词，它们的共同特点是语言通俗易懂，句子简洁明了，表达朴实无华，内容层次清楚，逻辑性强。然而，在文体上却还存在着细微的差别。第一篇为一名学者的讲话，所以措词平易，自然。第二篇是美国商业部长代表政府的讲话，语言相对而言更为正规，严谨，充满外交语言的特色。翻译时必须既注意彼此的共同点，又注意各自的特点，使译文的语言和风格尽可能地忠实于原文。如：第一篇的开场白译者采用了口语和书面语相结合的文体，译文也使用了自然平易的语言，反映出宾主之间亲切友好的关系。第二篇译文开场白中却用了"谨"这一词，不难看出这是正式的文体。又如：在两篇原文中同样出现了"your country"一词。在第一篇中译成"你们国家"，通俗自然，符合当时的场合与气氛。而在第二篇中则译成"贵国"，这样的措词更具有外交辞令的特色。

二、科坛演讲

科坛演讲常有特定的专题和专门的内容，在演讲的对象、手段、语言、方式等方面与其他类型的演讲相比也都有所不同。严谨的结构、精密的逻辑、科学的语言、专门的词汇及较强的学术性为此类演讲的文体特征。这就要求，译文同样逻辑周密、语言准确、表达科学。下面是一篇专业性与学术性均不强的一般知识性的讲话，虽不典型，却也常见。

Ladies and Gentlemen,

There are many problems connected with fixing faulty electrical appliances at home. *The first and greatest of them is* identifying the broken part. You can rarely tell just by looking at the outside. You have to take the appliance apart in order to find the difficulty.

Another problem is being able to find the extra part which is needed. Electrical appliances are imported, and spare parts are difficult to find.

Once the appliance is in a million parts, *still another problem becomes* obvious: How are all the pieces going to fit together again? There always seem to be extra pieces left over at the end.

Workers are *also* affected by spectators. It seems impossible to mend an appliance without attracting an audience that is full of well-meaning and contradictory advice. Workers must train themselves to ignore all such comments.

The lack of proper tools *is another problem*. Someone has disappeared with the screwdriver, the scissors are gone, etc. The hammer is of little use, and a knife doesn't work very well.

The electric shock which one can get from an improperly mended appliance is *also a serious problem* in this sort of work. Of course, if the shock is serious enough, you will have no more problems.

女士们,先生们:

在家里维修电器故障涉及到许多问题。首先最关键的问题是确定有故障的部件。寻找故障光靠外观检查还不行,必须把它拆开才能找到。

另外一个问题是要能够寻找到所需要的备件。但家用电器通常是进口的,所以不易找到备件。还有一个明显的问题,电器一旦被拆得七零八落,那么,怎么再将所有小零件装配在一起?重新装配后,似乎总会剩下一些多出的零件。

装配工作也时常受到围观者的影响。维修电器时似乎也不可能不吸引围观者,这些好心的围观者也总爱提些互相矛盾的意见。因此,修理者应培养自己不受这种干扰的能力。

缺乏必要的维修工具又成为一个问题。螺丝起子不见了,剪刀也不翼而飞了,等等。榔头用不上,而刀子又不好使。

在维修电器过程中,如果修理不得当,触电又是一个严重的问题。当然,如果严重触电,那么也就不会有更多的问题了。

在此篇演讲中,演讲者在讲述自己在家维修电器的难处时,相继使用了"The first and greatest of them"、"Another problem"、"still another problem"、"also"、"…is another problem"、"also a serious problem"等递进过渡词,使讲题层层展开,步步深入,结构严密,条理清楚,译文也体现了这一特点。

其次,科坛演讲辞在用词上的最明显特点是大量使用专门化的科技词汇。即使是许多常用词语在科坛演讲辞中也具有与平常不同的词义。譬如,此处"driver"就非"驾驶员",而为"螺丝起子"之义。

另外,科坛演讲所叙述的主体多为客观事物、现象或过程,所以常采用被动语态。这样做不仅可以使读者把注意力集中到叙述中的事物上,还给人以客观的感觉,而非演讲者本人的主观看法。翻译时也应予注意这一风格。

三、政治演讲

这类演讲语言精练,词汇丰富,深入浅出,佳句和警句迭出以鼓动人心。在翻译此类演讲词时,要特别注意词汇的选择,应尽量传达出原作的感情,要注意长句和短句、整句和散句的合理调配,以利于口头表达；还要注意保持原文中使用的各种修辞手法，以更好地体现原文的风格。

现举一篇林肯的演说词为例：

The Gettysburg Address

Fourscore and seven years ago our fathers brought forth upon this continent a new nation, conceived in liberty, and dedicated to the proposition that all men are created equal.

Now we are engaged in a great civil war, testing whether that nation, or any nation so conceived and so dedicated, can long endure. We are met on a great battlefield of that war. We have come to dedicate a portion of that field as a final resting-place for those who here gave their lives that that nation might live. It is altogether fitting and proper that we should do this.

But in a large sense we cannot dedicate, we cannot consecrate, we cannot hallow this ground. The brave men, living and dead, who struggled here, have consecrated it far above our poor power to add or detract. The world will little note nor long remember what we say here; but it can never forget what they did here. It is for us, the living, rather, to be dedicated here to the unfinished work which they who fought here have thus far so nobly advanced. It is rather for us to be here dedicated to the great task remaining before us: that from these honored dead we take increased devotion to that cause for which they gave the last full measure of devotion; that we here highly revolve that these dead shall not have died in vain; that this nation, under God, shall have a new birth of freedom; and that government of the people, by the people, and for the people, shall not perish from the earth.

葛底斯堡演说词

八十七年前,我们的先辈在这个大陆上建立了一个新国家,它孕育于自由之中,奉行人人生而平等的原则。

目前我们正在进行一场伟大的国内战争。战争考验着这个国家,或任何信奉自由、平等的国家,能否国基永固,长治久安。

今天我们在这场战争的一个伟大战场上隆重集会。我们来到这里,将战场的一角奉献给那些为捍卫国家生存而英勇捐躯的人们,作为他们最后安息之地。我们这样做完全是理所当然,义不容辞的。

但是,从更重大的意义上说,我们并不能使这片土地成为圣地,我们并不能使它流芳百世,我们并不能使它永垂不朽,因为在这里进行过斗争的、活着的和已经死去的勇士们,已经使这块土地变得这样圣洁,我们的微力已不足以对它有所扬抑了。我们今天在这里说的话,世人将不大注意,也不会长久记住,但勇士们在此的业绩,人们将永志不忘。而我们这些生存者所应该做的,就是在这里把自己奉献给勇士们为之忘我战斗,并一直大力推进的未竟事业,就是在这里把自己奉献给仍然留在我们面前的伟大任务:以这些光荣牺牲的烈士们的献身精神,投身于烈士们为之鞠躬尽瘁,死而后已的事业中去;在烈士墓前表示决心——一定让烈士们的鲜血决不白流,一定要让这个国家在上帝的保护下获得自由的新生,一定要让民有、民治、民享的政治制度永世长存。

这是美国总统林肯于 1863 年 11 月 19 日在葛底斯堡公墓落成典礼上发表的演讲,全文一气呵成,措词精练,语言生动,形象完美,文风朴实。译文较好地再现了原文的风貌。首先,选词精当,表达了原作的情感。例如演说词的结束语"government of the people, by the people, and for the people, shall not perish from the earth."译者成功地译为"一定要让民有、民治、民享的政治制度永世长存。""民有、民治、民享"的译法体现了原句的语言风格和修辞手法,成了一句有力的口号,而"永世长存"则传达了林肯对新政府充满希望和信心的感情。其次,为了使译文和原文一样行文流畅,层次清楚,译者还十分注意句子和段落之间的衔接连贯。比如:第二段的第二句"We are met on a great battle field of the war."译文中增加了"今天"二字,把当日的集会与正在进行的国内战争在时间上的联系交代清楚了,若没有这二字,则使人感到"集会"来得非常突然,前后文难以衔接。再次,这类正式演讲词偏向于书面语言,长句较多。译文有意识地拆成短句,这样更符合汉语习惯,读起来朗朗上口。如第二段的第三句:"We have come to dedicate a portion of that field as a final resting-place for those who here gave their lives that nation might live."译文重新安排语序,分成两个短句和一个短语:"我们来到这里,将战场的一角奉献给那些为捍卫国家生存而英勇捐躯的人们,作为他们最后安息之地。"最后,原文大量运用了排比句的修辞手段。译文也使用了同样的句型。

政治演说词除具有共同特点外,演讲者还有个人的风格,如肯尼迪的演讲以语言生动、感情奔放、鼓动性强取胜,而邱吉尔则以语言精辟、行文朴实、深入浅出著称。这些也是译者在翻译时要注意的。

附:练习
将下列演说词译成中文。

① Toast by the American Secretary of Commerce
Mr. Chairman,
Ladies and Gentlemen,
   We are delighted to be in your lovely city of Guangzhou. It is here that we will conclude what has been for all of us a memo-

rable visit to a magnificent country.

We have visited your historic, heroic capital city of Beijing.

We have visited Shanghai, the bustling industrial and port city through which much of the growing trade between our countries will flow. We have caught the magic and enchantment of Guilin, a place with complete serenity.

And we now come to Guangzhou for the close of the Guangzhou Fair, yet another symbol of the growing ties between our two countries.

We believe we have accomplished a great deal during our brief stay.

We have concluded six agreements—twice the number of all previous agreements between our two Governments. More importantly, we have seen and talked with your people. We have dined with you, drunk with you, bargained, worried and laughed with you. In all this, our respect has grown, our friendship warmed.

Now I should like to propose a toast

to the health of our host and the health of the Chinese people,

to our growing personal as well as commercial ties,

to our next visit to your beautiful country, and you to ours!

② ... Now, let's look back at our experiment. First, we made a hole in a cork and pushed into it a narrow glass tube. Then we pushed this into the neck of a bottle which we had filled with coloured water. When we did this, some of the coloured water went up in the tube. Then we put the bottle into a pan of hot water.

Almost at once, the water level in the tube went down a little, but then it started to go up, until the water poured out over the top.

The reason for this is that, when it gets hot, the volume of water increases. The reason why the water level went down at first is that the bottle became hot first and so it became a little bigger. When the water became hot, its volume increased. Nearly all liquids and solids get bigger like this when they become hot.

Next we emptied the bottle and left a small amount of coloured water in the tube. We put back the cork and we put the bottle back into the hot water. The water in the tube was at once blown out at the top. This is because, when the air in the bottle became hot, its volume increased a lot and very quickly when it gets hot...

③   Blood, Toil, Sweat and Tears

Winston Leonard Spencer Churchill

On Friday evening last I received from His Majesty the mission to form a new administration.

It was the evident will of Parliament and the nation that this should be received on the broadest possible basis and that it should include all parties.

I have already completed the most important part of this task. A war cabinet has been formed of five members, representing, with the Labour, Opposition and Liberals, the unity of the nation.

...

I now invite the House by a resolution to record its approval of the steps taken and declare its confidence in the new government. The resolution:

"That this House welcomes the formation of a government representing the united and inflexible resolve of the nation to prosecute the war with Germany to a victorious conclusion."

To form an administration of this scale and complexity is a serious undertaking in itself. But we are in the preliminary phase of one of the greatest battles in history. We are in action at many other points - in Norway and in Holland—and we have to be prepared in the Mediterranean. The air battle is continuing, and many preparations have to be made here at home.

In this crisis I think I may be pardoned if I do not address the House at any length today, and I hope that any of my friends and colleagues or former colleagues who are affected by the political reconstruction will make all allowances for any lack of ceremony with which it has been necessary to act.

I say to the House as I said to Ministers who have joined this government, I have nothing to offer but blood, toil, tears and sweat. We have before us an ordeal of the most grievous kind. We have before us many, many months of struggle and suffering.

You ask, what is our policy? I say it is to wage war by land, sea and air. War with all our might and with all the strength God has given us, and to wage war against a monstrous tyranny never surpassed in the dark and lamentable catalogue of human crime. That is our policy.

You ask, what is our aim ? I can answer in one word. It is victory. Victory at all costs — victory in spite of all terrors — victory, however long and hard the road may be, for without victory there is no survival.

Let that be realized. No survival for the British Empire, no survival for all that the British Empire has stood for, no survival for the urge, the impulse of the ages, that mankind shall move forward toward his goal.

I take up my task in buoyancy and hope. I feel sure that our cause will not be suffered to fail among men.

I feel entitled at this juncture, at this time, to claim the aid of all and to say, "Come then, let us go forward together with our united strength."

④   The Torch Has Been Passed
                  To A New Generation of Americans
                         John Kennedy

We observe today not a victory of party, but a celebration of freedom — symbolizing an end, as well as a beginning — signifying renewal, as well as change. For I have sworn before you and Almighty God the same solemn oath our forebears prescribed nearly a century and three quarters ago.

The world is very different now. For man holds in his mortal hands the power to abolish all forms of human poverty and all forms of human life.

And yet the same revolutionary beliefs for which our forebears fought are still at issue around the globe — the belief that the rights of man come not from the generosity of the state, but from the hand of God.

We dare not forget today that we are the heirs of that first revolution. Let the word go forth from this time and place, to friend and foe alike that the torch has been passed to a new generation of Americans — born in this century, tempered by war, disciplined by a hard and bitter peace, proud of our ancient heritage — and unwilling to witness or permit the slow undoing of those human rights to which this Nation has always been committed, and to which we are committed today at home and around the world.

Let every nation know, whether it wishes us well or ill, that we shall pay any price, bear any burden, meet any hardship, support any friend, oppose any foe, in order to assure the survival and the success of liberty.

...

In the long history of the world, only a few generations have been granted the role of defending freedom in its hour of maximum danger. I do not shrink from this responsibility — I welcome it. I do not believe that any of us would exchange places with any other people or any other generation. The energy, the faith, the devotion which we bring to this endeavor will light our country and all who serve it — and the glow from that fire can truly light the world.

And so, my fellow Americans, ask not what your country can do for you; ask what you can do for your country.

My fellow citizens of the world: Ask not what America will do for you, but what together we can do for the freedom of man.

Finally, whether you are citizens of America or citizens of

the world, ask of us here the same high standards of strength and sacrifice which we ask of you. With a good conscience our only sure reward, with history the final judge of our deeds, let us go forth to lead the land we love, asking His blessing and His help, but knowing that here on earth God's work must truly be our own.

第三章 新闻文体的翻译

新闻文体是英语中常见的实用文体之一,对它的理解可有广狭二义。狭义的新闻文体指的是新闻报道(news-reporting),广义的新闻文体则涉及报刊杂志上登载的各类文章。新闻中使用的语体种类比较丰富多样,各种体裁都有各自独特之处,但新闻刊物作为大众传媒的一种,其文章的写作目的与手法大体是一致的,即"用尽可能有趣的方式将一定的事实展现出来"。

第一节 新闻文体的语言特点与翻译方法

新闻文体因其自身特点和传播功能而在语言运用上形成了个性鲜明的特点。主要表现在以下几个方面:(一)用词新颖,精巧别致;(二)句式多样,富于弹性;(三)巧用时态,不拘呼应;(四)频繁使用被动语态,重点突出;(五)善用修辞,讲究效果。下文将用实例加以阐释,并提示相应的翻译要点。

一、用词新颖,精巧别致

1. 频繁使用新词

掌握某些词语的确切含义是理解与翻译报刊文字难点之一。这是因为新闻刊物不仅是报导新闻的媒介,而且是"使用新词的庞大机器和杜撰新词的巨大工厂"。频繁使用新词是新闻文体中的用词特点之一。

当今世界日新月异,科学技术迅猛发展,人类文明不断提高,在政治、经济、科技、文化乃至社会生活各个方面、各个角落都会产生新事物，出现新问题。一些新的表达法便伴随着特定的环境应运而生，以适应反映新的现实生活的需要。新词在构成与表现形式上大致有以下几种情况：旧词转新义，新事生新词，新近时髦词，派生出新词与临时新造词。

(1) 旧词转新义。指词的形式虽早已出现，但意思却发生变化，即旧词衍生出新义。这类旧词添新义的现象在新闻用语中屡见不鲜。在阅读时应有足够的敏感度，以免引起误解和误译。如：

The rapid-growing death toll of AIDS victims has posed a widespread panic across the States from gay bars in the west coast of California to the Fun City's red-light districts. 艾滋病患者死亡人数激增造成普遍恐慌。恐慌波及全国，从西海岸加洲的同性恋酒吧到逍遥城纽约的红灯区。

gay 的原意为"快乐的"，但现在在新闻报道中已转义为"同性恋的"或"同性恋者的"。此例中的 gay bar 是"同性恋者聚集的酒吧"，而不是"快乐酒吧"。又如：

Khomeini's curious blend of mysticism and activism still made him slightly suspect in the eyes of the Islamic *Establishment* — as a holy man who tried to run around with the Mob, one might say — but his following was growing steadily. 霍梅尼将神秘主义与激进主义古怪地相结合，使他在伊斯兰教当权派的眼中，仍有些许可疑之处——人们可能会说，他是个圣人，却与暴民搞在一起，可是他的信徒却越来越多。

Establishment 原意是"建立"、"确定"之义，后转义为"权势集团"、"当权派"或"领导核心"等。

(2) 新事生新词。指因新事物的出现而催生出的新词。这些新词往往伴随着特定的政治、社会等环境而产生，从而具有显著的社会性，也易于为读者所理解与接受。如：1969 年 7 月 20 日，美国阿波罗号（Apollo）宇宙飞船成功登月，各国报刊竞相报道，随之产生了大量有关的新词,现已在日常英语中广泛使用,如 moonwalk (月面行走),moonfall(登月),moonrock(月球岩石),moonscape (月面景色),moonship(月球飞船),space suit(宇航服),space travel(太空旅行),space shuttle(航天飞机),space race(太空竞争)等等。

Neil Armstrong and Edward Aldrin, who in 1969 became the first moonwalkers were among thousands of special guests viewing the spectacular blasting off of the space shuttle Columbia. 尼尔·阿姆斯特朗与爱德华·艾德林,这两位1969年首批月面行走者,与数千名特邀嘉宾一道,观看了哥伦比亚号航天飞机升空的壮观场面。

又如五十年代时某些美国青年不满当时的社会现状,以奇装异服、长发吸毒等放荡不羁的方式来反抗社会,表现个性。于是1953年出现了"hippie"或"hippy"一字,专指这类青年,译为"颓废派"或"嬉皮士"等。

I mentioned another hotel in the district, but this, he said, was full of hippies who bought and sold drugs such as heroin. 我提及该区的另一家旅馆,他却说这一家住满了买卖海洛因之类毒品的嬉皮士。

When he emerged from captivity, Niehous looked like a middle-aged hippie. He had lost 44 pounds and was dressed in ill-fitting jeans and sportshirt. 当尼霍士被释放时,他看起来就像一个中年嬉皮士。瘦了四十四磅,穿着不合身的牛仔裤和运动衫。

这类因新事物而出现的新词往往有特定的含义和相对固定的译法,且多为较大的辞典收录,翻译时可以按图索骥,一一对应。

此外,新闻英语中还有一种由"动词+-in 构成的新词,如 work-in, sit-in。这类词起源于六十年代的美国。当时的人民反对越战,黑人要求平等,各地学生罢课,开宣讲会,工人静坐罢工,因而美国最早使用了"sit-in"一词,见诸报端。现在这种构成新词的形式已成定格,以表示"有组织的抗议(或示威)"或"公开的集体行动"。如:bed-in/camp-in(露营示威),dial-in(电话示威),filth-in(乱倒垃圾示威),lock-in(封锁行动),sign-in(签名运动),smoke-in(吸毒聚会),teach-in(宣讲会),wed-in(集体婚礼),work-in(当班怠工示威)等。

Leaders of demonstrators accused the government of trying to hinder the teach-in by hastily organizing pop concerts and commandeering the city's mobile toilets. 示威领导者指责政府匆忙组织流行音乐会,强占城市流动厕所,企图以此阻扰宣讲会。

Subdued by the first blizzard of winter, Kabul was regaining a semblance of normality ... But the city was not the same. Soviet officers and political cadres were virtually in charge of the Defence and Interior Ministries. Most large police stations now had live-in Soviet advisers. 被冬天第一场暴风雪所压服的喀布尔,正在恢复正常的外貌。……但是这座城市已不再是原来的状况。苏联军官和政工干部实际上接管了国防部和内务部。多数警察局现在都有常驻的苏联顾问。

(3)新近时髦词。指的是在报刊杂志上和人们言谈中,一段时间内风行一时的字眼。这类词多数原为某些专门术语,报刊记者把它们作为一般词汇来用,使它们在含义上带有某种特点,增强了表现力。有些时髦词的词义逐渐得到扩展与引申,而使原意变得模糊。因此在阅读时应格外留心,仔细辨别,确定词义。例如:

But on decontrol of oil, we had extensive consultations not only with Congress, but also with the entire spectrum of outside groups:everything from oil companies and the business community to consumers and environmental leaders. 但是在取消石油管制方面,我们进行过广泛的协商,不仅与国会协商,而且与整个外

界各类集团协商:从石油公司、工商界到消费者以及环保方面的头面人物。

此处的"spectrum"原意为"光谱",属物理学名词,这里引申为"各种各样"。该词替代一般词汇增强了表达的形象感。

For days on end last week, Jimmy Carter secreted himself in the suddenly portentous stillness of Camp David to confront the converging traumas of inflation, recession and the energy crisis — to address what one official called "the last real chance to save his presidency..." 上周连续几天,吉米·卡特隐身于突然悄无声息的戴维营中,专心应付纷至沓来的难堪之事:通货膨胀,经济衰退和能源危机——致力于利用,如一位官员所称的,"真正的最后一次机会来保全他的总统宝座"。

"trauma"原意为身体上的创伤,属医学名词,用在这里转义为"心理冲击"或"精神创伤",暗示通货膨胀等一系列的问题给卡特带来的打击和危机。

Slippage is the ugliest and most dangerous, new buzz word in the United States. Slippage has been coined by the gay community in the US to refer to homosexuals who have slipped back to the sort of casual and promiscuous encounters spurned by most homosexuals when AIDS epidemic began to sweep America a decade ago. 倒退是美国新近流行的时髦词中最丑恶最危险的字眼。"倒退"一词是美国的同性恋社团新造的用来指那些倒退到重蹈随意杂交旧辙的同性恋者。这种杂交早在十年前艾滋病开始横扫全国时就被多数同性恋者所摒弃。

"slippage"的含义已由原来机械学里的"滑动"、"下降"扩展、引申为"倒退"、"道德沦丧"等新义。

(4)派生新构词。指把词根与前缀或后缀相结合所构成的新词。派生法是现代英语构词法中运用最多的形式,它所构成的新词占总数的 30—34％。用派生法构成的新词一方面可以补足原有英语词汇中缺少的词义，另一方面又能使文笔简练有力。如：

Anti-corruption and keeping a clean government remain a major task in the coming years, the Premier stressed. 总理强调说，反腐倡廉仍是今后几年的一项主要任务。

Mr. Moynihan used the job to build his constituency though he denies that charge, saying that the stories that he was running for senate from the UN were Russian "disinformation". 莫伊尼汉先生利用他的职位来争取选民投他的票，尽管他否认这种指责。他说，有关他站在联合国的席位上来竞选美国参议员的报道是俄国人的造谣。

新闻文体中派生新词使用的频率远超出其他文体。有些词的构成比较随意，甚至在一般词典中难以找到。如上例中的 disinformation，只在 Chambers Twentieth Century Dictionary 中有注解。对于这样的派生词应通过分析词缀来推断词义。再举一例：

In other words, asked the questioner, Sheikh Yamani was saying "that if we had such an overall settlement, we would be much better off oilwise?" 提问者舍克·雅玛尼说："也就是说，如果我们全面解决此事，那么我们在石油方面的境况就会更好吗？"

-wise 的意思很明确。有"in the direction of"，"with regard to" "in the manner of"之义。根据上下文可以将 oilwise 译为"石油方面"。由此可见了解一些新闻英语中比较活跃的词缀有助于对文章的理解与翻译。

（5）临时新造词。即英语中的"nonce words"或者"coinages"。它们是在写作过程中临时创造或拼凑而成的，且多为应时应景而用，未能风行开来成为"时髦词"，也未能成为新词由词典所收录，因此经常成为翻译与理解文章的"拦路虎"。其实它们并非凭空随意拼写出来，而是通过拼缀法派生而成，或用复合法组成，读者可

根据上下文推测其词义。如:

Khomeini thus established himself as leader of the revolution by calling upon the armed forces to overthrow the Shan. Hundreds of thousands of copies of the letter were distributed in Iran. As a Tehran University professor put it: "We are struggling against autocracy, for democracy by means of Xerocracy".
……霍梅尼就是这样通过号召武装部队推翻伊朗国王来确立自己为革命领袖地位的。这封信印了几十万份,散发到伊朗各地。正如一位德黑兰大学教授所说的那样:"我们反对专制,争取民主,武器就是复印机。"

Xerocracy 是即兴生造词,是在 Xerox 这一著名的复印机牌号后加上后缀-cracy 而成。意即借助复印机大量复制散发宣传品,来动员群众争取民主。此例的巧妙之处在于连用三个"-cracy"结尾的词,既谐音又俏皮,省略了许多不必要的话。

上例中的 Xerocracy 是通过派生法临时造就的。还有一些生造词是由几个词复合而成,如:

Manned lunar exploration for purely scientific reasons probably will not resume for many years. And when it does, it most likely will use a more low-keyed, cost-effective approach than the use-'em-up-and-throw-'em-away Apollo program. 纯粹为科学研究而进行的载人月球探险今后许多年都可能不会再搞了。再进行时极可能采取更有节制、花钱更有效的搞法,而不像阿波罗号那样,用完就扔掉。"

例中的 use-'em-up-and-throw-'em-away 是用复合构词法构成,虽然很长,但意思明确,可以理解,也容易翻译。对于临时新造词,主要依靠分析词的构成及上下文的语境来确定词义,翻译时应视实际情况作解释性的翻译,而不必刻意追求字面对应。

2. 借用各类语汇

报刊文字的用词新颖还表现在借用外来语，借用行话，借用人、物名称以及常用俚语等方面。其作用无非是引起读者的兴趣，更贴切地表达词义。

(1) 外来语 (loan words)。即从非英语的语言中借用一些词或词组。它们在新闻文体中经常出现，有些已被长期使用，在形式上与英语词汇无甚区别。如 blitz［德］闪电似的动作，encore［法］再演，加演，percent［拉丁］百分之……，visa［法］签证等。但仍有相当一部分外来语尚未完全英语化，在书写时多用大写字母或斜体形式标出。如：

Britain has hardened its stance over European Community (EC) economic and political union, indicating the sine qua non of the Maastricht summit next week would be prompt solution to the most contentious issues. 英国对欧共体经济与政治联盟的态度强硬。这表明下周于麦士的里支召开的首脑会议必须就最有争议的问题作出果断的解决。

句中 sine qua non 来自拉丁语，意为"绝对必要的条件"，"必备的资格"，此处可译为"必须"。

They have made fortunes from the sale of their scholarly certitude about the behaviour of homo economicus, but are stupefied by the unfamiliar phenomenon of increasing world-wide unemployment running parallel with bounding inflation. 他们以出售有关"经济人"行为的学术性确实资料而发了财，但在日益严重的世界性失业和跳跃式通货膨胀同时出现的这种陌生现象面前目瞪口呆。

句中的"homo economicus"出自拉丁语，意为英语中的"economic man"，因此可译为带引号的"经济人"。

The Second World War was another huge Volkerwanderung, it was accompanied by a vast dislocation of people. 第二次世界大战又是一次大规模的"民族迁移",随之而来的是千百万人流离失所。

Volkerwanderung 是德语词,意为"民族迁徙"。

多数报刊文章中出现的外来语可以在字典中找到释义,翻译时只需依据词义作适当处理,但有些专有名词必须用相应的专用表达法。如:

Mr. Yeltsin continued his own campaign against the Communist Party by stopping publication with the Russian republic of all its newspaper, including Pravda, because he said they had published only the conspirator's statements. 叶利钦先生继续进行他反对共产党的战役。他令俄国所有报纸,包括真理报停刊,因为他说他们只发表阴谋家的言论。

这里的"Pravda"为专有名词,译作"真理报"。

外来语的使用可以填补英语词汇的不足,翻译时应仔细品味这些词,准确地把握它们的表层意思及深层含义,用相应的汉语进行释译。

(2)俚语(slang)。俚语的使用是现代英语的趋势,它的发展迅速,使用范围不断扩大,不仅在日常口语中,而且在一些书面语言中频频出现,特别在新闻文体中更是倍受青睐。新闻写作人员常采用通俗的口语体语言,来增强与读者的"亲和性"。恰当地使用俚语,的确可以使语言显得自然亲切,生动诙谐,新颖时髦。如:

The New York Post summed up the spreading bewilderment by demanding in its blackest front—page: WHAT THE HECK ARE YOU UP TO, MR. PRESIDENT?《纽约邮报》用最大号的黑体字,在第一版以提问的方式概括了普遍存在的迷惑心态:"总统先生,您到底要干什么?"

句中的"the heck"是"the hell"的代称。

"If the airlines can fill every seat they can find at full fare", says one Washington aviation expert, "they'd be nuts to sell seat for 30 or 40 percent off." 华盛顿一位民航界专家说:"航空公司如果能以全价卖出每个座位的话,那么,削价百分之三十或四十去卖座位就是傻瓜了。"

俚语的翻译也是一道难题,在汉语中难以找到恰好相应的表达方式,往往只能"解其意",而难"传其神"。在翻译过程中应开动脑筋,搜索大致对应的汉语表达法,或在表述的语气上做文章,尽可能体现出俚语的"味"来,但切忌太过,以免媚俗。

(3)行话(Jargon)。指某一行业内人士常说的话,隔行者未必能懂。但很多行话在语言发展过程中逐步为大众所接受,成为通用的词语。报刊文字常借用各种行话,一方面可以迎合各行业人士的口味,使他们读后倍感亲切,另一方面,亦可增强语言的色彩和表现力。如:

El Salvador has made its way into the European news with the abduction of British bank managers and the seizure of Spanish Embassy — the only way that Europe can be asked to notice the existence of Central America outside O-level geography. 萨尔瓦多用劫持英国银行经理和占领西班牙大使馆的办法,成了欧洲报纸上的新闻——这是除了学生们上的地理课以外,唯一让欧洲人注意到还有个中美洲存在的办法。

此处的 O-level=Ordinary level,是英国学校里学习成绩达到及格水平的行话。

At the state level, deciding who's going to clean up (the waste) and who's going to pay (for the pollution) often becomes a jurisdictional black hole of fingerpointing and buckpassing. 在州一级,究竟由谁负责清理(废物),由谁(为污染)付费,往往有关方面互相指责推诿,形成一个管理上的黑洞。

black hole 原意为天文学中的"黑洞"。它具有巨大的引力场，转义为神秘不可测的、巨大的吞噬力量，可以消耗无穷的精力。这里用来表示环境保护上职责权限不明而引起的困扰，非常有力。

这些词语蕴含的信息量大，可借以引起联想，节省篇幅。在翻译时一般可根据原意直译，以保持语言精练的余韵，不必译得过于明白，以免使原句的蕴意失去原味，变得淡如白水。

(4)人、物名称。借用这些词来表达一定的含义，读来更加生动形象。如借用各国首都著名建筑物名称或政府首脑的姓名替代该国或其政府，或借用某个专有名词表示其特有的意义等。例如：

The Kremlin declined comment as Norway was expelling eight Soviet diplomats for activities incompatible with their status — the usual term for spying. 挪威驱逐了八名苏联外交官，因为他们从事了与其身分不符的活动——即常言所说的间谍活动，克里姆林宫对此拒绝发表评论。

Kremlin 在这里代表苏联政府。

Bonn has also told Damascus it did not intend to impound the tanks and expressed a desire to settle the issue cordially. 波恩也通知大马士革说，他们并不想扣押坦克，并表达了想要善处理事端的真诚愿望。

Bonn 和 Damascus 分别代替德国和叙利亚。

对于这类名词一般只需按字面翻译，不必作更详细的解释，因为他们在报刊上经常出现，属一般常识，读者一看便知。

3. 短词及缩略语

新闻英语的另一词汇特色是青睐小词、短词和广泛采用缩略形式，特别在标题制作上，尤显突出。新闻标题必须具备吸引读者，提挈内容的功效，因此特别强调简明扼要，经济达意。且报纸栏目狭窄，使用长词有失雅观。在报纸标题中，经常可看到字形短小的单音节词(monosyllabic words)、首字母缩略语(initialisms)和首字母拼音词(acronyms)以及"截除法"而产生的缩写词(abbreviations)。

(1)短词。词义宽泛,形体短小的词可以美化版面,简练文字,在新闻写作中十分常用。如:

①World eyes mid-East peace talks 世界关注中东和平谈判(eyes=watcher,observes)

②Family planning urged in India 印度急需计划生育(urged=promoted/advocated)

③With jobs cuts, New York is losing war of brooms 纽约裁减清洁工,环境卫生恶化(cuts=reduction)

④Australia makes bid to lure more Asian tourists 澳大利亚力图吸引更多的亚洲游客(bid=attempt)

(2)缩略词。一些常用的组织名称、事物名称和人的职位、职称等用省字母缩略形式来代替全称。如:

①START announced to begin June 29 裁减战略武器谈判于六月二十九日开始(START=Strategic Arms Reduction Talks)

②PC, Fax sales expected to soar 个人电脑、传真机销售有望猛增(PC=Personal Computer)

例1中的缩略词为首字母拼音词,即用首字母拼读成一个词,而例2中的缩略词为首字母缩略词,它保留原字母的发音。

当然缩略词的使用并非限于标题中,文章中也常出现。如:

One sign that it may be on the way was the announcement that Mr. Thomas Watson, the former head of IBM, who is interested in promoting trade with the Soviet Union, is to be the new American ambassador of Moscow. 积极促进对苏贸易的国际商用机器公司的前任负责人托马斯·华生先生将出任美国驻苏大使。这一消息的宣布,是可能出现某种情况的一个迹象。(IBM

=International Business Machines Corporation）

缩略词的意思都可以在字典中查到。有些缩略词的全称还可直接从上下文中找到,因此在翻译中不成为问题。

（3）简缩词。简缩词在英文报纸中十分活跃,构成方式也不尽相同,有截头法,有去尾法,有截头去尾法,有保留头尾法,还有一些不规则的裁剪词。如：Lib=Liberation, Copter=helicopter, flu=influenza, cric=critic, mic=microphone 等。现举实例如下：

1) EEC Warns Nuke Arms Spread 欧共体警告核武器扩散 (Nuke=Nuclear)。

2) Big biz eats others, small fry are eaten 企业大鱼吃小鱼 (biz=business)。

这类简缩词不仅出现在标题中,有时也用于新闻报道中。如：

A tennis pro in white shorts will place his racquet alongside the court at the sports club and say his prayer. 身穿白短裤的职业网球手会把球拍放在体育俱乐部的球场旁,然后祈祷(pro=professional)。

二、句式多样,富有弹性。

英美报刊的句法结构灵活多变,不拘一格。表现在富于变化和富有弹性两个方面。

第一,报刊文字中的句式富于变化。在新闻报道中有倒装句,有省略形式,有借助副词、动词变化的句式等。形式多样,变化无常的句式使新闻语言生动活泼,趣味盎然。例如：

Bucking the trends are much of the middle East and Sub-Sahara Africa. 撒哈拉南部非洲和中东许多地区的情况与这些趋势正相反。

此句为倒装句,正常语序是：Much of the Middle East and Sub-Sahara Africa are bucking the trends.

More important, it is questionable whether market forces will prompt private employers to make way for many older workers anytime soon. 更为重要的是，市场力量是否会促使私营雇主尽快向许多老工人让步还值得怀疑。

本句采用了省略形式，More important 等于 What's more important。

Already, the presence of large number of Third World immigrants produced chronic racial tension in Great Britain. 大批第三世界移民的拥入，已经造成了英国国内种族间剧烈的紧张关系。

此句中的 already 被置于句首，句式显得更为跳跃。

Says Dary Reading of Gowrie: "It makes you mad. We are good at what we do, but we still can't make a living." 高瑞的达里·雷丁说："这让你发疯。我们有本领干好我们的工作，但仍不能谋生。"

这是一个将动词 say 放在句首的句式。这种谓语动词位于句子开头、主语之前的句式是新闻报道文章所特有的。

新闻报道常用引语，这既可增加报道的真实感和生动性，又能提高所述内容的客观性，使读者确信记者未掺杂个人观点。转述或援引提供消息和发表意见人士所说的话，离不开使用"说"的句式。如一味用"某某人说＋引语"的句式未免显得单调，沉闷。因此老练的记者总是注意灵活运用不同句式，既可将"某人说"放在所说的话的前面，也可置于句中，还可以置于句尾。如：

Asked whether he was homosexual or bisexual, <u>she said</u>, "I know of no indication whatsoever that my husband had a male encounter." 当问到他是同性恋还是异性恋时，她说："我只知道没有任何迹象表明我丈夫有男性伙伴。"

"These things may seem kind of Mickey Mouse," <u>says William Damon</u>, chairman of the education department at

Brown. "这些事情看起来或许不重要", 教育部长威廉·戴蒙在布朗说。

An armed man who bolted past the Pentagon Security guards in an apparent dash toward the National Command Centre yesterday was shot and later died, *authorities said*. 权威人士说：昨天一名持枪男子闯过两名五角大楼卫兵, 似乎想冲向国家指挥中心。该男子被枪击中, 后丧命。

"For every American, this has to be the proudest day of our lives," the President told the astronauts. "For one priceless moment in the whole history of man, all the people on this earth are truly one." "对于每个美国人来说, 这一天定是我们一生中最值得骄傲的日子," 总统对宇航员们说, "在人类历史上极其珍贵的时刻, 地球上所有的人真正形成了一体。"

"He has never acted as anything but a candidate," says a senior Western diplomat. "He has always been an outsider looking in." "他一直在做候选人," 一位资深西方外交官说, "他总是站在局外, 却关注着局内。"

由于英汉语言表达的差异, 引语句式的多样化在译文中难以完全体现, 因为汉语中作为主语的人与谓语动词"说"的词序是不能颠倒的。翻译引语时仍应以符合汉语表达习惯为原则。

第二, 富于弹性是新闻文体句式的另一特点。句子长短不一, 松紧兼备。作者常紧凑句式, 浓缩信息, 具体表现为省略句式的普遍使用和高度浓缩的前置修饰。新闻报道中有时也会出现一些较为庞杂的句式, 其目的是提供丰富的背景材料, 反映相关人员的观点看法。表现形式为定语、状语结构的充分展开和插入语的适当镶嵌。

省略法是新闻报道中的惯用手段, 尤其是在标题的写作上。标题必须言简意赅, 故很多语法成分或词语常被省略, 主要是省虚词，留实词。大致有以下几种情况：

1. 省略冠词。如：

Patient loses heart, gets 3rd (＝A patient loses heart, gets the 3rd) 一病人两度移植心脏

37 killed in Italian plane crash (＝37 killed in an Italian plane crash) 一驾意大利飞机失事，37人丧生。

2. 省略系动词。如：

Courses on Practical Skill Popular with Students (＝Courses on Practical Skill Remain Popular with Students) 实用技能课程仍受学生欢迎

Cops under Fire (＝Cops are under Fire) 警察遭枪击

3. 省略代词。如：

Irish group kills ex-chief (＝An Irish group kills its ex-chief) 一爱尔兰团体杀死前首领

Anne and baby are well (＝Anne and her baby are well) 安娜和婴儿母子平安

4. 省略助动词。即构成各种时态的助动词常被省略。如：

Peking to fire test rocket to South Pacific (＝Peking is going to fire test rocket to South Pacific) 北京将向南太平洋发射试验火箭

Moscow's food prices soaring (＝Moscow's food prices are soaring) 莫斯科食品价格猛涨

5. 通常用逗号代替连词。如：

Belgium supports francs, denies it will quit "snake" (＝Belgium supports france and denies it will quit "snake") 比利时支持法郎，否认将退出"蛇形浮动"

6. 省略介词。即通常将介词短语中的介词省略，而将介词宾语提前，变成名词定语形式。如：

Anhui accelerates coal mine building (Anhui accelerates the building of coal mine) 安徽加速煤矿建设

为了浓缩结构，节省篇幅，新闻写作人员常使用前置修饰语(premodification)，或称前置定语。前置定语的使用可以避免因使用从句而带来的句式拖沓。美国专栏作家约翰·利奥把前置定语称为"新闻语言的基本成分"。从结构上看，前置定语大致可分为以下几类：

(1)名词短语作前置定语。如：

The talks to resolve the 43-year Arab-Israeli bitter conflict were launched on October 30 at a mostly symbolic session in Madrid Spain. (= the bitter conflict between Arab and Israeli which had lasted for 43 years) 十月三十日在西班牙马德里召开了一个非常有意义的会议，会上举行了谈判，旨在解决持续四十三年的阿以激烈冲突。

(2)动词短语作前置定语。如：

The crowds across the US that cheered the President's cease-fire announcement — and his declaration that "By God, we've kicked the Vietnam syndrome once and for all" — were celebrating far more than Saddam Hussein's defeat. (= the president's announcement that the fire had been ceased) 全美国的老百姓都为总统宣告停战——和他那"我们已经把越战失败综合症永远赶走了"的宣言而欢呼——他们庆贺的远不止击败萨达姆·侯赛因这件事本身。

(3)形容词短语作前置定语。如:

Only nine months after giving birth to her first child, Liz McColgan yesterday ended Britain's week-long wait for a gold medal at the world championship. (=ended Britain's wait that had lasted for a week)仅在第一个孩子出生九个月之后,莉兹·麦考根就于昨天在世锦赛上赢得了金牌,结束了英国为期一周的等待。

(4)分词短语作前置定语。如:

Yesterday, the troops were seen off by flag-waving, cheering crowds, their tanks strewn with flowers. (=by the crowds who were waving flags and cheering)昨天,人们挥舞旗帜,欢呼着为部队送行,坦克上撒满鲜花。

MANILA:Former Philippine first lady Imelda Marcos may return home one day earlier than expected, according to records of the state-run Philippine Airlines (PLA). (=the Philippine Airlines which is run by the state)马尼拉:据菲律宾国家航空公司的订票记录,前菲律宾第一夫人伊梅尔达·马科斯可能比预计提前一天回国。

(5)综合性词组或短语作前置定语。如:

Traditional department stores have suffered from poor business as customers have flocked to discounters and back-to-basics stores.(=the stores which sell basic goods.)传统的百货商店生意清淡,因为顾客纷纷拥向廉价品商店和生活基本用品商店。

(6)意思较为完整的句子作前置定语。如:

In an era of ubiquitous credit cards and write-yourself-a-loan checking accounts, saving has become as outdated as Ronald Reagan Movie. (=credit cards and checking accounts to which you yourself write a loan)在一个到处充斥信用卡和自写支票付

款的年代，节省已像罗纳德·里根的电影一样过时了。

从以上各例中可以看出，前置定语是精炼句式的有效手段，在翻译时也应体现出原文语言精练的特点，尽量保持字面的工整对应。当然必要时亦可适当增补词语，以求通顺晓意。

除运用前置修饰来浓缩句式之外，名词定语的使用亦有助于语句的精练。如：

①When wave after wave of newly homeless people rolled through the cities, emergency shelters seemed the surest and quickest way to get them off the streets. (=shelter for use in emergency) 当新的无家可归者一浪又一浪地席卷城市时，临时收容所看来是使他们离开街头最快也是最可靠的办法。

②Not only are such multipurpose centres more humane than warehousing people in welfare hotels, but they can also cost about half as much. (=centres serving for multipurpose) 这种多功能中心不仅比把人当作货物一样堆在福利旅馆内更为仁慈，而且还要便宜近一半。

但名词定语也有其局限性，它有时会使语义模糊，增加阅读难度，甚至造成误解。因此在翻译时应着重根据上下文和有关背景资料，弄清名词定语和所修饰的名词之间的语义关系。确定语义后，再选用基本对应的词语，将其深层含义表达出来。

新闻文体中有时也出现较为松散、庞杂的句式。具体表现为采用充分展开的定语和状语结构，以及酌情镶嵌插入语。新闻报道一般段落较短，有时一个段落只有一个句子。其基本句型多为 SV 或 SVO 类，但又夹用较长的定语和状语来提供背景材料和相关信息。以下列几句为例：

One Hundred Fish Recipes is a 64-page booklet that includes a comic strip on fish and fishing, instructions on how to clean and fillet a fish and a great variety of culinary tips illustrated with color photographs to whet the appetite. 《鱼类食谱一百种》是一本 64 页的小册子，包括描绘鱼类和捕鱼的连环图画，如何清洗、去骨切片的指示和用彩照作为插图以增强食欲的多样烹调知识。

Islamabad, April 15 (Xin Hua) — Afghan Muslim guerrillas and Soviet aggressor troops fought fiercely for three successive days <u>starting from April 12</u> for the control of Kandahar Headquarters of Kandahar Province <u>bordering Pakistan</u>, according to the Agency of Afghan Press today. 新华社伊斯兰堡四月十五日电——据阿富汗新闻社今日消息，阿富汗穆斯林游击队与苏联侵略军自四月十二日始进行了连续三天的激战，来争夺位于巴基斯坦边界的坎大哈省坎大哈总部的控制。

例 1 用很长的名词修饰语，详述了《鱼类食谱一百种》这本小册子所包含的内容，扩展了定语结构，交代了读者所关心的信息内容。例 2 则用两个分词修饰语，介绍了战斗的起始日期和地理位置。

插入语的使用亦可起到压缩信息的作用，同时还可替代一个从句，来简化句子结构。新闻报道中的插入语常用破折号标出，以示该插入语成分是句子主线之外的部分，而不像在其他文体中那样常用逗号标明。如：

There were immediate suspicious that Bill Clinton's decision last week to airdrop relief supplies over Bosnia — a step that had seemed like a low-risk humanitarian gesture — might have been answered in thunder by the Serbs. 立刻便有人怀疑，比尔·克林顿于上周决定向波斯尼亚空投救援物资——这一看起来风险很小的人道主义举动——可能引起塞族强烈反响。

大量使用嵌入结构的句子，如前所述的扩展定语、状语结构、插入语等，是新闻英语的特点。它的优点是浓缩信息，减少篇幅，但过多使用复杂的句式难免影响新闻写作的简洁性与准确性,有时甚至会因修饰成分过多过杂,盘根错节而造成误解。因此翻译时尤其要辨明关系,用明白、清晰的语言加以释译。

三、巧用时态,不拘呼应

时态的运用在新闻文体中有其独特之处,在标题中尤为突出。为生动简短起见,标题中常用一般现在时,不定式和现在分词分别表示过去、将来或正在进行的动作。用一般现在时表达已发生的动作,目的是为了增强报道的直接感和同时感。如:

US Journalism suffers rough year in credibility 一年来美国新闻界信誉下降

A Ground War Begins 一场地面战打响了

用不定式来表示将来的计划、安排和规定要发生的事。如:

Nippon steel to hold down production 日铁将降低产量

Largest Chinese trade delegation to visit US in Nov. 最大的中国贸易代表团将于11月访美

用现在分词来表示正在进行或发生的事,省略了助动词,如:

Yugoslav pianist stirring music world 南斯拉夫钢琴家震动乐坛

Deposits, loans rising in HK 存贷款额在港回升

除了标题中时态形式比较独特以外,在新闻报道的正文中也有不按传统规则使用时态的现象。传统的英语语法规定:时态应保持一致或呼应,宾语从句中的动词时态受主句动词时态的影响和制约。但在新闻英语中有时却不受这个规则的约束,有较大的"灵活性",试看例句:

Washington, April 1(UPI)--President Carter said Tuesday the decision of Iranian government to take custody of the American hostages is "a positive step", and "we don't intend to impose additional sanctions" against Iran.

But, Carter told reporters, the United States will continue the 'restraints' it imposed on Iran when the hostages were taken 150 days ago ……

He made it clear, however, that the freezing of Iranian assets and monitoring of Iranian students in this country would continue. "We will continue to monitor the situation very closely,"Carter said.

例句中既有按传统规则呼应之处"made … would continue,"也有从实际出发灵活运用的地方"told … will continue",和"said … is"。间接引语中用直接引语的动词形式增强了引语的真实感和现实性。

要正确理解英语标题中不同动词形式所表达的不同时态以及文章中不拘呼应的语法现象,翻译时必须加上表示不同时态的副词,如"了"、"将"、"正"、"已"等,将动作的前后关系表达清楚。

四、被动语态,频频出现

被动语态在新闻英语的使用频繁多于在其他文体中的使用。这是因为新闻报道中有时动作的接受者比执行者更为重要。如有关灾难、战争、骚乱、事故等方面的报道中,伤亡人员与人数往往是读者关心的中心。如:

More than 50 million acres of farmland have been submerged and grain store damaged. Thousands of peasants have been shown on television trying to save their grain by loading sacks into boats or trying to move them to higher ground. 五千多万亩粮田被淹,很多粮仓被毁。电视屏幕上,成千上万的农民在设法抢救粮食。他们或把麻袋装的粮食运到船上,或把它们移到高处。

值得注意的是,在标题中常省略助动词 to be,而用过去分词直接表示被动意义。如：

Coverage Denied 拒绝提供保险

20,000 feared dead in western Algerian quake 阿尔及利亚西部地震,死亡恐达二万人

英语新闻报道中的被动语态在译文中可作灵活处理,除非有必要突出动作接受者,否则不用被动语态。

五、善用修辞,讲究效果

新闻文体除了注重事实确凿,表达清晰外,还讲究语言的美感和韵味。因此常借助修辞手段,来增加新闻的可读性和吸引力。常用的修辞手段主要是比喻、借喻、夸张、双关语、成语、典故、叠词、押韵等。这与其他文体相似,不再赘述,仅举几例：

The Open Barn Door 敞开的粮仓大门(比喻美国的科技情报很容易获取)

The proposal to protect the hundreds of thousands of Kurdish refugees seemed dependent on the whims of Saddam Hussein or that it would have to be given muscle by a multinational force. 保护几十万库尔德难民的计划看来要依靠萨达姆·侯赛因的心血来潮,或者必须以多国部队的武力作后盾。(muscle 原意"肌肉",借以代替"力量"。)

This Quixote-lean, laser-eyed, lank-haired 33-year-old is no romantic Burton, no lyrical Gielgud, no protean Olivier. 这个身材瘦削有如堂吉诃德,目光锐利有如激光,头披直发的三十三岁的演员独具特点,他不像伯顿那样带有浪漫情调,也不似吉尔古具有田园风味,而且也有别于多才多艺的奥利维尔。(将目光夸张到如激光一样锐利。)

Climbers hold summit talks 登山运动员会师峰顶(Summit talks 原意是"首脑会议"。而这一则新闻报道了有关中国、日本、尼

泊尔三国登山运动员登上珠穆朗玛峰的情况。用在此处一语双关,增加了趣味性。)

All Work, Low Pay Make Nurses Go Away 工作辛苦,工资低廉,众多护士离职他去。(源自成语:All work and no play make Jack a dull boy. 略加改变,活泼俏皮,颇具讽刺性。)

Dare Devil who Dared 胆大包天的人(通过押头韵和使用叠词来增加语言的节奏感,起到强调的作用。)

各种修辞手段的运用反映了新闻语言的文学特征。在翻译时不仅要传达原意,而且必须尽力保持原文的风格。

第二节　各类体裁新闻的翻译

新闻体裁的分类多种多样,根据不同的标准,可以划分出不同的种类。如根据题材分类,可分为政治新闻、经济新闻、科技新闻、文化新闻、体育新闻、灾祸新闻、娱乐新闻、军事新闻以及社会新闻等等;根据篇幅的长短划分,又可分为简讯、短新闻、长消息、小记事、长篇报道等。又可根据时效性的强弱和表现手法、语言运用的不同,将新闻分为三个层次:即硬新闻、软新闻和中间层。硬新闻包括简讯、电讯稿等时效性特强的客观事实报道;中间层包括较为复杂的通讯报道、特写和各类新闻评论;软新闻则多为写法轻松自由、富有艺术感染力的社会新闻、科普文章、杂文小品等。不同层次的新闻体裁在写作手法和表现重心上各有不同,在翻译原文时应充分考虑到它们的不同特点和要求,使译文与原文不仅意义对等,而且文体相应。

一、硬新闻

这类新闻作品强调记实性和时效性,通常是一事一报,简洁明快,以事件的事实为主干,将最新的消息以最快的速度传播给读者。因此这类作品的文字简短、精练,表现手法上以叙述为主,结构多采用"倒金字塔"式。翻译此类新闻作品时要求准确、简明。

1. 简讯

又称单一事件报道(single-event coverage)是消息报道中最基本、最常见的形式。它往往篇幅不长,叙述简明扼要,文字平实流畅。下文是载于 1996 年 11 月 4 日的《澳大利亚人》报的一则简讯。

US missile targets Iraqi radar site

WASHINGTON: A United States Air Force F-16 fighter plane fired a missile at an Iraqi radar site after the jet was tracked electronically while in the "no-fly" zone over southern Iraq, the Pentagon said yesterday.

But the White House, explaining a long delay in announcing the strike, said it was unclear whether Iraqi radar has "locked on" to the plane on Saturday.

A Pentagon spokesman said the F-16 returned safely to its base in Saudi Arabia. It was not immediately known if the Iraqi site was damaged. The spokesman, confirming the strike about 18 hours after it occurred, said an investigation was under way. Iraq denied any such incident had taken place.

White House press secretary Mr Mike McCurry, travelling in Florida with the US President, said Mr Clinton had been briefed early on Saturday about the incident by a member of the National Security Council staff.

"There are no indications of changes in the status of anti-missile deployment" by Iraq, Mr McCurry said. He referred reporters to the Pentagon for further details.

The Pentagon spokesman read from a statement that said

the F-16 "fired a HARM (high-speed anti-radiation) missile at a radar site in southern Iraq after the aircraft was illuminated during a routine Southern Watch Mission".

The incident was first reported by The Washington Times. Only then was it acknowledged by the Pentagon and the White House.

Mr McCurry denied that the delay was designed to protect Mr Clinton from political fallout just before this week's presidential election. But he struggled to explain why the incident had not been announced sooner, telling reporters aboard Air Force One that he had assumed the Pentagon had announced it earlier in the day.

Asked about the delay, White house chief of staff Mr Leon Panetta said: "I think they were waiting to see whether he (the F-16 pilot) was locked on to (by Iraqi radar). They don't know the answer to that."

The missile firing was the first of its kind since September 4, when Iraqi forces confronted US flyers twice as the US jets began their patrols over an expanded no-fly zone for Iraqi aircraft that Washington unilaterally declared the day before.

美导弹击中伊拉克雷达基地

华盛顿：五角大楼昨日宣称：一架美空军F—16战斗机在伊拉克南部禁飞区被电子跟踪后，向伊一雷达基地发射了导弹。

但是白宫在解释拖延很久才公布这次打击行动的原因时称：星期六时尚不清楚伊雷达是否已"锁定"了这架飞机。

五角大楼的一位发言人说，该F—16战斗机已安全返回设在沙特阿拉伯的基地，伊雷达站是否被摧毁尚无法立刻得知。该发言人在这次打击行动发生18小时之后证实了此事，并说正在进行调查。伊拉克却否认有此事件发生。

正随美国总统在弗罗里达旅行的白宫新闻秘书迈克·麦考利说:星期六早晨,一位国家安全委员会工作人员已向克林顿先生简要汇报了此事。

"没有迹象表明伊反导弹部署情况有何变化,"麦考利说。详细情况他请记者向五角大楼查询。

这位五角大楼发言人宣读了一份声明说:这架F—16战斗机"在执行日常的南部警戒任务时遭到雷达跟踪后,向伊南部一雷达基地发射了一枚高速反雷达哈姆导弹。"

这次事件最早是由华盛顿时报报道出来的,到这时五角大楼和白宫才承认。

麦考利先生否认推迟公开此事是有意保护克林顿先生,以免在本周总统选举之前引起政治纠纷。他竭力解释为什么这次事件未更早公开的原因,对驻空军第一军的记者说,他以为那天早些时候五角大楼已公开了此事。

当被问及此次拖延时,白宫参谋长雷恩·潘尼特说:"我想他们是等等看他(F—16战斗机飞行员)当时是否被锁定。他们不知道这个问题的答案。"

这次导弹射击是9月4日以来这类行动的第一次。当时美方飞机开始在华盛顿前一天单方面宣布的扩大了的伊拉克飞机禁飞区内执行巡逻任务,伊拉克军方两次与美方飞机发生对抗。

这篇新闻报道全文仅三百余字,但事件的中心内容以及一些相关消息已尽现读者眼前。它围绕美军导弹击中伊拉克一雷达基地这个单一事件展开,在消息的开头交待了最重要的新闻事实:"一架美空军F—16战斗机在伊拉克南部禁飞区被电子跟踪后,向伊一雷达基地发射了导弹。"在文章的第二段报道了白宫对没有及时公开这次行动作了解释:"星期六时还不清楚伊拉克的雷达是否'锁定'了这架飞机"。至此,新闻的主要内容已全盘托出,后面的文字仅是对这部分报道的进一步补充。整篇报道以"倒金字塔"式展开,叙述简要,重点突出,语言晓畅。

译文也体现了原文的特点,准确流畅,简洁明了。在词汇的翻译上保持了原有一些词汇的形象性。如将 White House 和 Pentagon 直接译成"白宫"和"五角大楼"。又用"美"、"伊"代替"美国"和"伊拉克",符合汉语新闻报道的简洁要求。在句式处理上也较为灵活。如第一段原文是间接引语在前,发话者居后,而译文中互换了位置,译为"五角大楼昨日宣称……",这样更符合汉语的表达习惯。再如第三段中的一句"The spokesman, confirming the strike about 18 hours after it occurred, said an investigation was under way."译作"该发言人在这次打击行动发生18小时之后证实了此事,并说正在进行调查"。而不是拘泥原句句式,将它译成"该发言人在这次打击行动18小时后确认此事时说正在进行调查。"又如第四段中的"… said Mr. Clinton had been briefed early on Saturday about the incident by a member of the National Security Council staff."原句中的被动语态在译文中被转换成主动语态。句式上的灵活变动使译文读来更加流畅顺口,意义更加明确。

2. 电讯稿

这是由各大通讯社发送的新闻稿件。它弥补了记者无法到达事发现场作及时报道的不足。因此由当地通讯社发送的电讯稿便成了报纸的主要消息来源。它的体裁结构、写作风格与消息报道基本相同,翻译的要求也基本一致。但值得注意的是,电讯稿有一独特之处,即电头(dateline)。电头一般位于导语之前,由发稿地点、日期以及通讯社名称三部分组成,社名常用括号框起。在翻译电头时应特别注意英汉电头中三部分的不同排列顺序。英文电头的次序为地点、时间、社名,译成汉语时应改成社名、地点和日期的顺序。见下例:

Chinese Ambassador to Luxembourg Presents Credentials

Brussels, March 26 (Xinhua) — Chinese Ambassador Extraordinary and Plenipotentiary to the Grand Duchy of Luxembourg Zheng Weizhi today presented his credentials to the Grand Duke of Luxembourg H. R. H. Jean, according to a report from Luxembourg.

Grand Duke Jean held friendly talks with Ambassador Zheng Weizhi after the ceremony. In the afternoon, the Chinese Ambassador paid an official call on Prime Minister of Luxembourg Pierre Werner.

中国驻卢森堡大使递交国书

[新华社布鲁塞尔3月26日电]卢森堡消息:中国驻卢森堡大公国特命全权大使郑伟智今日向卢森堡大公吉恩殿下递交了国书。

仪式后,吉恩大公与郑伟智大使进行了友好交谈。下午中国大使正式拜会了卢森堡首相皮埃尔·唯勒。

附:练习

将下列新闻报道译成中文。

① British Joblessness Hit 10.2% in April

London — Unemployment in the United Kingdom topped 10% of the workforce in April, producing anguished new complaints from British labor and industry.

The April figures showed an increase in registered joblessness to a seasonally adjusted 2,466,000 persons from 2,380,800 the previous month and 1,456,200 the year earlier. The unemployment rate rose to 10.1 from 9.9% in March and 6% a year ago, the Department of Employment said.

Len Murray, General Secretary of Trades Union Congress, the British labor confederation, said the "figures set another dismay and depressing post-World War II record."

The Confederation of British Industry, a major employer group, described the jobless rise as a "matter of both regret and concern." The CBI said it already has predicted that the number of unemployed will rise to three million by the end of the year.

② Developing Nations Set Objectives

CARACAS, May 18(Reuter via Xinhua) — Foreign ministers and top representatives from 122 developing nations meet today to define their relations with industrialized countries and outline formulas for international co-operation.

Thirty-five foreign ministers from the "group of 77" developing nations will be present and other member-countries are expected to be represented by high-level non-ministerial delegations at the two-day meeting.

Over the past week, working commissions of the group have analysed common objectives on raw materials, energy, trade, development, finance, exchange of technology, and industrialisation.

The Group of 77 was set up as an informal grouping within the United Nations in 1964. It works closely with the UN Conference on Trade and Development (UNCTAD) to promote trade. The number of member-countries has since grown.

The commissions, whose members include countries in the Organization of Petroleum Exporting Countries (OPEC), agreed on a meeting of state-owned energy companies in Vienna next year.

The Group of 77 favours setting up its own multinational energy companies.

The two-day meeting in Caraballeda, near Caracas, will be opened by Venezuelan President Luis Herrera Campins.

③   Malaria Still Menaces Quarter of Humanity,
          says French professor

Rabat, April 12 (Xinhua) — About a billion people in the world today are still under the threat of malaria and nearly two million people die of the disease yearly, said Prof. Marc Gentilini of France in Agadir, according to local newspaper reports.

The statement was made at the first tropical medicine conference of French-speaking countries held in Agadir, Morocco, this week.

Prof. Gentilini pointed out that what even worse is that parasitoses are often associated with malnutrition and bacterial and virus diseases.

④   World's First Test-Tube Twins Born in Melbourne

MELBOURNE, June 8 (Reuter via Xinhua) — The world's first test-tube twins were born in Melbourne's Queen Victoria Hospital at the weekend, it was announced here.

A brief statement issued by hospital authorities said the mother went into labour shortly after doctors began inducing the birth of the twins — a boy and a girl.

She was in the 37th week of pregnancy, which would have

come to term in two weeks time.

Doctors said it was not unusual for twins to be born prematurely because of the special demands upon the mother.

The male half of the twins survived delicate heart surgery and doctors said he was out of danger and making "excellent progress."

The twins bring the number of test-tube births in Melbourne to six.

二、中间类新闻

居于中间层的非软非硬类新闻作品覆盖面甚广。既有大量采用叙事、描写、议论、抒情等多种表现手法,比较详细、形象地描绘事件发生与发展过程,刻画典型人物形象,或再现具有典型特征的片断的通讯和特写;也有侧重以事实为基础,阐发道理,表明观点的各类新闻评述。这类作品时效性要求低于硬新闻类作品,因此作者可有相对充裕的时间润色文字。通讯和特写往往显得生动、细腻,层次丰富,起伏跌荡;而新闻评论则以有理有据,逻辑严密,文笔庄重为其特点。

1. 通讯

或称较为复杂的消息报道,一般都比较完整地描写了事件发生的经过,具体揭示出矛盾发生发展的过程,有时还用工笔细描人物形象。其表现手法多种多样,文字讲究,结构丰满,力求趣味性与写实性和谐统一,以增加新闻的可读性。例如:

Gandhi's Assassination:"Bapu(father) Is Finished"

New Delhi, January 30 — Mohandas K. Gandhi was assassinated today by a Hindu extremist whose act plunged India into sorrow and fear.

Rioting broke out immediately in Bombay.

The seventy-eight-year-old leader whose people had christened him the Great Soul of India died at 3:45 P. M. (1:15 A. M. EST) with his head cradled in the lap of his sixteen-year-old granddaughter, Mani.

Just half an hour before, a Hindu fanatic, Ram Naturam, had pumped three bullets from a revolver into Gandhi's frail body, emaciated by years of fasting and asceticism.

Gandhi was shot in the luxurious gardens of Birla House in the presence of one thousand of his followers, whom he was leading to the little summer pagoda where it was his habit to make his evening devotions.

Dressed as always in his homespun, sacklike dhoti, and leaning heavily on a staff of stout wood, Gandhi was only a few feet from the pagoda when the shots were fired.

Gandhi crumpled instantly, putting his hand to his forehead in the Hindu gesture of forgiveness to his assassin. Three bullets penetrated his body at close range, one in the upper right thigh, one in the abdomen, and one in the chest.

He spoke no word before he died. A moment before he was shot he said — some witnesses believed he was speaking to the assassin — "You are late."

The assassin had been standing beside the garden path, his hands folded, palms together, before him in the Hindu gesture of greeting. But between his palms he had concealed a small-caliber revolver. After pumping three bullets into Gandhi at a range of a few feet, he fired a fourth shot in an attempt at suicide, but the bullet merely creased his scalp.

The shots sounded like a string of firecrackers and it was a moment before Gandhi's devotees realized what had happened. Then they turned on the assassin savagely and would have torn him to bits had not police guards intervened with rifles and drawn bayonets. The assassin was hustled to safekeeping.

Gandhi quickly was borne back to Birla House and placed on a couch with his head in his granddaughter's lap. Within a few moments she spoke to the stricken throng, among them Pandit Jawaharlal Nehru, premier of India: "Bapu (father) is finished."

Then Mani rose and sat crosslegged beside the body of the man whose life was forfeit for the cause of peace and humanity. She began to chant the two-thousand-year-old verses of the Bhagavad-Gita, the Hindu scripture.

Over all India the word spread like wildfire. Minutes after the flash was received in Bombay rioting broke out, with Hindu extremists attacking Moslems. A panic-stricken Moslem woman echoed the thoughts of thousands with a cry: "God help us all!"

In Delhi itself, in the quick-gathering gloom of the night, the news set the people on the march.

They walked slowly down the avenues and out of the squalid bazaars, converging on Birla House. There by the thousands they stood weeping silently or moaning a wailing. Some sought to scale the high walls and catch one last glimpse of the Mahatma. Strong troop contingents strove to keep order. Tonight in response to the insistent demand of the people, his body was shown to them.

The balcony window of the house opened and the body was borne outside. The people gasped and surged forward as it was placed in a chair, facing them. A brilliant spotlight blazed on the wrinkled, brown face. The eyes were closed, the face peaceful in repose. A white sheet covered the bloodstained loincloth.

Within Birla House there was grief and mourning which at least for the moment fused the dissident sects of India — the Hindus, the Moslems, and the Sikhs — into a community of sorrow.

But there were grave fears, heightened by the savage outbreaks in Bombay, that without her saint to hold passions in check, all India might be whirled into strife.

甘地遇刺:"爸爸死了"

合众社新德里一九四八年一月三十日电——穆罕达斯·K·甘地今天被一名印度教极端分子行刺身亡,此举使印度全国上下悲恸欲绝,惊恐不安。

甘地刚被刺,孟买就爆发了骚乱。

这位被人民尊称为"印度的伟大灵魂"的78岁领袖于当日下午3时45分(美国东部时间凌晨1时15分)头枕在他十六岁的孙女曼妮腿上死去。

就在半小时前,一个名叫拉姆·纳脱拉姆的狂热印度教徒用左轮手枪向甘地连开三枪,子弹射进了甘地那由于多年苦行和绝食而变得衰弱不堪的身躯。

甘地是在波拉宫优雅的花园内被枪击的。当时有一千多名他的信徒在场,他正带着这些人前往他经常做晚祷的一座夏日小塔。

甘地同平日一样,穿着宽松的土制印度袍,费力地拄着结实的木拐杖,在离塔仅几英尺远处遭到枪击。

甘地当即摔倒在地,按印度教的姿势,一手加额,表示宽恕凶手。三颗子弹在近距离射穿了他的身体,一颗在右胯,一颗在腹部,还有一颗在胸部。

死前他没说一句话。就在他被枪击前一刹那,他说:"你来迟了。"一些目击者认为这句话是他对凶手说的。

凶手曾一直站在花园小径旁,在他面前双手合十,作出印度教徒顶礼的样子。然而他的手掌间却藏着一支小口径左轮手枪。在几英尺外向甘地连开三枪后,又开第四枪,企图自杀,但子弹仅擦破了他的头皮。

枪声听起来像一串爆竹声,片刻后,甘地的追随者才意识到发生了什么事。他们立即发疯似地扑向凶手,要不是警卫人员用步枪和刺刀把他们隔开,他们也许早就把他撕成碎片了。凶手被押走,保护起来。

甘地迅即被抬回波拉宫,放在一个长沙发椅上,头枕在他孙女的腿上。过了一会儿,她对惊恐的人群说:"爸爸死了。"人群中有印度总理潘迪特·贾瓦哈拉尔·尼赫鲁。

然后曼妮站起来,盘膝坐在这位将一生献给和平事业和人类的伟人的遗体旁,开始吟诵流传两千年之久的印度教经文。

甘地遇害的消息犹如野火燎原,迅速传遍印度。消息传到孟买,那里立即就爆发了骚乱,印度教极端分子袭击了穆斯林。一位惊慌万状的穆斯林妇女喊出了千万人的心声:"真主保佑我们大家吧!"

在德里当地,在迅速变浓的阴暗的夜色中,这一消息使人们上街游行。

他们沿大街慢慢走着,走出肮脏的市场,在波拉宫会合。成千上万的人站在那里,悄悄啜泣,或哀声痛哭。有人设法爬上高墙,想最后看一眼圣雄。大批军队力图维持秩序。当晚在人们的一再请求下,甘地的遗体终于供人瞻仰了。

波拉宫阳台的窗户打开了,甘地的遗体被抬了出来,放在椅子上,面对人群,这时人们喘着气涌向前去。明亮的聚光灯照在甘地满布皱纹的褐色脸上,他的双目紧闭,面容安详。一块白布盖在血迹斑斑的长袍上。

在波拉宫内,悲伤与哀悼至少暂时弥合了印度各宗派之间的分歧,把印度教徒,穆斯林和锡克教徒融成忧伤的一体。

人们十分恐惧,害怕失去了圣雄,无人能控制民众的狂热,整个印度会卷入纷争之中。孟买发生的暴乱更加剧了这一恐惧。

这是一则综合新闻,记者不仅详细叙述了甘地遇刺这一在当时令世界震惊的事件,而且指出其后果,与印度的政局和教派纠纷紧密联系起来。整篇通讯结构合理,详略得当,脉胳清楚。在叙述事实的同时,用简练而又传神的笔触,勾勒出甘地这位"圣雄"的精神风貌,以及人们得知噩耗后的悲伤心情。有事实的叙述,有细节的描写,使得整篇报道有血有肉。在翻译时必须做到完整、传神,既要将新闻事实准确再现,又要将细节的描写译得细腻到位。

不难看出译文做到了这一点。如文中第四段中"pumped three bullets from a revolver into …"一句,pump 一词用得极为形象。原意为"把子弹打进"。若按字面意思译成:"把左轮手枪中的三颗子弹射入……"则既拖沓又别扭,简单译成"用左轮手枪向甘地连开三枪",译文就流畅得多,加上一个"连"字,更形象地再现了当时的情景。译文中还大量运用了汉语言中常见的四字辞格,如第一段中"sorrow and fear"译作"悲恸欲绝,惊恐不安";第四段中"frail"译成"衰弱不堪",第十三段中"wildfire"译成"野火燎原",第十五段中"weeping silently or moaning a wailing"译成"悄悄啜泣,或哀声痛哭",以及第十六段中"wrinkled","The eyes were closed, the face peaceful in repose","bloodstained"分别译作"满布皱纹"、"双目紧闭"、"面容安详"、"血迹斑斑"。这样处理使译文酣畅淋漓,文采飞扬,原文的感染力得到了保留甚至发扬。对某些用直译法难以清晰准确反映原意的词语用转译或释译法,使译文更加明白易懂。如第九段中"his hands folded, palms together"译成"双手合十"简洁明了,"in the Hindu gesture of greeting"译作"作出印度教徒顶礼的样子"使原句的含义昭然纸上。又如第六段"dressed as always"译成"同平日一样穿着"不仅译意准确,而且体现出甘地的性格与情操。第十五段中"this body was shown to them"译成"遗体供人瞻仰","瞻仰"一词译得十分妥贴,反映了印度人民对甘地的尊敬。可以说译文除了将原文的表层意思传达清楚外,还将其深层内涵与风格笔调传神地再现了出来。

附:练习

将下列通讯译成中文。

① The Two Americas as Seen from Detroit

A few blocks from the hotel is another America.

It is working class, integrated, mortgaged, and worried. Its wage earners are out of work. Millions are jobless across the country, but in Detroit the rate of unemployment is twice the national average. So many people have been laid off that dozens of extra unemployment offices have had to be opened.

I walked the unemployment lines the other day to talk to this America. It is depressed, pained and bewildered. But not self-pitying.

"All I want is my job back," a black woman, about 30, said to me. "I want to get out of this line and back on the assembly line." She lost her job at Ford almost nine months ago. She had applied in vain for 25 other jobs.

A white woman in her 50s had been standing in one line for an hour, holding her 10-year-old grandson by the hand. "I have been working all my life and this is the first time I've ever been laid off," she said. "I don't like having to get a handout from the government. I want to work."

A couple stood behind her — husband and wife, both auto workers, both out of work, both in their 50s. "It is not so bad for us," the woman said. "My husband can tinker with odd jobs around the neighbourhood and pick up a few dollars to go with relief, but it's hard on our two sons. One's been laid off and the other is about to be."

There are worse stories: stories of unemployed auto workers whose wives have miscarried under the pressure or have left home. One man, about 25, whose wife and child have left him, told a reporter for the Washington Post: "I cut back to the bitter bone. I've got such headaches and problems. I told my wife that it's not us, it's the system that is causing us problems. But she took my son and went back to live with her mother."

At another unemployment office I met a young black man who was discharged from the army last year and hasn't been able to find a job yet. "I served my country, man, and I can't find work. And I come down here and stand in this line to get my check and that line to cash it and I keep thinking, man: is this what it's about? Is this what it's come down to?"

There are two Americas, all right. They live next door and yet so very far apart.

②   Cops under Fire

It's a steamy Thursday night in central Dallas, and officers John Weiss and Jay James have been mired for 6 hours in an exasperating routine that belies the drama-saturated TV images of police. They have plodded through minor fender benders, stolen-car reports, false burglar alarms and disturbance calls in which little was disturbed. A small victory comes when they arrest a man in a baseball cap for possession of two tenths of a gram of crack: It takes them off the streets for more than an hour to book and process the helpless prisoner at the county jail. But at 10 p.m., the radio crackles with reports of a drive-by shooting. As James and Weiss pull up and begin coaxing information from a wailing Hispanic woman and angry bystanders, the red truck from which the shots were fired zooms by.

 The chase is on. James throws the patrol car into a transmission-shattering reverse. Tires spin and smoke. Within seconds, James and Weiss rocket down a side street, slam on the brakes at a stop sign and lay down rubber as they catapult onto a crowed thoroughfare. Moments later, they are careening in and out of traffic at 80 miles per hour, before the chase skids to a halt in a parking lot. As two other police cars converge, Weiss and James dive from their car, throwing open doors for protection while they draw and aim their guns in a single fluid motion. Meanwhile, to their surprise, other officers run right up to the truck — that "Old John Wayne BS," James will say later — and yank a chunky youth from the cab, hurling him to the pavement, their guns at his head. It is a typical weekday night shift in central Dallas. The weekends, of course, are more dangerous.

2. 特写

  特写是"再现"新闻事件、人物和场景的形象化的报道形式。与通讯相比，主题更加突出，焦点更加集中，叙述更加详细。它以描刻为主要手法，像电影中的特写镜头一样，抓住具有典型意义，富有特征的片断,绘声绘色地加以描述,使读者"如临其境,如见其人"。因此特写除了向读者提供事实外,更重要的是激起读者的兴趣。它不求完整全面,但求精彩动人。例如:

Anwar Sadat Assassinated at Cairo Military Review

CAIRO — Egyptian President Anwar Sadat, a modern-day pharaoh who attempted to lead the Arab world toward a permanent Mideast peace with Israel, was assassinated yesterday by a band of soldiers who attacked a military parade reviewing stand with automatic rifles and hand grenades.

The 62-year-old Sadat, who had been laughing heartily only a moment before, was mortally wounded by a bullet and a grenade fragment. An official medical bulletin later said: "There were two holes in the left side of the chest, a bullet in the neck just above the right collarbone, a wound above the right knee, a huge gash at the back of the left thigh and a complicated fracture of the thigh... (death was attributed to) violent nervous shock, and internal bleeding in the chest cavity, where the left lung and major blood vessels below it were torn."

Seven other persons were killed and 22 were wounded, including four Americans.

Sadat's death further jeopardized hopes of a lasting Mideast peace that has been stalemated for more than two years. Nevertheless, Sadat's hand-picked successor, Vice-President Hosni Mubarak, 52, was expected to continue the same domestic and foreign policies. Like Sadat, Mubarak has the strong backing of the Egyptian military. It was Mubarak who announced Sadat's death to the nation in a dramatic television appearance seven hours after the incident. He declared a year-long state of emergency.

According to Egyptian army officials, an army lieutenant and four enlisted men staged the attack that transformed a hot, sunny day of military muscle-flexing into a nightmare for thousands crowded into a massive concrete stadium. The attackers shouted, "Glory to Egypt! Attack ! You are agents ! You are intruders!" at the large crowd of dignitaries.

At least one of the attackers was killed by police and four others were reported to be under arrest. Military sources said the attackers were either Moslem fanatics or backers of a former Egyptian chief of staff, Lt. Gen. Saad Eddin ElShazli, who broke with Sadat over the peace treaty with Israel and is now in exile in Lebanon.

The parade was a grand show with both American and older Soviet hardware on display. No one enjoyed it more than Sadat, who smiled and laughed noisily for the watching press corps. Paratroopers had just successfully landed within a few feet of Sadat who was sitting behind a railing in the front row of the reviewing stand. All eyes turned upwards as six Egyptian Mirage jets roared over the reviewing stand, pulling up sharply in acrobatic rolls and turns that left plumes of red, white, blue and yellow smoke in their wake. It was just then — 12:40 p.m. local time (6:40 a.m. EDT) — that Associated Press photographer William Foley said: "All hell broke loose."

From a truck towing an artillery piece in the parade, a group of soldiers — one of them bare-headed — began firing what appeared, from photographs, to be Soviet-made AK-47 automatic rifles. "I thought it was part of the show at first," said AP reporter Steve Hindy. One of the soldiers jumped from the truck and lobbed a grenade at the reviewing stand. Others joined him. They held their rifles to their shoulders and, blazing away, began running toward the reviewing stand. A second grenade was thrown. One rifleman walked right up to the railing within four feet of Sadat and sprayed the reviewing stand. Eyewitness said the gunfire lasted at least a minute.

It took that long for the crowd to react. Those on the VIP platform tumbled from their chairs to the floor. Screaming and shouting erupted, and panic seized the crowd that began to flee in all directions. Many of them fell over one another, bodies littered the ground. Security guards or police — no one is sure — began firing, felling one of the attackers.

According to one government source, Sadat was unconscious moments after being wounded. He was flown from the site by helicopter to Maddi Military Hospital and arrived at 1:20 p.m. local time. Doctors said he was in a coma when he arrived. Sadat was finally pronounced dead at 2:40 p.m.

萨达特在开罗检阅部队，惨遭横祸

［开罗］：埃及总统安瓦尔·萨达特，这位试图带领阿拉伯世界与以色列实现中东持久和平的当代法老，昨天被一伙用自动步枪和手榴弹攻击军事检阅台的士兵打死。

就在片刻前，他还在开怀大笑。现在，这位六十二岁的总统被子弹和手榴弹碎片击中，造成致命伤。随后官方发表的一份医疗公报说："胸腔左部有两个洞，右锁骨上方的脖子里有一颗子弹，右膝上部被打伤，左大腿的后部有一个大伤口，并有严重的骨折……由于严重的神经性休克，以及左肺及左肺下面的主要血管破裂造成胸腔内出血，抢救无效，不幸去世。"

另外还有七人死亡,二十二人受伤,其中包括四名美国人。

萨达特总统的去世使僵持了两年多的中东持久和平更加渺茫。然而,人们预计萨达特亲手选定的接班人——五十二岁的胡斯尼·穆巴拉克副总统将继续执行他的内外政策。像萨达特一样,穆巴拉克也得到埃及军方的强有力的支持。刺杀事件发生七个小时后,正是穆巴拉克令人注目地出现在电视上,向全国公布萨达特去世消息的。他宣布为期一年的紧急状态。

据埃及陆军官员说,这次袭击是由一个陆军中尉和四名士兵发动的,对于成千上万聚集在巨大水泥体育场里的群众来说,这次行动将一个显示军事力量的阳光灿烂的炎热日子变成了一场恶梦。袭击者对着这一大群名流要人喊道:"光荣属于埃及,打啊!你们这些特务!你们这些侵略者!"

至少有一名袭击者被警察打死,据说有四人被逮捕。军方人士说,袭击者要么是穆斯林狂热分子,要么是埃及前参谋长萨阿德·艾丁·沙兹利中将的支持者。沙兹利中将在与以色列签订和约的问题上与萨达特闹翻,现在流亡在黎巴嫩。

这次军事检阅是一次隆重的力量展示,既有美国重型武器,也有老式的苏联武器。没有人比萨达特看得更开心了。为了做样子给在场的新闻记者看,他面带微笑,甚至放声大笑。萨达特坐在最前排,紧靠着检阅台的栏杆。伞兵成功地在他面前降落,离他只有几步远。随着人们仰望着天空:六架埃及幻影式喷气机从检阅台的上空呼啸而过,继而突然拉起,进行特技翻滚和转弯动作,尾部留下红、白、蓝、黄四种颜色的烟迹。就在这时——当地时间十二点四十分(美国东部夏季时间早晨六时四十分)——正如美联社摄影记者威廉·弗利所说:"乱得像地狱一样。"

在检阅中一辆拖着大炮的卡车上,一伙士兵——其中一人光着头——开火了。从照片看,他们使用的像是苏制AK—47型自动步枪。美联社记者史蒂夫·欣迪说:"开始我还以为是检阅的一部分哩!"一名士兵跳下卡车,向检阅台扔出了一颗手榴弹。另外几个士兵也跟了上来。他们端着自动步枪,一边射击一边冲向检阅台。又投了一枚手榴弹。一名士兵冲到离萨达特只有四英尺远的栏杆前,立即举枪对着检阅台扫射。据目击者说,射击至少持续一分钟。

良久,人们才反应过来。那些贵宾席上的人从椅子上跌倒在地。人群惊慌失措,有的呼喊,有的尖叫,东奔西跑,四处逃命。人跌倒压成一堆。地上满是躺着的人。保卫人员,或是警察——谁也不清楚——开始还击,打倒了一名袭击者。

一名政府人士说,萨达特受伤后便昏迷不醒。一架直升飞机把他从出事地点送往马迪军事医院,当地时间下午一点二十分抵达。医生们说,他被送来的时候,仍然处于昏迷状态。萨达特终于在二点四十分去世。

上文是载于1981年11月7日《每日新闻》上的一篇特写的节选。作者帕特里克·斯洛扬曾在合众国际社华盛顿分社和赫斯特报系的华盛顿分社工作十四年。自1981年起,一直任《每日新闻》伦敦分社社长。该篇报道曾被美国报纸主编协会评为优秀新闻获奖作品。文中对埃及总统萨达特遇刺这一突发事件及其后事作了极为细腻的描写,将许多戏剧性的场景与新闻事实巧妙地揉合起来,文笔娴熟,技法高超。与上一篇《甘地遇刺》通讯比较,叙事更加详细,描绘更加生动。以萨达特为中心,将事件整个过程的一切细节都囊括了进去。首先在导语部分,斯洛扬字斟句酌,将新闻的精华部分压缩在仅有四十来字的段落中,且将导语的各要素尽包其中:who(萨达特)、what(被打死)、whom(几个士兵)、when(昨天)、where(军事检阅台)、why(试图带领阿拉伯世界与以色列实现中东持久和平)、how(用自动步枪和手榴弹)。信息浓缩,语言凝炼。在紧接着的后五段中,又交待了一些相关的新闻事实。而从第七段始,他按时间顺序用高度戏剧性的手法记叙了这一事件,将一些具体的场面栩栩如生地展现在读者面前。特别是第八、九段,作者巧妙地采用动词的主动式,增添了事实的真实性和现实感。

译文也体现了其生动、细腻的风格。在前半部分,即自开头到第六段,译文沿袭了原文简洁紧凑、朴实平缓的文风,将相关新闻事实准确地传达出来。在后半部分,即第七至九段,则随原文笔调的改变而作相应的调整,通过选择准确恰当的词语,译出原文生动形象的特色。如第八段中的"One of the soldiers *jumped* from the truck and *lobbed* a grenade at the reviewing stand. Others *joined* them. They *held* their rifles to their shoulders and, blazing array, began *running* toward the reviewing stand. A second grenade was *thrown*. One rifleman *walked* right up to the railing within four feet of Sadat and *sprayed* the reviewing stand."斜体的动词均是动作性较强的词,且几乎都是单音节词,表明其急促、短暂,一个动作接一个动作,从而增加了原文如闻其声,如见其行的生动性和现场感。译成汉语时,译者都选用了单字词:"跳"、"扔"、"跟"、"端"、"冲"等,既简洁明快,又生动传神。这样的例子在第九段中也比比皆是。如将"tumbled from their chairs to the floor"译成"从椅子上跌倒在地"动作感十分强烈。译文除保持了原文生动细腻的特点外,在句式结构方面的处理亦有可圈可点之处。它既不完全拘泥原文,也不无端更改句式。如文章开头一段导语的翻译就是一例。原文将"埃及总统安瓦尔·萨达特"置于句首,突出了他作为新闻焦点的地位。接着说"这位试图带领阿拉伯世界与以色列实现中东持久和平的当代法老",点出了萨达特的历史地位,并暗示了其成为众矢之的的原因。译文沿用了这一结构,以保持萨达特作为新闻焦点的地位,在该句的后半部分则调整了语序,将时间状语置于动词之前,以符合汉语的表达习惯。另外为使语义明确,行文流畅,译文也作了相应的增词减词和句式转换。如第九段中"screaming and shouting erupted, and panic seized the crowd that began to flee in all directions"一句,原文中的Screaming and shouting，panic 作主语，在译文中变成了谓语，译成"人群惊慌失措，有的呼喊，有的尖叫，东奔西跑，四处逃命"。既体现了动作的瞬息感与连贯性，又增添了语言的文采和感染力。

附：练习
将下列特写译成中文。

① Soviet Union: The View from Shadrinsk

This city is a town of railroad workers and small factories, of weathered wooden cabins and log houses tumbling alongside the faceless post-war apartment blocks that march in uniform ranks along dusty streets. "A typical old Russian city," says Mayor Nikolai Ilyich Varlakov.

A friendly city too, but suspicious of foreigners. A colleague and I were the first Western correspondents in anyone's memory to visit Shadrinsk, and folks seemed as curious about us as we were about them. The townspeople were obviously determined to make a good impression. Our room at the Hotel Ural, the only lodging in town, smelled of fresh paint. A young clerk in a local shop said she had been forewarned that two Western journalists would be in town and had been told to look sharp and put the best goods up front.

Economic sanctions, such as the U.S. grain embargo, seem unlikely to rattle people in Shadrinsk, where shortages are a long-established fact of daily life. Perishable dairy goods and foodstuffs are continually in short supply; in state food shops, the only meats we saw were pigs' knuckles and snouts and sausages. The only fresh product we found in town was radishes and spring onions.

Near the town centre, it is a common sight to see women toting buckets away from street-corner pumps, or pushing hand-built carts, filled with laundry as they make their way to the muddy river bank. Even more startling are the small villages one passes as the Trans-Siberian rolls across the great Russian plain on its journey east: tiny settlements of leaning wooden huts, set among rutted dirt roads. When the train stops near such places, old women wrapped in timeless baggy dresses and head shawls crowd around the restaurant car to sell food and product.

② Emotionally drained King urges public to end violence

Los Angeles: Shaking and on the verge of emotional collapse, Mr Rodney King has pleaded with people to stop the riots.

Looking completely overwhelmed, Mr King went before the media on Friday and spoke publicly for the first time since the jury handed down not guilty verdicts on four LA police officers accused of beating him.

The public statement was extremely difficult for Mr. King, who was described by his lawyer, Mr Steve Herman, as being "completely unglued" because of his association with one of the worst riots in modern US history.

Mr King, a shy and inarticulate 26-year-old, took deep breaths before he addressed the media and was told to speak slowly.

Several times throughout his three-minute statement, made up as he went along, Mr King's voice broke as he verged on tears.

His message was clear, however — stop the looting, stop the arson, stop the violence.

3. 新闻评论

新闻评论是新闻机构所发布的言论的总称。它是报纸的声音、灵魂和旗帜,它集新闻性与政论性于一身,主要采用议论文的形式用道理来说服读者,据事立论,以理服人。文字上则比较庄重典雅,语气正统严肃,句式也较为复杂严谨。尤其是社论(editorial),一般用它来评论重大事件或政策,具有一定的指导性和权威性,故语言更加慎密准确,论述更加精辟透彻。例如:

The Energy Lesson

Ever since 1973, the energy policy pendulum has swung with depressing regularity from crisis to glut and back again. A steady resting point somewhere between has not been reached. That would be a point at which transient fluctuations in oil prices were not jarring, and at which U.S. policy would accept the reality of a permanent shift from $3-a-barrel oil to $30-a-barrel oil.

Now we are in the glut phase. Producers are being forced to drop prices sharply. And once again we hear that energy crisis is over. It is not. Economic recovery alone would soak up much of the excess in the oil market. Another war or revolution in the Gulf — which any prudent person must consider possible — could send the oil-importing nations back into crisis.

In the United States, imports have dropped by half in the past couple of years. Domestic production is up, and consumption is down. The administration uses this improvement to buttress its case for dissolving the Energy Department. But the appearance of less vulnerability to supply interruptions is deceptive and dangerous.

Some important changes in U. S. energy use have occurred. The price of oil has been decontrolled, the strategic petroleum reserve is finally being filled, industry is using energy much more efficiently and the gas guzzler is an endangered species. But the price of natural gas is still artificially low, consumers still have no reliable source of help for reducing energy use in their homes, mass transit compared with that of other advanced nation is terrible, and the lack of a substantial gasoline tax helps keep that unchanged.

Nevertheless, the Reagan administration argues that higher energy prices have led to energy conservation and that there is therefore no reason for further federal support of research and other conservation programs. But the real issue is how much of what would be economically beneficial is not happening, and will not happen, under current policies. Do most types of energy use — technologies for supply and distribution, consumer information, manufacturing processes and the rest — reflect the reality of expensive energy or the history of cheap energy? The answer varies by sector. Large businesses with access to expertise and capital have adjusted well. Most other sectors have not. In residential and commercial buildings, which consume a quarter of all the energy used in America, only a tiny fraction of the economically desirable savings is being captured.

In short, a good beginning has been made, but it is only a beginning. To abandon conservation programs and dismantle research efforts now is to save small amounts of federal dollars at a very large longer-range cost to the economy. And hopeful talk about the end of the energy crisis ignores the painful lessons of the past decade.

能源教训

自从 1973 年以来,我国能源政策就一直像钟摆一样令人沮丧地经常摆来摆去,从危机摆向过剩,又从过剩摆向危机。至今,钟摆还没有在两极之间某个稳定点上停下来;在这一点上,石油价格变化无常的波动才不致引起震动,美国的政策也才会正视石油价格从每桶三美元长期不断地上升为每桶三十美元的现实。

现在,我们正处在过剩阶段。生产者被迫大幅度降价。我们又一次听说能源危机已经过去。其实不然。不过只要经济回升,就能吸收石油市场上大部分的过剩石油。要是海湾地区再发生一场战争或革命(任何明智之士都一定认为这是可能的),石油输入国就可能重新陷入危机之中。

过去两三年中,美国石油进口已经减少了一半。国内产量上升,消费量下降。政府利用情况的改善来增强其撤销能源部的要求。从表面上看,供应中断的可能性减少了,但是,这只是一种危险的假象。

美国在能源利用方面的确有了一些重大变化。石油价格管制取消了,战略石油储备终于得到了充实,工业中的能源利用率大大提高,油老虎正在消亡。但是,天然气价格仍然人为地过低,消费者在家庭节能方面仍然得不到稳妥的帮助,公共交通同其他先进国家相比糟糕透顶,而且汽油税不高,情况至今仍无改变。

尽管这样,里根政府仍然辩白说,能源价格的提高已经使能源有所节约,因此,联邦政府已经没有理由再支持能源研究计划和其它节能计划了。但是,真正的问题是:究竟有多少事情从经济上来说本来是有利的,可是在现行政策下,却没有得到实现,而且将来也不会得到实现?大多数利用能源的环节——供应和分配技术、消费者情报、制造工艺等等——的现状又怎样呢?究竟是反映了能源昂贵的现实呢?还是反映了能源低廉的历史呢?答案视不同部门而定。拥有专门技术和资本的大企业已经作了妥善的调整。大多数其他部门还没有适应这种现实。居民住宅和商业建筑所消耗的能源占美国全部能源消耗量的四分之一。这些地方实行节约,在经济上是可取的,可是现已实现的节约却微乎其微,还大有潜力可挖。

　　总之,我们已经有了一个良好的开端,但是,这也仅仅是开端而已。现在就放弃节能计划,停止能源研究工作,可以给联邦政府节省少量开支,但从比较长远的观点来看,只能使经济蒙受重大损失。那种认为能源危机已经过去的乐观论调,忽视了过去十年的痛苦教训。

　　这篇评论讨论了一个全球面临的普遍问题——能源问题。文章一开头就提出了明确的论点,即能源政策停止摇摆不定,能源问题才能得到解决。然后逐步展开进行详细论述,指出过剩现象只是"一种危险的假相",能源情况虽然得到改善,但仍存在问题。最后得出结论:说能源危机已经过去的乐观论调是错误的,必须继续能源计划和能源研究工作。文章论述有理有据,语言严谨平实。无论从内容上还是文体上看都称得上是新闻评论的一个范例。

　　译文遵循了原文的风格,端庄严谨,选词考究,紧扣原文词句。如开篇第一句话:"the energy pendulum has swung with depressing regularity from crisis to glut and back again."译文为"能源政策就一直像钟摆一样令人沮丧地经常摆来摆去,从危机摆向过剩,又从过剩摆向危机。"完全再现了原句的结构和含义。又如第二段中的"soak up"译为"吸收",第三段中"to buttress its case"译成"增强其要求",都忠实地传达了原词的喻意。但有时为使语义更清晰,语流更顺畅,译文也有意地变换了句式。如第四段中"The price of oil has been decontrolled, the strategic petroleum reserve is finally being filled, industry is using energy much more efficiently and the gas guzzler is an endangered species."这一句中前两个分句是被动语态,后两个分句为主动语态,译文则全部采用相同的句型:"石油价格管制取消了,战略石油储备终于得到充实,工业中的能源利用率大大提高,油老虎正在消亡。"这样处理使句式更加工整,更符合新闻评论正式的语言风格和文体。

附:练习
将下列新闻评论译成中文。

① Washington, the Father or an Infamous Traitor?

Generally, there are two distinct philosophies on how to bring up the child so that in maturity he does not make a nuisance of himself.

The first and older of the two relies heavily upon training. Train the child. Train him so that when he grows up he will behave thereafter as he has been trained or indoctrinated to behave.

The second and more modern shifts the emphasis to education. Educate the child so that when he grows up he can think for himself and shape those values, attitudes and habits which serve him best in a rapidly changing environment.

Now this is a schematic distinction which clearly does not apply in the practice. The choice is not an "either-or". But one example, drawn from the textbook controversy, will suffice to illustrate the dispute over emphasis.

Most Americans have been brought up to esteem patriotism as the hallmark of their citizenship and good fortune. They were brought up, or trained, in this value because their parents and teachers wanted it that way. They wanted a generation of Americans conditioned to loyalty and duty. They did not want a generation educated to think freely about the conflicting values of patriotism and disloyalty and fall by error into the latter.

The mechanics of this indoctrination are familiar to everyone — the Pledge of Allegiance, the National Anthem, the salute to the flag. At this command decision, students are not educated to think it through and decide for themselves whether George Washington was, indeed, the Father of his Country or as millions of loyal Englishmen thought of him, the worst traitor to the crown since Oliver Cromwell. They learned the answer before they were old enough to think about it.

And at bottom, this is what the textbook wrangle is all about. Not to train the child in the values his parents have found enduring is to neglect him. Not to educate him is to condemn him to repetitious ignorance.

What is needed is an agreement upon the right mixture, and when this is reached the controversy will disappear.

② America's Careening Foreign Policy

Realities: It is unglamorous to articulate, and complex to conduct, a centrist policy. But only this course can marshal our resources, meet global realities and maintain domestic rapport. Since World War I our major achievements have been forged at the centre. American foreign policy must contain elements of both power and principle, to promote both security and justice.

For our adversaries we need firmness and negotiation. With

our allies we need to lead and to evoke greater contributions. For national security we must strengthen defences and search for arms control. In the developing world we must address the East-West dimension and the deeper roots of unrest.

Our permanent interests do not change every four years. The next administration, whether Democratic or Republican, should pursue a balanced policy from the beginning. It should acknowledge that sometimes its predecessor was right; appoint some members of the opposition; selectively use the Scowcroft Commission model, and strive for interagency coherence — in short, conduct our foreign policy in a non-partisan manner. Surely debates will continue. But they will be infused with a consciousness that all Americans are engaged in a common enterprise.

In this way America will demonstrate that if we are no longer young, neither are we old. If we are no longer innocent, neither are we corrupt. And if we are no longer paramount, neither are we pawns of destiny.

③ Should Drugs Be Legalized?

I find no merit in the legalizers' case. The simple fact is that drug use is wrong. And the moral argument, in the end, is the most compelling argument. A citizen in a drug-induced haze, whether on his back-yard deck or on a mattress in ghetto crack house, is not what the founding fathers meant by the "pursuit of happiness". Despite the legalizers' argument that drug use is a matter of "personal freedom", our nation's notion of liberty is rooted in the ideal of a self-reliant citizenry. Helpless wrecks in treatment centres, men chained by their noses to cocaine — these people are slaves.

Imagine if, in the darkest days of 1940, Winston Churchill had rallied the West by saying, "This war looks hopeless, and besides, it will cost too much. Hitler can't be that bad. Let's surrender and see what happens." That is essentially what we hear from the legalizers.

This war can be won. I am heartened by indications that education and public revulsion are having an effect on drug use. The National Institute on Drug Abuse's latest survey of current users shows a 37-percent decrease in drug consumption since 1985. Cocaine is down 50 percent; marijuana use among young people is at its lowest rate since 1972. In my travels I've been encouraged by signs that Americans are fighting back.

I am under no illusion that such developments, however hopeful, mean the war is over. We need to involve more citizens in the fight, increase pressure on drug criminals and build on anti-drug programs that have proved to work. This will not be easy. But the moral and social costs of surrender are simply too great to contemplate.

④   A Red Light for Scofflaws

Law-and-order is the longest-running and probably the best-loved political issue in U.S. history. Yet it is painfully apparent that millions of Americans who would never think of themselves as lawbreakers, let alone criminals, are taking increasing liberties with the legal codes that are designed to protect and nourish their society. Indeed, there are moments today — amid outlaw litter, tax cheating, illicit noise and motorised anarchy — when it seems as though the scofflaw represents the wave of the future. Harvard Sociologist David Riesman suspects that a majority of Americans have blithely taken to committing supposedly minor derelictions as a matter of course. Already, Riesman says, the ethic of U. S. society is in danger of becoming this: "You're a fool if you obey the rules."

Nothing could be more obvious than the evidence supporting Riesman. Scofflaws abound in amazing variety. The graffiti-prone turn public surfaces into visual rubbish. Bicyclists often ride as though two-wheeled vehicles are exempt from all traffic laws. Litterbugs convert their communities into trash dumps. Widespread flurries of ordinances have failed to clear public places of high-decibel portable radios, just as earlier laws failed to wipe out the beer-soaked hooliganism that plagues many parks. Tobacco addicts remain hopelessly blind to signs that say NO SMOKING. Respectably dressed pot smokers no longer bother to duck out of public sight to pass around a joint. The flagrant use of cocaine is a festering scandal in middle-and-upper-class life. And then there are (hello, Everybody!) the jaywalkers.

三、软新闻

这是新闻的第三个层次,主要包含一些杂文小品,讽刺性或文艺性文章,概称为时文(periodical essays)。其写法灵活自由,文体广泛多变,内容轻松活泼,语言诙谐幽默,常常具有知识性、趣味性和文艺性。它不同于社论的端庄稳重,以理服人,而是以其独具的魅力吸引读者,感动读者,让读者在轻松愉悦的心情中不知不觉地接受作者的观点。

下文是一篇就美国人在服饰、言谈、行为和人际关系诸方面的问题发表的杂感。文章通过有趣的典故、巧妙的比喻和含蓄的幽默以及夸张、押韵等多种修辞手法，将鲜明的观点表现出来。

The Decline of Neatness

Anyone with a passion for hanging labels on people or things should have little difficulty in recognizing that an apt tag for our time is the Unkempt Generation. I am not referring solely to college kids. The sloppiness virus has spread to all sectors of society. People go to all sorts of trouble and expense to look uncombed, unshaved, unpressed.

The symbol of the times is blue jeans — not just blue jeans in good condition but jeans that are frayed, torn, discolored. They don't get that way naturally. No one wants blue jeans that are crisply clean or spanking new. Manufacturers recognize a big market when they see it, and they compete with one another to offer jeans that are made to look as though they've just been discarded by clumsy house painters after ten years of wear. The more faded and seemingly ancient the garment, the higher the cost. Disheveled is in fashion; neatness is obsolete.

Nothing is wrong with comfortable clothing. It's just that current usage is more reflective of a slavish conformity than a desire for ease. No generation has strained harder than ours to affect a casual, relaxed, cool look; none has succeeded more spectacularly in looking as though it had been stamped out by cookie cutters. The attempt to avoid any appearance of being well groomed or even neat has a quality of desperation about it and suggests a calculated and phony deprivation. We shun conventionality, but we put on a uniform to do it. An appearance of alienation is the triumphant goal, to be pursued in oversize sweaters and muddy sneakers.

Slovenly speech comes off the same spool. Vocabulary, like blue jeans, is being drained of color and distinction. A complete sentence in everyday speech is as rare as a man's tie in the swank Polo Lounge of the Beverly Hills Hotel. People communicate in chopped-up phrases, relying on grunts and chants of "you know" or "I mean" to cover up a damnable incoherence. Neatness should be no less important in language than it is in dress. But spew and sprawl are taking over. The English language is one of the greatest sources of wealth in the world. In the midst of accessible riches, we are linguistic paupers.

Violence in language has become almost as casual as the possession of handguns. The curious notion has taken hold that emphasis in communication is impossible without the incessant use of four-letter words. Some screenwriters openly admit that they are careful not to turn in scripts that are devoid of foul language lest the classification office impose the curse of a G(general)rating. Motion-picture exhibitors have a strong preference for the R (restricted) rating, probably on the theory of forbidden fruit. Hence writers and producers have every incentive to employ tasteless language and gory scenes.

整洁之风的衰退

任何一个热衷于将人或物挂上标签的人不用费力就可知道我们这个时代的合适标签是"邋遢的一代"。我指的不单是大学里的学子。邋遢这种病毒已蔓延到社会各个阶层。人们用尽力气,不惜代价地显出一副不梳头、不刮脸、不烫衣的样子。

这个时代的象征就是蓝布牛仔裤——不只是完好的蓝牛仔裤,而且是磨损的、撕破的、褪色的牛仔裤。不是自然穿旧穿坏的,而是没有人要清爽、崭新的蓝牛仔裤。制造商们看清了这点,认识到大有市场,于是相互争先恐后地抛出做成像笨手笨脚的粉刷工穿了十年后扔掉的那种牛仔裤。褪色越厉害,看上去越旧,价钱就越贵。衣冠不整正是时髦,服饰整洁则已过时。

衣着舒适并没有错,只是这种流行的做法与其说是对自在的追求,勿宁说是盲目随大流的反映。没有哪一代人像我们这代人如此刻意装出一副随便、轻松、不在意的样子;也没有哪一代人取得如此出奇的成功,让每个人看上去就像饼干模子压出来的一样。这种避免显得穿着整齐,哪怕是干净一点的企图真有些不顾一切,使人感到这是刻意装出的假穷酸相。我们避免陈规陋习,但为了做到这一点,我们又都穿上了一致的制服。标新立异的外貌是自鸣得意的目标,于是大家都穿起特大号的运动衫和沾满泥的旅游鞋来追求实现这一目标。

言语杂乱如出一辙。词汇就像蓝色牛仔裤一样正在被夺去了色彩和特性。在日常言谈中使用完整的句子非常少见,就像在贝弗利山饭店漂亮的马球俱乐部的休息室里很少见到男人打着领带一样。人们用割裂的短语进行交流,依靠诸如:"你知道"或"我的意思是"这类哼哼哈哈的腔调来掩盖糟透了的语无伦次的现象。语言的简洁应与服饰的整洁一样重要。然而正在取而代之的却是随口胡说和杂乱无章。英语是世界上最大的宝库之一。我们置身于垂手可得的财富之中,却成了语言的穷汉。

语言的滥用变得几乎就像买支手枪一样地随便。有一种奇怪的看法已经根深蒂固,以为在谈话中要强调什么,不接连用粗话就不行。有些写电影剧本的人公开承认,他们在写剧本时非常小心,生怕不用下流话而被审查处定为 G 级(一般性)影片,那就糟了。电影院老板非常偏爱 R 级(限制性)电影,很可能是根据禁果的理论。于是作家与制片商们就有了一切动力来促使他们使用粗俗的语言和血腥的场面。

这是一篇具有强烈讽刺意味的小品文,从衣着谈到了语言,尖锐地攻击了美国当今社会的堕落风气。整齐清洁的仪表和正规流利的语言已经成为过去,而今流行的是故意做成磨损破旧的牛仔裤和满口的污言秽语。作者用讥讽的口吻,生动的描述来唤起读者的注意,发人深省。为求语言的动人,文中使用了大量的修辞手段,如暗喻:"The sloppiness virus has spread to all sectors of society."(第一段);明喻:"Vocabulary, like blue jeans, is being drained of color and distinction."(第四段);头韵:"uncombed, unshaved, unpressed."(第一段)和"spew and sprawl"(第四段);对偶:"Dishelved is in fashion; neatness is obsolete."(第二段);引典:"forbidden fruit"(第五段)等等。这些修辞手法的运用使文章读来妙趣横生,余味无穷,增强了文章的可读性。翻译此类文章时须充分考虑其语言活泼,文笔优美的特点,使译文读来也同样令人赏心悦目,引人入胜。

从本篇译文中不难看出译者努力做到了这一点。他在对修辞手法的处理方面尤为注意,保持了原文的风貌。如第一段中的头韵"uncombed, unshaved, unpressed"译成"不梳头,不刮脸,不烫衣。"既忠实原义,又重现原韵;将对偶句"Dishelved is in fashion; neatness is obsolete."译作"衣冠不整正是时髦,服饰整洁则已过时。"也很工整对称,与原文基本匹配。再如将上面所举的明喻译成"词汇就像蓝色牛仔裤一样正被夺去了色彩和特性",也传达了原句的语气。除了修辞手法处理得当外,译文的选词也很精确。这样的例子不胜枚举,此处仅举几例作一说明。第二段中用来修饰牛仔裤的"in good condition"译成"完好的";第四段中的"grunts and chants"译作"哼哼哈哈的腔调"都非常贴切、形象。此外有的句子为了求得译成的汉语更加生动和通顺,译者有意改变了词序和句式,如第四段中的一句:"But spew and sprawl are taking over."译文变成"然而正取而代之的是随口胡说和杂乱无章。"这样译法使得着重点更加突出,句子结构也显得稳重均衡。

附:练习
将下列文章译成中文。

① Electronic Mail
Communicating in the New Age

Friends and family scatter like dry leaves, drifting to different cities and countries. "I'll write," I promise solemnly. Alas, my good intentions produce only imagined letters never embraced by paper, never kissed by stamps.

Ah, but electronic mail has changed my ways. My computer has become an epistolary Pinatubo, erupting with letters and missives and memos whizzed around the world at warp speed. I share thoughts with pen pals in New Zealand, query strangers in Bombay, debate magicians in Manhattan.

Never having tried it, I used to scorn E-mail as boring high tech, the stuff of business communications. Then a friend insisted I investigate this "invisible world," as he called it, claiming that it is expanding exponentially. I logged on to CompuServe, a national on-line information service, and was hooked.

...

Sleepless nights. Yet the very features that make electronic mail appealing can sweep you into a vortex of E-reading and E-writing that gobbles up spare time, a hazard that's left me bleary-eyed on many a night. The near instant gratification makes letter writing fun, if not addictive. My circle of correspondents seems to expand geometrically, and my keyboard runneth over. I suppose I could set limits on my electro-effusiveness by chatting with only a few friends. But electronic mail is seductive precisely because it spurs me to investigate unexplored territory, to ask more questions and to establish contact with people half a world away.

That long reach can also draw families closer, says Rita Levine, a Pittsburgh parent. She swaps daily electronic notes with her daughter Erin, a freshman at the University of Delaware, where all students have Internet addresses. In the first two months of school, Levine got 53 E-mail missives from Erin, who drops her mom a few chatty lines whenever she is near a terminal. "It's funny,"says Levine. "We talk more now than when Erin lived upstairs."

② The Simple Life Comes Back

Goodbye to having it all. Tired of trendiness and materialism, Americans are rediscovering the joys of home life, basic values and things that last.

After a 10-year bender of gaudy dreams and Godless consumerism, Americans are starting to trade down. They want to reduce their attachments to status symbol, fast-track careers and great expectations of Having It All. Upscale is out; downscale is in. Yuppies are an ancient civilization. Flaunting money is considered gauche; if you've got it, please keep it to yourself — or give some away!

In place of materialism, any Americans are embracing simpler pleasures and homier values. They've been thinking hard about what really matters in their lives, and they've decided to make some changes. What matters is having time for family and friends, rest and recreation, good deeds and spirituality. For some people. that means a radical step: changing one's career, living on less or packing up and moving to a quieter place. For others, it can mean something as subtle as choosing a cheaper brand of running shoes or leaving work a little earlier to watch the kids in a soccer game.

③   Get What You Want Out of Life

Years before rising to nationally prominence as coach of Notre Dame's national ranked football team, Lou Holtz made a list of 107 things "to do before I die." It covered the gamut, from attending dinner at the White House to sky diving.

So far, Holtz has made it to go 91 — seeing all four of his children graduate college. "Set goal and follow through on them," he says. "You transform yourself from one of life's spectators into a real participant."

We all have dream and desires, but relatively few people have goals. Strongly held wishes — "I want to be rich" or "I wish I were thinner" — do not qualify. Though they begin as dreams, goals are specific objectives, attained only through concrete action. "If you can't measure it, rate it or describe it, it is probably not a goal," says Micheal LeBoeuf, a New Orleans business consultant.

Coach Holtz sees this firsthand. Nearly every freshman player dreams of professional football. He explains to them the distinction between goals and fantasies. "I tell them, lots of little goals lie between training camp and playing the NFL. First they have to make the Notre Dame team. Then one by one, they've got to clear the hurdles, and that's true of every goal we set."

As Holtz suggests, high achievers know exactly where they want to go. Here are the steps he and others have followed to fulfil their dreams.

Define your Objective.

Put It on Paper. Once you defined your goal, write it down. High achievers trace their accomplishment to the time they committed their goals to paper.

Map Your Strategy. Breaking a goal down into bite-size pieces makes achieving it seem less intimidating. A technique called backward planning consists of setting an objective and then retracing the steps needed to achieve it.

Set a Deadline. "A goal is a dream with a deadline," says motivational expert Zig Ziglar. "Deadlines provide a time frame for action and get us moving in pursuit of our dreams."

Commit Yourself.

Don't Fear Failure.

Persist, Persist. Along the way to any goal, you will be confronted with obstacles. Belief in yourself can act as an anaesthetic against these setbacks.

It's Never Too Late. Age is not a barrier to achievement. As we grow older and learn more, we gain the confidence to take on new challenges.

④ The Decline of Neatness

Untidiness in dress, speech and emotions is readily connected to human relationships. The problem with the casual sex so fashionable in film is not that it arouses lust but that it deadens feelings and annihilates privacy. The danger is not that sexual exploitation will create sex fiends but that it may spawn eunuchs. People who have the habit of seeing everything and doing anything run the risk of feeling nothing.

My purpose here is not to make a case for Victorian decorum or for namby-pambyism. The argument is directed to bad dress, bad manners, bad speech, bad human relationships. The hope has to be that calculated sloppiness will run its course. Who knows, perhaps some of the hip designers may discover they can make a fortune by creating fashions that are unfrayed and that grace the human form. Similarly motion-picture and television producers and exhibitors may realize that a substantial audience exists for something more appealing to the human eye and spirit than the sight of a human being hurled through a store-front window or tossed off a penthouse terrace. There might even be a salutary response to films that dare to show people expressing genuine love and respect for one another in more convincing ways than anonymous clutching and thrashing about.

Finally, our schools might encourage the notion that few things are more rewarding than genuine creativity, whether in the clothes we wear, the way we communicate, the nurturing of human relationships, or how we locate the best in ourselves and put it to work.

第四章 广告文体的翻译

广告在当今这个已进入信息时代的商品社会中可谓无处不在,无孔不入。对广告文体的研究具有十分重要的现实意义和实用价值。广告的翻译如同广告的写作一样应使读者在阅读之后,知晓商品的有关信息,产生购买的欲望和冲动。现从广告文体的劝说功能入手,介绍广告的翻译要求与标准,并通过介绍广告的语言特点提示在广告翻译中应注意之处。

第一节 广告文体的语言特点与翻译方法

广告文体在语言运用上富有鲜明的特色。无论在词汇、语法或修辞方面均有其不同一般之处,翻译时不可不加注意。

一、广告的词汇特点

广告的词汇丰富多彩,但每一个词的选择与使用都服务于"推销商品"这一最终目的,因此它们往往具备鼓动性和感染力。归纳起来主要表现在如下几方面:

1. 形容词及其比较级、最高级的使用

用词方面都倾向于美化所述商品,有大量的褒义形容词频繁出现,以加强描述性和吸引力。

① *Famous world-wide* gourmet cuisine. *Excellent daily* specials and *mouthwatering* desserts。世界有名的美食烹调。精美的每日特色饭菜和令人垂涎的点心。

此例为一则餐馆广告,形容词占了整个广告的一半,十分具有诱惑力。

② *Tender* tailoring. *Feminine* but far from *frilly* … *gentle* on your budget, too. 做工,精巧细致;式样,娇美自然;价格,低廉宜人。

这则女性服装的广告,用 tender, feminine, frilly, gentle 等形容词来描述商品,特别符合女性读者的口味。

为了使更多的消费者购买自己的商品,商品广告常通过比较来抬高自己。虽不直接贬低别人,却常用形容词的比较级来修饰与突出自己的商品。例如:

① Tasters *richer* … *mellower* … *more satisfying*. 口味更浓……更醇……更令人满意。

② For the first time, there's a remarkable gel that can give your hair any look you want—*sleeker, fuller, straighter, curlier, more natural*, even wet—without a drop of alcohol or oil. 一种前所未有,不同寻常的发乳问世了。它可以使您的头发随心所愿——更光滑,更丰茂,更平直,更卷曲,更自然,甚至保持湿度——却不含一滴酒精或油脂。

有时形容词还以最高级的形式出现,以增强购买者的信心。

① And along the way, you will enjoy the *warmest, most personal* service. 一路上您将享受最热情、最周到的服务。

② Our philosophy is simple. To give you the *most important* things you want when you travel: the *best* location, the *best* standards and the special attention a businessman needs. 我们的宗旨很简单。让您在旅行中得到企业家最想要的一切:最好的地点,最高的标准和特别的服务。

2. 创造新词、怪词以引起新奇感

广告中常用一些杜撰的新词、怪词,以突出产品的新、奇、特,满足消费者追求新潮、标榜个性的心理,还可取得某种修辞效果。

① TWOGETHER

The ultimate all inclusive one price sunkissed holiday. 两人共度一个阳光灿烂的假日,一切费用均包括在单人价格之内。

TWOGETHER 既取 together 之音,又取"两人"之意比 together 更形象,倍添情趣。

② What could be delisher than fisher? 还有什么比钓鱼更有味?

delisher 来自 delicious,这样的处理与后面的 fisher 造成押韵的效果,增添了韵律美。

还有一些商品名称,通过加前后缀,合成新词,生动有趣,意味深长。如以-ex 结尾的商标就有 kleenex(一种手巾纸)、windex(一种擦窗清洁剂)、rolex(手表)等。据说-ex 来自 excellent 一词,加上此后缀可以暗示产品的品质优良。又如根据法语词 boutique(妇女时装用品小商店)一词在广告中演绎出类似的新词,如 footique, bootique 表示专卖女鞋的商店。这些合成的新词既营造了新奇、独特的气氛,又给人一词多意的凝炼感。

3. 缩略词和复合词以节省广告篇幅

广告写作中常尽可能缩短篇幅,以降低成本。使用缩略词和复合词的使用比比皆是。

① Where to leave your troubles when you fly JAL. 乘坐日航班机,一路无烦恼。

JAL 是 Japan Airlines 的缩略形式。

② Even at just over $100 per person per day, our thrill-of-a-lifetime trips are cheap. 即使每人每天一百多美元,我们那

令人终生难忘的极富刺激的旅行仍然便宜。

4. "雅"语、"俗"语平分天下,色彩缤纷

广告宣传的商品不同,推销的对象不一,因此广告的用词也"雅"、"俗"各异。"雅"指优雅而正式的书面语,"俗"则指口语、俚语和非正式用语。口语体的词汇在广告中常常出现,易懂、易记;俚语、非正式用词的运用则使广告更加生动活泼。"俗"语常见于一般消费品广告中,如食品、饮料、日用小商品等。此类广告很合乎一般大众的口味。优雅正式的书面语常用来描述豪华汽车、高档化妆品以及名烟名酒等奢侈品。这类商品的消费者多为富足并受过良好教育的人,所以用雅致和富有文彩的字眼既能烘托商品的高贵品质,又满足了这类消费者讲究身分、追求上乘的心理。如:

① The home of your dreams awaits you behind this door. Whether your taste be a country manor estate or a penthouse in the sky, you will find the following pages filled with the world's most elegant residences. 打开门,等着您的就是梦寐以求的家。无论您想要一座乡间宅第,或者是一间摩天大楼的顶屋,翻开下面几页就可以看到世界上最美的住宅,供您挑选。

广告中的 await, be, manor, elegant, residence 均是正式语汇,代替了口语体的 wait, is, house, nice, place。

② *Moms* depend on Kool-Aid like *kids* depend on *moms*. 妈咪依赖果乐,就像宝宝依赖妈咪一样。

用俗语 moms, kids 代替 mothers 和 children 使广告读来更加亲切,缩略了距离,符合儿童的特点。

广告中用词不拘一格,色彩纷呈。在翻译时就要尽可能贴近原文,注意将描述性和鼓动性强的形容词译巧译好。而新词、怪词的翻译只需适当体现,不必生译硬译,重要的是将词的意思表达清楚。缩短词和复合词的翻译也应注意简短,减少篇幅,但不能因简

伤意,必要时仍须用全称。此外,还须在译文中体现原文的语言色调。原文中使用了精致的雅语,译文中就不能用俚语、俗语。原文用较轻松随意的口语,译文中也应一致,要通俗易懂,琅琅上口。

二、广告的语法特点

1. 简单短句多,醒目易懂。例如:
① Coca-Cola is it. 还是可口可乐好!
② Fresh Up with Seven-Up 请饮七喜,倍添精神。

2. 并列句多,简洁明了,易于理解;平行结构,加深印象。例如:
① Introducing FITNESS magazine. It's about health, it's about exercise, it's about your image, your energy, and your outlook. 向您推荐《健康》杂志:说健康,说锻炼,说形象,说精力,说展望。
② The Olympic challenge is ours, and so is the human challenge. Samsung is forging ahead in electronics, and the race into a new age is about to begin. 奥林匹克是对我们的挑战,也是对全人类的挑战。三星电子在前进,迈入新时代的比赛即将开始。

3. 省略句多,语言凝炼。例如:
① You'll enjoy relaxed sunny days. Warm, crystal clear lagoons. Cool, green foliage. Waterfalls. Flowers. Exotic scents. Bright blue skies. Secluded beaches. Graceful palms. Breathtaking sunsets. Soft evening breezes. And food that simply outstanding. 您会享受这阳光明媚的轻松日子。温暖、清澄的环礁湖,清凉、碧绿的树叶,瀑布,花丛,异样的芬芳,明亮的蓝天,幽静的海滩,优美的棕榈,壮丽的日落,轻柔的晚风。还有那绝妙的食物。

从"温暖、清澄的环礁湖"到"轻柔的晚风"一连串名词短语代替了 You'll enjoy…的句子,既简洁紧凑,又鲜明有力。

② It's a moment you planned for. Reached for. Struggled for. A long-awaited moment of success. Omega, for this and all your significant moments. 这是您计划的时刻,期望的时刻,争取的时刻,长久等待的成功时刻。欧米茄,记下此刻,和所有重要时刻。

4. 祈使句多,具有强烈的鼓动色彩。例如:

① So come into McDonald's and enjoy Big Mac Sandwich 走进麦当劳,享用大三明治。

② For more of America, look to us 想更多了解美国,来找我们。

5. 否定句少,即便使用否定句式,也多为了用其他商品来反衬,或从反面突出产品特性。如:

① We would never say the new Audi 100 is the best in its class, We *don't* have to. 我们根本不必说新型奥迪 100 是同类车中最好的。没有这个必要。

② Q: Where in America can you find a better pair of Men's Twills for ﹩32.50?
　A: Nowhere that we know of.
问:你能在美国其他地方花 32.50 美元买到一条更好的斜纹布男裤吗?
答:据我们所知,不能。

③ If you can't relax here, you can't relax. 此地不能放松,无处能放松。

6. 常用主动语态和现在时,给人一种直接感,并暗示商品的持久性和永恒性。例如:

① Harmony of style and performance set this new 626 apart. Qualities *are* at the heart of every Mazda. 式样与性能的协调一致使新型626与众不同。质量是马士达的核心。

② The Charisma of the Filipina, It *comes* from somewhere within. And it *shines* on every flight. 菲律宾航空公司的魅力,来自内在本质,在每一次飞行中熠熠生辉。

在翻译中应充分考虑原文语法特点并加以体现,无论是句型、时态、语态均应尽量取得一致。但这并不意味着亦步亦趋,照搬原文。有时应稍加变通,使语义明确,语流顺畅,达到易读易懂,深入人心,有利促销的目的。

三、广告的修辞特点

广告有"半文学体"之称,因此广告中常使用修辞手段。如:

① Featherwater: light as a feather 法泽瓦特眼镜:轻如鸿毛。(明喻)

② To spread your wings in Asia. Share our vantage point. 在亚洲展开您的双翅,同我们一起飞高望远。(暗喻)

③ My Paris in a perfume 巴黎恰在香水中。(借喻)

④ I'm More satisfied! 我更满意摩尔牌香烟。(双关语)

⑤ We take no pride in prejudice. 我们不以偏见为荣。(典故,源于简·奥斯汀的名著 *Pride and Prejudice*。)

⑥ We've hidden a garden full of vegetables where you'd never expect. In a pie. 我们在您想不到的地方藏着整个菜园。就在馅饼里。(夸张)

⑦ Flowers by Interflora speak from the heart. 植物园培育的鲜花倾诉衷肠。(拟人)

⑧ Dish after dish after dish. People expect us to be better. 一盘一盘又一盘。人们盼望我们更好。(重复)

⑨ My mother wanted me to have piano lessons.
My father wanted me to go to Harvard.
My teacher wanted me to become a lawyer.
My wife wants me to stay at home.
Aren't your desires just as important?
……
Cars that are created to impress only yourself.
母亲要我学钢琴,
父亲要我进哈佛,
老师要我当律师,
妻子要我留家中。
你自己的愿望不也一样重要吗?
……
只有汽车为你而造,让你喜欢。(排比)

⑩ A contemporary classic. A timeless timepiece. 当代的经典作;永久的计时器。(对偶)

⑪ Hi-Fi、Hi-Fun、Hi-Fashion, only from Sony. 高保真,高乐趣,高时尚,只来自索尼。(头韵)

修辞手段在广告文体中的广泛运用,造成翻译的困难。由于英汉语言的差异和文化背景的不同,英语中用词奥妙之处有时很难用汉语再现。翻译者应分析其相同点与不同点,在译文中,尽可能采用相同或相似的修辞手段,但切不可一成不变,因文害义,应根据汉语表达习惯和中国读者的审美情趣作相应的变化。

第二节 不同类型广告的翻译

广告可以从不同的角度分成若干类。按其所使用的传播媒介来分,可分为报纸广告、杂志广告、广播广告、电视广告、电话广告、演出广告、赛场广告、张贴广告、路牌广告、车船广告、橱窗广告、邮件广告、电子广告等等。按其内容不同又可分为商业广告、金融广告、工业广告、招聘广告、公益广告等等。商业广告又可细分为若干种。如果从广告的制作手段和文体来分,则可归纳为两大类,即"硬卖"类和"软卖"类。它们在立意、构思和语言运用方面各有特色,在翻译时必需采用不同的手法来保持各自的风格,以取得良好的广告效果。第一,"硬卖"类广告以传递信息为侧重点,主要通过介绍有关商品的优点特性,以理服人,促进消费。在文体风格上接近于具有信息功能的新闻体和科技体,语言准确清晰、朴实客观,语气平稳冷静,循循善诱。第二,"软卖"类广告则以情动人,在商品与消费者之间建立感情联系,激发购买的冲动。文体风格接近于文学体裁,语言较华丽雅致,色彩丰富,形象生动,语气夸张,诱惑力强。试比较以下两则广告:

Cholesterol has natural enemies

In the battle against Cholesterol, it seems man has a natural ally.

Deep-sea, cold-water fish contain a special oil called Omega-3. An oil that recent studies indicate helps control Cholesterol.

Now Squibb brings you Omega-3 in a dietary supplement.

Introducing Proto-chol.

A natural oil from only deep-sea, cold-water fish rich in Omega-3, And it's concentrated in an easy-to-swallow sealed gelcap, so there is no fishy taste or smell.

Of course, Proto-chol should be part of a complete cholesterol control program, which includes regular exercise, foods low in saturated fats and regular medical checkups.

So start your cholesterol control program today.

Cholesterol is one enemy you should fight everyday.

1987 E. R Squibb&Sons, Inc.
Princeton, N. J.

胆固醇的天然克星

在与胆固醇的抗争中,人类似乎有个天然的盟友。

深海冷水鱼类体内含有一种称为"欧米加—3"的特别油脂。经新近科学研究表明,这种油脂有助于抑制胆固醇。

斯贵博公司现奉献给您含有"欧米加—3"的营养补充食品,隆重推出"降胆固醇油"。这种油脂仅取之于含有丰富"欧米加—3"的深海冷水鱼类,浓缩后置于便于吞服的密封胶内,故无鱼腥味。

当然,服用"降胆固醇鱼油"只是抑制胆固醇整个方案的一部分,还需经常锻炼,食用低脂肪食品和定期到医院检查。

劝君采取行动,早日降低胆固醇。

胆固醇是您必须每日与之斗争的顽敌。

美国新泽西洲普林斯顿市
斯贵博父子公司

Tomorrow will be a reflection of tonight

Nightime is a special time, a time of rest and renewal. Your body begins to relax to unwind from the activity of the day and slip into the softer rhythm of the night. It is when your body turn the energy needed for the smiles and laughter of the day into the magical replenishment of the night. This is the time your skin needs special care.

Night of Olay is special night care cream, created to make

the most of the magic of the night. It is greaseless and remarkably light to touch, a sheer pleasure on your skin, allowing it to breathe naturally while it absorbs this special nighttime nourishment.

Hour after quiet hour all through the night. Night of Olay enhances your skin's own natural renewal by bathing it in continuous moisture, easing tiny dry wrinkle lines and encouraging the regeneration of softer younger looking skin.

Night of Olay tonight will be reflected in your youthful radiance tomorrow.

Night of Olay.

明天是今夜的映象

夜晚是一段特别的时间——休息和更新的时间。您的身体开始放松,由白天的紧张活动松驰下来,转入夜晚轻柔的韵律。白天您的笑容和笑声所消耗掉的精力要由夜晚魔术般地来补充。这时您的皮肤需要特别护理。

奥莱夜霜是一种夜晚使用的特别护肤霜,能充分发挥夜晚的魔力。无油脂,轻柔,舒适,让皮肤一面自然呼吸,一面吸收奥莱夜霜的特殊营养。

一夜之中,每时每刻,奥莱夜霜使您的皮肤始终保持湿润,增强皮肤的自然再生能力,舒展细微的皱纹,让您的皮肤显得更柔软更年轻。

今夜擦的奥莱夜霜明天变成您青春的明艳。

奥莱夜霜

例1是一则介绍降低胆固醇的食品——深海鱼油的广告。它将商品的名称、用途、特点等信息用十分平白的语言直截了当,清楚明白地一一进行事实性的叙述,整篇广告信息量大,有科学的可信度。广告使用了一些意思准确、形式简洁、带有专业性色彩的词汇。如 deep-sea，cold-water，easy-to-swallow，Proto-chol 等合成词和 cholesterol，Omega-3，dietary supplement，saturated fats，medical checkup 等专业词汇，使广告的笔调显得专门化、内行、令人信服。

例2是美容用品广告。它针对女性渴望青春永驻，以美丽动人的形象出现在人前的心理，提出了打动人心的口号："今夜擦的奥莱夜霜明天变成您青春的明艳。"它不像例1那样具体介绍化妆品的成分以及作用，而是通过激发人们内心对美的渴望来促销。广告开头两段先将夜晚的特点提示出来："夜晚是一段特别的时间——休息和更新的时间。""身体开始放松"，"转入夜晚轻柔的韵律"。接着自然过渡到商品的介绍："白天您的笑容和笑声所消耗掉的精力要由夜晚来补充。这时您的皮肤需要特别的护理……奥莱夜霜是一种夜晚使用的特别护肤霜，能充分发挥夜晚的魔力。"然后才介绍商品本身的特点："无油脂、轻柔、舒适"以及功效："特殊营养"、"保持湿度，增强皮肤的自然再生能力，舒展细微的皱纹"等等。词汇方面选择了一些意义较为广泛，但颇具诱惑力的字眼来吸引读者，从而促进销售。如文中多次出现 special 一词，以突出其与众不同，两次使用 natural（naturally）以迎合消费者回归自然的心理，两次使用与"年轻"相关的词组——younger looking，youthful radiance 来满足消费者永葆青春的愿望，另外还有 magic，magical，softer rhythm，remarkably light，sheer pleasure 等词语都是些较能激发读者购买欲的字眼。

以上两例表明"软卖"类广告注重情感的激发，"硬卖"类广告侧重信息的传递。对于不同类型的广告在翻译时须注意保持原文的特点，概括说来，"硬卖"类广告的翻译应重表意，而"软卖"类广告的翻译侧重传情。

前者译文不求词藻华丽，但求真实简明。在结构处理与表达方式上一般无须作较大变动。它更强调语义对等。下例为一则"硬卖"类广告,试比较原文与译文。

SINGER
Presses out the Iron Age
The Magic Steam Press reduces ironing time
by as much as 50%

  The Singer Magic Steam Press will give your garments an instant, fresh-from-the-cleaners look.

  An innovation in household ironing, it has a pressing surface ten times the size of most handheld irons and pressure over 100 lbs. The magic Steam Press provides exactly what you want——ease, speed and professional results.

* Burst of Steam features for stubborn wrinkles
* Easy one-hand operation, either sitting or standing
* Variable temperature control adjusts temperature according to fabric selected
* Portable and easy to store
* Protects fine fabric
* Huge ironing pad surface
* Non-stick ironing pad surface
* 100 lbs, of even ironing pressure
* Automatic safety shut-off

140 Years of Innovation
SINGER

Singer's worldwide retail and distribution system covers 100 countries.

胜家熨斗,开创熨斗新时代
——神奇的蒸汽熨斗可节省一半熨烫时间。
神奇的蒸汽熨斗使您的衣服笔挺,犹如刚从洗衣店取回。

这是家用熨斗的一次创新。它的熨烫面比多数家用熨斗大10倍,具有100余磅压力。神奇的蒸汽熨斗给予您企求的效果——时间短,操作简便,效果好。
- 喷出的水蒸汽可烫平任何顽固的皱褶;
- 一只手操作。操作时可坐着,也可站着;
- 设有温度控制器,可根据不同的衣料调整温度;
- 携带、存放两便;
- 自动保护精细面料;
- 熨烫板宽大;
- 熨烫板表面不粘连;
- 熨烫压力为100磅,压力均匀;
- 自动安全开关。

胜 家 公 司
140年的创新历史
批发零售网点遍及100多个国家和地区

这则广告用电报式的短语结构将商品的特点清晰简要地介绍给读者。译文沿袭了原文的句式,保持了说明性风格,语义清楚,明白易懂,反映了"硬卖"类广告简明真实的特点。其中商品名称SINGER译成"胜家"既渲染了产品的出类拔萃的品格,提高了广告语言的鼓动性和诱惑性,也非常符合汉语广告的语言习惯,可谓音意合一。当然译文中尚有可进一步推敲和润色之处。例如将品名译成神奇的蒸汽熨斗就割裂了名称,应译成"胜家神奇蒸汽熨斗"。再如将protects fine fabric译成"自动保护精细面料"就不符合汉语习惯,如改译成"不伤精细面料"则好得多。又如"The Magic Steam Press provides exactly what you want——ease, speed and professional results"一句,译文显得过于拘泥原文,若译作:"神奇蒸汽熨斗恰恰遂您心愿——方便,快捷,奇效。"似乎更符合汉语的表达习惯。"Easy one-hand operation, either sitting or standing"一句译得也不够简洁,可译作:"单手操作,可坐可站。"总之这类广告的翻译应以达意为主要标准,兼顾汉语的表达习惯。

"软卖"类广告的翻译侧重情感的传递。译文应生动形象,富有色彩,传神传情,以求得接受效果的等值。下面这则广告就属以情动人的"软卖"类广告。

I came back

I came back to softness and comfort.

I came back to Dr. White's.

And I wonder why I ever went away.

Because only Dr. White's gives me two kinds of comfort. The super-comfort of their cotton-wool content that makes them so much softer. And the comfort of a safer, more absorbent towel, with a flush-away design, too, for even more convenience.

I tried the rest, but I came back.

Isn't it time you came back to Dr. White's?

Dr. White's
Two kinds of comfort

[译文 A]

我回来了

我回到了 Dr. White's 身边。

我又感到了柔软与舒适。

真奇怪!我为什么曾离它而去。

因为只有 Dr. White's 能给我两种舒适。内含的棉絮使它们更加柔软,尤为舒适。有"冲洗"设计的吸水性特强的毛巾使它们更安全,更方便。

我曾经试过其他的,但是我又回来了。

您也该回到 Dr. White's 身边来了吧?

[译文B]

我归来了

归来享受柔情与安乐。
归来再与白仕重相聚。
真不懂我为何会离去。
唯有白仕让我获得双重享受。
棉絮内衬,分外柔软。
吸水毛巾,更加安全。
易冲易洗,方便无比。
我也曾作过别的尝试,
但我还是归来了。
难道您不该也归来吗?
白仕,
让您拥有双重享受。

这是一则为白仕牌妇女卫生巾所做的广告。对比A和B两种译文,不难看到孰优孰劣。译文A绝对忠实于原文,将原文的意思用直译法译出,译文字字紧贴原文,可以说语义对等这一层次已经达到,但在功能对等与效果对等这两个层面上显然远不如译文B出色。译文B没有像译文A那样逐字逐句对应,而是使用了符合汉语修辞习惯的排比句,极富诗情画意,保持了原文的感染力,激发了读者的兴趣。整篇译作意到神到,可谓妙手天成。由此可见,"软卖"类广告的翻译应以传神传情为重点,既不以词害义,也不因意损文,真正做到曲尽其意,韵味悠长。

附:练习:

将下列广告译成中文。

一、硬卖类

①   Press the Button

The camera automatically focuses, sets the exposure, shoots, and hands you a developing picture.

Polaroid's SX-70 Sonar One Step

Now all you have to do to get a precisely-focused, properly-exposed picture is simply press one button on Polaroid's SX-70 Sonar One Step, the world's finest instant camera.

Sonar automatically measures the distance to your subject. The 4-element glass lens rotates to the precise focus——from as close as 10.4 inches to infinity. The single-lens reflex viewfinder previews your subject. The automatic exposure control makes the exposure. And the built-in motor hands you the developing picture. All in only a second and a half. Never before has precision picture-taking been so simple.

②   The Showplace that Goes Places

There are two fundamental reasons for buying any motorhome.

Driveability

And livability.

A GMC Motorhome is designed to supply both in abundance.

Consider GMC's front-wheel drive. It means there's no driveshaft running from the front to the rear. This allows for a low center of gravity. Thereby contributing to a stable ride.

And in the rear, the wheels are arranged in tandem, one behind the other, rather than side by side.

This arrangement offers several advantages:

First, when combined with GMC's air suspension system, it helps to make for a smooth and stable ride. Second, it allows the use of six brakes rather than four, one at each wheel. And third, it provides impressive room inside. Because when the rear wheels are in tandem, they intrude less on interior space.

Then there's the livability factor. A GMC is not only pleasant to look at. It's a pleasure to live in, as well.

The interior is orderly and efficient.

The galley has all the conveniences you could want. Including a roomy 7½-cubic-foot refrigerator with freezer. An efficient and convenient range. And a stainless steel sink with double bowl.

And as you can see, the seating area is a joy to behold. With a choice of beautifully coordinated colors, fabrics and floor plans.

③   Executive Backchair

Engineered for customized orthopedic support to prevent and relieve back pain.

* Forward-tilt feature
* Adjustable neck rest
* built-in adjustable lumbar support

New!
To fit individuals from 5'22" to 6'6"
Backsaver

④   We keep up with the high cost of burning down

We know it's hard for you to keep abreast of the cost of replacing your home——the way its value is increasing. So we do it for you. We're the homewatchers, the Farmers Agents. We'll check your present coverage. We'll see that you have the right kind of insurance. We'll cover you for today's higher replacement costs. And we'll provide adequate coverage in the future, automatically, through our Value Protection Program. What's more, we can also provide a mortgage protection policy which pays off the mortgage if the bread-winner should pass away. It's all part of our fast, fair, friendly service.

FARMERS INSURANCE GROUP

The Homewatchers

We have a growing concern for you

⑤   *HOW TO RELIEVE ARTHRITIS PAIN AND INFLAMMATION*

Take Bufferin to relieve minor arthritis pain fast. Bufferin goes to the heart of the pain and works where you hurt to quickly relieve minor arthritis pain. So you feel better for hours.

Take Bufferin to reduce inflammation that Tylenol can't effectively reach. Many people with arthritis pain, swelling and stuffiness don't realize that inflammation is the primary cause. And Many don't know that while Tylenol works on pain, it doesn't effectively reduce inflammation. But Bufferin does. Taken regularly, Bufferin reduces inflammation, so after several days you begin to feel relief from the swelling and persistent pressure around joints.

Arthritis can be serious. If pain persists more than 10 days or redness is present, consult your doctor immediately.

  BUFFERIN FOR THE PAIN AND
  INFLAMMATION OF ARTHRITIS
   Used only as Directed.
   BRISTOL—MYERS CO.

二、软卖类

①   AUSTRALIA FEEL THE WONDER

  The Aborigines believe that this entire country was sung into existence by the Spirits.

    Come, listen to the music.

  Listen to the laughter of Kookaburras in premeval forests. To the pulsing hum of Aboriginal music at ancient ceremonies which reenact the creation of the world. To tell tales in outback pubs. Listen to the muffled thunder of our surf. Listen, finally, to the kind of music people say you can hear even when it's absolutely quiet.

②   Where Visual Drama Meets Audio Ambience

  One glance is all it takes. You're at the edge of creative innovation. Where the sense blends in a sea of expressive experience——waves of lucid sound, landscapes of sensuous form, all for your personal enjoyment. Now listen closely. At first it seems that you're in a jazz club, then a cinema, then a cathedral … what will be the next?

  The ambience keeps shifting as your fingers switch through the six options on the UD-90 remote control.

KENWOOD
Vision of Sound

③ Recently I had to go to St. Louis for a meeting. Instead of flying, as I have been doing for the past four years, I decided to take an overnight Pullman. It happened to be raining when I left. No matter. The train was exactly on time, and what's more, I didn't drenched before boarding.

By the time I reached my roomette, my suitcase was there waiting for me. I hung my suit in the locker and changed into a pair of slacks. Then I settled back in that big, comfortable seat and managed to get more work done —— in an hour—— in the privacy of my roomette than I am able to accomplish in my own office in half a day.

I couldn't have slept better.

We arrived at the St. Louis station 30 seconds early. When I left the train. I was fortified with a good breakfast, and unwrinkled suit, shined shoes and a serene disposition. The cab ride to my engagement was a matter of seconds. What all this adds up to is that a journey I usually consider an ordeal turned out to be a pleasurable event. I am looking forward to many more trips by Pullman.

④   Minolta: "Photography that brings people together"

We began inflating at dawn, preparing for our silent drift across a doll-like landscape, the most unforgettable of times.

Photography brings people together, and makes the world laugh, and think, and cry. No one knows this better than Minolta, for we've been mirroring the world, now, for over fifty years.

⑤   Berried Treasure

It's the shortcake you have been longing for. Ruby red strawberry in a light syrup over *fluffy* yellow cake. The crowning touch? A *pearly* puff of whipped topping.

And while you're treasuring every morsel, imagine this: German Chocolate Cake, richly wrapped in a *chunky* coconut walnut icing and strawberry cheesecake——smooth, *silky* sensational.

Sweet dreamers. *Weight Watchers* make desserts that'll make your day. And berried or not, you'll treasure them all.

Weight Watchers
Weight Watchers International Inc. 1986®

第五章　科技文体的翻译

第一节　科技英语的特点

科技英语(English for science and technology)是英语的各种文体中之一种。它是随着科学技术的产生、发展而出现、发展的,并且逐步地引起科学界和语言学界的关注和重视。现在全世界有许多国家设有科技英语研究中心,专门从事科技英语语言的研究。我们国家也分别在北京和上海设立了科技英语语言研究中心。国内外许多大学开设了科技英语这门课程,有的学校还专门设立科技英语专业或系科。科技英语大致可分为七类:(一)科技著述,科技论文和报告,实验报告和方案;(二)各类科技情报和文字资料;(三)科技实用手段,包括仪器、仪表、机械、工具等的结构描述和操作说明;(四)有关科技问题的会谈、会议、交谈的用语;(五)有关科技的影片、录相等有声资料的解说词;(六)科技发明、发现的报道;(七)科学幻想小说。

科技英语虽已发展成为一门独立的文体而为人们所研究,但在语言本质上,即构成语言的三大要素——语音、词汇和语法,与普通英语没有区别。在语音上,科技英语和普通英语共有一个语音系统;在词汇上,科技英语中有虽大量专业技术词汇和术语,但其基本词汇都是普通英语中固有的,一般的科技书刊中出现的绝大部分词汇都是普通词汇(通常称为半科技词汇)。即使在科技性极强的科技文章里,普通词汇的使用率也远远超过专业词汇。此外,许多专业词多来源于普通词,虽被赋予新义,但仍能看出与基本词义间相互的关系。例如 head 一词,其基本意义为"头",但在科技英语中根据不同的专业译为"磁头"、"水头"、"源头"、"机头"、"弹头"、"船头"、"压力头"等。凡此种种均未离开该词的基本意义。在语法上,科技英语虽然有明显的特点,如用被动句式、句子结构复杂冗长、多名词化结构等等,但都在英语语法规则的范围之内,并没有构成新的语法规则,只不过某些语法现象出现频率较高,从而形成科技英语的特色而已。

一、词汇特点

科技英语中大量使用科技词语。在这些词语中,有些是纯科技词,有些是通用科技词,或者称为半科技词,还有些词是表达抽象概念的词。在词形上,科技英语词汇多派生词和缩写词。这些都是科技英语的词汇特点。

1. **纯科技词**。指的是那些仅用于某个学科或某个专业的词汇或术语。不同的专业有不同的专业技术词汇或术语。由于科学的发展,新的学科和领域不断产生,新的发明和创造层出不穷,新的术语和词汇也就随之诞生了。每门学科和专业都有一系列含义精确且相对狭窄的语汇。如:hydroxide(氢氧化物)、anode(阳极)、annealing(退火)、isotope(同位素)等。如果不懂得某一特定领域内的一套专门词汇和术语,就无法阅读和翻译该领域的科技文献。

2. **通用科技词汇**。这类词汇系指不同专业都要经常使用的通用词汇,但在不同的专业中却有不同的含义,如 transmission 一词可译成:"发射、播送"(无线电工程学);"传动、变速"(机械学);"透射"(物理学);"遗传"(医学)。又如 operation 一词可译成"操作",通用于许多专业,但也有特定的词义,例如,在计算机科学中则指"运算",在医学中指"手术",而在军事方面则指"作战"。即便在同一专业中,同一个词又有多种概念。如 power 一词仅在机械力学这个专业里就有"力"、"电"、"电力"、"电源"、"动力"、"功率"等含义。这类专业意义多样化的词往往是基础科学中通用和常用的词汇,词义纷繁,用法灵活,搭配形式多样,使用范围广泛,翻译时需慎重。

　　3. 派生词。英语的构词法主要有合成、转化和派生三大手段。这三种手段在科技英语的词汇构成中都得到大量的运用,其中派生词,也就是加前、后缀构成的词出现的频率远远高于其他手段构成的词。例如,前缀 anti-(反,抗)构成的科技词有:anti-aircraft(高射兵器)、anti-auxin(抗生素)、anti-missile(反导弹)、anticatalyst(反催化剂)、anti-coherer(散屑器);前缀 micro-(微、微观)与 macro-(大、宏观)派生出来的词有:microbiology(微生物学)、microchemistry(微量化学)、microcircuitry(微型电路技术)、microelectronics(微电子学);macroclimax(大气候)、macrocosm(宏观世界)、macromolecule(大分子)、macrospore(大孢子)等。此外还有 hydro-(水,氢化的,氢的),hyper-(超出,过于,极度,过)hypo-(在……之下,低下,次,亚)等前缀,还有具有否定意义的前缀,如 dis-,mis-,un- 以及表示数量和数目的前缀 uni-,tri-,dec-等。由后缀构成的词也很繁杂。以-logy 结尾的词表示某种学科,如 biology(生物学),ecology(生态学),psychology(心理学),futurology(未来学),planetology(太阳系星体学),anthropology(人类学);-ics 结尾的词也表示某个学科,如:physics(物理学),electronics(电子学),cybernetics(控制论),phonetics(语音学),genetics(遗传学),economics(经济学)。还有些后缀表示行为、性质、状态等抽象概念,如-tion, -sion, -ance, -ence, -ity, -ment, -ure 等构成的词 insulation, expansion, maintenance, interference, activity, movement, fracture 等等。

　　4. 缩写词。科技英语中含有大量的缩写词,而且新的缩写词还在不断涌现。缩写词有其经济、简便的优点。但同时,由于同一个缩写形式可代表不同的词组,这也给阅读科技文章带来了困难。科技英语的缩写词有以下几个特点。第一,结构上,由词组中的首字母构成,如:ddda — decimal digtal differential analyzer(十进位数字微分方程解算器),HIT — Health Indication Test(健康检查);也有些缩写词由词组中的第一个字母或前两、三个字母组成,或由音节中的首字母组成,如 RADCM — radar countermeasure(反雷达措施);NAVWPNSCEN — naval weapons center(海军武器中心)。可见,缩写词的缩写形式不是单一的而是多样化的。第二,书写形式上,有时全用大写,有时全用小写,有时则大小写兼用。有时字母间用点".",分开,有时用连字符"-",有时则用斜线"/"。如 AB 这个缩写词有 ab,a/b,a&b,aB,AB,Ab,A-B,A·B,A/B,这八种不同的表达形式。第三,词义上,缩写词常存在同形异义的现象,以 LVP 为例,它分别代表 low-voltage protection(低压保护),left ventricular pressure(左心压),launch vehicle programs(运载火箭计划),而 MA 可代表 machine account,machine accountant,manufacturing assembly,map analysis,mechanical advantage,mental age,mill annealed,milliampere 等。通常,字形越短词义就越多,字形越长,异义便越少。还有很多的缩写词为外来语首字母的缩写,如 aB 为德语 auf Bestelling 意为 on order(已订购但尚未交货的),A/B 为瑞典语 Aktiebolag 一词,意为 limited company(有限责任公司)。

二、句法特点

1. **被动结构**的大量使用。这是科技英语中最为显著的特征。据国外的语言学家统计,科技英语中有 1/3 以上的动词为被动形式。从下面的两例可见被动结构的使用特点:

① The coolant is *circulated* through the annular spaces between the fuel elements and the moderator, absorbing heat as it passes, and the heat so absorbed *is conveyed* out of the core to the heat exchanger. Very large quantities of heat *are generated* by fission, and in order that these *may be* rapidly *dissipated*, a large volume of coolant *is required*. It *is* therefore frequently *pressurized*, especially where a gaseous coolant *is used*, to increase its density. A number of different coolants *have been employed*, including water, carbon dioxide and liquid metals. 冷却剂在释热元件和缓和剂之间作环形循环,循环时吸收热量,并把吸收过来的热量从反应器中心向热交换器传递。裂变产生大量的热量。为使这些热量快速消散,需要大量的冷却剂。因此,要不停地加压(尤其使用气体冷却剂时),以便增加其密度。现已使用的冷却剂有若干种,其中包括水、二氧化碳和液态金属等。

② As oil *is found* deep in the ground, its presence *cannot be determined* by a study of the surface. Consequently, a geological survey of the underground rock structure *must be carried out*. If it *is thought* that the rocks in a certain area contain oil, a "drilling rig" *is assembled*. The most obvious part of a drilling rig *is called* "a derrick". It *is used* to lift sections of pipe, which *are lowered* into the hole made by the drill. As the hole *is being drilled*, a steel pipe *is pushed* down to prevent the sides from falling in. If oil *is struck* a cover *is* firmly *fixed* to the top of the pipe and the oil *is allowed* to escape through a series of valves. 石油埋藏于地层深处。因此,仅仅靠研究地层表面,无法确定有无石油,必须对地下的岩石结构进行地质勘测。如果确定了某一区域的岩石蕴藏着石油,就在此安装钻机。钻机最明显的部分是机架,用以提举一节一节的钢管。这些钢管被压入井孔。一边钻井,一边下钢管,以防周围土层塌陷。一旦出油,就紧固管盖,让油从各个阀门喷出。

在上面两篇短文的11个句子里,出现了23个谓语动词,其中有21个动词为被动形式。这足以说明被动结构在科技英语中的广泛使用。

2. **大量使用非谓语动词形式**。科技英语中大量使用分词、动名词和动词不定式,现举两例:

① Today the electronic computer is widely used in *solving* mathematical problems *having* to do with weather forcasting and *putting* satellites into orbit. 今天,电子计算机广泛地运用于解决一些数学问题,这些问题与天气预报和把卫星送入轨道有关。

这是一个简单句,含有三个动名词短语和一个现在分词短语。

② Numerical control machines are most useful when quantities of products *to be produced* are low or medium; the tape *containing* the information *required* to *produce* the parts can be stored, reused or modified when *required*. 少量地或中量地生产产品时,数控机是极为有用的,录有生产零件必须资料的磁带可以存放起来,需要时,还可重新使用或修改。

在科技英语中,上述例句俯拾皆是。这些非谓语动词形式之所以如此普遍地使用,是因为它们能正确和严密地反映句子各成分的内在联系。

3. **名词化倾向**。它指的是广泛使用名词词组(表动作意义的名词+of+名词+修饰语),这种词组往往起到从句的作用,通常被称为名词化结构。例如:

① *The testing of machines by this method* entails some loss of power. 用这种方法测试机器会浪费一些能量。

② *The substitution of some rolling friction for sliding friction* results in a very considerable reduction in friction. 用滚动摩擦代替滑动摩擦,会大幅度减少摩擦力。

③ The ultrosonic metal inspection is *the application of ul-*

trasonic vibrations to materials* with elastic properties and the observation of the resulting action of the vibration in the materials. 金属超声波探伤就是把超声振动施于弹性金属材料之上,并观察振动在材料中产生的作用。

这种名词化结构,文字明了,句型简洁,结构紧凑,表意客观,信息量大,在很多情况下可以省去过多的主谓结构,所以科技文章中常使用这种结构。

此外,科技英语中还存在"名词连用"的情况,即中心名词之前有一个以上其他名词,它们皆为中心名词的前置修饰语。以简化句子结构,便于理解。例如:

① illumination intensity determination 照明强度测定

② breast cancer survey program evaluation 乳腺癌普查计划实施总结

③ interferon spray concentration processing 干扰素喷药浓缩剂加工法

④ computer programming teaching device manual 计算机程序编制教学装置

⑤ 3-feet glass manhole door 三英尺玻璃孔门。

4. 普遍使用形容词短语作**后置定语**。这是语法结构的需要,起到定语从句的作用,可视为定语从句的省略形式,目的是为了简化句子结构和对被修饰词严格限定和说明。例如:

① Non-mobile robots, *capable of learning to perform an industrial task and then of being left to perform it tirelessly*, are even now in use in industrial plants all over the world. 能学会做工,并能孜孜不倦地工作,但不能行走的机器人,今天在世界各地的工厂里都得到了应用。

② Consequently, the suggested procedures must be viewed

only as the best *presently available* in the opinion of the specialists who worked on this chapter. 因此,根据编写本章的专家们的意见,建议的程序必须仅被看作目前所能获得的最好程序。

③ For units *smaller than a meter* the decimal system is applied so that the meter is devided into decimeters(dm), centimeters(cm),millimeters(mm),etc., which makes measuring really simple. Moreover, 1000 meters makes one kilometers (km), the unit *available for measuring long distances*. 对于小于米的单位,十进制是这样应用的:米被分成分米(dm)、厘米(cm)、毫米(mm)等等,使测量变得非常简单。此外,1000米合成1公里(km),作为用来测量长距离的单位。

5. 常用结构复杂的**长句**。长而复杂的句子结构是科技英语句法的又一典型特征。有些句子达数行,数十行,包含几十个甚至上百个单词,长长的一段仅有一个句子。这种现象在标准、规范和专利说明书中尤其多见。翻译时必须弄清句子的结构,按照汉语习惯,分割成若干句子,以便清晰地表达原意。例如:

① The materials of producing a transparent copolymer plastic of the BSBS type, as herein before defined, are butadiene and styrene, which copolymer contains substantially 60 to 90 weight per cent total block styrene and 40 to 10 weight per cent block butadiene-styrene, which method comprises the two-step process of first polymerizing in the ratio of 0.077 to 0.57 moles of butadiene per mole of styrene in benzene or cyclohexane solvent in the absence of polar additives to produce a solution with a total polymer content of 6 to 15 per cent and using an initiator the whole of the initiator being added in the first step, 0.02 to 0.1 weight per cent based on the total weight of monomers to be polymerized of an alkyllithium in which the alkyl contains 4 to 8 carbon atoms, at a temperature of 50 to 120℃, and when this first step of the polymerization is substantially completed, in the second step, adding additional monomers in the ratio of 0.12 to 1.48 moles of butadiene per mole of the styrene, the amounts of butadiene added in the second step being greater than that added in the first step and the amounts of styrene added in each step being substantially constant and continuing the polymerization at a temperature of 50 to 120℃, until the reaction is substantially completed. 如前所述,生产 BSBS 型透明共聚物塑料是以丁二烯和苯乙烯为原料的。这类共聚物主要含有 60—90%的苯乙烯和 40—10%的丁二烯——苯乙烯。其生产方法分为两点。第一点是聚合。聚合比例为每个摩尔的苯乙烯含 0.077—0.57 个摩尔的丁二烯 1。苯或环乙烷这种熔剂不用极性添加剂,而用引发剂,就能制取含有 6~15%的聚合物溶液。在这一步,引发剂的用量为 0.02~0.1%。引发剂用量的多少取决于由烷基锂聚合成的单体的重量。烷基锂在 50~120℃时含 4—8 个碳原子。第一步的生产过程以后,就开始第二步。第二步是添加单体,比例为每个摩尔的苯乙烯加入 0.12—1.48 个摩尔的丁二烯单体。丁二烯的添加量,第二步比第一步大。苯乙烯的添加量,两步基本相等。在 50—120℃时,丁二烯和苯乙烯继续聚合,直至整个反应完成为止。

② A further inference was drawn by Pascal, who reasoned that if this "sea of air" existed, its pressure at the bottom (i.e. sea level) would be greater than its pressure further up, and that therefore the height of mercury column would decrease in proportion to the height above sea-level. 帕斯卡作了进一步推论,他说,如果这种"空气海洋"存在的话,其底部(即海平面)的压力就会比其高处的压力大。因此,水银柱的高度降低量与海拔高度成正比。

6. 有限时态种类。在科技英语中陈述句居多,很少用感叹句、疑问句时态多采用一般现在时,只在叙述过去的实验和发现时使用一般过去时,间或也使用现在完成时以表示与现在有直接联系。

第一,一般现在时用来叙述真理,原理和定律以及一般结论。

① Electronics is the basis of all tele-communication systems. 电子学是所有电信系统的基础。

② The fourth column of table 5 represents the dry weight of tops. 表5第四栏表示菜叶的干重。

③ Tin has resistance to corrosion by air or water. 锡具有防空气和水的耐腐蚀性。

④ The earth is one of the nine planets. They all go round the sun the same way. Each of them also turns on its own axis. The earth makes a complete journey round the sun in one year. It turns once on its axis in 24 hours. The sun rises and sets because the earth is turning.

There are two planets nearer the sun: Mercury and Venus. Mercury is small and it is very near the sun. It turns on its axis 3 times for every 2 times it goes round the sun. Its year is $1\frac{1}{2}$ days long. Mercury is too hot and too small and has no air, so nobody can live on it.

地球是九大行星之一。所有的行星都以同样的方式绕着太阳运行,同时,每颗行星又绕着各自的轴自转。地球绕太阳运行一周需时一年,自转一周需要二十四小时。因为地球总是在转动,所以有日出和日落。

有两颗行星比地球更靠近太阳:水星和金星。水星是颗小行星,离太阳又很近。它每绕太阳公转两周,本身就自转三周,所以水星的一年就是它的一天半。水星温度太高,体积太小,又没有空气,所以没有人能在水星上生活。

第二,一般过去时用来介绍过去的工作,如实验、发明创造等。
The Wrights flying machine, made of pieces of wood and clothes, looked too fragile to fly. But at 10:35 o'clock in the morning, the brothers began their final tests. The machine's first two attempts at a takeoff ended in failure. But finally came success. 莱特兄弟的飞行器由木块和布料制成,外观单薄,似乎不能飞行。但在上午10时35分,两兄弟开始了最后的试验。前两次起飞均告失败,最后一次却成功了。

第三,一般将来时用来叙述计划要做的工作,预期获得的结果和规律性的倾向。

① Liquids will expand and contract like gasses. 液体像气体一样膨胀和收缩。

② A gas under compressing will become hotter. 受压缩的气体的温度将会升高。

③ The presence of an open mine will have a significant effect on underground water surrounding the mine. 露天矿的存在对矿山周围的地下水将产生重要的影响。

7. 条件句较多。科技英语中,在说明事理、提出设想、探讨问题或推导公式时,常常涉及到各种前提、条件和场合。因而,条件句使用较多,包括真实条件句和虚拟条件句两种。前者为可以实现的条件,而后者为不能实现的条件。为避免武断,科技英语往往从假定、猜测、建议和怀疑的角度出发,因而需要使用虚拟语气,同时也可使口吻显得委婉和谨慎一些。

① If electron moves, it produces a magnetic field. 如果电子运动的话,它就会产生磁场。

② If air is passed through a drying agent the moisture will be removed. 如果让空气通过干燥剂,其水分就会失去。

③ If the lead and the return from the main supply touched each other at any place, the whole potential difference of the supply would send a very great current through the wires. 如果主电源上的导线和回线在任何一个地方相接触，那么整个电源的电位差将通过线路送出非常强大的电流。

④ If there had not been any air in the cooling system, the effect of cooling would not have been affected and the temperature could not have been kept so low. 如果冷却系统中没有空气存在，冷却效果就不会受到影响，温度也不可能保持这样低。

⑤ If the cover should have a crack in it, the harmful gas would come out and cause pollution. 要是盖子上有裂缝，有害气体就会泄漏而造成污染。

8. **祈使语气**使用也较多。常见于说明书、操作规程、作业指导、程序建议和注意事项等资料中。有时也用"should"和"must"来表示这种语气。

① Allow the water to cool for ten minutes and then take the temperature. 让水冷却10分钟，然后再测温度。

② Grip handles as far as possible from blades. 紧握手柄，尽量离刀口远些。

③ The machines should be handled with great care. 这些机器应小心轻放。

④ The results of the experiment should be plotted on a graph. 实验结果应在图上标出。

⑤ The surface must be cleaned. 表面必须清扫干净。

⑥ Flux must be applied. 必须涂上助熔剂。

9. 常用**省略**、**倒装**、**割裂**等句式。科技文章中残缺不全、语序颠倒、成分割裂的句子随处可见。这不仅是句法上的需要，同时也是一种修辞手段。

第一，省略。省略是指句子成分被省略，以避免重复，使语言更为精练。下列句子中括号里的词皆被省略：

① Oxygen has an ionic valence of -2, and chlorine (has an ionic valence) of -1. 氧的化合价为－2，而氯的化合价为－1。

② Since (it is) composed of several different pure substances, air is a mixture. 空气由几种不同的纯物质组成，故是一种混合物。

③ The earth attracts the moon and the moon (attracts) the earth. 地球对月球有引力，而月球也对地球有引力。

此外，有许多固定的省略句型，如：

As compared above	如前所述
As indicated in Fig. X	如图所示
As noted later	如后所述；从下文可看出
As previously mentioned	前已提及
As shown in Table X	如表 X 所示
If necessary	必要时；如有必要
If possible	如果可能
If any (anything)	如果有的话；即使需要
If required	需要时；如果需要
When needed	需要时；如果需要
When in use	在使用时；当工作时

第二，倒装句。倒装是指句子成分排列不同于正常的顺序，以达到强调句首部分的目的，可分为完全倒装和部分倒装两种。

① Important physical properties for distinguishing one gas from another are color, odor, density, and solubility. 颜色、气味、密度和溶解度是一种气体区别于其他气体的重要物理特征。

② The form of matter made up of two or more materials not chemically combined we call mixture. 由两种或两种以上的物质组成,而非化合而成的物质形式,称为混合物。

③ A thermometer put in the water can tell us the temperature of the water, but in no way does it show the amount of heat the water contains. 放在水中的温度计能测出水温,但是它无法表明水中含有的热量。

第三,割裂。这是一种特殊的表达形式,常常伴随着长句出现。由于长句多是科技英语的特色之一,因此,科技英语中的割裂现象也较多。起割裂和隔离作用的主要有:①介词短语、分词短语、不定式短语等;②各种从句;③句中的附加成分,如插入成分、同位语和独立成分。

① A body consisting of molecules that contain atoms of different chemical properties is called a compound. 物质若其组成分子含有不同化学性质的原子,则称为化合物。(主谓为分词短语所分割)

② Experiments show that there is a definite relationship between the electrical pressure that makes a current flow, the rate at which the electricity flows and the resistance of the object or objects through which the current passes. 实验表明,使电流流动的电压,电流流动的速率与电流所通过的物质的电阻这三者之间确有一定的相互关系。(pressure, rate 和 resistance 三词为各自后面的从句所割裂)

③ Many forms of motion are highly complex, but they may in all cases be considered as being made up of translations and rotations. 很多运动的形式是非常复杂的,但在所有情况下,都可认为是由平移和转动构成的。(复合谓语为介词短语 in all cases 所分割)

三、科技术语的翻译

随着新科学、新技术、新材料、新设备、新工艺的不断出现,科技新词也大量涌现,层出不穷。对于这些科技术语可采取意译、音译、混译、形译和像译等方法。

1. 意译,即根据原文的含义译为相应的汉语。这是最基本的方法。如:

cybernetics	控制论
microelectronics	微电子学
guided missile	导弹
flowsheet	流程图
holography	全息摄影(术)

2. 音译,即按英语的发音译成相应的汉语。科技英语中很多词汇,如计量单位、材料名称等,是以发明者的名字来命名的。在这种情况下,音译是唯一可行的办法。

volt	伏(特)
ampere	安(培)
joule	焦耳
herts	赫(兹)
radar	雷达
copy	拷贝
aspirin	阿司匹灵
engine	引擎(发动机)
vitamin	维他命(维生素)
penicillin	盘尼西林(青霉素)
laser	镭射(激光)

3. 音意混译，即某些术语的一部分音译，另一部分则意译。

  kilowatt   千瓦
  decibel   分贝
  Magnus moment 马格努斯力矩
  Einstain equation 爱因斯坦方程

4. 形译，即译成汉语时使用原词形。如：

  J-particle   J-粒子
  X-ray   X 射线
  Q-meter   Q 表
  G-line   G 线

5. 像译，即将科技术语中代表某一几何图形的原文字母用在汉语中，以体现其形状。如：

  O-ring   O 形环
  C-clamp   C 形夹钳
  S-turning   S 形弯道
  T-bolt   T 形螺栓

6. 符号和公式在译文中均保持不变。如：

$$Q = kiA = C_1 \frac{HA}{L}$$

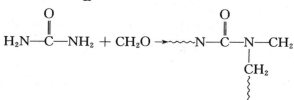

第二节 科技报道

科技报道通常由标题和正文两部分组成。标题与正文各有其语言特点在翻译时应区别对待。

第一,标题。读者阅读报刊杂志往往总是快速浏览新闻的标题,新闻标题必须具备简明、新奇的特征。文字简短,往往在一行左右,常省略冠词,甚至谓语动词。在有限的空间里让读者了解报道的内容梗概。例如:

① Airlines studies Jet Fuel Contamination. 航空公司正研究喷气燃料受污染问题。

② Underground Test in U.S. 美国进行了一次地下核试验。

③ French optimistic about adoption of digital T. V. standard. 法国对采用数字式电视标准表示乐观。

以上标题均简明扼要地点出了报道的内容。译成汉语时也要简短精练,同时又要清楚明确。如例 1 中,若将 contamination 译成"污染"会造成误解,译成"受污染",则意义清楚明了。例 2 中原标题是一个名词短语,省略了不定冠词"an"。译成"美国的地下核试验"会给读者一个笼统的印象。其实,这是指的最近的一次核试验。译成"美国进行了一次地下核试验"虽增添了字数,却给人以鲜明的印象。例 3 中并无谓语动词,将形容词短语 optimistic about 改译成汉语的动词短语"对……表示乐观"则更加符合汉语的习惯。

第二,正文。紧跟在标题下面的便是科技报道的正文。其要点和结论一般都在第一段集中反映出来,将人物、事物、时间、场所、原因、方法、结果均交待清楚。详情则在下面进一步分段说明。科技报道的文体特征是简短,用词造句比较通俗易懂,具体准确,且有吸引力,较口语化,表达较为自由。翻译科技报道时,在语言风格上应符合原文的特点。

科技报道大致分成一般性的科技报道和专业性较强的科技报道两类,包括科技简讯、科技评论、会议消息、人物介绍、新产品专栏、书评等。

一、一般性的科技报道

此类报道虽涉及科技方面的内容,甚至只限于某一专业,但仍属一般性报道。其对象为一般读者,对专业性知识涉及不深。所用的词汇大都属一般性词汇,即使用到专业性词汇,也都为该专业中的基础性词汇。体裁风格与报章杂志上的一般新闻报道相似。主要特点为简练明确,通俗易懂。翻译此类报道对翻译者的专业知识水平要求不高,但必须清楚地了解不同专业所使用的术语。

①   Underground Test in U. S.

NEW YORK, Thurs. , APP—A nuclear device as powerful as 90,000 tons of TNT was detonated a mile beneath the Colorado Rockies today in an experiment aimed at loosening vast stores of natural gas.

The explosion of the device's three 30-kiloton atomic mechanism went smoothly.

It was the largest nuclear blast so far in the Atomic Energy Commission project to stimulate massive stores of natural gas locked in rock formations.

The AEC said only background levels of radiation normally found in the environment was recorded at a monitoring station at the blast site.

The blast shock the ground at an observation area 11 miles from the site and street light go miles away in Montrose, Colorado.

Residents of Rifle, about 30 miles from the site of the detonation, said they felt nothing.

The AEC had predicted that the buildings in the town would shake.

The National Earthquake Centre 180 miles away at Boulder recorded the blast 40 seconds after it was set off.

Center spokesman Jim Lander said seismographs recorded the jolt at 5.3 on the Richter Scale, which has no top limit.

Mr. Lander said the tremor would be classed as a "locally severe earthquake which would cause damage."

美国的一次地下核试验

[美联社纽约星期四电]今天,在科罗拉多落基山区地下一英里处,爆炸了一个能量为九万吨的三硝基甲苯炸药的核装置。这是一次以释放储量丰富的天然气为目的的实验。

该装置三个三万吨级原子结构的爆炸进行顺利。

到目前为止,这是原子能委员会开发蕴藏在岩层中大量天然气工程的一次最大的核爆炸。

原子能委员会说,爆炸现场监测站记录到的只是当地环境所常有的基本辐射强度。

这次爆炸震动了离现场11英里处观察区的地面和90英里外科罗拉多州蒙特罗斯城街灯。

距爆炸现场大约30英里的莱福镇居民说,他们毫无感觉。

原子能委员会曾预计该镇的建筑物会发生震动。

180英里外的布尔德国家地震中心四十秒后记录到这次爆炸。

该中心发言人金·兰德说,地震仪记录的震动强度为里氏5.3级,这种震动没有强度极限。

兰德先生说,可把该震动列为"有破坏性的局部严重地震"的类别。

这是美联社的一篇通讯报道,主题是美国为开发天然气进行的一次地下核试验,虽涉及核爆炸和产生的地震这些科学范畴,但只是一般性的客观报道,并不包含深奥的专业理论。所使用的词汇大都为一般性常用词汇,少量的科技词汇也属于基础性的。每一自然段表达一个中心思想,特点为仅一句话,但句子不长,结构简单,让人一目了然。译文保持了原文的风格与格式。每段仍为一句话,意思明确、结构完整。所使用的汉语词汇亦皆为一段性或科技基础性词汇。全文通俗易懂,明白晓畅。

② Fiber Optics Shows Mettle in
Watery Application for Navy

Fiber optics continues to be the transmission line of choice for harsh environments. The latest example: ITT's electro-Optical Products in Roanoke, Va., has installed a six channel 4-km cable underground in what it refers to as a "generally water-filled duct." Though such immersion might be sudden death for a convetional electrical cable, the fiber, made of electric material, is not bothered. More than 10 Mb/s can be handled by the installation at the Navy airstation in Norfolk, Va.

光导纤维在海军
多水环境中应用出色

光导纤维仍然是用于恶劣环境下的优等传输线。最新例证为:弗吉尼亚州罗恩诺克布的 ITT 公司下属的电子光学产品分公司敷设了一条四公里长的六信道光缆,埋在地下一个被称为"经常浸满水的管道中"。普通电缆这样浸泡在水中就会立即损坏。然而,由电力材料制成的光缆则不会出现此问题。弗吉尼亚州诺福克海军航空站的光缆装置传输能力可大于 10Mb/s。

这是一篇光导纤维不受水的浸蚀、性能优越的简短报道。光导纤维属专业性较强的新型通讯材料。但报道并未涉及其专业理论和知识,只是与普通电缆作了对比来突出其优良的质量,使一般读者都能了解,以便推广应用。但由于与通讯技术有关,文中仍有不少科技词汇,如 fiber optics(光导纤维), transmission line(传输线),six channel(六信道),electrical cable(电缆),electric material(电力材料)等。语言风格也较正式,使用了 choice, harsh environments, installed, immersion 等这些正式文体中才出现的词汇。读起来使人感到其专业性较上一篇报道要强一些,但仍在读者的理解能力之内,依然属于一般性科技报道。译文注意体现了正式文体这一风格。除了按专业要求准确译出科技词汇外,也用正式文体的汉语词汇分别将上面所列举的词汇译为:"优等"、"恶劣环境"、"敷设"、"浸泡"等。

③   Theory of Heat Treatment of Metals

Aptly titled, this text concentrates on the physical metallurgy of heat treatment, whereas most physically metallurgy texts are not directed specifically at heat treatment phenomena, even in part, this complete text is devoted solely to the topic. The industrialist will be disappointed that many aspects of heat treatment, such as atmosphere production and control, and properties of quenchants, are missing. Indeed, gas carburizing is dismissed in less than 2 pages, but principles of annealing, hardening and tempering, and age-hardening are adequately covered. In view of the low price, this text may well be worth acquiring by those closely concerned with industrial heat treatment practice who lack an adequate physical metallurgy textbook. The omissions and, to a lesser extent, the obvious problems involved in translating from Russian should be borne in mind.

金属热处理理论

这本教科书书名贴切,集中介绍了热处理物理冶金学。大多数物理冶金学教材未专门阐述热处理现象，甚至连部分阐述也没有，而这本完整的教科书却专门论述了这一课题。企业家们会感到失望的是，热处理的许多方面，例如气氛的产生和控制，以及淬火剂的性能等，均未列入。气体渗碳也的确仅占两页不到的篇幅，但是，对退火、淬火和回火以及时效硬化等方面的原理都作了充分的讨论。由于本书价格低廉，很值得那些与工业热处理技术密切相关而又缺少合适的物理冶金学教科书的人员购买。缺漏的内容以及次要一些的俄文翻译过程中出现的明显问题，敬请见谅。

　　这是一则简短的科技教科书的书评。书评虽短，内容却很充实，具有实事求是的科学性。译文对原文中出现的有关冶金学方面的词汇，按专业要求准确地译成汉语术语，如：将 physically metallurgy of heat treatment 译成"热处理物理冶金学"，将 Atmosphere 译成"气氛"，这是冶金学中使用的专门术语。将 annealing, hardening and tempering and age-hardening. 译成"退火"、"淬火和回火"、"时效硬化"，这些都是汉语中标准的冶金专业词汇。

二、专业性较强的科技报道

　　此类报道的最大特点为专业性较强，某些一般性词汇甚至已转意而具有特殊的内涵。此类报道往往刊登在带有学术性的专门刊物上，文体较正式，没有一定专门知识的读者难以读懂。其读者群为专业从事这一专业研究的人员。翻译这类报道要求译者具有较深的专业知识基础，才能将原文准确地用汉语表达出来。在翻译过程中应特别注意专业词汇的翻译，切不可望文生义，此外，译文的文体也应正规稳重。现举两例：

① 　　　　Modicon Upgrades Programming Panel

　　Gould Inc.'s Modicon division in Andover, Mass., has upgraded its P180 programming panel to offer an optional ladder-listing feature and to make it compatible with many RS-232-C or current-loop display terminals and printers. The option in the Deluxe P180 provides hand-copy listings of relay ladder programs resident in any Modicon 484 industrial process controller. The Deluxe version is priced at $ 1,895; the basic P180 can be updated in the field to offer the Deluxe's features.

莫迪康公司提高
编程板的性能

古尔德公司设在马萨诸塞州安道弗市的莫迪康公司改进了P180编程板的性能,使其具有可选阶梯式列表特性,并能与多种RS-232-C型或与四路式显示终端及打印机兼容。Deluxe 180这种可选功能可提供Modicon 484工业程控机中所固有的转发梯式程序硬拷贝列表。Deluxe型的单价为$1,895,P180原型可当场加以改进,使其具有Deluxe型的性能。

这是一篇有关提高编程板性能的报道,牵涉到计算机的专业知识和技术。文中所用的科技词汇皆为计算机专业的术语。译文用了汉语中与其对应的专业术语,使从事计算机专业的人员一目了然。一些产品型号如果在汉语中尚无固定译法,可直接引用原文,以免因不熟悉而引起误解。

② Colour Maps of Vision in the Brain

Cells in the visual cortex—the surface layers at the back of the brain—have two important jobs to do. They have to analyse the depth of objects in the visual world, and they have to detect discontinuities between one object and another. The same cells are involved in both processes—but how are the two overlapping systems organized? Using a new technique, Gary Blasdel and Guy Salama of the University of Pittsburgh in the US have produced pictures of the visual cortex of macaque monkeys that demonstrate the two systems in action.

The method they used was to expose a portion of the monkey's cortex and flood it with a voltage-sensitive dye. The amount of dye taken up into a cell depends directly on that cell's activity; the more impulses the cell fires, the more strongly it will be marked by the dye. They then filmed the pattern of the dye in the cortex as the monkey watched stripes of different orientations presented to either eye.

Blasdel and Salama found that it was difficult to see any pattern at all using the image of the cortex actually seen by the camera. But by subtracting one image from another to cancel out non-specific staining, they produced clear pictures illustrating the phenomena known as "ocular dominance" and "orientation selectivity", which are thought to underlie perception of depth and edge detection respectively.

Subtracting the image of the activity produced by one eye from that produced by the other gave stripes of light and dark areas, each about half a millimetre wide. These correspond exactly to the "ocular dominance bands" already described by the Nobel prizewinners David Hubel and Torsten Wiesel. Although they each receive inputs from both eyes, cells in one band respond best to the right eye, those in the next band to the left and so on.

Hubel and Wiesel had also described how cells in the cortex were organized into columns, each column responding best to lines at a certain orientation, while the column next door preferred a slightly different orientation. But the techniques they used did not allow them to study ocular dominance and orientation selectivity in the same area at the same time. They also had little evidence to show how the columns were grouped in order to provide the necessary analysis throughout the visual field. One suggestion was that the orientation columns were organised into slabs, perhaps at right angles to the ocular dominance bands, each slab covering all possible orientations for a different part of the visual field.

Blasdel and Salama's results suggest a variation on this theme. When they tested the cortex for its response to a horizontal line, for example, they found that the dye was distributed in small patches throughout the area they studied. Using a computer to combine the responses to six different orientations and colour-coding them, they found that patches representing related orientations were ususlly grouped together. But there was no overall "rainbow" appearance as there would be if orientation columns were in continuous slabs. Instead, the areas of gradual change were occasionally interrupted by sudden shifts in orientation preference of more than 45 degrees. These "fractures" appear to break up the cortical surface into a number of small, irregularly shaped modules. Superimposing the pattern of fractures on the ocular dominance bands in the same area showed that they seemed to run down the centres of the bands, or across them. This appears to ensure that each module will receive input from both eyes.

It would make a beautifully tidy story if each of these modules represented an area of visual space. At the moment that seems unlikely; the modules are not large enough to accommodate cells responding to all possible orientations. But it could be the case that they are submodules of larger compartments.

Whatever the outcome, this study has introduced a new technique for visualising the neuroscientist's toolbox.

大脑内的彩色视觉图象

脑后部的表层,即脑视觉皮层中的细胞承担两项重要任务:要分辨视觉世界所现万物的景深,又要分辨物与物之间的界限。同一种视觉细胞要起两种作用,这两种重叠的机制如何彼此协调呢?美国匹兹堡大学的加里·布莱斯德尔和盖伊·萨拉姆使用一种新技术摄制了猕猴视觉皮层的照片,展现了这两种机制的运作情形。

他们采用的方法是把猕猴的一部分视觉皮层暴露出来,并染上一种对电压敏感的颜色。每个视觉皮层细胞吸收的染色量直接取决于这个细胞的活动程度,细胞激起的行动愈强,细胞染色愈浓。猕猴用两只眼分别观看到方向各异的条纹,他们就在此时拍摄下这只猕猴的视觉皮层呈现出的染色图案。

布莱斯德尔和萨拉姆发现,在使用照相机实际拍摄的视觉皮质的图像上,很难看出任何图案。但他们通过从一个照片上的图像中消去另一图像,以删去非特别染上的颜色,这样一来,便获得了一些十分清晰的照片,说明了被称之为"视觉显性"和"定向选择性"的现象。人们认为这两种现象分别是感知景深和察觉物体边缘的基础。

在从一只眼获得的活动图像上消去从另一只眼获得的活动图像后,便得到明暗相间的条纹。每条条纹宽约半毫米。这些条纹与诺贝尔奖获得者戴维·休伯尔和托斯顿·威斯尔曾经描绘过的"视觉显性条纹"恰好完全相符。虽然每一个细胞所接受的输入信号都来自双眼,但某一条纹上的细胞与右眼最相呼应;而相邻条纹上的细胞却与左眼最相呼应,如此等等。

休伯尔和威尔斯还描述了视觉皮层中的细胞是如何排成纵列的,每一列对某一特定方向的物体线条反应最强,而相邻纵列的方向却略有不同。但是,他们使用的技术却不能让他们在同一区域内同时观察研究视觉显性和定向选择性。他们也没有证据可以表明这些纵列是如何组成，以便在整个视野内提供必要的分析。有一种看法认为，这些有方向性的纵列组成片状，可能与视觉显性条纹垂直，每一片覆盖某一部分视野内的各个方向。

布莱斯德尔和萨拉姆对这个问题的研究得出了不同的结果。例如，当他们实验视觉皮层对水平线条的反应时，发现染色呈斑点状遍布在他们研究的区域内。他们应用计算机综合了视觉皮层对6个不同方向的反应情况，并作上彩色标记。他们发现，代表相关方向的斑点常聚在一起。人们曾认为，如果方向纵列呈连续的片状，就会出现总的"彩虹"，但结果并非如此。相反，那些逐渐变化的区域在方向的选择上有时会被45°以上的骤变所隔断。这些"裂痕"似乎把视觉皮层的表面分割成了许多形状不规则的小块。将这些裂痕的图案置于同一区域的视觉显性条纹之上即可看出它们似乎占据条纹的中部或穿越条纹。这一点看来可以令人们首肯，每一小块都会从双眼接受输入信号。

如果这些小块中的每一块都代表视野范围内的一个区域，那将是多么美好的事呀！目前，似乎还不能得出这样的结论。这些小块还不够大，无法容纳下对一切方向都能反应的所有细胞。但也许情况是这样：这些小块只是更大一些块片内的次一级的小块。无论结果如何，这项研究已提供了一种新技术，将大脑的运作显现出来。很明显，它将为神经学家增添一种颇有价值的科研手段。

这是一篇专业性较强的科技报道。其读者多为该专业的研究者或技术人员。报道的内容详细、具体，具有理论性。文章结构严谨，逻辑性强。长句多，有的句子结构较复杂。文中充满专业词汇，有的术语也许只有专业人员才能明白。本篇译文注意做到了这一点，在文体上也体现了原文的科学性、逻辑性和正规性的风格。

附：练习

将下列文章译成中文。

① The Ozone Problem

Thirty-one countries have taken a first step toward an international agreement to protect the earth's atmosphere. They have proposed some limits on the production and use of chemicals that destroy ozone. Dr. Mustapha Tolba of Egypt is Director of the United Nations Environment Program. His group organized a recent meeting in Geneva, Switzerland on the ozone problem. He said a final agreement to protect the atmosphere could be signed by September.

The proposed agreement calls for limiting production of chemicals called chloro-fluorocarbons. These chemicals are commonly called CFCs. Countries signing the agreement would not produce any more CFCs than they produced in 1986. The restriction would take effect beginning in 1990. A 20% cut in production and use of CFCs would take place a few years later. Dr. Tolba said the delegates at the Geneva meeting agreed that the world is facing a serious problem with the loss of protective ozone. But, he said, they also agreed that industry needs time to make changes.

Ozone is a kind of oxygen found mainly in the upper atmosphere. It blocks much of the sun's ultraviolet light from reaching earth. Large amount of ultraviolet light can damage crops and cause skin cancer. So we need ozone to protect against these dangers.

Scientists say CFCs and other chemicals used in many industrial products destroy ozone. In the late 1970s. Canada, Finland, Norway, Sweden, and the United States banned the use of CFCs in aerosol containers. But CFCs continue to be used in other countries and in other products. An American State Department official said the proposed international agreement on ozone is very important. He said it shows there can be international cooperation in dealing with a threat to the environment before it happens.

②   The Greenhouse Effect

An environmental group, the World Resources Institute, recently released a report that deals in part with the same issue discussed in Geneva. The report warns about the effects of changes in the atmosphere. It says the world must act immediately to halt these changes, or temperatures on earth will rise to dangerous levels. A scientist for the World Resources Institute, Irving Mintzer, used a computer to study the changes in the atmosphere called the greenhouse effect.

A greenhouse is a glass building that traps heat so plants can be grown inside even in cold weather. CFCs, carbon dioxide, and other gases in the atmosphere act like a greenhouse. They permit heat from the sun to reach earth, but they trap the heat and prevent it from escaping back into space.

Mr. Mintzer's study showed that average temperatures might rise more than 4 degrees Celsius if present industrial policies are not changed. That increase in temperature, he says, could come within 45 years. The higher temperatures could melt ice at the North Pole and South Pole. Average sea levels could rise as much as one meter, causing severe floods along coastal areas.

The problem is not expected to be so bad, Mr. Mintzer says, if governments approve strong measures to limit the greenhouse effect. Those measures include reducing the use of CFCs, producing less carbon dioxide by burning less oil and gas, and replanting rain forests that will help remove carbon dioxide from the atmosphere.

③　　　　　　The Treatment of Waste Water

An American researcher has successfully tested a way to clean waste water without chemicals. The technique uses green plants. Researcher William Jewell is an agricultural engineer at Cornell University in New York State. He calls his cleaning method the nutrient film technique. He says it is very simple. It is based on fact that waste water is an excellent plant food.

The United States Enviromental Protection Agency is supporting Professor Jewell's experiments. The tests were carried out at an existing waste water treatment center in the northeastern state of New Hampshire. The scientists put plants in narrow containers inside a glass building. One end of each container was a little higher than the other end. Waste water was directed down the containers through the plants' thick roots. As expected, the roots trapped the wastes in the water and used them for food. At the same time, the plants produced natural gas. The gas could be collected and sold as fuel.

Professor Jewell says his nutrient film technique is more effective than most chemical systems. He also says it can produce clean water for about half the cost. And he says the technique can be used in treatment centers fueled by the sun. Four places in Florida already are using green plants to clean their waste water.

④   Tar May Not Be the Killer in Cigarettes

New evidence that low-tar cigarettes may not be safer cigarettes has emerged from studies in the US. Scientists from the University of Kentucky have exposed the cells of mice to smoke from cigarettes. They say that standard filters, which reduce the amount of tar inhaled by smokers, do not make the smoke less toxic to the cells. Robert Griffith, from the university's college of pharmacology, says: "These observations are of great potential importance for design of cigarettes. Too much emphasis has been placed on the importance of tar alone."

The heart of the issue is the fact, acknowledged on all sides, that standard filters, made of acetate fibre, are efficient at reducing particulate matter, such as tar, from cigarette smoke, but are no good at removing gases. Britain's Tobacco Advisory Council said that a typical filter will reduce the amount of tar inhaled by a smoking machine by 40—75 per cent.

It has generally been assumed that tar, which contains a number of chemicals that cause cancer, is the most lethal constituent of cigarette smoke. Government thinking behind encouraging cigarette companies to reduce the tar delivered in a mouthful of cigarette smoke relies on this. Tar tables published by governments imply that low-tar cigarettes are safer. But the

American research undermines this approach.

Scientists led by Griffith exposed cultures of mouse cells to smoke from various kinds of cigarette. They report in the Archives of Toxicology (vol 58, P120) that "acetate filters had little effect on cell mortality. The results indicate that the gas phase of smoke may be of major importance in generating the observed toxic effects."

Modern cigarettes with the lowest tar delivery below 10 miligrams may help rescue the real toxicity of cigarettes somewhat, however.

These cigarettes have porous paper and sometimes tiny holes, made by lasers, in the paper round the filter. Wendall Moore, a British scientist, says that the purpose of this ventilation of the cigarette is to allow a denser filler without making the smoker's task of drawing too onerous. The ventilation of the filter means that a third of a puff will be fresh air. He says. "These techniques are used in all low-tar brands giving less than 10mg of tar." Griffith found in his study that this dilution did reduce the toxicity of the smoke. One problem is that many people puff more at a lowtar cigarette, thus negating the beneficial effect of the dilution.

第三节 科技论文

科技论文是科技研究人员研究成果的直接记录,包括理论性论文和实验性论文两大类,或阐明理论、或描述实验,内容均较专门、很深,文字也均较正规、严谨。科技论文的结构已成格式化。一般包括标题、提要、引言、正文、结论以及致谢这几部分。

第一，**标题**。语言精练，主题明确，在结构上以名词短语居多。例如：

① Effects of Combustor Inlet Conditions on Flame Stability 燃烧室进口条件对火焰稳定性的影响

② Pretension Diagrams for Bolted Joints 螺栓结合的预张力图

以上两个标题的中心词皆为名词，通过介词与后面的定语联系起来。在翻译时必须首先弄清标题的语法结构以及各个词语之间的相互关系，才能准确地译出标题。当然也有其他形式的标题。例如：

New Technology for the Next Generation of Commercial Transports — Real or Imaginary 下一代商用运输机的新技术是现实还是幻想？

这一标题虽然以名词为中心词，但整个结构却是一省略的疑问句。可见标题的格式并非完全一致，视表示的含义而定。有时标题过分简练，或含专业术语缩略语，意思一时不易弄清，可读完全文后再译，更有把握。

第二，**提要**。它是论文的必要部分，是论文内容的概括和总结。读者往往先读提要，再决定是否值得通读全文。科技刊物一般都在论文的上方登载提要作为提示。有些刊物甚至专门刊登摘要。通常，提要所占篇幅不到全文的 10%，要求文字精练，陈述客观，提纲挈领，突出精华。句型以扩展的简单句居多，结构紧密。时态大都用一般现在时。现以 On Optional Correction of Gunfire Errors（《论射击误差的最佳修正》）一文为例：

[Abstract]

Control of stochastic error in a discrete System is analyzed for an error model comprised of zero mean uncorrelated and Markovian processes plus a random bias of known functional form. It is known that the optimal solution in the sense of miniun mean square error is realized with a Kalman filter, a linear predictor. and a storage-feedback device. The system used to illustrate this application is a gun system, and performance comparisons are given for it.

[提　要]

　　本文对一误差模型在离散系统中的随机误差的控制进行了分析。该误差模型由零平均非相关过程和马科夫过程以及已知函数式的随机偏差组成。分析表明,可用一卡尔曼滤波器、一线性预测器和一存储——反馈装置求得最小均方误差的最佳解。用来具体说明这种应用系统是一火炮系统,并对其操作进行了比较。

　　这篇提要共由三个句子组成,几乎每句都是被动句式,还有 it 引导的主语从句。翻译这样的文字通常应用句型转换法,将被动结构译成以"本文"为主语的主动句式,这样才符合汉语的行文习惯。上面的译文体现了这一要求。

　　第三,**引言**。它是科技论文的开头部分,介绍论文所涉及课题的研究目的、背景、情况、范围和重要性,以及研究的结果和方法,以便让读者了解全文。引言与提要的区别在于,提要是全文的缩影,引言则是全文的主题与总纲。语言特点是被动语态多,第三人称多。下面的两段引言就是例证:

[Purpose]

　　In local areas, highway engineers have found it necessary to use deposits of basalt rock as a source of aggregate for the base course of highways. Some of these deposits yield an aggregate that entirely deteriorates rapidly, causing failure of the highway base within a year or two.

　　To cope with this condition the Highway Materials Testing Laboratory has developed tests intended to indicate in advance whether basalt aggregate from any particular source will degrade rapidly. Also, it has carried on experiments to see whether treating aggregates with asphalt emulsion would slow down the deterioration of those known to be unsatisfactory in their natural condition. The purpose of this report is to present the results of these tests and experiments.

Sources of Information

Information on the sources of aggregates that have not held up as should be expected was obtained from the State Highway Department. The techniques of twisting were based in part on work done in other states, as indicated by the citation of references. Most of the facts presented were obtained, however, by the direct testing and experimentation done in the laboratory.

[目 的]

在某些地区，道路建筑工程师们发现有必要使用玄武砂石作为公路底层铺设用的骨料。有些玄武矿石加工成的骨料是用于公路底层十分理想的材料，而另一些玄武矿石加工出来的骨料却质量迅速退化，不到一两年的时间就造成公路基础的损坏。

针对这一情况，公路材料实验室进行了一些实验，目的是为了事先弄明来自各个具体产地的玄武矿石是否会在质量上迅速退化。实验室还进行了其它的一些实验以证明那些已知不理想的骨料经过沥青乳液处理后是否能够减缓自然状态下骨料的退化过程。本文的目的是陈述这些试验和实验的结果。

[信息来源]

有些产地的骨料不如预期的那样结实，有关这些产地的信息来源于广州公路局。试验的技术有一部分是根据其他州的工作成果，引用的参考材料已说明了这一点。但这里所提出的大部分事实都是来自实验室里所作的直接试验和实验。

第四，**正文**。它是论文的主题，一般包括：一、实验部分（实验材料和实验装备，实验程序或实验方法）；二、结果；三、结果讨论。下面以 Stress Concentration in Rectangular Cut-outs under Pure Sheer(《在纯剪刀状态时矩形切口的应力集中》)一文为例。

1. Experimental Work

Photoelatic models made from moulded Araldete Sheets were loaded in pure shear by means of a shear loading attachment. This attachment was essentially a four bar link mechanism loaded along a diagonal. The models were fixed to the loading attachment using 3/32 in diameter pins at half-inch spacing. Cut-out, sizes, $2a \times 2b$, considered were 2 in $\times$ 1 in, 2 in $\times$ 2 in and 4 in $\times$ 2 in. Each cut-out was investigated for various corner radii. In the neighborhood of cut-outs, square grid patterns were inscribed on the models.

To determine the tangential stress distribution along the boundary of a cut-out, it was only necessary to obtain the fringe orders at the grid points at the boundary. The tardy compensation method was used for the determination of fractional fringe order and for accurate observation a telemicroscope was used.

An attempt was also made to obtain the maximum stress ratio in a crack of 2 in length by determining the maximum stress ratio in openings of 2 in length with semicircular ends of various radii.

2. Results And Discussion

Figure 2 gives a plot of stress ratio against 0 for a cut-out of ratio $a/b = 1$ for various r/b ratios and shows the distribution of tangential stress along the boundary of a square cut-out. The maximum tangential stress occurs at the corners ($0 = 45°$) and conforms with the result obtained by Houghton and Rothwell. The variations are sharp for small corner radii and the sharpness reduces with increasing corner radii. Boundary stresses at the middle of the sides are zero. The ratio $r/b=1$ represents a circular hole for which the maximum stress ratio is 4 at $\theta=45°$C. The theoretical value for the maximum stress ratio for a circular hole is also 4.

For rectangular cut-outs the boundary stress distribution is not symmetrical with respect to the axes of symmetry of the openings and maximum stress concentrations occur in two opposite quadrants. Figure 3 shows the boundary stress distribution in a rectangular cut-out of $a=1$ in, $b=1/2$ in ($a/b=2$) for various corner radii in the quadrant of maximum stress concentration. Boundary stresses are zero at the middle points of the longer sides but not so at the middle points of the shorter sides ($\theta=90°$) of the cut-out. The maximum stress concentration occurs at the corners ($\theta=45°$).

Figurt 4 gives a plot of maximum stress ratio against r/b for $a/b=1$ and 2. It shows that a very high stress concentration is obtained when the corner radius is small. A minimum stress concentration occurs in a circular hole or a cutout with semicircular ends. The maximum stress ratio for $a/b=1$, $r/b=0.12$, is found to be 6.85 against theoretical and experimental values of 9.54 and 6.3 respectively obtained by Houghton and RothWell. These authors used the method of conformal transformation for a square cut-out.

For cut-outs with semicircular ends the variation of maximum stress ratio with increasing a/b ratio is asymptotic when the length of the opening is kept constant. In such a case, for a large a/b ratio the opening represents a crack and the asymptotic value gives the maximum stress ratio for a crack of known length. Figure 5 shows such a plot for a=1 in from which it is observed that the maximum stress ratio for a crack of 2 in length is 7 under pure shear.

1. 实验工作

由模制环氧树脂板制作的光测弹性模型是用剪刀加载装置进行纯剪力加载的。该装置主要是一个四连杆机构、沿对角斜线承受载荷。光测弹性模型是由直径为3/32英寸的销钉每隔半英寸固定在加载装置上的。假定的切口尺寸(2a×2b)各为 2in×1in、2in×2in、以及 4in×2in。对各切口的转角半径进行了研究。在模型上面，切口附近，画出方格网图形。

为确定切口边缘的正切应力分布，只需要得到边缘格点的边纹相重数即可。可采用塔迪补偿法来测定相对比例边纹相重数，并采用遥测量微镜以便精确观察。

还曾经通过测定长度为 2 英寸、不同半径的半圆形终点的开口的最大应力比，设法求出长度为 2 英寸的裂纹最大应力比。

2. 结果和讨论

图 2 是根据各种 r/b 比的 a/b=1 比切口 0 角绘出的应力比并且示出正方形切口边缘上的正切应力分布情况。最大正切应力在 θ=45°角时出现。这符合豪顿和罗斯维尔的实验结果。小圆角时变化明显迅速，随着圆角加大，急剧程序明显降低。各边中心点的边缘应力为零。r/b=1 比表示为一圆孔，在 θ=45°时，它的最大应力比为 4。圆孔的最大应力比的理论值也为 4。

矩形切口的边缘应力分布不与开口的对称轴对称，而且最大应力集中发生在两个对应的 1/4 圆周处。图 2 示出最大应力集中 1/4 圆周处各种圆角的矩形切口(a/b=2, a=1 in, b=1/2 in)的边缘应力分布。边缘应力在切口的较长两边中点为零,但在较短两边中点$(\theta=90°)$就不这样。最大应力集中在$\theta=45°$角时出现。

图 4 是根据 a/b＝1 和 2 时的 r/b 绘出的最大应力比。该图表明,在圆角较小时,可得出很大的应力集中。最小应力集中则在圆孔或具有半圆角的切口上出现。a/b＝1,r/b＝0.12 时的最大应力比达到 6.85,而豪顿和罗斯维尔得出的理论值和实验值分别为 9.54 和 6.3。这两位论文作者对正方形切口采用了保角变换法。

对于具有半圆角的切口来说,开口长度不变时,最大应力比随着 a/b 比增大而发生的变化是渐近的。在这种情况下,大 a/b 比的开口为一裂纹,而渐近值可指出已知长度裂纹的最大应力比。图 5 所示是 a＝1 英寸时观察到的纯剪力状态下 2 英寸长度裂纹最大应力比为 7 的曲线图。

上面这段文字包括了实验工作与结果和讨论这两个部分,专业性极强,典型地代表了科技论文的特点。结构严谨完整,语言准确科学,完全是客观的事实描述,不带任何感情色彩。实验部分都用简单过去时,表示过去的事实。结果和讨论部分则全用现在时态,以表示其经常性与真理性。句子一般均较长,大都为扩展的简单句,多数通过介词来联接并表明词汇或短语之间的关系。有时也出现复合句。有时为了表达清晰明确起见,重复或转换句型在所难免。有些结构复杂的长句,译前应仔细分析各部分的关系,获得正确理解后再下笔。原文中出现的公式或表格图形,可原封不动地移入译文,因为这些已是中外通用的形式。本篇译文较好地达到了准确、科学这一基本要求,语言朴实无华,明确达意,可作为翻译这类文章的借鉴。

第五,**结论**。它是科技论文全文的总结,其目的在于总结和突出研究的成果。结论是经过由实践到认识的完整过程之后而得出的,必须符合事理和逻辑,经得起考验。因此,结论的语言特点是:肯定准确,简明扼要。

The investigation shows that the boundary stress distribution in a square cut-out conforms with the theoretical stress distribution. For a rectangular cut-out the boundary stress distribution is not symmetrical with respect to the axes of symmetry of the cut-out. The stresses are zero at the middle points of the longer sides but not so at the middle points of the shorter sides. A maximum stress concentration occurs at the corners of square or rectangular cut-out and it increases with decreasing corner radii. A minimum stress concentration occurs in a circular hole or a cut-out with semicircular ends.

研究表明,正方形切口的边缘应力分布符合理论的应力分布。对矩形切口来说,边缘应力分布并不与切口的对称轴对称。在较长两边的中点,应力为零;但在较短两边中点,却不这样。最大应力集中在正方形切口或矩形切口的圆角处出现,并且随着圆角减小而增大。最小应力集中在圆孔或具有半圆角的切口上出现。

第六,**致谢**。作者常在结论之后或引言之前用简短的词句对协作者、指导者或帮助者表示感谢。这段文字可长可短,可以用第一人称也可以用第三人称(the author)。

I am grateful to Ernest M. Scheuer and Sidney H. Miller of the RND corporation for a number of helpful suggestions, emendations, and additions of the manuscript. I wish also to thank Captain Joseph Cerny, SAC, who first introduced me to the problems of maintenance analysis.

我谨对兰德研究公司的欧内斯特·M·肖尔和西德尼·H·米勒给予原稿的许多建议、订正和补充表示感谢。战略空军司令部的约瑟夫·塞尼上尉曾最先向我介绍了维修分析问题,我也向他表示感谢。

此外,在科技论文之后,作者尚需列出参考书籍和论文的目录，这也是科技论文一般不可缺少的一部分。在译文之后亦应附上，可保持原状，不必一一译出。这里不再举例说明。

附：练习

将下列文章译成中文。

Stabdump—A Dump Interpreter Program to
Assist Debugging

D. R. Mc GREGOR AND J. R. MALONE

Department of Computer Science,
University of Strathclyde, Glasgow, Scotland

[summary]

Program development can be greatly speeded by a dump analysis program which makes the state of a program more visible to the programmer. A single comprehensive analysis presenting as much of the relevant material in as concise a manner as possible has proved superior in use to the alternative of interactive analysis one item-at-a-time. The methods adopted in the STAB utility to achieve comprehensive and concise output are described. The system and compiler modifications necessary to support this type of system are discussed.

    key words: program, development, differential, dump, debugging aids

[Introduction]

This paper describes a programming tool which we have been using for nearly two years. It is very effective, both for finding 'bugs' and also for checking that a program is in fact operating correctly. The tool works in conjunction with our STAB

—1 program development system (STAB—1 is a software writing language derived originally from BCPL). A similar tool could be constructed for use with virtually any language or program development system. Here we would like to direct attention to what we believe are the major advantages of this type of tool, and to indicate which features have been most successful, and which we think are worth incorporating in other similar systems.

[Program Philosophy]

The major difficulty in finding errors in programs often occurs because the programmer is trying to work from inadequate evidence. By the time an error is detected—or a program crashes—the computer may well have executed many statements. Finding the original error may well be beyond the programmer's powers of deductive reasoning. Life can be made much easier if his development system can render the workings of his program more visible. What we want is to provide the maximum insight to the programmer. One of the traditional methods of debugging is for the programmer to obtain (and waste much time analysing) a large, crude store dump (in hexadecimal or octal). The major disadvantages of this method are that the information is not presented in terms of the source language program, much irrelevant detail is supplied, and the format of the data may be unhelpful, requiring the programmer to do conversions into other representations.

Given that one wishes to be able to examine the dump in the terminology of the source program, that is using the symbolic names how much detail should be presented? Should it be presented interactively one item-at-a-time? Or should we attempt to give a comprehensive report? Several systems provide symbolic names for extracting information from the dump, but with rather a small 'window' of visibility.

Three interactive systems which do this are the 'debugger' in the Unix system, the recently described system for BCPL, and an earlier version of the STAB system. Our experience is that the limited visibility provided by this kind of system makes them rather difficult to use. However, we do not want the programmer to be swamped by masses of irrelevant detail. The ideal system would show only all of what was significant and relevant.

[System Requirements]

The tool we are describing is a symbolic dump interpreter, which can fully describe the state of the program at the time the dump was taken. First the dump itself.

In all operating environments for the STAB system, the detection of a program malfunction (by the operating system, library routines or the user program) results in a store image of the program being dumped into a backing store file. It is also convenient to be able to produce this store image voluntarily by a call from the program without subsequent termination of the run. The automatic dump facility is already found in some operating systems. (The earliest known to us being a system at the Livermore Research Establishment some 10 years ago. Others include Strathclyde Front End Processor and the Bell company's well-known Unix system.) We would strongly recommend it as an essential aid to program development on any system. It is not difficult to get the desired effect on most systems.

A major advantage of this method of obtaining information

about a program's malfunction is that there is virtually no runtime overhead in either space or speed. No extra trace routines are neccessary and the dump interpreting software is a separate system utility which is only used when required. This is a facility which remains effective when a program has passed into production use and is very effective in 'nailing' those occasional bugs in a production environment.

[Compiler Requirements]

The contents of the compiler symbol table must be preserved in some convenient machine-readable form so that a separate dump analyser can use them to interpret the binary store image.

[Stabdump Program]

The STABDUMP dump analysis program picks up the program's symbol table information (preserved for it by the compiler), the store image, and returns dump values for all variables including the contents of data-structures such as arrays and records. The STAB language has global variables as well as own (static) and local (stack-based) variables and the STABDUMP program has corresponding sections each of which carries out one stage of the analysis of the dump file. The first is the stack interpreter which 'unwinds' the stack, printing out the current routine calling sequence, and the contents of all local variables and calling parameter values. The second deals with the STAB language globals and own variables. For each global variable the program prints the name, address and the contents (for a simple variable in decimal and octal, for an array in decimal and characters). This degree of display is unusually large compared to other systems. We should like to stress however that it is very valuable to have all the information presented in this variety of ways. Many problems can be solved after only a cursory inspection of the dump report and the programmer does not require to convert information from one form to another. In order to present a concise and comprehensible report at this level of detail, however, we have to take steps to reduce the amount of irrelevant information being output.

First, only the initial sections of dynamic records — referenced by pointer variables — are printed. These will anyhow be printed in full when the array in which they reside is itself dumped. Second, replicated lines on the dump are not printed. The printout merely prints one line and indicate how may times it is repeated. Third (and the most important), we make the dump *differential*. That is, the dump being analysed is compared with the dump of the program at an earlier state of the run. Only where the later dump differs will any information be printed out for the programmer to examine. In the simplest and most common mode of use, the dump program would be required to compare the postmortem or check point with the image of the program at the initial load time. We have found the differential principle to be very beneficial both in reducing the volume of information and also in directing the programmer's attention to those areas where there is an error. It is most effective during initial testing of programs. It is not uncommon to find that a full dump of 15—20 pages has been reduced by the differential dump to only 2—3 pages. Despite this large reduction, such is the completeness of the differential output that the full dump is no longer used any more.

There are also special-purpose sections which interpret a number of named buffers in the store image. These buffers are only present if various trace or monitor packages have been compiled into the source program. This is a useful and convenient technique for organising the output of this kind of information. One section interprets a buffer containing retrospective trace information (when the trace package was present in the program). Another interprets a buffer containing counts of the number of times particular routines and statements were obeyed, producing histograms and tables of counts.

[Conclusion]

To summarize our experience:

1. Systems should be arranged so that it is not possible for a program to terminate incorrectly without producing a store image dump in a backing-store file. The more automatic this is , the better. The overhead is low and well worth incurring provided the necessary dump analysis aids are available.

2. A comprehensive postmortem analysis is more convenient and more effective than an interactive item-at-a-time one.

3. The printout should indicate the contents of all variables —not merely simple (scalar) variables.

4. Data selection by the 'differential dump' principle and compression of repeated information is worthwhile.

5. Even in systems which do not have global variables the desired effect could be obtained by making the program checkpoint after the variables have been initialized. In our own department the differential dump principle has recently been extended

to our microprocessor development stations in which the micro's store content can be dumped back into the host development machine for comparison with the initial contents loaded.

Acknowledgements

Many people have contributed to the development of the STAB－1 system over the last seven years. We should like to thank our colleagues in the Department of Computer Science for their advice and helpful discussions.

第四节 专利文献

专利文献(Patent Literature)是专利制度的产物,是一种重要的科技信息资料。

专利文献的核心部分是专利说明书(Patent Specification),人们平常所说的专利文献,主要指的是专利说明书。它是申请人向专利局申请专利权时,用以说明自己发明的目的,发明的要点,发明的详细内容以及要求取得的权利要求范围的文件。即专利说明书是新发明、新技术、新工艺、新材料、新产品、新设备等的记录。

专利说明书的编写格式比较统一,篇幅长短不一,通常大都在5000字左右。专利文献虽然是技术文件,但具有浓厚的法律色彩,有一套专用词汇。常用词如:

royalty	使用费,版税
prior art	现行技术水平
block diagram	方框图
sectional view	剖视图
accompanying drawing	附图
Ser. No.	申请号,登记号
in situ	在原处

preferred embodiment	最佳实施方案
hereby	特此，由此
hereinabove	在上文
heretofore	直到此时，在这之前
hitherto	迄今，至今
thereafter	此后，其后
whereat	在该处

专利文献中句子通常较长，结构复杂，并有一些常用句型，如：

① This invention generally relates to … 关于，涉及

This invention relates to methods for audio signal amplification and to audio amplifier circuit and power supplies therefor. 本发明介绍的是音频信号放大的方法、音频放大电路及其电源。

② Reference is made to …请参阅

Reference is made to our corresponding application No. 25838/78 filed 3lst May 1978. 请参阅我们在 1978 年 5 月 31 日登记的与此有关的 No. 25838/78 申请书。

③ …embodiment of … 例子

Figure 1 is an embodiment of the present invention. 图 1 是本发明的具体结构。

④ According to the present invention, there is provided… 本发明提供的是…

According to another aspect of the invention there is provided a complementary MOS type semiconductor device. 本发明的另一个方面是提供一种互补 MOS 型半导体器件。

⑤ The invention will further be described (illustrated, explained)…进一步说明(解释)…

This invention will further be explained in the examples that follow wherein all temperautres are on ℃ unless stated otherwise. 我们将通过下列实例进一步解释本发明。在各例中除另有说明外，所有的温度都用℃作单位。

专利文献除大量使用复合长句外，还常用被动句式和非谓语动词形式。例如：

① The prescribed proportions of PbO, TiO_3, ZrO_2, Sb_2O_3 and Nb_2O_5 constituting a basic composition, and ThO_2, CeO_2 or mixtures thereof forming an auxiliary composition were exactly weighed out, with the proportions of $PbTiO_3$ included in said basic composition fixed at 48 mol percent, the proportions of $Pb(SbNb)_{0.5}O_3$ included therein varied to 26, 20, 14, 10, 6 and 0.5 mol percent and the proportions of $PbZrO_3$ similarly included therein varied to 26, 32, 38, 42, and 51.5 mol percent.

按规定的比例称出 PbO, TiO_2, ZrO_2, Sb_2O_3, Nb_2O_5，由它们构成基本成分。然后称出 ThO_2, CeO_2 或其混合物，由这些物质构成辅助成分。含于上述基本成分中的 $PbTiO_3$ 的组成比例固定在48摩尔％上；含于上述基本成分中的 $Pb(SbNb)_{0.5}O_3$ 的组成比例的变化范围是 26、20、14、10、6、0.5 摩尔％；同样含于上述基本成分中的 $PbZrO_3$ 组成计算的变化范围是 26、32、38、42、48、51.5 摩尔％。

② The specification of patent No. 1,012,052 describes and claims a body of polycrystalline dielectric ceramic material having a lead zirconate—lead titanate—lead stannate composition falling within the area ABCEF of the triaxial diagram 1d of the drawings accompanying this specification and containing at least one substitutional additive ingredient selected from the group consisting of elements having respective ionic radii sufficiently close to the ionic radius of one of the elements lead, tin, titanium, zirconium and oxygen to permit of substitution, and a valence state differing from that of said one element by less than three units, the aggregate quantity of additive ingredient amounting to from 0.1 to 5 percent of the replaced ion on an atom basis, each additive ingredient present in said material being in ionic form and substituting for a finite percentage of the ions of a particular one of the elements lead, tin, titanium, zirconium and oxygen with the respect to which it conforms with regard to ionic radius and valence state, said additive ingredient replacing a quantity of said elements having in the aggregate an equal number of valence units.

第1012052号专利说明书介绍一种含有锆酸铅、钛酸铅、锡酸铅的多晶陶瓷介质材料，其组成在说明书附图1d三元相图中处于ABCEF的区域内。该组成至少还含有一种置换添加物，这种添加物的离子半径应接近于铅、锡、锆和氧这些元素中任何一种的离子半径，以利于互相置换，而化学价之差应小于三价。在原子的基础上该添加物的总量为被替换离子的0.1—5％。上述材料中的每种添加物是以离子的形式存在的，它以一定的百分数置换铅、锡、钛、锆、氧中的某一元素的离子。添加物在离子半径和价数上必须类似于上述任一种元素，并且置换添加物的量与被置换的元素在总体上具有相等的化合价数。

根据对上述专利文献的语言特点的分析，将这类长句译成汉语时要做到语言准确、清晰、简洁十分不易。要实现这一要求，必须综合地运用各种翻译技巧，才能使译文明白易懂。

一份完整的专利文献一般由下面几个部分组成：专利文摘(abstract of disclosure)、发明背景(background of invention)、发明摘要(summary of the invention)、附图简述(brief description of the drawing)、发明详述(detailed description of the invention)、专利权利要求范围(claims)、引用文献(references cited)等。

一、专利文摘。这是该发明全部技术原理的摘要，通常由专利申请人撰写,技术性较强。皆用极为精练、极为概括的语言写成,介绍本发明的主要内容。以下列文摘为例,文摘仅分两小节,由三个句子组成。译文也使用了带有明显技术性与法律性的正式而精炼的文笔。

SINTERING FERROELECTRIC
MATERIALS SUCH AS BARIUM
TITANATE IN A VACUUM

Abstract of the Disclosure

The dielectric properties of ferroelectric materials such as barium titanate are upgraded by sintering the dry pressed shapes in a vacuum having partial air pressures of 1 to 1000 microns. Maintaining the vacuum during cooling is optional.

The invention described herein may be manufactured, used, and licensed by or for the Government for governmental purposes without the payment to us of any royalty thereon.

真空烧结钛酸钡等铁电材料

[内容简介]

提高钛酸钡等铁电材料介电性能的一种方法是在真空1至1000微米空气分压下煅烧干压成形。在冷却期间,是否保持真空可任意选择。

凡政府机构或为政府机构效力而使用本发明的,均可以发给特许证,免交纳专利使用费。

二、发明背景。用来介绍该发明所属技术领域的发展情况和存在的问题,有助于启发科技人员的思路。发明背景一般分为两部分:发明的专业范围(field of the invention)和原先技术的说明(description of the prior art)。下面的例证即分为这两个部分,前者简略,后者详细。

Background of the Invention

This invention relates in general to a method of upgrading the dielectric properties of ferroelectric materials and in particular to a method of upgrading the dielectric properties of barium titanate.

Both kiln firing and hot pressing have been known as techniques of treating ferroelectric materials in order to obtain a ceramic of high dielectric constant. In the case of kiln firing, various atmospheres have been used during firing as for example, oxygen, steam, carbon dioxide, etc. The difficulty with kiln firing of ferroelectric materials is that the resulting ceramic has not been characterized by a sufficiently high dielectric constant and dielectric losses have been high. At present, ceramics produced by hot pressing ferroelectric materials have exhibited properties superior to any of those produced by kiln firing. However, hot pressing is expensive and not efficient in producing large quantities of useable ceramics for electrical applications as for example, for capacitors.

[发明背景]

本发明介绍一种提高铁电材料介电性能的方法,并且具体介绍了提高钛酸钡介电性能的方法。

大家都知道,为了得到高介电常数的陶瓷,窑炉烧结和热压是处理铁电材料的两种方法。就窑炉烧结而言,煅烧时使用了各种气氛,例如氧气、蒸汽、二氧化碳等等。用窑炉煅烧铁电材料存在的问题是,所得到的陶瓷介电常数不够高,并且介质损耗大。现在,热压铁电材料方法所生产的陶瓷已显示出优于窑炉烧结所生产的陶瓷。但是,热压价钱昂贵,而且在电子陶瓷的大量生产(例如电容器瓷)方面效率不高。

三、发明摘要。这一部分扼要指出该发明能够解决的问题及其主要优点,然后再从技术上介绍该发明的目的。

下列的例子中,原文句子长而结构复杂,第二段仅由一个很长的复合句构成,故译者采用拆译法将这一长句分译成两个独立的句子,以达到译文的清晰通顺。

Summary of the Invention

The general object of this invention is to provide a method of treating ferroelectric materials so that ceramics having superior electrical properties are obtained. A further object of this invention is to provide such a method that will be economic.

It has now been found that ceramics of improved dielectric properties can be obtained economically by dry pressing the ferroelectric material and then firing the dry pressed ferroelectric material in such partial air pressures that no reduction of the ferroelectric material occurs. Partial air pressures used are dependent on the particular ferroelectric material being treated and in the range of the partial pressure where reduction of the ferroelectric material would occur.

[发明概况]

本发明总的目的是提供处理铁电材料的一种方法,以获得电性能优良的陶瓷。本发明进一步的目的是采用一种经济的方法。

现已发明,在铁电材料不发生还原的空气分压的情况下煅烧已干压的铁电材料,就能获得价钱便宜、介电性能良好的陶瓷。所使用的空气分压取决于具体的铁电材料,但必须在铁电材料不发生还原的空气分压的情况下进行。

四、发明评述。该部分应为最佳实施方案的详述,是专利说明书中对发明的技术原理介绍得最详细和最完整的部分。它通过附图上的数字标号和相应注码,将具体装置各部分的作用,相互关系等实质性内容以及具体的应用方法,都表述得清清楚楚。

由于专利文献的语言的一大特色是句子长,结构复杂,含有很多的非谓语动词,在翻译时最有效的办法是先理顺从句间的相互关系和修饰语与被修饰语之间的关系,然后按照逻辑顺序进行拆译。下面的译文正是采用了这种方法取得了明白、易懂的效果。

Detailed Description of the Preferred Embodiment

The raw powder of a typical ferroelectric material, to wit, a commercially available barium titanate is first dry pressed and then fired to maturity under controlled atmospheric conditions. In this instance, the dry pressed barium titanate is fired in tube furnace in moderate vacuum of about 1 micron to about 1000 microns. This vacuum is applied through the peak temperature of 1200 degrees C. to 1400 degrees C. and through subsequent cooling to ambient temperature. The peak temperature is reached in about 7 hours. The moderate vacuum may be initiated at furnace startup. However, the influence of vacuum is considered minimal at the lower temperatures. In addition, the vacuum may be discontinued during the cooling cycle. In a systematic study of the effect of partial firing pressures, an appreciable improvement in dielectric constant is obtained for samples of barium titanate treated by the above described methods. This improvement amounts to a 47 percent increase; from 2550 with samples fired in oxygen to 3750 with samples fired in a 20 micron vacuum. The dissipation factor traverses a minimum and the DC resistivity a maximum for samples fired in an 85 micron vacuum. One particular firing at about 1350 degrees C. utilizing a moderate vacuum of about 1 micron to about 1000 microns in which the vacuum was discontinued during cooling yielded a dielectric constant of 7520 and a dissipation factor of 0.004 when measured at 1 kilohertz; and a dielectric constant of 5450 and a dissipation factor of 0.022 when measured at 1 megahertz.

Other ferroelectric materials amenable to the treatment of his invention include alkaline earth titanates such as strontium titanate, zirconates such as calcium zirconate, niobates such as potassium niobate, and stannates such as barium stannate.

In addition, other means of obtaining partial air pressures besides vacuum are contemplated as coming within the scope of the invention as for example, the use of CO/CO_2 mixtures, hydrogen, and partial inert gas atmospheres.

The initial fabrication of the ferroelectric material is accomplished by means well known in the art as for example dry pressing, doctor blading, etc.

The time and temperature of firing is dependent upon the particular ferroelectric material being treated and it readily determinable by one skilled in the art.

It should also be pointed out that the invention aids in the elimination of voids in the resulting densified body.

Thus, the instant invention provides an economic means of upgrading the dielectric properties of ferroelectric materials by the use of vacuum or partial air pressures during firing without the onset of reduction.

The foregoing description is to be considered merely as illustrative of the invention and not in limitaion thereof.

[最佳实施方案详述]

首先把一种典型的铁电材料(即工业用的钛酸钡)的原料粉末

进行干压,然后在控制气氛条件下烧成。在本例中,干压的钛酸钡在1~1000微米的中等真空度下,装在管形炉里煅烧。真空烧结的峰值温度为1200至1400℃,达到峰值温度约七小时,然后冷却到环境温度。窑炉开始工作时中等真空便开始。不过,在较低温度下,真空的作用很小。此外,在冷却期间,可以停止真空。在系统研究部分烧结压力的作用方面,已发现,通过上述方法处理的钛酸钡试样介电常数明显提高,提高量约47%。在氧气气氛中烧结的试样介电常数为2500,而在20微米真空下烧结的则为3750。在85微米真空下烧结的样品,损耗因数为最小值,直流电阻率为最大值。在1350℃、大约1微米至1000微米的中等真空度下进行煅烧,并在冷却期间停止真空,结果在1千赫兹的频率下测出的介电常数为5720,损耗因数为0.004;在1兆赫兹的频率下,测出的介电常数为5450,损耗因数为0.022。

本发明也适于处理其他铁电材料,包括碱土金属钛酸盐,例如钛酸锶;锆酸盐,例如锆酸钙;铌酸盐,例如铌酸钾;锡酸盐,例如锡酸钡。

此外,除真空外,获得空气分压的其他方法也属本发明的范围,例如使用CO/CO_2混合物、氢气、惰性气体气氛。

制造铁电材料最初的工艺采用大家所熟知的方法,例如干压、刀刮等。

煅烧的时间和温度取决于特定的铁电材料,技术熟练的人很容易测定。

应当指出,本发明有助于消除致密瓷体的孔隙。

如上所述,在烧结时使用真空或空气分压,而不使其还原,这就是本发明提高铁电材料介电性能的经济实惠的方法。

上述内容仅仅是本发明的例证,并不局限于此。

五、专利权利要求范围。在这一部分中往往按顺序编号列出各权项。文字严谨、精确,具有法律条款的特点,是专利重点保护之所在。第一项通常是全部专利的概括,其余各项是专利的局部特点和变化情况。技术内容上与前重复。在翻译时,除对文字有强烈的专业技术性的要求之外,应特别注意其法律性文体的特点:即清晰、明确、逻辑性强。

What is claimed is:

1. In a method of making a barium titanate ferroelectric article comprising dry pressing commercially available barium titanite, firing the dry pressed form to maturity, and cooling; wherein the improvement comprises firing the dry pressed form at about 1200 to 1400 degrees C. while applying a vacuum in the range of partial air pressures preceding the partial pressure where reduction of the barium titanate would occur and in the range of between about 1 to 1000 microns and cooling to ambient temperature to upgrade the dielectric properties of the barium titanate.

2. The method according to claim 1 wherein said vacuum is maintained while cooling to ambient temperature.

[本专利权利要求范围]

1. 制造钛酸钡铁电材料的方法是:干压工业用钛酸钡,然后将其烧结、冷却。其中改进之处是:把已干压好的制品在1200至1400℃下、在钛酸钡不被还原、真空度为1至1000微米空气分压下煅烧,然后冷却到环境温度,从而提高钛酸钡的介电性能。

2. 权利要求1所述的方法中,在冷却到外界温度时,保持真空。

从上面这份完整的专利说明书(省略了附图简述与引用文献两项)可以看出,专利说明书是技术性,专业性与法律性极强的文献。在翻译这类资料时,不仅要注意其中的专业词汇,同时也要特别注意译文表达的准确性和逻辑性。

附：练习

将下列专利文献译成中文。

Socket wrench with interchangeable sockets stored in handle Background of the Invention

A very popular and useful wrench is a socket wrench of the type which is a handle, a head at one end of the handle with a socket mounting stub, and a set of interchangeable socket members of different size which are adapted for individual selective mounting on the stub. Usually called "socket wrench sets", they are commonly packed in a box which has a compartment for the handle and a compartment, or separate compartments, for the interchangeable socket members. In addition, it is quite common for such a socket wrench set to include an extension member which has one end portion that seats on the stub and a second end portion comprising a stub to selectively receive the interchangeable socket members.

Socket wrench sets are often used in connection with service work on machinery or vehicles; and it is a common experience of a person doing such work to find that he needs to change socket members when the case containing them is not readily at hand; and this causes undesirable delay and, sometimes, frayed nerves.

Many interchangeable socket members are lost because they are not immediately returned to the case; especially when, for example, the person removes from the case two or three socket members that he expects to need on a particular job and then misplaces one or more of them.

[Summary of the Invention]

The principal object of the present invention is to provide an improved socket wrench of the type having interchangeable sockets by constructing the wrench handle in the form of an arcuate longitudinal wall defining a cavity and which has an entrance opening along one side through which socket members may be inserted into the cavity. The said cavity has portions of different sizes each of which is adapted to frictionally grip one of the socket members of said set; and said wall has an access opening operatively associated with each portion of the cavity permitting application of force to the socket member in said portion to remove it through said entrance opening.

[The Drawings]

Figure 1 is a perspective view of a socket wrench embodying a first form of the invention, shown with the entrance opening to the storage cavity uppermost;

Figure 2 is a perspective view of the embodiment of Fig. 1 with the entrance opening lowermost;

Figure 3 is a fragmentary longitudinal sectional view taken substantially as indicated along the line 3-3 of Fig. 1;

Figure 4 is a sectional view taken on the section line in Fig. 3 looking in the direction of the arrows 4-4;

Figure 5 is a sectional view taken along the section line in Fig. 3 looking in the direction of the arrows 5-5;

Figure 6 is a view like Fig. 1 of a second embodiment of the invention;

Figure 7 is a transverse sectional view taken substantially as indicated along the line 7-7 of Fig. 6; and

Figure 8 is a perspective view similar to Fig. 2 illustrating a third embodiment of the invention.

[Detailed Description of the Invention]

Referring to the drawings in greater detail, and referring first to Figs. 1 to 5, a socket wrench indicated generally at 10, includes a handle 11, a head 12 at one of the handle, a socket mounting stub 13 on the head, a set of interchangeable socket members 14 through 20 which are of different sizes and which are adapted to be individually selectively mounted on the stub 13, and an extension member 21 which has one end portion 22 that seats on the stub 13 and a second end portion 23 comprising a stub to selectively receive any of the socket members 14 through 20.

The handle 11 comprises a longitudinal, arcuate wall 24 defining a cavity 25 with an entrance opening 26, and the wall 24 tapers from a broad outer end 27, having an end plate 28, to a narrow neck 29 which is immediately adjacent the head 12.

The cavity 25 has a plurality of portions 30 through 36 (Fig. 2) which are adapted to receive and frictionally retain the socket members 14 through 20, respectively. In addition, the cavity 25 includes a neck portion 37 in which the extension members 21 is frictionally held. The portions 30 through 37 of the cavity 25 are defined by transverse webs, such as the webs 38 and 39 in Figs. 3 and 4, which thus cause the several portions 30 through 37 of the cavity to serve as compartment for the members 14 through 21. The compartment for the socket member 20 is, of course, defined by the web 39 and the end wall 28 of the handle. The webs have chamfered or rounded margins to facilitate insertion of the socket members into the compartments.

Each of the portions, or compartments 30 through 37 is provided with an access opening, numbered 40 to 47, respectively, consisting of a laterally elongated hole which is on the longitudinal median line of the wall 24. Each of the access openings permits pressure to be applied to the member which is frictionally retained in the compartment with which the access opening is associated, so as to remove the member from the compartment through the entrance open 26. As seen from the enlarged sectional views of the holes 45 and 46 in Fig. 3, the margins of the holes are care fully finished to a rounded cross section so that a person applying finger pressure to remove one of the members cannot damage a finger or push it through the hold and find himself unable to withdraw it.

The compartments 30 through 37 are provided with resilient means, which, as illustrated in the drawings, consists of a pair of strips 48 of a soft, elastomeric material which are close to the upper edges 49 of the wall 24 which define the entrance opening 26.

As seen in Fig. 4 and 5, the longitudinal wall 24 has a radius of curvature in the area of any of the compartments 30 through 37 which is greater than that of the member stored in the compartment, but the upper margins 49 of the wall 24 are above the pivot axes of the members and curve inwardly above the diameters of said members which are stored in the handle with their pivot axes extending longitudinally. Thus, the wall in cross section is a segment of a circle in excess of 180°, and the resilient means 48 is slightly above a horizontal diameter of each of the members so as to afford firm frictional gripping of all the members, each of which is stored with its diameter inwardly of the minimum span across the resilient means 48. It is clear that the cavity might have a resilient strip on only one side, with the socket member snapping past the margin of the wall on the other side; or that with proper selection of wall material and thickness the socket members could snap into place without the separate resilient means.

The interchangeable socket members 14 through 20 are of standard type. Each has a square hole, like the hole 19a seen in Fig. 4, at one end; and a hexagonal socket, like the socket 20b seen in Fig. 5, at the other end. The square holes adapt the socket members for individual selective mounting on the stub 13 or on the extension member stub 23, as the case may be.

Referring now to Figs. 7 and 7, the second embodiment of the invention is similar to the first, except that the access openings in the form of holes along the median line of the handle wall 124 are eliminated; and a handle wall 124 is provided with access openings in the form of an arcuate recess at each of the margins 149 of the wall. The recesses are given the reference numerals 140 through 147 in Figs. 6 and 7, corresponding to the numbers 40 through 47 of the access holes in the first embodiment. As seen in Fig. 7, the arcuate recesses are provided with margins which are rounded in cross section to avoid possible finger injury. The recesses permit force to be applied to a socket member by gripping it between the fingers in order to remove it from the cavity through the entrance opening, as is the case with the first embodiment.

The only difference between the first and second embodiments is that in the latter the arcuate recesses make it necessary for the resilient means to be in the form of single pads 148 bonded to the wall 124 between the recesses, rather than the continuous strips of the first embodiment.

Referring now to Fig. 8, the third embodiment of the invention has a handle provided with an arcuate wall 224 which is much like the wall 24 of the first embodiment in that it defines a storage cavity with an entrance opening along one side and has holes the axes of which are along the longitudinal median line of the wall 224. In the third embodiment, the socket members 14 through 20 and the extension member 21 are stored with their respective axes of rotation effectively on the longitudinal median plane of the entrance opening, and the access holes 240 through 247 are of different sizes so that each is adapted to have a part of one of the members extending therethrough. As in the first and second embodiments, transverse webs (not shown) divide the storage cavity into separate compartments, each of which receives and frictionally grips one of the members 14 through 21. Thus, force may be applied to the projecting end of any one of the members 14 through 21 when it is desired to remove that member from the cavity through the entrance opening.

If desired, the wall 224 may be modified so that it is deeper, in which event the members 14 through 21 may be completely enclosed within the cavity, and in that case the unit is provided with access holes like the holes 40 through 47 of the first embodiment.

The foregoing detailed description is given for clearness of understanding only and no unnecessary limitations should be understood therefrom, as modifications will be obvious to those skilled in the art.

[Claims]

1. In a socket wrench of the type which has a handle, a head at one end of the handle with a socket mounting stub, and a set of interchangeable socket members of different sizes which are adapted for individual selective mounting on said stub, the improvement comprising:

said handle has an arcuate longitudinal wall defining a cavity which has an entrance opening along one side;

said cavity has portions of different sizes each of which is adapted to frictionally engage with one of the socket members of said set;

and said wall has an access opening operatively associated with each protion of the cavity permitting application of force to the socket member in said portion to remove it through said entrance opening.

2. The improvement of claim 1 in which the access openings are holes along the longitudinal median line of the wall.

3. The improvement of claim 2 in which the holes are 1 aterally elongated, have rounded margins, and are large enough to accommodate the end of a finger for applying force to the socket member.

4. The improvements of claim 3 in which each portion of the cavity is adapted to receive and frictionaly engage with a socket member which has its axis of rotation lengthwise of the handle.

5. The improvement of claim 2 in which each portion of the

cavity is adapted to receive and frictionally engage with a socket member which has its axis of rotation substantially centered on the hole.

 6. The improvement of claim 5 in which each hole is adapted to have an end portion of a socket member projecting through it for application of force to the socket member.

 7. The improvement of claim 1 in which said access opening is in the form of an arcuate recess at each margin of the wall, so that force may be applied to a socket member by gripping it between the fingers.

 8. The improvement of any of the preceding claims in which the cavity includes a neck portion immediately adjacent the socket head which is constructed to frictionally engage with an extension member which has one end portion that seats on the stub and a second end portion comprising a stub to selectively receive the socket members.

 9. The improvement of any of the preceding claims in which the handle tapers substantially uniformly from the large outer end to a narrow neck portion adjacent the head.

 10. The improvement of any of the preceding claims which includes integral transverse, webs between adjacent portions of the cavity defining compartments for the members.

第五节　科普读物

  简单地说,科普读物是普及科学常识的读物,它包括对宇宙万物的各种自然现象的解释及自然科学中各学科的基本知识,涉及的面十分广博,诸如物理、化学、天文、地理、生物、医学等无所不包。科普读物的形式也多样化,有科学小丛书、百科全书、科普文摘、科学史、科学家传记等。

科普读物的读者主要是青少年,内容上着重常识性、知识性和趣味性,语言上通俗易懂,深入浅出,语句简短,多用普通词汇。在翻译这类读物时应忠实于原文风格,用生动灵活、浅显易懂的汉语普及科学知识,让读者感兴趣。例如:

The Beginnings of Astronomy

Early men were also greatly interested in the stars they saw twinkling in the sky at night. What they did not realize was that the stars were also present during the daytime, but their light was not visible because of the brilliance of the sun. How did they discover this?

There is one event which does enable us to see the stars in the daytime. It is the total eclipse of the sun, when the moon passes in front of the sun and hides it from view. When this happens, the sky becomes dark enough for the stars to be seen. Total eclipses of this kind do not occur very often and are not likely to be seen from the same area more than once every fifty four years. One can imagine what an awe-inspiring sight it must have been for an early man, who would remember the event for the rest of his life.

So man watched the movements of the sun, the moon and the stars and wondered about them. It was practising the oldest branch of science—astronomy.

早期天文学

古人也对夜晚所见天空中闪烁的群星怀有浓厚的兴趣。他们还不知道白天星星也在那里,只是看不见它们的闪光,因为太阳光太强了。人们怎么会发现这一点的呢?

只有一种情况能让我们在白天看见星星,那就是日全食。月亮走到太阳前面,把它遮住。这时天空变暗,便可看见星星了。这种日全食并不常见,同一个地区也许每隔五十四年只会碰上一次。我们可以想象,对于古人来说,这该是一种多么令人心惊胆战的景象啊,他们一生中永远也不会忘记。

人类就是这样观察太阳、月亮和星体的运动,并产生疑问的。人们在思考它们是什么,以及他们在干什么的时候,其实就是在从事对科学的最古老的学科——天文学的研究。

这是一段有关天文学起源的叙述。作者并未涉及多少理论,而是从太阳,月亮,星星说起,特别描绘了日全食的景象。这些都是极普通的天文现象,人人都能理解。作者使用通俗易懂、口语化的文字来表述,使一般读者,特别是小读者都能接受。文章里并无枯燥抽象的说教,只有生动而形象的描绘。如讲到星星,就用"twinkling"来形容其星光闪烁;讲到日全食,就用"月亮走到太阳前面,把它遮住"的具体事实来说明道理。有些词甚至带有文学风味,如awe-inspiring, wonder about 等,再与"what they were and what they did"这一类通俗的口语结合在一起,使文字既活泼又有美感。译者十分注意原文的这种风格,在译文中用对应的汉语生动流畅地再现了原文的风貌。

Something about Radar

Radar is a new development in Radio Science. It plays an increasingly important part in the navigation of ships and aircraft as well as in the meteorology for cloud and thunderstorm detection. Radar is also very important for military purposes. So, it is also very interesting and helpful to have some knowledge about how radar works.

Let us begin with the reflection of sound waves and light waves as well as their uses in finding objects.

Suppose that you are standing on a flat piece of open land, on which there is a house some distance away. You shout "Hello" and a little later an answering "Hello" is heard. You recognize the answering "hello" as an echo and decide that the house must be acting as the reflector of the sound. This phenomenon offers a way to find the range of a target which plays its part here as a reflector. Nevertheless the speed at which sound travels is too low for such a purpose. Thus this sound-wave echo method has its limitation in practical use.

Now, turn our attention to the reflection of light waves. When you switch on your flashlamp, the light went out by the flashlamps returns from the object on which the light falls and reaches your eyes. In other words, light waves bear great similarity with sound waves in this respect. And since the speed of light is about a million times as great as that of sound waves, the reflection of light waves may very well be applied in detecting a target and its range. However, we must not forget that this very method is affected on a great extent by weather conditions such as fog, cloud, rain, snow and the like.

Wireless waves, as we know, belong to the same big family as sound waves and light waves. They have many fundamental features in common. Among them the most important is that wireless waves can also be reflected. The speed at which wireless waves travel is as great as that of light waves. Moreover they are, for all practical purposes, completely unaffected by temperatures, barometric pressure, darkness, daylight or weather conditions. So wireless waves are just the waves most suitable to be used in detecting a distant target and finding its range. And this is exactly what radar set, the equipment that sends out wireless signals and receives their echoes, bases on.

关于雷达

雷达是无线电科学的一项新发展。它在舰船和飞机的导航以及对云层和雷雨的气象探测中,起着日益重要的作用。雷达在军事上也很重要。因此,了解一些雷达的工作原理,既很有趣也很有益。

让我们由声波、光波的反射及其在探测目标方面的用处开始谈起吧。

设想你站在一块开阔的平地上,不远处有一幢房屋。你高喊:"喂!",一会儿就可以听见回答:"喂!"。你觉察到这回答"喂"是回声,并且断定:这幢房屋一定起着声音反射物的作用。这种现象,对起反射物作用的目标,提供了一种测量其距离的方法。然而用来测量目标的距离,声音走的速度太慢。因此,这种声波回声测距法在实际应用中有其局限性。

现在我们把注意力转向光波的反射。你打亮手电筒时,它射出的光,从照射的物体上反射回来到你眼里。换句话说,光波和声波在这一方面具有很大的相似之处。由于光速大约为声速的一百万倍,因此光波的反射现象很可以用来探测目标及其距离。但是,我们不要忘记:这种方法在很大程度上要受到雾、云、雨、雪等这类天气条件的影响。

我们知道,无线电波和声波、光波属于同一大类。它们具有许多基本相同点。其中最重要的是无线电波也能反射。无线电波的传播速度和光速一样快。此外,在实际应用上,它完全不受温度、气压、黑夜、白昼或天气条件的影响。因此,无线电波正是最宜用来探测远距离目标及其距离的有效波类。这正是雷达装置——发射无线电信号和接收其回波的设备赖以运作的基础。

这是一篇完整的有关雷达工作原理的短文,用浅显通俗的语言解释了如何使用雷达来探测物体距离的道理。文章未直接论述有关雷达的理论,而是采用与听得见的声波和看得见的光波的对比来说明雷达——无线电波相同的反射性能和它独具的优越性。语言十分口语化,好似一位老师正面对着学生们讲课一样。不仅句子结构简短,并使用了"Let us begin","Suppose","Now, turn our attention to"等这一类讲课中常用的起转折和连结作用的词汇和表达方式。在人物上直接用"we"和"you"来缩短与读者的距离,恰似面对面谈话一样,如 Suppose that you're standing on a flat piece of open land …","you shout 'Hello'","You recognize …"和"We must not forget","as we know",等。这种叙述体而非论说体的风格在本文中显得十分突出。译文较好地体现了原文的风格,将上列的词汇短语和句子直接译为"让我们从……开始谈起吧","设想你在一块开阔的平地上","现在我们把注意力转向…","你高喊'喂'","你觉察到","我们不要忘记","我们知道"。这些也都是汉语口语中常用的词汇,短语或句子。科普读物的普及和简易的原则在原文和译文中均较好地体现了出来。

Michael Faraday

During the first half of the 19th century scientists began to acquire a better understanding of electricity. We owe much to people like Volta, Ohm and Ampere whose names are associated with the various units of electrical measurement, and to Michael Faraday whose later discoveries laid the foundation for our modern electrical industry.

Farady was one of the world's greatest experimenters and he set himself the task of finding out more about light, heat, electricity and magnetism. He had the idea that if electricity flowing through a wire it could create a magnetic field around it (a fact discovered by Ampere) then the field around a magnetic might be used to produce electricity. His experiments with two magnets, an iron core and a coil of wire proved his idea to be correct.

From these early experiments in electro-magnetism came eventually the development of the electric generator which produces electricity for our homes and factories. They also resulted in the invention of the electric motor to drive machinery and provide power for electric trams and trains. The electric telegraph, the telephone and many electrical facilities owe their development to the original work of Michael Faraday.

米迦勒·法拉第

十九世纪上半叶,科学家们开始对电有了更清楚的了解。这应归功于像伏特、欧姆、安培这些人。他们的名字已和电的各种测量单位联系在一起。也应归功于米迦勒·法拉第。他的发现奠定了现代电力工业的基础。

法拉第是世界上最伟大的实验物理学家之一。他立志要进一步弄清楚光、热、电和磁力的特性。他认为既然电在通过电线时会在电线周围形成磁场(这是安培发现的),那么,磁体周围的磁场就一定可以用来产生电。他用两块磁体、一个铁心和一组线圈进行试验,结果证明他的想法是正确的。

后来为家庭和工厂生产电力的发电机最终就由这些早期的电磁实验发展而来。这些实验也导致了能开动机器,和为电车与电气火车提供动力的电动机的发明。电报、电话以及许多电器设备的发明也都归功于米迦勒·法拉第的创造性劳动。

介绍科学家的文章和书籍是科普读物的一个重要组成部分。这篇短文就是对著名英国物理学家法拉第的简略介绍,主要提到他对电力工业和电器发明所作出的巨大贡献。文中虽提到他曾用"两块磁体,一个铁心和一组线圈"进行"试验",但并未阐说发电的原理和他是如何作试验的,因为对科学家的介绍虽涉及科学内容,但如人物传记一样,着重在介绍人物,特别是他在科学发展方面做出的功绩。如过多涉及科学的专门知识不仅使普通读者难以读懂，也会喧宾夺主，反将科学家本人置于次要地位。故文章作者只用最基本的科技词汇，如 light, heat, electricity, magnetism, magnetic field, iron core, coil of wire, generator, motor 等。这些都在一般读者的知识的范围之内，不会带来理解上的困难。此外文章的风格比较正式，选用的词汇短语也比较正规，如 associated with, laid the foundation for, resulted in, owe … to 等。译文也用相同的较正式的汉语词汇，短语来翻译这些基本科技词汇和正规文体的表达方式。如光、热、电、磁力、磁场、铁心、线圈、发电机、电动机，以及"联系在一起"、"奠定基础"、"导致"、"归功于"等等，较准确地体现了原文的风格。

附：练习

将下列科普文章译成中文．

① Energy Conversion

The conversion of mechanical energy to heat is by no means new to us. We are also familiar with other transformations of energy. Chemical energy is converted into heat when fuel burns. Electrical energy is transformed into heat and light in electrical lamps and electrical stoves. Radiant energy turns into heat when sounlight strikes an object which absorbs it. "All contradictory things are interconnected; not only do they coexist in a single entity in given conditions, but in other given conditions, they also transform themselves into each other." In a word, all energies may be converted from one form to another and what is more, they all can transform into heat by themselves. Heat is an energy of irregular motion of particles in a substance, at ordinary temperature it is less usable than any of the other energies.

However, at high temperatures heat energy may be converted into energy of more usable forms. Some people have made different kinds of machines to convert heat into mechanical energy. Diesel and gasoline engines are designed to convert heat that is developed by the burning of fuel into mechanical energy for running tractors, trucks, and cars. The mechanical energy transformed from heat in a steam turbine is made to operate generators. And the generators, in turn, convert the mechanical energy into electrical energy. All these transformations are taking place every minute and everywhere in our daily life and production.

② Of all the sciences, biology has the greatest relevance to the understanding of man. It was slightly more than a century ago, in 1859, that Darwin set forth the revolutionary idea which this book encompasses — that man, together with every other living thing, is a product of a process of evolutionary development. But man has not only evolved, he is still evolving. Human evolution is not all in the past. It is also an actuality and a concern for the future. The problem of possible genetic damage to human populations from radiation exposures, including those resulting from the fallout from testing of atomic weapons, has quite properly claimed much popular attention in recent years.

3: Many of the materials listed above as examples of organic compounds were once believed to be products of living organisms—and so were called organic. Following much laboratory experimentation, however, chemists were able to demonstrate that certain products, which had previously been considered the results of vital or living processes, could be produced in the laboratory. One of the classical examples of this type of work was Wöhler's synthesis of urea. In the year 1828, Wöhler, a German chemist, produced urea, a decomposition product of proteins, by heating ammonium cyanaet, a compound of inorganic origin:

$$NH_4CNO \cdots\cdots CO(NH_2)_2$$

This was the beginning of a new era in the synthesis of carbon compunds which scientists had previously thought impossible to prepare in the laboratory. The vital-process idea was discarded. Today, rapid strides are being made in the preparation of sugars, vitamins, and related compounds. Every day, new compounds are produced in the laboratory by the synthetic organic chemist, and many of these compounds have an important bearing on our everyday life.

In the discussion of the conductivities of aqueous solutions of acids, bases, and salts, it was pointed out that, as a group, they were relatively good conductors of the electric current.

In marked contrast to this is the fact that aqueous solutions of alcohol, sugar, glycer, and the like are very poor conductors. These facts suggest that there is little or no ionization in the case of organic compounds. Thus, although ionic inorganic reactions proceed almost instantaneously, organic reactions frequently require, even under the most favorable conditions, considerable time before they approach completion.

第六节 科幻小说

科学幻想小说(science fiction)是以科学的某方面内容为故事

情节或背景的小说。这类作品一般通过科学的想象对未来作大胆的推测和设想,引导读者走进新的境界,激励人们去探索科学和其中所蕴藏的无数的可能性,因而具有一定的科学启示作用。由于作者把科学和幻想通过小说这种艺术形式有机地结合起来,融为一体,故科学幻想小说充满了丰富的想象、神秘的情节和离奇的人物,十分耐人寻味。

由于科学幻想小说是以科学事实、科学学说和科学推论为依据,采用小说这种文学形式通过情节和人物将科学幻想表现出来,奉献给读者,因此,它兼具科学和文学双重特点。要想翻译好科学幻想小说,译者也同样要具备基本的科学知识和文学素养,并掌握小说翻译的基本要领。

科学幻想小说属于通俗读物的范畴,读者大都为平民百姓,其中一大部分为中小学生,其目的除普及科学知识外,也给读者以娱乐和享受。科学幻想小说的语言比较通俗易懂,口语化,易于为广大读者,特别是中小学生所接受。所涉及的科学现象与科学原理也用简单明了的日常语言来加以解释,很少使用科技论文或著作中那种复杂、正式、专业性很强的文字。在翻译科学幻想小说时,也要充分体现原作的语言风格,强调通俗易懂,同时也要将原作生动、活泼、有趣的描述再现出来,以引起读者的兴趣。

The object of Mr. Cavor's search was a substance that should be unaffected by all forms of radiant energy. "Radiant Energy," he made me understand, was anything like light or heat, or X-Ray, or gravitation. All these things, he said, radiate from centres and act on bodies at a distance. Now almost all substances are unaffected by some form or other of radiant energy. Glass, for example, is transparent to light, but less so to heat, and alum is transparent to light, but blocks heat completely.

Now all known substances are affected by gravitation. You can cut off light or heat from anything; but nothing will cut off the attraction of the sun or the moon. Yet why there should be nothing is hard to say. Cavor did not see why such substance should not exist, and showed me by calculations on paper that it was possible. It was an amazing piece of reasoning, but it is impossible for me to reproduce it here. All I can say is that he believed he might be able to make this substance out of a complicated mixture of metals and a new element called Helium, which was sent to him from London in sealed stone jars.

Anyone with the least imagination will understand the extraordinary possibilities of such a substance. Whatever use it is put to, one came on miracles. For example, if one wanted to lift a weight, however enormous, one had only to get a sheet of this substance beneath it, and one might lift it with a straw.

凯沃先生研究的对象是一种不受任何形式的辐射能影响的物质。他向我解释说："辐射能"指的是像光、热、X射线或地心吸引力一类的能量。他说，这一类能量都从中心点向外辐射，作用于远处的物体。几乎所有物质都有不受某种辐射能影响的特性。比如玻璃能透光，但传热就差些，而明矾能透光，却完全不传热。

目前所有已知的物质都受地心引力的影响。你可以将任何东西隔断光和热，但没有任何东西可以切断太阳和月亮的引力。而为什么这样，现在还无法解释。凯沃认为不受太阳和月亮引力的物质没有理由不存在，并且在纸上演算给我看，证明这种物质有可能存在。这是一种令人惊异的推理。但要我在这里把它复述出来，是不可能的。我能说上来的只是：他相信他能利用多种金属和一种叫做氦的新元素混合而成的复杂的混合物造出这种物质来。他所用的氦是用密封的石罐从伦敦运来的。

即使最缺乏想象力的人也可以懂得这样一种物质可能具有的非同一般的神奇力量。不论把它用在何处,都会创造出奇迹来。比如,如果你想举起一件重物,无论多么大,只要把一片这样的物质放在它的下面,你就可以用一根稻草把它提起来。

以上这段文字选自经 L·多斯缩写的威尔斯所著的《月球探险记》第一章。威尔士的科幻小说大多创作于 19 世纪末,航空的时代还远没有到来。在这样的年代,他便能幻想着去太空旅行,到月球上去探险,这种超前的科学预见实在难能可贵。这一段主要谈论了物理学上的辐射能的问题,特别是引力问题。并预见到不受太阳和月亮引力的物质的存在可能性。虽然在地球上仍未发现这种物质,但在太空中引力的变化是巨大的,产生了失重现象。作者关于这一物理现象的解释并未使用多少科技性或专业的词汇,却用极其普通的语言,浅显易懂地作了说明。因此,在翻译中也要避免使用过大的词汇,而用明白晓畅,通俗浅显的语言将原文的风格再现出来。

I started to unscrew the glass lid of the manhole. The danser air within our sphere began to escape singing like a kettle. Cavor stopped me. It was evident the pressure outside was very much less than it was within. My blood vessels began to beat in my ears, and the sound of Cavor's movements decreased. I was breathless and dizzy. Cavor sat with a cylinder of oxygen at hand to restore our pressure. He prepared a drink and insisted on my sharing it with him, before he permitted me to resume unscrewing. I lifted the glass lid and laid it carefully on the bundle. I knelt beside the edge of the manhole, and peered over it. Beneath, within a yard of my face, lay the untrodden snow of the moon.

Cavor thrust his head through the hole in his blanket and

wrapped it about him. He sat down on the edge of the manhole, hesitated for a moment, then dropped down and stood on the soil of the moon. Then he drew himself together and leapt.

It seemed to me to be an extremely big leap. He seemed twenty or thirty feet off. He was standing high upon a rock and signalling to me. Perhaps he was shouting, but the sound did not reach me.

......

I found myself flying through the air, saw the rock on which Cavor stood coming to meet me, and clutched it in a state of utter amazement. Cavor bent down and shouted in piping tones for me to be careful.

我动手拧松舱口玻璃盖板的螺丝。球体内部浓度较高的空气开始发出水壶冒气的咝咝声向外逃逸。凯沃叫我停下来。很显然，外面的气压比里面低得多。我的耳朵听到自己身上的血管在咚咚地跳，凯沃的动作所发出的声音听不清了。我感到呼吸短促，头晕目眩。凯沃坐在那里，身边放了个氧气瓶，准备恢复球体内的气压。他配了一杯饮料，坚持要我和他一起喝了之后，才让我继续旋开舱口螺丝。我卸掉了玻璃盖挡板，轻手轻脚地把它放在包袱上，然后跪在舱口边上往外看。下面，离我的脸不到一码远，就是月球上从未有人践踏过的积雪。

凯沃把头伸出毯子领口，然后把毯子紧紧裹在身上。他坐在舱口旁边，踌躇了一会，跳了下去，站在月球的土地上。然后他纵身一跳。

我觉得他这一跳真远，似乎跳到二、三十英尺开外。他高高地站在一块岩石上面向我打手势。也许他在喊叫，可我听不到他的声音。

......

我觉得自己在空中飞,看见凯沃站着的那块岩石向我迎来。在极度惊讶的心境中,我一把抓住了它。凯沃弯下腰来,尖声叫着,叫我当心。

以上这一段取自《月球探险记》第二章。作者对从未有人登临过的月球作了符合科学的预见——月球上空气稀薄。人在月球上因舱内外压差而产生了各种生理反应,如浑身的血液在沸腾,呼吸短促,头晕目眩等。踏上月球后又因缺少引力,人轻轻一跳便是二三十码远。此外因为空气的稀薄,二三十码远外的喊叫声都无法听到。原文的描写很生动、细微,煞有其事地把整个过程和具体的感觉都一一描绘出来,甚至把舱内较浓的空气发出的声音比喻成水壶冒气的咝咝声,真使人有如临其境之感。译文也尽量使用生动、形象的语言,再现了原文的风貌,如用了一些四字词,"呼吸短促,头晕目眩"。译文将"coming to meet me"译成"向我迎来"不仅更符合原文的用词,也将这一跳的距离与速度描绘得有声有色。此外译文中还加用了"咝咝"这样的象声词,使故事的叙述格外生动具体。

He was not alone.

There was noting to indicate the fact but the white hand of the liny gauge on the board before him. The control room was empty but for himself, there was no sound other than the murmur of the drivers—but the white hand had moved. It had been on zero when the little ship was launched from the *stardust*, now, an hour later, it had crept up. There was something in the supplies closet across the room, it was saying, some kind of a body that rediated heat.

It could be but one kind of a body—a living, human body.

He learned back in the pilot's chair and drew a deep breath, considering what he would have to do. He was an EDS pilot, inured to the sight of death since accustomed to it and to viewing the dying of another man with an objective lack of emotion, and he had no choice in what he must do. There could be no alternative——but it required a few moments of conditioning for even an EDS pilot to prepare himself to walk across the room coldly, deliberately , to take the life of a man he had yet to meet.

He would, of course, do it. It was the law, stated very bluntly and definitely in grim Paragraph L, Section 8, on International Regulations: *Any stowaway discovered in an EDS shall be jettisoned immediately following discovery.*

不只是他一人。

除了仪表板上刻着刻度的测试仪上的白色指针之外没有任何东西能说明这一事实。控制室里除他以外,别无他人;除了发动机的嗡嗡声之外,也别无其他声响——但白色指针已经移动了。当这一小的急救飞船从巡航飞船星尘号上发射出来时,指针指在零上。现在,一个小时过去了,指针向上移动了。这表明船舱一边的贮藏室里有东西,有某种散发热量的活体。

只可能有一种活体——活的人体。

他靠在驾驶座上,深吸了一口气,思考着该怎么办。他是名急救飞船的飞行员,由于看惯了死亡的景象,客观地对待别人的死不动感情,因此对死已熟视无睹。他也没有别的选择——但即使是这样一个急救飞船的飞行员要平静走过机舱,有意地去结束他要见到的那个人的生命,也需要有几分钟的时间作思想上的准备。

他当然会干掉他。这是法律,无情的星际条例第八章第L款明确无误地规定:急救飞船内一经发现偷渡者,应立即抛出舱外。

本段文字选自美国当代著名的科学幻想小说家汤姆·戈德温(Tom Godwin)所创作的《冷酷的方程式》(The Cold Equation)的开头部分。根据星际条例:急救飞船内一经发现偷渡者,必须即刻抛出舱外。这是太空拓荒所必不可少的法令。飞船刚从星尘号发射出来一小时之后便发现散发体热的偷渡者。飞船驾驶员正要按章执行这令人扫兴的差使时,却意外地发现偷渡者是位少女。故事便围绕这个执法观念与人道主义的矛盾展开了。小说的一开头便布置了悬念,He was not alone. 如何翻译这句话,既符合原意又保持悬念呢？译者将其译成"不只是他一人"。这一句话读来唐突,却能引起读者兴趣和好奇,而且在句子长度上也与原文相符。这种译法是十分成功的。这虽是一部科幻小说,讲的是太空航行,其实幻想只是作为一种背景,其主题却是情与法的斗争,与一般小说无异。这一类的科幻小说文学味更浓一些。在翻译时完全可以像对待其他通俗小说一样来处理。

附：练习

将下列科幻故事译成中文。

① Theremon nodded thoughtfully and held out his glass for more liquor. Sheerin grudgingly allowed a few ruby drops to leave the bottle.

"It was twenty years ago," he continued after remoistening his own throat, "that it was finally demonstrated that the Law of Universal Gravitaion accounted exactly for the orbital motions of the six suns. It was a great triumph."

Sheerin stood up and walked to the window, still clutching his bottle. "And now we're getting to the point. In the last decade, the motions of Lagash about Alpha were computed according to gravity, and *it did not account for the orbit observed*; not even when all perturbations due to the other suns were included. Either the law was invalid, or there was another, as yet unknown, factor involved."

Theremon joined Sheerin at the window and gazed out past the wooded slopes to where the spires of Saro City gleamed bloodily on the horizon. The newsman felt the tension of uncertainty grow within him as he cast a short glace at Beta. It glowed redly at zenith, dwarfed and evil.

"Go ahead, sir," he said softly.

Sheerin replied, "Astronomers stumbled about for years, each proposed theory more untenable than the one before——until Aton had the inspiration of calling in the Cult. The head of the Cult, Sor 5, had access to certain data that simplified the problem considerably Aton set to work on a new track."

"What if there were another nonluminous planetary body such as Lagash? If there were, you know, it would shine only by reflected light, and if it were composed of bluish rock, as Lagash itself largely is, then in the redness of the sky, the eternal blaze of the suns would make it invisible——drown it out completely."

Theremon whistled, "What a screwy idea!"

"You think *that's screwy*? Listen to this: Suppose this body rotated about Lagash at such a distance and in such an orbit and had such a mass that its attraction would exactly account for the deviations of Lagash's orbit from theory——do you know what would happen?"

The columnist shook his head.

"Well, sometimes this body would get in the way of a sun." And Sheerin emptied what remained in the bottle at a draft.

(*Nightfall*, by Issac Asimov)

② Tommy Dort went into the captain's room with his last pair of stereo-photos and said:

"I'm through, sir. These are the last two pictures I can take."

He handed over the photographs and looked with professional interest at the visiplates which showed all space outside the ship. Subdued, deep-red lighting indicated the controls and such instruments as the quartermatster on duty needed for navigation of the spaceship *Llanvabon*. There was a deeply cushioned control chair. There was the little gadget of oddly angled mirrors——remote descendant of the back-view mirrors of twentieth century motorists——which allowed a view of all the visiplates without turning the head. And there were the huge plates which were so much more satisfactory for a direct view of space.

The *Llanvabon* was a long way from home. The plates, which showed every star of visual magnitude and could be stepped up to any desired magnification, portrayed stars of every imaginable degree of brilliance, in the startingly different colors they show outside of atmosphere. But every one was unfamiliar. Only two constellations could be recognized as seen from Earth, and they were shrunken and distorted. The Milky Way seemed vaguely out of place. But even such oddities were minor compared to a sight in the forward plates.

There was a vast, vast mistiness ahead. A luminous mist. It seemed motionless. It took a long time for any appreciable nearing to appear in the vision plates, though the spaceship's velocity indicator showed an incredible speed. The mist was the Crab Nebula, six light-years long, three and a half light-years thick, and outward-reaching members that in the telescopes of Earth gave it some resemblamce to the creature for which it was named. It was a cloud of gas, infinitely tenuous, reaching half again as far as from Sol to its nearest neighbor-sun. Deep within it burned two stars; a double star; one component the familiar yellow of the sun of Earth, the *other an* unholy white.

(*First Contact*, by Murray Leinster)

③ And he got results. He was lucky to begin with and even luckier when he formularized the law of probability and reduced it to such low terms that he knew almost to the item what experiments not to try. When the cloudy, viscous semifluid on the watch glass began to move itself he knew he was on the right track. When it began to seek food on its own he began to be excited. When it divided and, in a few hours, redivided, and each part grew and divided again, he was triumphant, for he had created life.

He nursed his brain children and sweated and strained over then, and he designed baths of various vibrations for them, and inoculated and dosed and sprayed them. Each move he made taught him the next. And out of his tanks and tubes and incubators came amoebalike creatures, and then ciliated animalcules, and more and more rapidly he produced animals with eye spots, nerve cysts, and then—victory of victories—a real blastopod, possessed of many cells instead of one. More slowly he developed a gastropod, but once he had it, it was not too difficult for him to give it organs, each with a specified function, each inheritable.

Then came cultured mollusklike things, and creatures with more and more perfected gills. The day that a nondescript thing wriggled up an inclined board out of a tank, threw flaps over its gills and feebly breathed air, Kidder quit work and went to the other end of the island and got disgustingly drunk. Hangover and all, he was soon back in the lab, forgetting to eat, forgetting to sleep, tearing into his problem.

He turned into a scientific byway and ran down his other great triumph—accelerated metabolism. He extracted and refined the stimulating factors in alcohol, cocoa, heroin, and Mother Nature's prize dope runner, *cannabis indica*. Like the scientist who, in analyzing the various clotting agents for blood treatments, found that oxalic acid and oxalic alone was the active factor, Kidder isolated the accelerators and decelerators, the stimulants and soporifics, in every substance that ever undermined a man's morality and/or caused a "noble experiment." In the process he found one thing he needed badly——a colorless elixir that made sleep the unnecessary and avoidable wasted of time it should be. Then and there he went on a twenty-four-hour shift.

(*Microcosmic God*, by Theodore Sturgeon)

第六章 文学文体的翻译

第一节 文学文体的语言特点与翻译

文学作品不同于应用文、新闻、广告和科技材料。后四者皆为实用性的体裁,有其明确的目的和具体的用途。文学作品不拘一格,很难限于某一特殊的目的和用途。

文学可以说是语言的艺术。科学语言是直指的,它要求语言符号与其所指的对象完全吻合,因此科学语言趋向于使用类似数学或符号逻辑学那种标志系统。文学语言则更偏向于形象性。它远非仅仅用来指称或说明什么,它还有表意传情的一面,说明作者或人物的态度和语气,甚至强调文字符号本身的意义,强调词语的声音象征,如格律、音韵等。

在文学作品中,语言被用来写景,渲染气氛;写人,塑造形象;写心,分析心理;写情,呼唤人性;写物,树立象征;写事,制造悬念。文学语言具有形象、抒情、含蓄、幽默、讽刺性、象征性和韵律感等特征。翻译者要忠实、正确、流畅、优雅地将文学作品翻译成功,精确传达原作者的思想情感。文学翻译可以说是一种在原作严格限制下的再创作。

以美国文学的开拓者华盛顿·欧文(Washington Irving)的散文《圣诞之夜》(*Christmas Eve*)的一些段落为例:

It was a brilliant moonlight night, but extremely cold; our chaise whirled rapidly over the frozen ground; the postboy smacked his whip incessantly, and a part of the time his horses were on a gallop. "He knows where he is going," said my companion, laughing, "and is eager to arrive in time for some of the merriment and good cheer of the servants' hall. My father, you must know, is a bigoted devotee of the old school, and prides himself upon keeping up something of old English hospitality. He is a tolerable specimen of what you will rarely meet with nowadays in its purity, the old English country gentleman..."

...

We had passed for some time along the wall of a park, and at length the chaise stopped at the gate. It was in a heavy magnificent old style, of iron bars, fancifully wrought at top into flourishes and flowers. The huge square columns that supported the gate were surmounted by the family crest. Close adjoining was the porter's lodge, sheltered under dark fir—trees, and almost buried in shrubbery.

...

The most interesting couple in the dance was the young officer and a ward of the squire's, a beautiful blushing girl of seventeen. From several shy glances which I had noticed in the course of the evening, I suspected there was a little kindness growing up between them; and, indeed, the young soldier was just the hero to captivate a romantic girl. He was tall, slender, and handsome, and like most young British officers of late years, had picked up various small accomplishments on the Continent—he could talk French and Italian—draw landscapes, sing very tolerably—dance divinely; but, above all, he had been wounded at Waterloo:—what girl of seventeen, well read in poetry and romance, could resist such a mirror of chivalry and perfection!

The moment the dance was over, he caught up a guitar, and

lolling against the old marble fireplace, in an attitude which I am half inclined to suspect was studied, began the little French air of the Troubadour. The spuire, however, exclaimed against having anything on Christmas eve but good old English; upon which the young minstrel, casting up his eye for a moment, as if in an effort of memory, struck into another strain, and, with a charming air of gallantry, gave Herrick's "Night-Piece to Julia."

The song might or might not have been intended in compliment to the fair Julia, for so I found his partner was called; she, however, was certainly unconscious of any such application, for she never looked at the singer, but kept her eyes cast upon the floor. Her face was suffused, it is true, with a beautiful blush, and there was a gentle heaving of the bosom, but all that was doubtless caused by the exercise of the dance; indeed, so great was her indifference, that she amused herself with plucking to pieces a choice bouquet of hot-house flowers, and by the time the song was concluded the nosegay lay in ruins on the floor.

这是一个月明之夜，十分寒冷；我们的马车在冰冻的路上急驰，车夫不停"吧，吧"地挥动鞭子。一段时间马在飞奔。我的朋友笑着说："马夫知道回哪里，他急着到家好及时参加仆人们在大厅中的一些热闹活动，分享欢乐。你应该知道我的父亲是一个顽固不化的老古板，以保持英格兰古老的好客传统而自豪。他是当今你很少能遇见的一位差强人意的纯粹样板，古老英格兰的乡绅……"
……

我们的马车沿着花园围墙走了一段时间，最后停在大门前。门是古式的，宏伟、笨重，用铁条铸成，顶部盘成奇特的花样。巨大的方形门柱顶上是家族的徽记。门房就在旁边，藏在枞树的暗阴影下，几乎隐没于灌木丛中。

……

最有趣的一对舞伴是年轻的军官和受乡绅监护的一位十七岁的美丽的红颜少女。我注意到在晚会过程中姑娘好几次向他投去含羞的目光。由此我猜想俩人之间正产生一些亲密之感。的确,这位年轻军官正是征服多情少女的英雄。他身材颀长,面容英俊,像近年来大多数年轻的英国军官一样,在欧洲大陆学到了各种各样的细巧才能:他能讲法语和意大利语,会画风景画,歌唱得也不错,舞跳得神乎其神,而最重要的是他在滑铁卢战场上受过伤:——哪一个熟读诗歌和爱情故事的十七岁少女能抗拒这样一位英勇完美形象的化身呢!

舞一跳完,他立即拿起一把吉他,斜靠在古老的大理石壁炉边,弹起了特鲁巴杜的法国小曲,那种姿态我颇为怀疑是故意摆出来的。然而乡绅却高声反对在圣诞前夕弹奏别的乐曲,只准奏古老美妙的英国音乐。于是这位年轻的吟唱诗人抬眼思索了一会儿,似乎在回想什么,随即弹起另一首歌谣,带着动人的豪放姿态唱起了赫里克的"献给朱丽娅的夜曲"。

这首歌也许不是故意唱来恭维漂亮的朱丽娅的,因为我发现他的舞伴正好叫朱丽娅,然而她却肯定不知道歌的用意,因为她一直不望唱歌的人,垂下两眼只盯着地板。她的脸涨得通红,楚楚动人,这倒是真的,胸部也在轻轻地起伏。不过这一切无疑是由于跳舞运动引起的。的确她一点不在意,只是埋头把一束暖房里培养出来的漂亮鲜花撕成一瓣瓣,歌唱完时整个花束全都毁去,洒在地板上。

从这篇优美的散文中,不难看出文学语言的一些基本特征。

第一,形象性。作者用生动的语言描绘出各种栩栩如生的形象,给读者以具体而深刻的印象。写景时,一幅幅真实的图画呈现在读者的眼前,创造出一种作者着意渲染的气氛。例如文章的第一句话:"这是一个月明之夜,十分寒冷;我们的马车在冰冻的路上急驰,"就将隆冬的乡间夜景生动地嵌在了画面上。天上是一轮明月,脚下是冰冻的道路,一辆马车在急驰,似乎你可以听见只有那嗒嗒的蹄声打破这清冷的寂静。写人时,则将一个个真实的人物勾勒出来,使读者如闻其声,如见其人。文中对年轻军官与十七岁少女的描绘就是一个典型的例子。军官的大胆炫耀与姑娘的娇羞作态形成有趣的对比,形象分外鲜明。

第二,抒情性。文章的最后一段有一段十分抒情的描述:

……I had scarecely got into bed when a strain of music seemed to break forth in the air just below the window. I listened, and found it proceeded from a band, which I concluded to be the waits from some neighboring village. They went round the house, playing under the windows. I drew aside the curtains to hear them more distinctly. The moonbeams fell through the upper part of the casement, partially lighting up the antiquated apartment. The sounds, as they receded, became more soft and aerial, and seemed to accord with the quiet and moonlight. I listened and listened — they became more and more tender and remote, and, as, they gradually died away, my head sunk upon the pillow, and I fell asleep.

我刚要上床睡觉,一串乐声似乎就在窗下响起。我侧耳倾听,发现是一个乐队在演奏,我断定是邻村来的圣诞乐队。他们绕着屋子走,在窗下奏乐。我拉开窗帘以便听得更清楚。月光透过落地窗的上部,部分地照亮了这一古旧的房间。随着乐声的远去,声音变得更加轻柔飘渺,似乎和谐地与四周的宁静及月光相伴。我倾听着倾听着——乐声越来越微弱,越遥远,逐渐地逝去。我的头落在枕上,安然睡去。

这一段作者用抒情的笔调描绘了轻柔的音乐和静谧的月光,更描绘了音乐和月光在人物心中留下的印象。作者虽未明确告诉读者人物在想什么,但从开始的"倾听"到最后的"倾听"又"倾听"的动作中,不难猜出人物的快乐与宁静的心情。这种将客观环境与主观心理相结合、将情与景相结合的描写手法是抒情的典型手段。

第三,含蓄性。好的文学作品既然是启示性的,就要求读者有更大的参与性。作者往往不把意思明白地说出而尽量留有余地,让读者自己去思索、去寻找结论。从大的方面说,任何人、物或事都需要通过读者自己去认识,作者本不应把个人的看法强加给读者。从小的方面说,一句话如果表达得太直也就失去了回味的余地。点到即止,暂不说破,岂不更能引起读者的兴趣?例如本文作者通过对青年军官与美丽少女的神态表情、行为举止的描述已使读者领悟到两者之间的情感,但作者并未直截了当地道出,而故意含蓄地说:"I suspected there was a little kindness growing up between them."此句中的"kindness"一词,并非常见的"和善、仁慈"之意,而是相互间的"喜爱",但又不能公然译出,一语道破,而必须既保留原文的含蓄性又能使读者悟出其真实的意思。译文所用的"亲切之感"一词既表达了作者的原意,又不失其幽默感。

第四,幽默感。本篇散文对年轻军官与少女的描绘不仅生动地突出了两者的形象,更使读者感受到了字里行间作者的幽默感。例如军官在欧洲学到的各种才能正是征服上流社会女性的本领,其实这些才能并无多大意义,作者幽默地用"small"一词来形容。特别是他在滑铁卢受过伤,这使他在姑娘心目中变成了英雄,而这位姑娘恰恰又"熟读诗歌和爱情故事",情窦初开,自然轻而易举地被他征服了。这是上层社会中常见的现象,作者用幽默笔调使其变成了一种令人好笑的事。这种笑是一种会心的笑。

第五,讽刺性。这种讽刺性指的是反语法,即 irony,说的是一回事,其含义却是另一回事,字面的意思和深层的含义正好相反。这是文学作品中常用的一种修辞手段。它可以使文字分外生动,深化表达的思想,给读者以强烈印象,同时也是创造幽默的一种方式。本文作者在描绘朱丽娅激动的感情时故意说"然而她却肯定不知道歌的用意,因为她一直不望唱歌的人,垂下两眼只盯着地板。她的脸涨得通红,楚楚动人,这倒是真的,胸部也在轻轻地起伏。不过这一切无疑是由于跳舞运动引起的。的确她一点不在意……。"她真的不懂歌的用意吗?脸红和呼吸急促真的仅是跳舞运动的结果吗?她真的一点都不在意吗?当然不是。恰恰相反,她的心中正掀起感情的波涛,却故意装出一副漠不关心的样子。读者们决不会被这些句子的表面词义所欺骗,他们会心中暗笑这位天真多情的姑娘。

第六,象征性。大而化之,我们甚至可以将明喻、暗喻、转喻等修辞手段都概括在这一项目之内。象征是用某一具体事物来表示某种抽象的意义。例如人们通常以玫瑰来象征爱情,白雪来象征纯洁等。在文学作品中除了这些通常为大家所接受的象征外,在不同的上下文中某些具体事物具有作者所赋予它的特殊意义。例如本文中的滑铁卢已经不只是地名,也不只是战场的名字,它已成了英雄行为的代名词,象征着英勇无畏。于是每个参加了这一战役的军人都成了击败拿破仑的英雄,受人崇敬,自然更受年轻姑娘的崇拜。象征是一种十分重要的文学手段。它不仅简练具体,给人以感觉得到的形象,更能深化含义,表达出只能意会而不可言传的思想和感情。

第七,韵律感。文学语言不同于一般实用性的语言,不仅在于内容美,也在于形式美,即语言形式本身的美。这种美主要表现在语言的韵律和节奏上。最具有韵律美的文学形式自然首推诗歌。它对韵律有特别严格的要求。即使是散文作品,其强烈的节奏感也会使人对语言表达的意义留下深刻的印象。例如本篇第一句话"It was a brilliant moonlight night, but extremely cold; our chaise whirled rapidly over the frozen ground; the postboy smacked his whip incessantly, ..."其中 moonlight 和 night 是非常和谐的尾韵,而"smacked his whip incessantly"使人几乎听到了那"吧,吧"

的连续鞭子声。在翻译这句时应尽可能将这种节奏与响声传达给读者。本文中更具韵律的是那首《献给朱丽娅的夜曲》。在译文中须相应体现歌词的韵味。如歌词的第一节为:

Her eyes the glow-worm lend thee,
The shooting stars attend thee.
   And the elves also,
   Whose little eyes glow
Like the sparks of fire befriend thee.

你的眼睛像清亮的萤火,
你的眼睛似灿烂的流星。
   还有那小精灵
   永远关照你
目光中闪耀着火一般的真情。

以上七个方面,只是文学语言的一般特征,远未能概括其所有方面,但至少在翻译文学作品时应注意这些特征。文学作品的译文同样必须也是文学作品。它必须将原作的文学特征忠实地、一丝不苟地传达给译文的读者,不仅是思想感情,还包括语言形式,即不但要达到信息上的等值,还应达到艺术上的等值。做到这一点是十分不容易的。这就是为什么人们常把翻译看成是一个再创造过程的缘故。

一般说来,文学体裁共分为四大类,即诗歌、散文、戏剧、小说。无论在英语中还是汉语中,诗歌均是最古老的文学体裁。这是容易理解的,因为在有文字记载之前,最早的文学形式是口头文学,而诗歌就是直接从口头文学发展而来的。真正意义上的小说无论在汉语中还是英语中都是最年轻的文学体裁。下面按散文、小说、戏剧、诗歌的次序,分别论述这四种体裁文学作品的翻译。

第二节 散　文

英语散文作为正式的文学体裁，起始于16世纪末，17世纪初。第一位英国散文家是弗朗西斯·培根(Francis Bacon)。英语散文一词"essay"是从法国散文家蒙田(Montaigne)为自己的散文集所取的题名"Essai"移植而来。培根也将essays作为自己散文集的名字。18世纪是英语散文蓬勃发展、群星璀璨的时代。一大批散文家崛起文坛，争奇斗艳。19世纪的浪漫主义运动更推动了英语散文的发展，在散文文体上有很大的突破。以查尔斯·兰姆(Charles Lamb)为代表的浪漫主义散文家在原有的非正式散文体的基础上进一步创造了自由自在、无拘无束、表达个人思想感情的小品文。20世纪以来科学技术的迅猛发展对散文文体产生了重大的影响，通俗的口语和谈话式的风格十分显目地引入到散文中，使散文更加接近人民大众，更加有力地干预生活，更加直接地反映普通人民的思想感情。

英语散文的文体一般可分正式散文体和非正式散文体两大类。前者采取客观的态度讨论问题，说理透彻，逻辑性强，结构严谨，用词讲究，风格凝重。有的作品浓缩到几乎句句皆可成为座右铭的程度。培根就是典型的代表。后者则是个人思想感情的抒发。作者让自己的想象力自由地翱翔，时而谈到这一点，时而又转到那一点，像春蚕吐丝，若即若离，婉转曲折，点到即止，主题虽小，意义深刻。文章结构散漫，语言浅近，风格自由，生动幽默，轻松自然，作者的个性跃然纸上。

如今这两种散文的区别已不是那样泾渭分明。正式散文的作者也常常在作品中表现出强烈的个性，非正式散文的作者却往往用轻松的文笔来探讨一个严肃的主题。

在翻译正式散文时，必须注意使译文的笔调适合原文的庄重风格。以培根的散文《谈读书》为例,这是一篇具有典范性的正式散文。主题严肃,形式凝重,句法严谨,词藻绚烂,语言准确,反映出作者无穷的智慧与冷静的观察。经过精雕细琢的一字一句几乎都可以成为一条格言,洗练含蓄,意味无穷,每句话都可以作为一篇文章的标题,演绎发挥。

OF STUDIES

Studies serve for delight, for ornament, and for ability. Their chief use for delight is in privateness and retiring; for ornament, is in discourse; and for ability, is in the judgment and disposition of business. For expert men can execute, and perhaps judge of particulars, one by one; but the general counsels, and the plots, and marshalling of affairs come best from those that are learned. To spend too much time in studies is sloth; to use them too much for ornament is affectation; to make judgment wholly by their rules is the humor of a scholar. They perfect nature, and are perfected by experience; for natural abilities are like natural plants, that need pruning by study; and studies themselves do give forth directions too much at large, except they be bounded in by experience. Crafty men contemn studies, simple men admire them, and wise men use them; for they teach not their own use; but that is a wisdom without them, and above them, won by observation. Read not to contradict and confute, nor to believe and take for granted, nor to find talk and discourse, but to weigh and consider. Some books are to be tasted, others to be swallowed, and some few to be chewed and digested: that is, some books are to be read only in parts, others to be read, but not curiously; and some few to be read wholly, and with diligence and attention. Some books also may be read by deputy and extracts made of them by others; but that would be only in the less important arguments and the meaner sort of books: else distilled books are like common distilled waters, flashy things.

Reading makes a full man, conference a ready man, and writing an exact man. And, therefore, if a man write little, he had need have a great memory; if he confer little, he had need have a present wit; and if he read little, he had need have much cunning to seem to know that he does not. Histories make men wise, poets witty, the mathematics subtle, natural philosophy deep, moral grave, logic and rhetoric able to contend. *Abeunt studia in mores* (Studies are transformed into manners). Nay, there is no stone or impediment in the wit but may be wrought out by fit studies: like as diseases of the body may have appropriate exercises. Bowling is good for the stone and reins, shooting for the lungs and breast, gentle walking for the stomach, riding for the head, and the like. So if a man's wit be wandering, let him study the mathematics, for in demonstrations, if his wit be called away never so little, he must begin again; if his wit be not apt to distinguish or find difference, let him study the schoolmen, for they are *cymini sectores* (hair-splitters). If he be not apt to beat over matters and to call up one thing to prove and illustrate another, let him study the lawyers' cases: so every defect of the mind may have a special receipt.

谈 读 书

读书足以怡情,足以博彩,足以长才。其怡情也,最见于独处幽居之时;其博彩也,最见于高谈阔论之中;其长才也,最见于处世判事之际。练达之士虽能分别处理细事或一一判别枝节,然纵观统筹,全局策划,则舍好学深思者莫属。读书费时过多易惰,文采藻饰太盛则矫,全凭条文断事乃学究故态。读书补天然不足,经验又补读书之不足,盖天生才干犹如自然花草,读书然后知如何修剪移接;而书中所学,如不以经验范之,则又大而无当。有一技之长者鄙读书,无知者羡读书,唯明智之士用读书,然书并不以用处告人,用书之智不在书中,而在书外,全凭观察得之。读书时不可存心诘难作者,不可尽信书上所言,亦不可只为寻章摘句,而应推敲细思。书有浅尝者,有可吞食者,少数则须咀嚼消化。换言之有只须读其部分者,有只须大体涉猎者,少数则须全读,读时须全神贯注,孜孜不倦。书亦可请人代读,取其所作摘要,但只限题材较次或价值不高者,否则书经提炼犹如水经蒸馏,淡而无味矣。

　　读书使人充实,讨论使人机智,笔记使人准确。因此不常作笔记者须记忆特强,不常讨论者须天生聪颖,不常读书者须欺世有术,始能无知而显有知。读书使人明智,读诗使人灵秀,数学使人周密,科学使人深刻,伦理使人庄重,逻辑修辞之学使人善辩:凡有所学,皆成性格。人之才智但有滞碍,无不可读适当之书使之顺畅,一如身体百病,皆可借适宜之运动除之。滚球利睾肾,射箭利胸肺,慢步宜肠胃,骑术利头脑,诸如此类。如智力不集中,可令读数学,盖演题须全神贯注,稍有分散即须重演;如不能辨异,可令读经院哲学,盖是辈皆吹毛求疵之人;如不善求同,不善以一物阐证另一物,可令读律师之案卷。如此头脑中凡有缺陷,皆有特药可医。

(王佐良　译)

　　译出这样一篇词语精练、含义深刻的正式散文,实在不是一种易事。王佐良先生的这篇译文从精神到形式都精确而优美地传达了原文的思想和风格,做到了既形似又神似。17世纪培根的散文,恰似汉语中的古典文言文一样。第一,用词简练、准确,常常难以增减,也无法替换,词小而意深。以第一句为例,delight, ornament

和 ability 分别代表了读书的三种功能,意义明确,一字千钧。王先生的译文也用了三个词,"怡情"、"博彩"和"长才",恰好一一对应起来,几乎完美无缺,很难找到其他词来替代。若换之以较长的词语,如"娱乐身心"、"美化谈吐"和"增长才干",其意思虽然相似,但由词而增长至短语,其分量就大不一样了。又如原文的"Crafty men contemn studies, simple men admire them, and wise men use them."一句中 contemn, admire 和 use 三个词分别译为"鄙"、"羡"、"用",给人以精至不可再精的印象。

第二,句子结构紧凑,绝无赘语,可以说到了一字不可减的程度。如原文的"Reading makes a full man, conference a ready man, and writing an exact man."每个从句仅四到五个词。"makes"在后面两个从句中都省略掉了。译文也同样用简练的短句译出:"读书使人充实,讨论使人机智,笔记使人准确。"每句六字,短小有力,结构谨严,意义明确。

第三,在修辞上最突出的特点为平行结构。可以说通篇文章都由许多排句构成,给人以平衡美。再以第一句为例,作者连用了三个 for 短语。第二句又接着重复地用了上句的三个 for 短语,后面接着三个 in 短语。这样的排列不仅形成了均衡的结构,更深化了意义。在翻译这两句时,也必须采用同样的平行结构,才能传达出原文的形式美。第一句译文连用了三个"足以",第二句在三个"其"这一词后又连用了三个"最见于"短语,十分传神地表达原文的文风。

第四,在声律上节奏感强烈。由于句短词精、结构均匀、轻重音节相间,故读上去铿锵悦耳,掷地有声。仍以第一句为例,"for delight, for ornament, and for ability"后两个为三音节词,delight 虽为二音节,由于"i"为长音,故读上去几乎音长一样,这就达到了几乎同样的节奏。第二句话在 in 短语的设计上,作者用两个长的短语夹住一个短的短语,即"in privateness and retiring","in discourse"和"in the judgement and disposition of business",最后的短语最长,以便给全句一个稳重的结尾。最值得一提的是王佐良先生的第二句译文,三个从句的字数完全一样,而在结尾时分别用了"之时","之中","之际"三词,不仅使音节数量相同,而声韵上又有变化,达到了既均衡又丰富的音律美。

非正式散文的语言风格不同于正式散文,而兰姆所创造的小品文更加将非正式的风格推向极致,其最大的特征为幽默和倾吐作者的心怀。现以他写的《梦中儿女》(*Dream children, a Reverie*)为例,一篇约1500字的散文竟未分段落,一气呵成。并非作者标新立异,故作惊人之举,实为内容与形式的需要。一个冬日的夜晚,作者坐在炉旁,对围绕膝边的孩子们讲起了往事。从房屋讲到了祖母,讲到了自己的童年,讲到幼年时调皮的伯父,最后讲到孩子死去的母亲。整篇散文就是这一叙述的记录。作者滔滔不绝地讲下去,完全没有考虑去划分段落,也没有必要这样做。在转换话题时作者使用了"Then I went on to say how …"或者"I told how …"的句型,并夹之以记下孩子们的反应,使读者一目了然,清楚地了解文章的转折与发展。读者读完后会深深被这生动描绘的父母、夫妻、子女、和兄弟姐妹之间的亲情所感动。出人意外的是读到末尾读者才发现这原来是作者的一场白日梦。作者从未结过婚,更谈不上有孩子。兰姆向读者开了一个大玩笑,这正是作者幽默之所在。然而在这玩笑背后却隐藏着作者深沉的悲哀和叹息,反映了他的辛酸的人生经历。

这里仅摘一段,可见非正式散文风格之一斑。

Alice spread her hands. Then I told what a tall, upright, graceful person their great-grandmother Field once was; and how in her youth she was esteemed the best dancer—here Alice's little right foot played an involuntary movement, till upon my looking grave, it desisted—the best dancer, I was saying, in the county, till a cruel disease, called a cancer, came and bowed her down with pain; but it could never bend her good spirits, or make them stoop, but they were still upright, because she was so good and religious. Then I told how she was used to sleep by herself in a lone chamber of the great lone house; and how she believed that an apparition of two infants was to be seen at midnight gliding up and down the great staircase near where she slept, but she said "those innocents would do her no harm"; and how frightened I used to be, though in those days I had my maid to sleep with me, because I was never half so good or religious as she—and yet I never saw the infants. Here John expanded all his eyebrows and tried to look courageous.

……接着我告诉他们太奶奶菲尔德是一个高个子的女人,性格正直,举止优雅;在年轻时候大家都认为她舞跳得最好——这时艾丽丝小巧的右脚不由自主地动了起来,直到我脸上显出严肃的表情才停止——我是说在全县她的舞跳得最好,后来她染上了可怕的疾病,叫作癌症,让她受着痛苦的折磨,但疾病压不垮她的坚强意志,也不能让她低头,她仍然精神抖擞,因为她非常善良,非常虔诚。接着我告诉他们通常她独自睡在这幢孤寂的大屋中一间孤寂的房间里;她相信半夜里会看见两个幼童的鬼魂在她卧室旁边的大楼梯上溜上溜下,但她说"这两个天真的小家伙不会伤害她。"而我那时尽管总和保姆睡在一起,却常感到害怕,因为我连她的一半善良和虔诚都赶不上——不过我从来未见过这两个孩子的鬼魂。这时约翰展开眉毛,努力装出一副勇敢的样子。

这是一篇典型的风格轻松自由、结构散漫随意的非正式散文。第一,从结构上看,所选的这一段仅包含三个句子,前两个长句主要由并列分句组成,间以主从分句,结构松散,这正是口语的特征。最后一短句实为插语,叙述约翰的反应,为这一段叙述的内容作一结尾,下面好转入另一主题。虽然全文未分段落,然转折清晰,使读者能方便地跟上作者的思路。在翻译时必须采用同样的结构,并注意使用"接着我告诉他们……"这一不断出现的标志性用语。

第二,原文十分口语化,流利自然,句子结构简单,所用的词汇大都为日常的普通用语,因此在翻译时也必须使用口语化的语言,多用短句,多用普通词汇。例如将 apparition 译成"鬼魂"就比"幽灵"要更通俗一些。将"make them stoop"译成"让她低头"就既为日常用语又符合原文创造的形象。

第三,这毕竟是一篇具有很高文学品位的散文,作者用词十分讲究,有些词汇颇为文雅,如 upright, graceful,因此在翻译时也必须译出其优美的风格,不能一味追求口语化,否则就会流于粗劣。译文使用了"性格正直,举止优雅"两个短语,较好地传达了原文的意韵。

从散文的写作目的和手法出发,散文大致可分为四大类,即记叙文、描写文、说明文和议论文。

一、记叙文

记叙文大多记叙作者本人的亲身经历或者他听到或读到的故事传说、奇闻轶事。

其实在记叙文中具有重要意义的往往不是叙述的故事而是叙述者即作者本人。因为通过叙述故事他主要将自己的印象与体验传达给读者,让读者也感受到其中的意义。一个好的叙述者会选择一个有利的角度、采取一种动听的语调,使用某些生动的语言,来营造一种特有的气氛,使故事具有作者特殊的个性。就像一个老人,冬日黄昏坐在炉边向周围的人讲述往日的故事一样,他的声调、他的表情、他的手势使故事具有了特殊的风味,成了他表现个性的一个重要手段。听众也许早已听过这一段故事,甚至是听他本人说过,然而再听一遍时,仍然兴味盎然。因此在翻译时要特别重视原作的文风,要突出原作者的个性,要传达他所使用的独特语调,要表现某些词汇和语句的特殊用法。总之,要将原作的风格和韵味传送给读者。

以史蒂文森(Robert Louis Stevenson)的《牵驴旅行》(*Travels with a Donkey*)中的一段为例:

In a little place called Le Monastier, in a pleasant highland valley fifteen miles from Le Puy, I spent about a month of fine days. Monastier is notable for the making of lace, for drunkenness, for freedom of language, and for unparalleled political dissension. There are adherents of each of the four French parties—Legitimists, Orleanists, Imperialists, and Republicans—in this little mountain-town; and they all hate, loathe, decry, and calumniate each other. Except for business purposes, or to give each other the lie in a tavern brawl, they have laid aside even the civility of speech. 'Tis a mere mountain Poland. In the midst of this Babylon I found myself a rallying-point; every one was anxious to be kind and helpful to the stranger. This was not merely from the natural hospitality of mountain people, nor even from the surprise with which I was regarded as a man living of his own free will in Le Monastier, when he might just as well have lived anywhere else in this big world; it arose a good deal from my projected excursion southward through the Cevennes. A traveler of my sort was a thing hitherto unheard of in that district. I was looked upon with contempt, like a man who should project a journey to the moon, but yet with a respectful interest, like one setting forth for the inclement Pole. All were ready to help in my preparations; a crowd of sympathizers supported me at the critical moment of a bargain; not a step was taken but was heralded by glasses round and celebrated by a dinner or a breakfast.

在位于中央山脉 15 英里之外的风景宜人的高原山谷中,有一个名叫蒙纳斯梯尔的小地方。我在那里消磨了大约一个月的晴朗日子。蒙纳斯梯尔以生产花边、酗酒无度、口无遮拦和空前绝后的政治纷争而闻名于世。在这个山区小镇里,法国的四大政党——正统派、奥尔良党、帝制党与共和党——都各有党徒。他们相互仇恨、厌恶、攻击、诽谤。除了谈生意,或者在酒馆的口角中互相指责对方说谎之外,他们说起话来一点不讲文明。这里简直是个山里的波兰。在这个巴比伦似的文明之都,我却成了一个团结的中心。所有人都急切地想对我这个陌生人表示友善,愿意帮忙。这倒不仅是出于山区人民的天然好客精神,也不是因为大家惊奇地把我看成是一个本可以住在这一大世界的任何一个地方,却偏偏自愿选中蒙纳斯梯尔的人。这在很大程度上是因为我计划好了要向南穿过塞文山脉旅行。像我这样的旅行家在全区内简直是一个从未听说过的怪物。大家都对我不屑一顾,好像一个人计划要到月球旅行似的,不过又带有一丝敬重和兴趣,就像我是一个将出发到严寒的北极去冒险的人。大家都愿意帮助我作各种准备;在讨价还价的关键时刻,一大群同情者都支持我。在采取任何步骤之前都要先喝一顿酒,完了之后还要吃一顿晚饭或早饭。

这是一篇典型的叙事文,作者叙述了自己的一段亲身经历。他用幽默、讽刺的笔调将这一段很有趣的经历记叙出来,其目的并不是单纯地为了保存这一段记忆或娱乐读者。它反映了作者对世界、对人生以至对政治的看法。描述的虽是细微的事物,却反映了深刻的社会现象。在一个偏僻的山区小镇里,人民过着封闭落后的生活,与外界隔离,连外出旅行也被看成了是一个无法想象的冒险。然而带有讽刺性的是这样一个原始的小地方却仍然摆脱不了政治的影响,也被卷入了激烈的政治纷争。所幸者人们依然保持了天然的纯朴和热诚。作者的讽刺是善意的,更多的是幽默。

在翻译本篇散文时应十分注意传达出作者轻松幽默的笔调,这样才能反映出作者玩世不恭的风格。例如:"Monastier is notable for the making of lace, for drunkenness, for freedom of language, and for unparalleled political dissension."作者故意将不相关的四个方面放在一起,造成一种滑稽可笑的印象。有的词语是直截了当的表述,如"for drunkenness",有的却又使用委婉的说法,如"for freedom of language",有的又用夸张的语气,如"for unparalleled political dissension"。在翻译时也必须尽量使用相同的表达方式。译文译成:"蒙纳斯梯尔以生产花边、酗酒无度、口无遮拦和空前绝后的政治纷争而闻名。"不仅将原文的风格再现了出来,并且有意识使用了四个字的词语来表现原文连续使用四个"for"短语的平行结构。再以"a rallying-point"为例,如果只照字面意思译成"集中点"尚不足以表达原文的幽默含义。当地的人向来政见不一,四分五裂,吵闹不休,而"我"却成了一个中心,把不同意见的人集合起来,大家对我的态度却完全一致。故译成"团结的中心"就将深层的幽默含意准确地表达出来。而将"Babylon"扩译成"巴比伦似的文明之都"不仅使读者易于理解原词的意义,也反映出作者的讽刺意味。再以"a crowd of sympathizers"为例,如求汉语通俗化,本可译成"一群支持者",但如直译为"同情者"不但意思更为深刻,也更好地保留作者原有的幽默感。

再以华盛顿·欧文(Washington Irving)的《作者自叙》(*The Author's Account of Himself*)的开头部分为例:

I was always fond of visiting new scenes, and observing strange characters and manners. Even when a mere child I began my travels, and made many tours of discovery into foreign parts and unknown regions of my native city, to the frequent alarm of my parents, and the emolument of the town-crier. As I grew into boyhood, I extended the range of my observations. My holiday afternoons were spent in rambles about the surrounding country. I made myself familiar with all its places famous in history or fable. I knew every spot where a murder or robbery had been committed, or a ghost seen. I visited the neighboring villages, and added greatly to my stock of knowledge, by noting their habits and customs, and conversing with their sages and great men. I even journeyed one long summer's day to the summit of the most distant hill, whence I stretched my eye over many a mile of terra incognita, and was astonished to find how vast a globe I inhabited.

This rambling propensity strengthened with my years. Books of voyages and travels became my passion, and in devouring their contents, I neglected the regular exercises of the school. How wistfully would I wander about the pier-heads in fine weather, and watch the parting ships bound to distant climes! With what longing eyes would I gaze after their lessening sails, and waft myself in imagination to the ends of the earth!

我一直喜爱游历新的景点,见识新奇的人物和习俗。很小的时候我就开始旅行,许多次到本城陌生的区域和偏僻的地方去漫游,去探索。我的父母常常被害得为我担忧。当地的地保却因找到我而受到赏赐。我长大了一些的时候,观察的范围也随之扩大。每逢假日的下午,我总到附近的乡村去漫步。我对所有历史名胜或神话传说的地方都很熟悉。我知道什么地方发生过凶杀或抢劫,什么地方出现过鬼魂。邻近的村庄我都去过,留心各处的风俗习惯,并和当地的德高望重者交谈,这大大增长了我的见识。在一个漫长的夏日,我甚至登上了最远的山顶,极目四望,周围许多英里内全是不认识的地方。我惊奇地发现我居住的地球多么巨大。

随着年岁的增加,我喜爱漫游的脾气更盛。阅读有关航海和旅行的书籍成了我的爱好。我贪婪地读着,连学校的正课练习都耽误了。我多么渴望在晴朗的日子里到码头去漫步,眺望离去的船只驶向远方。我的眼睛充满向往,目送渐渐渐小的船帆,在幻想中我自己也随之漂向天涯海角!

　　这是一篇具有抒情风格的记叙文,语调显然与上一篇大不相同。作者想表达的不是玩世不恭的态度,而是从童年时代即怀有的对旅行的喜爱和对航海的向往。这是一种高尚有益的爱好,故作者从正面来叙述,所用的语言十分正规,态度积极,决无挖苦调笑之语。为了表达内心的情感,作者使用了优美的语言和抒情的笔调。这是翻译者必须牢牢掌握的基本特征。这种田园诗般的风格也增加了翻译的难度。

　　为了抒发情怀,作者对遣词构句十分着力。例如在开头第一句话中作者使用了"was fond of"一语,而未用更普通的"like"一词,因为其表达情感的深刻与文雅程度大不一样。因此在翻译这一短语时,用"喜爱"一词就比"喜欢"更适合。作者也十分注意句子结构的均衡。例如在第二句中就有两对平行的短语,第一对是"foreign parts and unknown regions",第二对是"to the frequent alarm of my parents, and the emolument of the town-crier"。好的译文应将这种平行结构的形式也表现出来。将其译成"陌生的区域和偏僻的地方"和"我的父母常常被害得为我担忧,当地的地保却因找到我而受到赏赐"大致可再现其原韵。又如"added greatly to my stock of knowledge"完全可译成"大大增加了我的知识",但如译成"大大增长了我的见识"却显然与上文更贴切一些。因为上文说的是"noting"和"conversing",其结果恰恰是"见识",而这个词也更雅一些。最具抒情格调的是最后一句话,"How wistfully would I wander about the pier-heads in fine weather, and watch the parting ships bound to distant climes! With what longing eyes would I gaze after their lessening sails, and waft myself in imagination to the ends of the earth!"作者不仅描绘出一幅美丽辽阔的图画,而且表达了内心的强烈情感和渴望。情与景融成一体。在翻译这一句时,千万不可损害其风格,必须也使用抒情的语言。译文的最后一句使用了"渴望"、"漫步"、"眺望"、"向往"、"目送"、"渐远渐小"和"天涯海角"等词语,比较忠实地向读者再现了原文的画面和作者内心的情感。

附:练习

将下列记叙文译成中文。

① My first visit to the school was when I was seven. A strapping girl of fifteen, in the customary sunbonnet and calico dress, asked me if I "used tobacco"—meaning did I chew it. I said no. It roused her scorn. She reported me to all the crowd, and said:

"Here is a boy seven years old who can't chew tobacco."

By the looks and comments which this produced I realized that I was a degraded object, and was cruelly ashamed of myself. I determined to reform. But It only made myself sick; I was not able to learn to chew tobacco. I learned to smoke fairly well, but that did not conciliate anybody and I remained a poor thing, and characterless. I longed to be respected, but I never was able to rise. Children have but little charity for one another's defects.
(*The Autobiography of Mark Twain*, edited by Charles Neider)

② When I reached the age of twelve I left the school for ever and got my first full-time job, as a grocer's boy. I spent my days carrying heavy loads, but I enjoyed it. It was only my capacity for hard work that saved me from early dismissal, for I could never stomach speaking to my "betters" with the deference my employer thought I should assume.

But the limit was reached one Tuesday — my half holiday. On my way home on that day I used to carry a large basket of provisions to the home of my employer's sister-in-law. As her house was on my way home I never objected to this.

On this particular Tuesday, however, just as we were putting the shutters up, a load of smoked hams was delivered at the shop. "Wait a minute," said the boss, and he opened the load and took out a ham, which he started to bone and string up.

I waited in growing impatience to get on my way, not for one minute but for quite a considerable time. It was nearly half-past two when the boss finished. He then came to me with the ham, put it in the basket beside me, and instructed me to deliver it to a customer who had it on order.

This meant going a long way out of my road home, so I looked up and said to the boss: "Do you know I finish at two on Tuesday?" I have never seen a man look more astonished than he did then. "What do you mean?" he gasped. I told him I meant that I would deliver the groceries as usual, but not the ham.

He looked at me as if I were some unusual kind of insect and burst into a storm of abuse. But I stood firm. He gave me up as hopeless and tried new tactics. "Go out and get another boy," he yelled at a shop-assistant.

"Are you going to deliver them or not?" the boss turned to me and asked in a threatening tone. I repeated what I had said before. "Then, out of here," he shouted. So I got out.

This was the first time I had serious trouble with an employer.   (*Revolt on the Clyde*, by William Gallacher)

③ I first heard this story in India, where it is told as if true — though any naturalist would know it couldn't be. Later I learned that a magazine version of it appeared shortly before the First World War. This account, and its author, I have never been able to track down.

The country is India. A colonial official and his wife are giving a large dinner party. They are seated with their guests — army officers and government attaches and their wives, and a visiting American naturalist — in their spacious dining room, which has a bare marble floor, open rafters and wide glass doors opening onto a veranda.

A spirited discussion springs up between a young girl who insists that women have outgrown the jumping-on-the-chair-at-the-sight-of-a-mouse era and a colonel who says that they haven't.

"A woman's unfailing reaction in any crisis," the colonel says, "is to scream. And while a man may feel like it, he has that ounce more of nerve control than a woman has. And that last ounce is what counts."

The American does not join in the argument but watches the other guests. As he looks, he sees a strange expression come over the face of the hostess. She is staring straight ahead, her muscles contracting slightly. With a slight gesture she summons the native boy standing behind her chair, and whispers to him. The boy's eyes widen, he quickly leaves.

Of the guests, none except the American notices this or sees the boy place a bowl of milk on the veranda just outside the open doors.

The American comes to with a start. In India, milk in a bowl means only one thing — bait for a snake. He realizes there must be a cobra in the room. He looks up at the rafters — the likeliest place — but they are bare. Three corners of the room are empty, and in the fourth the servants are waiting to serve the next course. There is only one place left — under the table.

His first impulse is to jump back and warn the others, but he knows the commotion would frighten the cobra into striking. He speaks quickly, the tone of his voice so arresting that it sobers everyone.

"I want to know just what control everyone at this table has. I will count three hundred — that's five minutes — and not one of you is to move a muscle. Those who move will forfeit 50 rupees. Ready!"

The 20 people sit like stone images while he counts. He is saying "... two hundred and eighty ..." when, out of the corner of his eye, he sees the cobra emerge and make for the bowl of milk. Screams ring out as he jumps to slam the veranda doors safely shut.

"You were right, Colonel!" the host exclaims. "A man has just shown us an example of perfect control."

"Just a minute," the American says, turning to his hostess. "Mrs. Wynnes, how did you know that cobra was in the room?"

A faint smile lights up the woman's face as she replies: "Because it was crawling across my foot."

(*Reader's Digest*, *1974*)

④ I was born in the working-class. Early I discovered enthusiasm, ambition, and ideals; and to satisfy these became the problem of my child-life. My environment was crude and rough and raw. I had no outlook, but an uplook rather. My place in society was at the bottom. Here life offered nothing but sordidness and wretchedness, both of the flesh and the spirit; for here flesh and spirit were alike starved and tormented.

Above me towered the collosal edifice of society, and to my mind the only way out was up. Into this edifice I early resolved to climb. Up above, men wore black clothes and boiled shirts, and women dressed in beautiful gowns. Also, there were good things to eat, and there was plenty to eat. This much for the flesh. Then there were the things of the spirit. Up above me, I knew, were unselfishness of the spirit, clean and noble thinking, keen intellectual living. I knew all this because I read "Seaside Library" novels, in which, with the exception of the villains and adventuresses, all men and women thought beautiful thoughts, spoke a beautiful tongue, and performed glorious deeds. In short, as I accepted the rising of the sun, I accepted that up above me was all that was fine and noble and gracious, all that gave decency and dignity to life, all that made life worth living and that remunerated one for his travail and misery.

But it is not particularly easy for one to climb up out of the working-class—especially if he is handicapped by the possession of ideals and illusions. I lived on a ranch in California, and I was hard put to find the ladder whereby to climb. I early inquired the rate of interest on invested money, and worried my child's brain into an understanding of the virtues and excellencies of that remarkable invention of man, compound interest. Further, I ascertained the current rates of wages for workers of all ages, and the cost of living. From all this data I concluded that if I began immediately and worked and saved until I was fifty years of age, I could then stop working and enter into participation in a fair portion of the delights and goodnesses that would then be open to me higher up in society. Of course, I resolutely determined not to marry, while I quite forgot to consider at all that great rock of disaster in the working-class world—sickness.

(*What Life Means to Me*, by Jack London)

⑤ Life in the White House is active and intense. For one thing, it is a city home and there is always the sense and sound of traffic outside. Sometimes there would be the sound of demonstrations. Inside, it often seemed as if there were never any real privacy as the household staff went about their work, and in the basement the kitchens were constantly bustling with preparations for the steady stream of breakfasts, luncheons, teas, receptions, and official dinners.

We tried at the beginning to cut back on some of the trappings. Pat and I agreed that we should reduce the number of stewards and aides who surround a President wherever he goes. I told Haldeman to have the two Navy medics who had served full time as the President's masseurs reassigned to some more productive duty. I immediately stopped what was to me the almost incredible practice of having the President's bed from the White House flown ahead whenever he traveled outside Washington so that he would never have to sleep in a strange bed. I said that I would need only Manolo and possibly one steward to take care of my clothes and meals when I went on weekend working trips to Camp David or Key Biscayne. We ordered the decommissioning of the two large Navy yachts that had been maintained exclusively for the President's use. We also tried to cut down on the numbers and security requirements of the Secret Service who were always with us.

But even so, life in the White House was confining, and this made the home we bought in summer 1969 for our retirement in San Clemente even more special for us. It is an old Spanish house situated on a beautiful high point directly above the beach. The constant sound of the waves gives it serenity and the palm and eucalyptus trees surrounding it provide natural protection that made it possible for us to take at least semi-private walks. We named the house La Casa Pacifica—the Peaceful House. A small complex of offices was built on the Coast Guard station next door, and these became the Western White House.

Because of the distance we were able to visit San Clemente only a few times a year. More often we would go for a weekend to Key Biscayne or Camp David. In some respects, Pat ran three households — in Washington, California, and Florida — and she made each of them a home for us even if we were there for only a few days.

(*The Memoirs of Richard Nixon*, by Richard Nixon)

二、描写文

描写文以"写感受"为核心。写景为的是创造气氛,寄托作者的心境,抒发作者的情怀。写物为的是托物言志,以物来比喻人的精神,寄托作者的志趣。写人为的是树立人的形象,表达作者对生活的感受和认识。

描写文常常具有极强的抒情风格。一切被描写的对象都是作者情怀的外在体现。内心的情和外部的景水乳交融在一起。抒情的方式大致有两类,一为直接抒情,一为间接抒情。作者直抒胸臆,用明快的语言道出自己的感情为直接抒情。然而描写文一般多采用间接抒情的方式,通过对客观的人、物或景的描绘间接地表现作者主观的感情、意志、愿望和理想。

为了生动、具体、有感染力地表达作者的印象和情怀,描写文中所使用的语言必须具有形象性、直觉性和情感性。这是描写文对语言的特殊要求,也是翻译描写文时应特别下功夫之处。和其他类散文比来,描写文的语言更加清新、美丽、饱含诗意。它是一幅用语言勾勒出的画。要将其中的诗情画意忠实而生动地体现出来,译文的语言也必须达到同等的优美程度。

以英国作家亨利·梅杰·汤姆林森(Henry Major Tomlinson)的散文《船长》(*The Master*)为例:

This master of a ship I remember first as a slim lad, with a shy smile, and hands that were lonely beyond his outgrown reefer jacket. His cap was always too small for him, and the soiled frontal badge of his line became a colored button beyond his forelock. He used to come home occasionally—and it was always when we were on the point of forgetting him altogether. He came with a huge bolster in a cab, as though out of the past and nowhere.

...

Of course, he was a delightful fellow. He often amused us, and he did not always know why. He was frank, he was gentle, but that large vacancy, the sea, where he had spent most of his young life, had made him—well, slow. You know what I mean. He was curiously innocent of those dangers of great cities which are nothing to us because we know they are there.

...

The skipper went to gaze down a hatchway. He walked to the other side of the ship, and inspected something there. Conned her length, called up in a friendly but authoritative way to an engineer standing by an amidship rail above. He came back to the mate, and with an easy precision directed his will on others, through his deputy, up to the time of sailing. He beckoned to me, who also, apparently, was under his august orders, and turned, as though perfectly aware that in this place I should follow him meekly, in all obedience.

Our steamer moved out at midnight, in a drive of wind and rain. There were bewildering and unrelated lights about us. Peremptory challenges were shouted to us from nowhere. Sirens blared out of dark voids. And there was the skipper on the bridge, the lad who caused us amusement at home, with this confusion in the dark about him, and an immense insentient mass moving with him at his will: and he had his hands in his pockets, and turned to tell me what a cold night it was. The pier-head searchlight showed his face, alert, serene, with his brows knitted in a little frown, and his underlip projecting as the sign of the pride of those who look direct into the eyes of an opponent, and care not at all. In my berth that night I searched for a moral for this narrative, but went to sleep before I found it.

我记得这位船长最早是一个瘦长的小伙子,带着羞怯的微笑,一双手孤零零地露在已经嫌短的水手服外面。帽子总是显得太小,帽上肮脏的海员帽徽变成了一个变了色的钮扣,顶在前额的鬈发上。他偶尔回家一次,总是在大家快要完全忘记他的时候才回来。他夹着一个大包坐着驿车回来了,好像是从过去的时代和不知道的地方冒出来的。

……

当然他是一个可爱的家伙,常常使大家都觉得有趣,他自己却往往不知道这是为什么。他直爽坦白,文质彬彬。他在海洋这个巨大的空间里度过了年轻的大半生,这使他变得——嗯,迟钝。你知道我的意思。真奇怪他连大城市里的种种危险都不知道。我们却清清楚楚,因为我们知道这些危险的确存在。

……

船长走过去,弯身望望舱口下面,他又走到船的另一侧,查看了一下。他从船头至船尾巡视一周,用亲切但又是权威的口吻对站在船中部上层甲板栏杆旁的机械师大声招呼了一声。然后他走回到大副身边,通过他的这位副手,轻松而准确地按自己的意志指挥别人,一直到开船时为止。他向我抬抬手,显然我也要按他威严的命令行事。他转过身去,似乎非常清楚在这条船上我会十分恭顺地完全跟随他。

午夜,在一阵狂风暴雨中我们的船出港了。周围闪烁着令人头昏目眩、杂乱无章的灯光。不知道从什么地方传来对我们专横的喝问。暗空里响起了汽笛声。船长站在舰桥上,就是在家乡让大家好笑的那个小伙子。周围的黑暗中一片混乱,而脚下毫无知觉的庞然大物正按照他的意志移动。他的手插在口袋里,转身对我说今晚真冷。码头的探照灯照亮了他的脸,机警,沉着,眉毛微皱,下唇突出,正是那些敢于正视对手眼睛而毫不在意的人的自豪姿态。那晚我睡在铺上,想从我叙述的这一切中引出一些教训,但还未等找到,就睡着了。

这是一篇十分成功的人物素描。作者通过对比的手法描绘了一位人们眼中笨拙、羞怯、不谙世事的毛头小伙子如何出落成一个能干果断的船长。语言准确洗练、朴质无华,寥寥数笔,一个活生生的形象跃然纸上。作者使用的对比是多方面的,将主人翁与周围的人对比,将主观猜测与客观实际对比,将行为举止与环境背景对比,将过去与现在对比,将外表面貌与内在品质对比。通过这种种的对比手法烘托出人物形象,使其分外鲜明,令人难以忘怀。

在翻译这篇散文时应特别注意忠实生动地用对应的汉语描绘出人物的形象。第一句中的"a slim lad","a shy smile","and hands that were lonely",三个短语是作者对于这一人物的突出印象,不仅指人物客观的外形,也指作者的主观感觉。译文分别译成"一个瘦长的小伙子","羞怯的微笑"和"一双手孤零零地"。其中特别是"lonely"一词比较难译,因为它特别体现了作者的感受。如译成"孤单"或"寂寞",不仅与"手"难以搭配,也不足以表达出其形象和给人的印象。译成"孤零零地"一语,并改作状语用,则通顺而恰到好处地译出了原文的双重意义。第二句写了有关人物的衣着。前一句提到了外套,这一句再讲帽子和帽上的帽徽。作者虽未详细描绘人物的各个方面,但由于精心选择与突出了他与众不同的外形和衣着,已清晰地塑造了这一人物的形象,而不需再多费笔墨。译文也同样抓住这一要点,用准确、简练、通俗的语言传达了原文的风韵。

最后一段作者着意描绘了周围艰难混乱的环境,恰好与人物指挥若定的大将风度形成尖锐的对比,显出人物的高大形象。这是一段精彩的描写。译文将"a drive of wind and rain"译成"一阵狂风暴雨","bewildering and unrelated lights"译成"令人头昏目眩、杂乱无章的灯光"和"peremptory challenges"译成"专横的喝问","an immense insentient mass"译成"毫无知觉的庞然大物",所用的词汇不仅生动、正式、绚烂,符合原文风格,也准确地营造出原文渲染的气氛。至于有关人物的表情的描写,译文形象传神地译为:

"探照灯照亮了他的脸,机警、沉着,眉毛微皱,下唇突出,正是那些敢于正视对手眼睛而毫不在意的人的自豪姿态。"其中将"direct"译成"敢于",更符合原词的内涵。

原作的结尾既简单自然又意义深远。作者只客观地描绘了人物的形象,至于从中可以学到什么,留给读者自己去思考。正如中国有句古话说:"人不可貌相,海水不可斗量。"这是一条待人接物的真理。译文的最后一句,和原文一样简短通俗:"还未等找到,就睡着了,"较好地传达了作者的幽默。

下面为美国著名作家亨利·大卫·梭罗(Henry David Thoreau)的名文《动物乡邻》(*Brute Neighbors*)中的一段:

The mice which haunted my house were not the common ones which are said to have been introduced into the country, but a wild native kind not found in the village. I sent one to a distinguished naturalist, and it interested him much. When I was building, one of these had its nest underneath the house, and before I had laid the second floor, and swept out the shavings, would come out regulary at lunch time and pick up the crumbs at my feet. It probably had never seen a man before; and it soon became quite familiar, and would run over my shoes and my clothes. It could readily ascend the sides of the room by short impulses, like a squirrel, which it resembled in its motions. At length, as I leaned with my elbow on the bench one day, it ran up my clothes, and along my sleeve, and round and round the paper which held my dinner, while I kept the latter close, and dodged and played at bopeep with it; and when at last I held still a piece of cheese between my thumb and finger, it came and nibbled it, sitting in my hand, and afterwards cleaned its face and paws, like a fly, and walked away.

出没于我屋中的小鼠不是人们所说的从外面带到本地来的那种普通老鼠,而是一种村里看不到的本乡本土的野鼠。我送了一只给一位著名的生物学家,他很感兴趣。在我盖房子时,一只小鼠在屋下筑了一个窝。我铺好二层楼的地板、扫去刨花之前,一到午饭时刻,它就准时出来,在我的脚边拣面包屑吃。它可能以前从未看见过人,但很快就熟悉了,在我的鞋子和衣服上跑来跑去。它能像松鼠一样一跳一蹦方便地爬上房间的墙壁,动作真像松鼠。末了有一天,我用肘支在板凳上向前倾着身子。这时它窜上了我的衣服,沿着袖子跑,围绕装着我饭食的纸包转来转去。我把纸包包紧,闪避开,和它玩躲猫猫。最后我用拇指和食指捏着一块奶酪不动,它跑过来坐在我手上,一点一点咬下来吃掉,然后像苍蝇一样弄干净脸和爪子走开去。

　　这是一段描写动物的文字,将小鼠的习性、动作、神态十分生动地再现在读者面前,并在字里行间表明了作者与小鼠间的亲密友好的关系和作者天真未泯的童心。在翻译时首先必须使用适当的语言词汇来描绘小鼠的形象,应特别注意一些表示小鼠动作的词,如"pick up"、"by short impulses"、"round and round the paper"、"nibbled it"和"cleaned its face and paws"等。译文分别将这些短语译为"拣"、"一跳一蹦"、"围绕纸袋转来转去"、"一点一点咬下来吃掉"和"弄干净脸和爪子",较好地表现了小鼠的神态。其次由于原文使用了一种简朴平常的语调,句子简短,词汇短语皆为普通日常用语,因此在翻译时也应避免使用华词丽藻和复杂长句,用朴素的语言来传达原文的风格。如将"haunted"译成"出没于"既忠实地表达了原词的意思,在风格上又不过分典雅,仍属常用语。"introduced"通常可译成"引进",但放在此处未免过分正式。译成"带到"则显得自然而妥贴。原文中这一长句"When I was building, one of these had its nest underneath the house, and before I had laid the second floor, and swept out the shavings, would come out regularly at lunch time and pick up the crumbs at my feet.",整句虽长,却由一些短小的从句组成,清楚流畅。译文也同样使用了一连串的短句:"在我盖房子时,一只小鼠在屋下筑了一个窝。我铺好二层楼的地板、扫去刨花之前,一到午饭时刻,它就准时出来,在我的脚边拣面包屑吃。"读上去通顺畅达,把原文的节奏较好地体现出来。

艾伦·莫尔赫德(Alan Moorhead)所写的《蓝尼罗河》(*The Blue Nile*)是一篇典型的写景的描写文。现摘其第一段为例:

The Blue Nile pours very quietly and uneventfully out of Lake Tana in the northern highlands of Ethiopia. There is no waterfall or cataract, no definite current, nothing in fact to indicate that a part at least of this gently moving flow is embarked upon a momentous journey to the Mediterranean, 2,750 miles away. The actual outlet lies in a bay at the southern end of the lake, and it would be quite possible for a traveller to miss it altogether. The shore line unobtrusively divides into low islands fringed with black lava boulders and overgrown with jungle, and the grey-green water slips in between. There are no villages here, and except for a few fishermen paddling about on their papyrus rafts like water-boatmen in a pond, no sign of civilization at all. The silence is absolute. One sees a few spry grey monkeys on the rocks, and the black and white kingfisher, fluttering ten feet above the water before he makes his dead-straight drop upon a fish. Pythons are said to live in these regions, and they grow to a length of twenty feet or more and are adorned in patterns of black and many colours. If you are very lucky you might catch sight of one of them swimming to new hunting grounds along the shore, but more often they are to be found in the low branches of trees, and from that safe hiding place among the leaves they lash out to grab and demolish a monkey or a small unsuspecting antelope coming down to the river to drink...

蓝尼罗河从埃塞俄比亚北方高原的塔那湖安稳平静地流出。没有瀑布或急湍,没有确定的水流。实际上毫无迹象表明至少有一部分这样缓缓淌去的流水正踏上一个重要的旅程,流向2,750英里之外的地中海。实际的出口在位于塔那湖南端的小湾内,旅行者很可能会完全忽略过去。河岸线毫不显眼地断成一个个低矮的小岛,四周镶着火山石,岛上长满丛林,岛间流着灰绿色的河水。此地没有村庄,只有几个渔夫在附近划着用纸莎草编成的筏子,就像水虫在池塘水面上滑行一样,除此之外毫无文明的痕迹。万籁俱寂。人们看见岩石上有几只矫健的灰猴,黑白相间的翠鸟在离水面10英尺的空中扇动着翅膀,然后笔直投入水中去抓鱼。据说巨蟒就生长在这些区域,长大后长达20余英尺,身上布满黑色和各种色彩的花纹。如果幸运的话,可以看见一条巨蟒沿着岸边游向新的捕食地方,但更常见的是它们盘在树木的低枝上。从树叶中安然藏身的地方它们会突然窜出来猎取和吞噬来河边喝水的猴子或失去警惕的小羚羊。

原文对景色的描写既有静态的刻画,又有动态的描绘。静态为景物的状态、外观和环境。动态则为其动作、行为和举止。在多数情况下写静稍易而写动则难得多。在翻译时必须十分注意用词,要将原文的静与动的不同形象充分再现出来,尤其应注意动词的翻译。另一方面也应使译文清丽动人,具有诗情画意,以符合原文的风格。原文的第一句话既写了河流的动态,也描写了河流的静态。"pours"是动作,"quietly and uneventfully"虽然形容"pours",实际上指的是状态。译文译成"安稳平静地流出"将动态与静态较好地结合在一起,颇为得体。在"is embarked"这一短语中,"embarked"虽为过去分词,通常指状态,而此处却有较强的动作意味,译文用"踏上"一词译出，颇能传达出原词的动感。"like waterboatman in a pond"既为介词短语，似应指状态，其实它比喻着"paddling"的动作。译文在其后加上"滑行"一词，变成"就像水虫在池塘水面上滑行一样"，这样就将筏子的动态十分生动、形象地呈现在读者面前。原文用动词短语"lash out"来描绘蛇的动作。原意为"快得像鞭子一样挥出"。这样翻译不仅文字太长，也失去了简短明快的力量。将它译成"窜出"既保留了原词的动感，又符合汉语的习惯，将蛇的突然动作完全表现出来。而将"grab and demolish"译成"猎取和吞噬"也符合蛇的天性。如按通常惯例，将"grab"译成"攫取"或"抓住"，将"demolish"译成"摧毁"或"吃光"则不符蛇的生理特征。

在描写静景时，作者使用了过去分词短语，如"fringed with black lava boulders and overgrown with jungle"，译文译成"四周镶着火山石，岛上长满丛林"。特别是带有总结性的这一短句："The silence is absolute."译文将其译成"万籁俱寂"，不仅文字精练优美，更烘托出了原句创造的气氛。

附：练习

将下列描写文译成中文。

① He was an undersized little man, with a head too big for his body — a sickly little man. His nerves were bad. He had skin trouble. It was agony for him to wear anything next to his skin coarser than silk. And he had delusions of grandeur.

He was a monster of conceit. Never for one minute did he look at the world or at people, except in relation to himself. He was not only the most important person in the world, to himself; in his own eyes he was the only person who existed. He believed himself to be one of the greatest dramatists in the world, one of the greatest thinkers, and one of the greatest composers. To hear him talk, he was Shakespeare, and Beethoven, and Plato, rolled into one. And you would have had no difficulty in hearing him talk. He was one of the most exhausting conversationalists that ever lived. An evening with him was an evening spent in listening to a monologue. Sometimes he was brilliant; sometimes he was maddeningly tiresome. But whether he was being brilliant or dull, he had one sole topic of conversation: himself. What *he* thought and what *he* did.

He had a mania for being in the right. The slightest hint of disagreement, from anyone, on the most trivial point, was enough to set him off on a harangue that might last for hours, in which he proved himself right in so many ways, and with such exhausting volubility, that in the end his hearer, stunned and deafened, would agree with him, for the sake of peace.

(*The Monster*, by Deems Taylor)

② The mirth of the company was greatly promoted by the humors of an eccentric personage whom Mr. Bracebridge always addressed with the quaint appellation of Master Simon. He was a tight brisk little man, with the air of an old bachelor. His nose was shaped like the bill of a parrot; his face slightly pitted with the smallpox, with a dry perpetual bloom on it, like a frost-bitten leaf in autumn. He had an eye of great quickness and vivacity, with a drollery and lurking waggery of expression that was irresistible. He was evidently the wit of the family, dealing very much in sly jokes and innuendoes with the ladies, and making infinite merriment by harpings upon old themes; which unfortunately, my ignorance of the family chronicles did not permit me to enjoy. It seemed to be his great delight during supper to keep a young girl next to him in a continual agony of stifled laughter, in spite of her awe of the reproving looks of her mother, who sat opposite. Indeed, he was the idol of the younger part of the company, who laughed at everything he said or did, and at every turn of his countenance. I could not wonder at it; for he must have been a miracle of accomplishments in their eyes. I was let briefly into his history by Frank Bracebridge. He was an old bachelor, of a small independent income, which, by careful management, was sufficient for all his wants. He revolved through the family system like a vagrant comet in its orbit; sometimes visiting one branch and sometimes another quite remote; as is often the case with gentlemen of extensive connections and small fortunes in England. He had a chirping buoyant disposition, always enjoying the present moment; and his frequent change of scene and company prevented his acquiring those rusty unaccommodating habits with which old bachelors are so uncharitably charged. He was a complete family chronicle, being versed in the genealogy, history, and intermarriages of the whole house of Bracebridge, which made him a great favorite with the old folks; he was the beau of all the elder ladies and superannuated spinsters, among whom he was habitually considered rather a young fellow, and he was master of the revels among the children; so that there was not a more popular being in the sphere in which he moved than Mr. Simon Bracebridge.

(*Christmas Eve*, by Washington Irving)

③ He rolled the ball gently over the grass. The kitten watched it, fascinated. It flattened itself on the grass, stretched out its neck, cocked its ears, stared with wide eyes, and moved its tail in cruel anticipation. Then it dashed towards the ball, and, just as it reached it, made a sideways spring with arched back and avoided it, and sat down and began to lick its right foreleg from the knee downwards, as though it had forgotten all about the ball. "Well," said my friend with self-satisfaction, "what do you think of Oliver Cromwell? Isn't he a beauty?" I agreed that he was. "Look, look," his wife interrupted us, and, as the kitten began to flatten himself into position for another rush at the ball, she gurgled as if to herself: "Oh, he was such a darling! He was such a darling!" This time the kitten did leap on to the ball, caught it in its front paws, lifted it in the air, turned a back somersault with it, rolled on the grass, and then, as if in terror, fled for all it was worth into the Solomon's seal in the flower border, and hidden among the stalks, looked out on its late prey, like a tiger concealing itself in the jungle.

(*The New Cat*, by Robert Lynd)

④ While we were still on very high ground, and before the descent toward Argentiere began, we looked up toward a neighbouring mountain-top, and saw exquisite prismatic colours playing about some white clouds which were so delicate as to almost resemble gossamer webs. The faint pinks and greens were peculiarly beautiful; none of the colours were deep, they were the lightest shades. They were bewitchingly commingled. We sat down to study and enjoy this singular spectacle. The tints remained during several minutes — flitting, changing, melting into each other; paling almost away for a moment, then reflushing — a shifting, restless, unstable succession of soft opaline gleams, shimmering over that airy film of white cloud, and turning it into a fabric dainty enough to clothe an angel with.

By and by we perceived what those super-delicate colours, and their continuous play and movement, reminded us of: it is what one sees in a soap-bubble that is drifting along, catching changes of tint from the object it passes. A soap-bubble is the most beautiful thing, and the most exquisite, in nature: that lovely phantom fabric in the sky was suggestive of a soap-bubble split open and spread out in the sun.

(A Tramp Abroad, by Mark Twain)

三、说明文

说明文在散文中占有很大比重,就某一主题进行阐述和发挥的一般性文章皆属说明文的范畴。

一般说来,说明文结构严整,逻辑力强,用词精确,翻译时必须把握住这些特征,特别应注意在用词组句上多下功夫。既不可将精练的定义用啰嗦的文字译出,又不可过分求简洁而不能精确地传达出原意。有些富有哲理的警句最难翻译,然而它们又是文章精华之所在,需不断推敲,再三润色。好的译文不仅形似,也能神似,所谓神形兼备,这正是翻译者孜孜以求的境界。

以约翰·亨利·纽曼主教(John Henry Newman)的《绅士的界说》(*Definition of a Gentleman*)一文为例:

Hence it is that it is almost a definition of a gentleman to say he is one who never inflicts pain. This description is both refined and, as far as it goes, accurate. He is mainly occupied in merely removing the obstacles which hinder the free and unembarrassed action of those about him; and he concurs with their movements rather than takes the initiative himself. His benefits may be considered as parallel to what are called comforts or conveniences in arrangements of a personal nature: like an easy chair or a good fire, which do their part in dispelling cold and fatigue, though nature provides both means of rest and animal heat without them. The true gentleman in like manner carefully avoids whatever may cause a jar or a jolt in the minds of those with whom he is cast — all clashing of opinion, or collision of feeling, all restraint, or suspicion, or gloom, or resentment, his great concern being to make every one at their ease and at home. He has his eyes on all his company; he is tender towards the bashful, gentle towards the distant, and merciful towards the absurd; he can recollect to whom he is speaking; he guards against unseasonable allusions, or topics which may irritate; he is seldom prominent in conversation, and never wearisome. He makes light of favors while he does them, and seems to be receiving when he is conferring. He never speaks of himself except when compelled, never defends himself by a mere retort; he has no ears for slander or gossip, is scrupulous in imputing motives to those who interfere with him, and interprets everything for the best. He is never mean or little in his disputes, never takes unfair advantage, never mistakes personalities or sharp sayings for arguments, or insinuates evil which he dare not say out.

　　如把绅士说成是一个从不伤害别人的人,这大概就是绅士的定义。这种说法既精练,本身也准确。他主要关心的事在于排除妨害周围人自由自在行动的障碍。他支持别人的行为,自己却不采取主动。大家认为他的长处就像是一张安乐椅或一堆温暖的火,为个人提供了舒适和方便的安排,起到驱除寒冷和疲乏的作用,尽管没有椅子和火堆,大自然也给了人以休息的手段和人体本身的热量。同样,真正的绅士也会小心翼翼地避免在一起相处的人心中引起不快或抵触,例如意见的冲突,感情的不和,压抑,疑惑,忧郁或愤恨等。他十分关注于让大家都感到心情舒畅,无拘无束。他留意所有的同伴,对羞怯的人温柔体贴,对疏远的人和蔼可亲,对荒唐的人宽宏大度。他能记得在对谁说话,随时警惕不作不恰当的暗示,也不谈令人生气的话题。在谈话中他很少显示自己,但也从不令人生厌。他帮别人的忙毫不在意,倒像别人在帮他的忙。除非被迫,否则他从不谈及自己,也从不反唇相讥来为自己辩护。他不听诽谤和闲话。有人妨害了他,他总谨慎对待,不去怪罪他们,而从最好的方面来解释一切。他在争论中从不偏狭小气,从不利用不公平的优势,从不把人身攻击或尖锐言词错当成辩论,也从不含沙射影地暗示他不敢说出的坏话。

《绅士的界说》是一篇典型的说明文,这是其中的一段。文章给绅士下了一个简短、精练、不同凡响的定义,颇出人意外,使人为之耳目一新。绅士是"一个从不伤害别人的人。"这是总的界说。然后作者从各个具体方面来例举其表现。主要讲的是他的人际关系和待人接物的态度,这样就和定义密切呼应起来。在翻译时必须牢牢把握住这一角度,才能对一些词和句有正确的理解,也才能将其恰如其分地译成汉语。例如在"he concurs with ... initiative himself"一句中"concurs with their movements"和"takes initiative"是一双相对的短语,表明了两种不同的态度。译文译成"支持别人的行为,自己却不采取主动"较好地表达了对立的含义。下一长句"His benefits ..."比较难译。如将"His benefits"按字面译成"他的利益"必然会引起误会。从整个句子来看,"他"被比作"一张安乐椅"或"一堆温暖的火",可见是对别人而言,故译文译成"他的长处",后面的"arrangements of a personal nature"也不能直译为"个人性质的安排",而应译成"给个人提供了安排"。在"He is never mean ... say out."这一句中,"mean"和"little"是两个极普通、常见的形容词,但这里却有特别的意义,因为它们被用来形容在辩论中对待别人的态度。译文译成"偏狭小气"正是从这一角度出发的。最后一句中的"personalities"为复数形式,不同于其一般的用法,此处应为"攻击"、"诽谤"的意思。译文将其译成"人身攻击"较准确地表达了原词的含义。从以上例子中,可以看出在翻译说明文时,对词、句精确意义的研究十分重要。而要想深刻地理解词句以做到精确的翻译,不可不从宏观上掌握全篇的主旨和作者写作的角度。

在本文中作者使用的一个突出的修辞手段为平行结构,以体现均衡的艺术美。在翻译时必须尽量将这优美的形式再现出来。例如将"clashing of opinion, or collision of feeling"译成"意见的冲突或感情的抵触",将"at their ease and at home"译成"心情舒畅,无拘无束",将"tender towards the bashful, gentle towards the distant, and merciful towards the absurd"译为"对羞怯的人温柔体贴,对疏远的人和蔼可亲,对荒唐的人宽宏大度"等,均较成功地再现了原文的平行结构。

再以贝特兰·罗素(Bertrand Russell)所写的《我生活的目的》(*What I Have Lived For*)一文为例:

Three passions, simple but overwhelmingly strong, have governed my life: the longing for love, the search for knowledge, and unbearable pity for the suffering of mankind. These passions, like great winds, have blown me hither and thither, in a wayward course, over a deep ocean of anguish, reaching to the very verge of despair.

I have sought love, first, because it brings ecstasy—ecstasy so great that I would often have sacrificed all the rest of life for a few hours of this joy. I have sought it, next, because it relieves loneliness—that terrible loneliness in which one shivering consciousness looks over the rim of the world into the cold unfathomable lifeless abyss. I have sought it, finally, because in the union of love I have seen, in a mystic miniature, the prefiguring vision of the heaven that saints and poets have imagined. This is what I sought, and though it might seem too good for human life, this is what—at last—I have found.

With equal passion I have sought knowledge. I have wished to understand the hearts of men. I have wished to know why the stars shine. And I have tried to apprehend the Pythagorean power by which number holds sway above the flux. A little of this, but not much, I have achieved.

Love and knowledge, so far as they were possible, led upward toward the heavens. But always pity brought me back to earth. Echoes of cries of pain reverberate in my heart. Children in famine, victims tortured by oppressors, helpless old people a hated burden to their sons, and the whole world of loneliness, poverty, and pain make a mockery of what human life should be. I long to alleviate the evil, but I cannot, and I too suffer.

This has been my life. I have found it worth living, and would gladly live it again if the chance were offered me.

在我生活中起支配作用的有三种简单却又极为强烈的情感：对爱情的渴望，对知识的追求和对人类苦难的无比同情。这些情感像大风一样吹来吹去，方向不定，越过深沉痛苦的海洋，直达绝望的边缘。

我追求爱情，首先因为它使人陶醉——陶醉到往往使我愿意牺牲我的余生来换取几小时这样快乐的程度。其次我追求爱情是因为它使人摆脱寂寞——那种可怕的寂寞，好似人带着一种颤抖的意识，站在世界的边际，俯视下面无底的死亡深渊一样。最后我追求爱情是因为在爱情的结合里我看见了在圣徒和诗人的想象中所预见到的天堂的神奇缩影。这就是我的追求，尽管这似乎是人生过度的奢望，但它正是我最终找到的东西。

我怀着同样的热情追求知识。我渴望了解人心。我渴望懂得星星为什么发光。我竭力想弄清使数字成为变化主宰的毕达哥拉斯的力量。我获得了一点结果，但成绩不大。

爱情和知识在一定的范围内通向天堂，而怜悯却总把我带回人间。我的心里回响着痛苦的呼唤。忍饥挨饿的孩子们，遭到压迫者折磨的受苦者，成了儿辈们讨厌负担的无依无靠的老年人，以及整个寂寞、贫穷、痛苦的世界，所有这一切对于人类应过的生活是一种嘲弄。我盼望减轻这些罪恶，但无能为力。我自己也在受苦受难。

这就是我的生活，我觉得过这样的生活值得。如果有机会，我会高兴地再这样活一遍。

这是一篇分类阐述的说明文，一开始作者就将自己的情感划分成三类，分别一一道来，不仅详细解释了原因，并举出具体的例子来说明。在第二段中作者列出了追求爱情的三个原因。第三段则从三个具体方面来说明所追求知识的内容。第四段作者用感情的目光来观察世界，描述了人世间种种苦难的现象，以引起人们的怜悯。翻译本文时必须有意识地分门别类列出各个要点，使人一目了然。

第一段作者用了三个平行的短语列出了三种情感。译文也同样用了三个均衡的平行结构十分清晰而明确地译出了这三个主要方面："对爱情的渴望，对知识的追求和对人类苦难的无比同情。"在第二段里，译者将"first"，"next"，"finally"译成"首先"，"其次","最后"并分别置于句首,这使得三个原因分外醒目。译者在译"one shivering consciousness"这一短语时,前面加了一个主语,成为"好似人带着一种颤抖的意识",这和下文的动词"站在"与"俯视"放在一起更符合汉语习惯。在第三段里,译文用了两个"我渴望"和一个"我竭力"来和原文相应,引导出三个句子,表明了知识的三个方面。

与前两段不同,在第四段里原文充满了富有感情的句子和词汇。译文较忠实感人地译出了原句和原词所包含的情感,如"通向天堂","带回人间","心里回响着痛苦的呼唤"等。接着原文列举了四个方面的人世苦难。译文将其译为:"忍饥挨饿的孩子们,遭到压迫者折磨的受苦者,成了儿辈们讨厌负担的无依无靠的老年人,以及整个寂寞、贫穷、痛苦的世界,"较好地反映了作者的怜悯之心。

约翰·布鲁克斯(John Brooks)写的《电话》(*The Telephone*)是一篇阐述因果关系的说明文。现节录如下:

What has the telephone done to us, or for us, in the hundred years of its existence? A few effects suggest themselves at once. It has saved lives by getting rapid word of illness, injury, or famine from remote places. By joining with the elevator to make possible the multistory residence or office building, it has made possible—for better or worse—the modern city. By bringing about a quantum leap in the speed and ease with which information moves from place to place, it has greatly accelerated the rate of scientific and technological change and growth in industry. Beyond doubt it has crippled if not killed the ancient art of letter writing. It has made living alone possible for persons with normal social impulses; by so doing, it has played a role in one of the greatest social changes of this century, the breakup of the multigenerational household. It has made the waging of war chillingly more efficient than formerly. Perhaps (though not provably) it has prevented wars that might have arisen out of international misunderstanding caused by written communication. Or perhaps — again not provably — by magnifying and extending irrational personal conflicts based on voice contact, it has caused wars. Certainly it has extended the scope of human conflicts, since it impartially disseminates the useful knowledge of scientists and the babble of bores, the affection of the affectionate and the malice of the malicious.

　　自有电话以来的百年中,电话对我们有什么影响,或者有什么作用呢?可以立刻举出一些效应。由于通过电话能从远方迅速获得有关疾病、伤痛、灾荒的消息,因而挽救了许多生命。电话和电梯合在一起使建筑多层住宅楼和办公楼成为可能,不管是好是坏,这使建设现代都市成为可能。由于电话使各地的讯息传递在速度与便利程度上有了量的飞跃,从而大大加快了工业上科技变化和发展的速度。毫无疑问,电话使得写信这一古老技巧即使未完全失去生命力的话也大大受到了削弱。电话使有和社会正常交往愿望的人可以独自居住;这样一来,电话就在本世纪最大的社会变化之一——多代人家庭的解体方面发挥了作用。令人不寒而栗的是电话使进行战争比过去更加方便有效得多。也许(不过这无法证明)电话还能防止由于书信往来造成国际间误解而引起的战争。也许——这同样也无法证明——由于电话中互相能听见声音而加重与扩大了个人的无理冲突,反而会导致战争。由于电话不偏不倚地既传播科学家的有用知识,也散布饶舌者的闲言碎语,既送来亲人的爱,也带来恶人的恨,无疑它扩大了人们的冲突范围。

　　文章一开头就提出了电话对人有什么影响的问题。这是一个总的原因,总的根源。接着作者一一列出电话所产生的影响,即其后果。既有正面的成绩,也有负面的效应。原文在第一句话中使用了"telephone"一词以后,一直用"it"来代替。译文为了清楚地分别列出各种不同的影响起见,都译成"电话"而避免直接译成"它",这不仅更符合汉语习惯,也使文章结构条理分明,充分体现了说明文的特点。

译文在用词上十分注意汉语的通顺。例如将"crippled"译为"受到了削弱",将"kill"译成"失去了生命力",将"impartially"译成"不偏不倚地",既符合原词的含义,又使汉语通畅易懂。原文最后使用了两对互相对仗的短语,"disseminates the useful knowledge of scientists and the babble of bores, the affection of the affectionate and the malice of the malicious."译文也使用了两对同样的对仗结构:"既传播科学家的有用知识,也散布饶舌者的闲言碎语,既送来亲人的爱,也带来恶人的恨",十分忠实生动地传达了原文的韵律。

附:练习

将下列说明文译成中文。

① Poetry speaks for itself. But poets, curiously enough, do not; and so it is time that someone speak for them and say what they would say if they spoke in prose. It is time that they be defended against the silent charge—all the more damning because it is so silent—that they are a special race of men and women, different from all other creatures of their kind and possessed of faculties which would make them, if we knew them, only too wonderful to live with, not to say too embarrassing. I should like to relieve them from the burden of being queer. Poets are supposed to be a suffering race, but the only thing they suffer from is the misapprehension that they are endowed with a peculiar set of thoughts and feelings — particularly feelings — and that these endowments are of the romantic sort. It consists, to speak for the moment historically, in the notion that the poet has always and must always cut the same figure he has cut during the past hundred years or so. It consists in expecting him to be a Shelley, a Keats, a Byron, a Poe, a Verlaine, a Swinburne, a Dowson. He may be another one of those, to be sure; but he also may be any kind of person under the sun. My only conception of the poet is that he is a person who writes poetry. That may sound absurdly simple, but it is arrived at after reflection upon the innumerable kinds of poetry which poets have written, and upon the baffling variety of temperaments which these poets have revealed.

(*What Is a Poet?* by Mark Van Doren)

② I can see three different types of composers in musical history, each of whom conceives music in a somewhat different fashion.

The type that has fired public imagination most is that of the spontaneously inspired composer — the Franz Schubert type, in other words. All composers are inspired, of course, but this type is more spontaneously inspired. Music simply wells out of him. He can't get it down on paper fast enough. You can almost tell this type of composer by his prolific output. In certain months, Schubert wrote a song a day. Hugo Wolf did the same.

Beethoven symbolizes the second type — the constructive type, one might call it. This type exemplifies my theory of the creative process in music better than any other, because in this case the composer really does begin with a musical theme. In

Beethoven's case there is no doubt about it, for we have the notebooks in which he put the themes down. We can see from his notebooks how he worked over his themes — how he would not let them be until they were as perfect as he could make them. Beethoven was not a spontaneously inspired composer in the Schubert sense at all. He was the type that begins with a theme; makes it a germinal idea; and upon that constructs a musical work, day after day, in painstaking fashion. Most composers since Beethoven's day belong to this second type.

The third type of creator I can only call, for lack of a better name, the traditionalist type. Men like Palestrina and Bach belong in this category. They both exemplify the kind of composer who is born in a particular period of musical history, when a certain musical style is about to reach its fullest development. It is a question at such a time of creating music in a well-known and accepted style and doing it in a way that is better than anyone has done it before you.

(*Different Types of Composers*, by Aaron Copland)

③ My mother's mother probably made the best apple pies I ever tasted. As a tiny girl, I used to watch my Granner make them, and I marveled at her sure, swift movements. Granner needed no recipes, yet her pies always came out delicious, fragrant with love and goodness. I was never too interested in making the crust, but by the time Granner brought out eight plump red apples, she had my full attention.

Peeling the apples was my job, and each round, firm apple yielded up its crisp skin in a long spiral. Meanwhile, Granner quartered and cored the apples I had peeled and began slicing them into the crust-lined pans. Often, I pilfered a thick, tangy slice and popped it into my mouth, but she pretended not to notice.

When the two pans were heaped full of apples, Granner dusted them generously with cinnamon, then sprinkled a scoopful of sugar over the cinnamon. Next, she dotted each pie with small squares of butter, sprinkled on a pinch or two of ground nutmeg and cloves, then drizzled on the juice of half a lemon.

Finally, Granner was ready to place the top crust. She did this by folding the rolled-out dough in half, slipping it over the pie, then flipping the folded half into place. I always felt quite capable and efficient as I then carefully trimmed the excess crust from around each rim and slit six steam holes in each pie-top. When I proudly handed the perfect pies over to Granner, she smiled and slid them into a 375° oven.

After twenty minutes, the spicy warmth crept into the living room and enticed us toward the kitchen. My eager taste buds were convinced that the pies were ready, but Granner said it would be twenty minutes more. Finally, it was time to take the steamy prizes from the oven, and I could scarcely wait for them to cool. But with that first bite, I was in a child's heaven, eating in the nippy-sweet warmth of that kitchen, surrounded by an aura of well-being and love.

(Rhetorical Models For Effective Writing,
by J. K. Nicholas and J. R. Nicholl)*

④ Why, you may wonder, should spiders be our friends? Because they destroy so many insects, and insects include some of the greatest enemies of the human race. Insects would make it impossible for us to live in the world; they would devour all our crops and kill our flocks and herds, if it were not for the protection we get from insect-eating animals. We owe a lot to the birds and beasts who eat insects but all of them put together kill only a fraction of the number destroyed by spiders. Moreover, unlike some of the other insect eaters, spiders never do the least harm to us or our belongings.

Spiders are not insects, as many people think, nor even nearly related to them. One can tell the difference almost at a glance for a spider always has eight legs and an insect never more than six.

How many spiders are engaged in this work on our behalf? One authority on spiders made a census of the spiders in a grass field in the south of England, and he estimated that there were more than 2,250,000 in one acre; that is something like 6,000,000 spiders of different kinds on a football pitch. Spiders are busy for at least half the year in killing insects. It is impossible to make more than the wildest guess at how many they kill, but they are hungry creatures, not content with only three meals a day. It has been estimated that the weight of all the insects destroyed by spiders in Britain in one year would be greater than the total weight of all the human beings in the country.

(*Spare that Spider*, by T. H. Gillespie)

⑤ Why does the idea of progress loom so large in the modern world? Surely because progress of a particular kind is actually taking place around us and is becoming more and more manifest. Although mankind has undergone no general improvement in intelligence or morality, it has made extraordinary progress in the accumulation of knowledge. Knowledge began to increase as soon as the thoughts of one individual could be communicated to another by means of speech. With the invention of writing, a great advance was made, for knowledge could then be not only communicated but also stored. Libraries made education possible, and education in its turn added to libraries; the growth of knowledge followed a kind of compound-interest law, which was greatly enhanced by the invention of printing. All this was comparatively slow until, with the coming of science, the *tempo* was suddenly raised. Then knowledge began to be accumulated according to a systematic plan. The trickle became a stream; the stream has now become a torrent. Moreover, as soon as new knowledge is acquired, it is now turned to practical account. What is called 'modern civilization' is not the result of a balanced development of all man's nature, but of accumulated knowledge applied to practical life. The problem now facing humanity is: What is going to be done with all this knowledge? As is so often pointed out, knowledge is a two-edged weapon which can be used equally for good or evil. It is now being used indifferently for both. Could any spectacle, for instance, be more grimly whimsical than that of gunners using science to shatter men's bodies while, close at hand, surgeons use it to restore them? We have to ask ourselves very seriously what will happen if this twofold use of knowledge, with its ever-increasing power, continues.

(*The Personality of Man*, by G. N. M. Tyrrell)

四、议论文

西方的议论文起源于古雅典元老院雄辩的演说,其主要特点为深思熟虑的逻辑推理,目的在于让元老们信服发言者观点的正确性与合理性而加以采纳。今日的议论文同样具有真诚、客观、合乎逻辑的特征。一般说来议论文由以下四个部分组成。首先,提出问题并对问题作简短的介绍和分析。介绍必须中肯,分析必须客观。如果问题本身就有谬误,那么就失去了议论的前提。其次,应明确、概括地摆出解决问题的办法。既可紧跟在提出问题后立刻说明,然后再仔细分析,也可在文章最后作为总结性的归纳提出。应尽可能用一、两句话简练明确地表达出来,利于读者领会。第三,任何观点都必须有充分的事实作为依据,即必须举出有关的典型例证来支持自己的论点。事例越具体越实在越好。决不可使用无关的或不典型的例证,也不可仅根据个别例证而得出一般性的结论,否则将犯逻辑错误。第四,在肯定自己的论点同时,必须对对方的论点进行批驳。批驳时应记住不能绝对化。任何问题都有其两面性。不可能一方绝对正确,另一方完全错误。只能衡量优劣,以此作为选择的标准。辩论的态度应公正而宽宏大度,对方的正确方面需予以承认,而对其谬误也应采取宽容的态度,才能赢得读者的信任与支持。

为了使自己的文章有征服人心的力量,作者往往一方面用逻辑推理的方法来诉诸读者的理性和智力,而另一方面也用打动人心的论点来诉诸读者的知觉与情感。逻辑推理的主要方式为归纳、演绎与类比。而要打动人心则必须充满感情,塑造形象,做到文情并茂。

以上特点在翻译议论文时必须十分注意。特别是需相应地用简练明确的文字译出提出的问题、解决的办法和得出的结论。严谨、精练、准确、逻辑性强是翻译议论文必须遵守的原则。但同时也不能忽略文字所包含的情感因素,以便更好地打动读者的心。现举例如下:

This is a sceptical age, but although our faith in many of the things in which our forefathers fervently believed has weakened, our confidence in the curative properties of the bottle of medicine remains the same as theirs. This modern faith in medicines is proved by the fact that the annual drug bill of the Health Services is mounting to astronomical figures and shows no signs at present of ceasing to rise. The majority of the patients attending the medical out-patients departments of our hospitals feel that they have not received adequate treatment unless they are able to carry home with them some tangible remedy in the shape of a bottle of medicine, a box of pills, or a small jar of ointment, and the doctor in charge of the department is only too ready to provide them with these requirements. There is no quicker method of disposing of patients than by giving them what they are asking for, and since most medical men in the Health Services are overworked and have little time for offering time-consuming and little-appreciated advice on such subjects as diet, right living, and the need for abandoning bad habits, etc., the bottle, the box, and the jar are almost always granted them.

Nor is it only the ignorant and ill-educated person who has such faith in the bottle of medicine, especially if it be wrapped in white paper and sealed with a dab of red sealing-wax by a clever chemist. It is recounted of Thomas Carlyle that when he heard of the illness of his friend, Henry Taylor, he went off immediately to visit him, carrying with him in his pocket what remained of a bottle of medicine formerly prescribed for an indisposition of Mrs Carlyle's. Carlyle was entirely ignorant of what the bottle in his pocket contained, of the nature of the illness from which his friend was suffering, and of what had previously been wrong with his wife, but a medicine that had worked so well in one form of illness would surely be of equal benefit in another, and comforted by the thought of the help he was bringing to his friend, he hastened to Henry Taylor's house. History does not relate whether his friend accepted his medical help, but in all probability he did. The great advantage of taking medicine is that it makes no demands on the taker beyond that of putting up for a moment with a disgusting taste, and that is what all patients demand of their doctors—to be cured at no inconvenience to themselves.

(*Patients and Doctors*, by Kenneth Walker)

这是一个充满怀疑论的时代。但是尽管我们对祖先笃信的许多事物的信心减弱了,我们对药瓶子的疗效的信任程度却仍和他们一样。卫生部门的年度药费正达到天文数字,并且目前尚无停止上升的迹象。这一事实证明了现代人对药物的信赖。到医院门诊部就诊的大多数病人如果不能带一些看得见、摸得着的药物,如一瓶药水、一盒药丸或一小罐药膏回家的话,就会觉得未得到充分的治疗。而负责门诊的医生也非常愿意满足他们的要求。病人要什么药就给什么药,再没有比这更快的处理病人的办法了。因为卫生部门的大多数医务人员都劳累过度,几乎没有时间在饮食、健康的生活和需要克服的坏习惯等方面提出既费时又不讨好的忠告,所以几乎总是把瓶子、盒子和罐子塞给病人。

不仅无知的和缺乏教育的人对药瓶子如此信赖,尤其是在聪明能干的药剂师用白纸把它包扎起来再用一点红腊封好时。据说托马斯·卡莱尔有过这样的事：当他听到他的朋友亨利·泰勒生病时，他立即跑去看他，衣袋里带着原来卡莱尔夫人不舒服时服剩下的一瓶医生开的药。卡莱尔根本不知道口袋中的瓶子里装的是什么药，也不知道朋友害的什么病，更不知道妻子原来生的什么病。一种药对一种病既然这样有效，肯定对别种病同样有好处。他匆匆赶往亨利·泰勒家去，想到给朋友带去帮助，心里颇感欣慰。结果他的朋友是否接受了他药物上的帮助，没有下文，很可能接受了。服药的巨大好处是只要服药者忍受一下苦味就行了。这正是所有病人对医生的要求：治好病又不要给自己带来多少麻烦。

这是一篇典型的议论文，主题是人们对药物的盲目信任。文章开门见山地提出问题，指出在这个怀疑一切的时代人们对药瓶子的信任程度却丝毫未变。接着作者摆出一般的事实来证明他的论点，即年度医药费的上升和大多数病人到医院看病目的就是要拿回一点药，而医生也乐得满足他们的要求。一般的事实尚不够有力，作者更举出了著名英国作家卡莱尔的具体例子，让读者看到像卡莱尔这样有知识有修养的人居然也完全盲目地相信药物的疗效。这就充分证明了作者的论点，使读者感到信服。

译者在翻译本文时，不仅注意清晰忠实地译出原文的说理，如为了表达清楚，译者将"This modern faith ... ceasing to rise."这句话分作两句来译，并颠倒次序："卫生部门的年度药费正达到天文数字，并且目前尚无停止上升的迹象。这一事实证明了现代人对药物的信赖。"此外译者还特别注意到原文所使用的讽刺性的笔调，并在译文中较好地表现出来。如将"There is no quicker method ... asking for,"这句话译成"病人要什么药就给什么药，再没有比这更快的处理病人的办法了"。又如"the bottle, the box, and the jar are almost always granted them"这句话中的"granted"一词，译者将其译为"塞给"，十分合乎汉语习惯，较传神地表达了原词的讽刺意味。此外，译者对某些词句的译法颇有独到之处。如原文第三句中"tangible"一词,译者译为"看得见,摸得着的"。这比原词虽长得多,却给读者以具体入微的生动感觉。又如在本文的倒数第二句话中有一从句:"History does not relate"如果译成"历史没有说明"则用词过大。译者译为"没有下文"较贴切地表达了原意,汉语又十分通俗易懂。再如译者将最后一句话中"a disgusting taste"一语译为"苦味",十分符合中国人对药的传统描述,易为读者接受。

Many people in industry and the Services, who have practical experience of noise, regard any investigation of this question as a waste of time; they are not prepared even to admit the possibility that noise affects people. On the other hand, those who dislike noise will sometimes use most inadequate evidence to support their pleas for a quieter society. This is a pity, because noise abatement really is a good cause, and it is likely to be discredited if it gets to be associated with bad science.

One allegation often made is that noise produces mental illness. A recent article in a weekly newspaper, for instance, was headed with a striking illustration of a lady in a state of considerable distress, with the caption 'She was yet another victim, reduced to a screaming wreck'. On turning eagerly to the text, one learns that the lady was a typist who found the sound of office typewriters worried her more and more until eventually she had to go into a mental hospital. Now the snag in this sort of anecdote is of course that one cannot distinguish cause and effect. Was the noise a cause of the illness, or were the complaints about noise merely a symptom? Another patient might equally well complain that her neighbours were combining to slander her and persecute her, and yet one might be cautious about believing this statement.

What is needed in the case of noise is a study of large numbers of people living under noisy conditions, to discover whether they are mentally ill more often than other people are. The United States Navy, for instance, recently examined a very large number of men working on aircraft carriers: the study was known as Project Anehin. It can be unpleasant to live even several miles from an aerodrome; if you think what it must be like to share the deck of a ship with several squadrons of jet aircraft, you will realize that a modern navy is a good place to study noise. But neither psychiatric interviews nor objective tests were able to show any effects upon these American sailors. This result merely confirms earlier American and British studies: if there is any effect of noise upon mental health it must be so small that present methods of psychiatric diagnosis cannot find it. That does not prove that it does not exist; but it does mean that noise is less dangerous than, say, being brought up in an orphanage—which really is a mental health hazard.

(*Non-auditory Effects of Noise*, by D. E. Broadbent)

工业部门和军队中的许多人对噪音有实际体验。他们认为对此问题作任何调查研究不过是浪费时间。他们甚至不愿承认噪音可能对人有影响。另一方面，那些讨厌噪音的人有时却会用极不充分的证据来支持他们对更宁静的社会环境的要求。这是件憾事，因为减少噪音的确是件好事，但如果与并不恰当的科学联系在一起，就可能得不到人们的信任。

常常有人断言噪音引起精神病。例如一份周报最近刊登了一篇文章，篇头有一幅醒目的插图，图中是一位十分苦恼的女士，解说词说"她是又一个牺牲品，变成了一位尖声喊叫的废人"。当人们急切地去读正文时,才知道这位女士是个打字员,她感到办公室里打字机的声音越来越使她烦躁不安,最后她不得不进了精神病院。当然这种事的症结在于因果难分。究竟噪音是病因,还是抱怨噪音只不过是病后的一种症状呢?另一个病人也许同样可以有理由抱怨说她的邻居联合起来诽谤她、迫害她,不过对这种说法人们都不会轻信的。

至于噪音,需要对大量生活在噪音条件下的人进行研究,来发现他们是否比别人更常患精神病。例如美国海军最近检查了在航空母舰上工作的许许多多的人。此项研究被称为安乃因工程。人们住在哪怕距离飞机场有好几英里远的地方都可能感到不快。如果你想一下和几个中队喷气机同呆在一条船的甲板上是什么滋味的话,你就会了解现代海军是一个研究噪音的好地方。但是无论进行精神病学方面的采访还是作客观的测试都不能证明噪音对这些美国水兵有任何影响。这样的结果只证实了美国和英国早期的一些研究:如果噪音对心理健康有任何影响的话,那也一定很小,以致目前的精神病诊断方法尚无法发现。这并不证明不存在影响,但它的确意味着噪音的危险性比不上例如在孤儿院里长大来得厉害——孤儿院才真正对心理健康有危害。

本篇议论文的中心议题是对噪音的看法,重点在于反驳那种以为噪音会引起精神病的说法。作者认为反对噪音的人提出的证据不充分,并举报纸上的一个具体例子为证:一个女打字员因听不得打字机的噪音而进了精神病院。但究竟是噪音导致了精神病还是因精神病而害怕噪音,因果关系不清。作者自己却举出了强有力的例证来说明噪音对心理健康并无多大影响。这是对噪音极大的美国海军航空母舰上的水兵调查的结果。这种对比式的批驳方法,是十分雄辩有力的。

译者在翻译本文时十分注意词句的逻辑性和准确性。如将"This is a pity, … with bad science." 译成:"这是件憾事,因为减少噪音的确是件好事,但如果与并不恰当的科学联系在一起,就可能得不到人们的信任。"在此句中,将"good cause"译成"好事","bad science"译成"并不恰当的科学"和"discredited"译成"得不到人们的信任",不仅表达得通顺易懂,符合汉语习惯,也将逻辑性体现得十分清楚。又如将"yet one might be cautious about believing this statement"译成"不过对这种说法人们都不会轻信的",并没有完全按原文直译,却较好地传达了原意。

Some old people are oppressed by the fear of death. In the young there is a justification for this feeling. Young men who have reason to fear that they will be killed in battle may justifiably feel bitter in the thought that they have been cheated of the best things that life has to offer. But in an old man who has known human joys and sorrows, and has achieved whatever work it was in him to do, the fear of death is somewhat abject and ignoble. The best way to overcome it—so at least it seems to me—is to make your interests gradually wider and more impersonal, until bit by bit the walls of the ego recede, and your life becomes increasingly merged in the universal life. An individual human existence should be like a river—small at first, narrowly contained within its banks, and rushing passionately past boulders and over waterfalls. Gradually the river grows wider, the banks recede, the waters flow more quietly, and in the end, without any visible break, they become merged in the sea, and painlessly lose their individual being. The man who, in old age, can see his life in this way, will not suffer from the fear of death, since the things he cares for will continue. And if, with the decay of vitality, weariness increases, the thought of rest will be not unwelcome. I should wish to die while still at work, knowing that others will carry on what I can no longer do, and content in the thought that what was possible has been done.

死亡的恐惧压在一些老人心上。其实青年有这种感觉还情有可原。有理由害怕在战争中阵亡的年轻人想到生活提供给他们的最好东西被骗走时感到痛苦是无可非议的。但是尝过人生的欢乐和痛苦、完成了力所能及的任务的老人恐惧死亡就有些可悲可鄙了。至少在我看来,最好的克服办法是让你的兴趣逐渐扩大,更加超越个人圈子,直到自我围墙一点一点萎缩,自己的生命日益溶入宇宙的生命之中为止。个人的存在应该像一条河,开始很小,狭窄地局限在两岸之间,急促地奔腾,流过巨石,越过瀑布。河面渐渐变宽,两岸后移,水流更为平静,最终滔滔不绝地汇入大海之中,毫无痛楚地失去了个体的存在。人在老年时能这样看待自己的生活,就不会遭受死亡恐惧的折磨,因为他所喜爱的事物仍会继续下去。如果随着精力的衰退,疲惫日增,那末想到安息也就不会觉得不快了。我希望在工作中死去。知道别人会继续我未竟的事业,再想到我已竭尽了所能,也就感到心满意足了。

本篇议论文主要谈论老年人对死亡恐惧的心理。作者不仅作了分析并与年轻人进行了对比,更提出了解决这一问题的方法,如让"兴趣逐渐扩大,更加超越个人圈子",将"自己的生命日益溶入宇宙的生命之中"等。最后作者更以自己为例,提出了个人的感受:"知道别人会继续我未竟的事业,再想到我已竭尽了所能,也就感到心满意足了。"文章不仅说透了道理,并用贴切的比喻和个人的心愿来打动读者的感情。文笔生动形象,亲切感人。

在翻译本文时译者将"An individual human existence … their individual being."这两句话译成:"个人的存在应该像一条河,开始很小,狭窄地局限在两岸之间,急促地奔腾,流过巨石,越过瀑布。河面渐渐变宽,两岸后移,水流更为平静,最终滔滔不绝地汇入大海之中,毫无痛楚地失去了个体的存在。"生动优雅地表现了原文的风格。本句中的"recede"被译成"后移",而上句中的"recede"却译成"萎缩",都比较符合汉语习惯,较贴切地表达了原词的意思。在本文的最后一句话中,译者将"content"一词的翻译放在句尾,并用一较长的短语"也就感到心满意足了"来表达,作为全文的结束语。这样做避免了结尾过分突兀,而达到了文章结构的完整与均衡。

附:练习
将下列议论文译成中文。

① Parents have to do much less for their children today than they used to do, and home has become much less of a workshop. Clothes can be bought ready made, washing can go to the laundry, food can be bought cooked, canned or preserved, bread is baked and delivered by the baker, milk arrives on the doorstep, meals can be had at the restaurant, the works' canteen, and the school dining-room.

It is unusual now for father to pursue his trade or other employment at home, and his children rarely, if ever, see him at his place of work. Boys are therefore seldom trained to follow their father's occupation, and in many towns they have a fairly wide choice of employment and so do girls. The young wage-earner often earns good money, and soon acquires a feeling of economic independence. In textile areas it has long been customary for mothers to go out to work, but this practice has become so widespread that the working mother is now a not unusual factor in a child's home life, the number of married women in employment having more than doubled in the last twenty-five years.

With mother earning and his older children drawing substantial wages father is seldom the dominant figure that he still was at the beginning of the century. When mother works economic advantages accrue, but children lose something of greet value if mother's employment prevents her from being home to greet them when they return from school.

(*Education*, by W. O. Lester Smith)

② What characterizes almost all Hollywood pictures is their inner emptiness. This is compensated for by an outer impressiveness. Such impressiveness usually takes the form of a truly grandiose realism. Nothing is spared to make the setting, the costumes, all of the surface details correct. These efforts help to mask the essential emptiness of the characterization, and the absurdities and trivialities of the plots. The houses look like houses; the streets look like streets; the people look and talk like people; but they are empty of humanity, credibility, and motivation. Needless to say, the disgraceful censorship code is an important factor in predetermining the content of these pictures. But the code does not disturb the profits, nor the entertainment value of the films; it merely helps to prevent them from being credible. It isn't too heavy a burden for the industry to bear. In addition to the impressiveness of the settings, there is a use of the camera which at times seems magical. But of what human import is all this skill, all this effort, all this energy in the production of effects, when the story, the representation of life is hollow, stupid, banal, childish?

(*The Language of Hollywood*, by James T. Farrell)

③ In the organization of industrial life the influence of the factory upon the physiological and mental state of the workers has been completely neglected. Modern industry is based on the conception of the maximum production at lowest cost, in order that an individual or a group of individuals may earn as much money as possible. It has expanded without any idea of the true nature of the human beings who run the machines, and without giving any consideration to the effects produced on the individuals and on their descendants by the artificial mode of existence imposed by the factory. The great cities have been built with no regard for us. The shape and dimensions of the skyscrapers depend entirely on the necessity of obtaining the maximum income per square foot of ground, and of offering to the tenants offices and apartments that please them. This caused the construction of gigantic buildings where too large masses of human beings are crowded together. Civilized men like such a way of living. While they enjoy the comfort and banal luxury of their dwelling, they do not realize that they are deprived of the necessities of life. The modern city consists of monstrous edifices and of dark, narrow streets full of petrol fumes, coal dust, and toxic gases, torn by the noise of the taxi-cabs, lorries and buses, and thronged ceaselessly by great crowds. Obviously, it has not been planned for the good of its inhabitants.

(Man, the Unknown, by Alexis Carrel)

④ I am always amazed when I hear people saying that sport creates goodwill between the nations, and that if only the common peoples of the world could meet one another at football or cricket, they would have no inclination to meet on the battlefield. Even if one didn't know from concrete examples (the 1936 Olympic Games, for instance) that international sporting contests lead to orgies of hatred, one could deduce it from general principles.

Nearly all the sports practised nowadays are competitive. You play to win, and the game has little meaning unless you do your utmost to win. On the village green, where you pick up sides and no feeling of local patriotism is involved, it is possible to play simply for the fun and exercise: but as soon as the question of prestige arises, as soon as you feel that you and some larger unit will be disgraced if you lose, the most savage combative instincts are aroused. Anyone who has played even in a school football match knows this. At the international level sport is frankly mimic warfare. But the significant thing is not the behaviour of the players but the attitude of the spectators: and, behind the spectators, of the nations who work themselves into furies over these absurd contests, and seriously believe—at any rate for short periods—that running, jumping and kicking a ball are tests of national virtue.

(*The Sporting Spirit*, by George Orwell)

⑤ Walking for walking's sake may be as highly laudable and exemplary a thing as it is held to be by those who practise it. My objection to it is that it stops the brain. Many a man has professed to me that his brain never works so well as when he is swinging along the high road or over hill and dale. This boast is not confirmed by my memory of anybody who on a Sunday morning has forced me to partake of his adventure. Experience teaches me that whatever a fellow-guest may have of power to instruct or to amuse when he is sitting in a chair, or standing on a hearth-rug, quickly leaves him when he takes one out for a walk. The ideas that come so thick and fast to him in any room, where are they now? where that encyclopaedic knowledge which he bore so lightly? where the kindling fancy that played like summer lightning over *any* topic that was started? The man's face that was so mobile is set now; gone is the light from his fine eyes. He says that A (our host) is a thoroughly good fellow. Fifty yards further on, he adds that A is one of the best fellows he has ever met. We tramp another furlong or so, and he says that Mrs A is a charming woman. Presently he adds that she is one of the most charming women he has ever known. We pass an inn. He reads vapidly aloud to me: 'The King's Arms. Licensed to sell Ales and Spirits.' I foresee that during the rest of the walk he will read aloud any inscription that occurs. We pass a milestone. He points at it with his stick, and says 'Uxminster. II Miles.' We turn a sharp corner at the foot of the hill. He points at the wall, and says 'Drive Slowly.' I see far ahead, on the other side of the hedge bordering the high road, a small notice-board. He sees it too. He keeps his eye on it. And in due course 'Trespassers,' he says, 'will be Prosecuted.' Poor man! —mentally a wreck.

(Going Out for a Walk, by Max Beerbohm)

第三节 小 说

小说创作种类繁多,有社会小说、心理小说、侦探小说、科幻小说、哲理小说、荒诞派小说、意识流小说、魔幻现实主义小说等等;然而不管是哪一种类型的小说,都离不开人物、情节、语言、风格这些创作要素。

小说的创作离不开人物的塑造和情节的安排。人和人的生活是文学的主要表现对象,而塑造丰满鲜明的人物形象,则是小说家共同的艺术追求。小说中的人物不仅具有典型性,而且是真实可信的。小说作者把人物放在特定的环境中、放在故事的情节中加以刻画。高尔基曾说过,情节是人物性格的发展史。作者按照自己的意图来安排小说的情节,以达到传达思想感情的目的。因此,人物形象是否丰满鲜明,故事情节是否引人入胜,常常是衡量一部小说成功与否的重要标志。

语言作为一种符号,不仅仅是小说创作的工具或外壳,它是小说创作中不可缺少的重要的参与者。小说语言具有极大的包容性,吸收各种文学艺术语言之长作者驾驭语言的能力直接影响到小说的创作,很难想象一个语言贫乏的人能创作出好的小说来。

不同的人有不同的创作风格。小说作为一种语言艺术,它的风格主要是通过人物形象、故事情节、语言运用等方面来集中体现的。美国的马克·吐温(Mark Twain)、海明威(Ernest Hemingway),我国的鲁迅、钱钟书等人都有各自鲜明的创作风格。

小说文体的主要特征对小说的翻译提出了特别的要求和应遵循的原则以及需加注意的问题。一篇好的小说译文从内容到风格都必须尽量贴近原文。

那么,具体来说,在翻译小说的过程中,应该注意哪些问题呢?下面将分别从语境的传译、人物描绘的传译、总体风格的传译、和写作技巧的传译等四个方面来加以说明。

一、语境的传译

语境(context),即语言环境,指的是运用语言进行交际的一定的具体场合。小说的语境都是特定语言创设的语境,语境转译比语义转译困难得多,有时语义虽然正确,但却并不能切合原作的语境。在进行语境的翻译时,不仅要注意选词的问题,而且还牵涉到使用什么样的句式以及选用哪种表达方式的问题。由于小说语境的形成受到许多因素的影响,如词语的选用,句式的调整,作者的意图和修养等等,因此在翻译过程中,译者必须把握原作的总体语境和个别语境,选用最佳表达方法,忠实地再现原文的语境。

以张谷若所译狄更斯长篇小说《大卫·考波菲尔》片断为例:

It was Miss Murdstone who has arrived, and a *gloomy looking* lady she was; dark, like her brother, whom she greatly resembled in face and voice; and with very heavy eyebrows, nearly meeting over her large nose, as if, being disabled by the wrongs of her sex from wearing whiskers, she had carried them to that account. She brought with her two *uncompromising* hard black boxes, with her initials on the lids in hard brass nails. When she paid the coachman she took her money out of a hard steel purse, and she kept the purse in *a very jail of a bag* which hung upon her arm by heavy chains, and shut up *like a bite*. I had never, at that time, seen such a *metallic* lady altogether as Miss Murdstone was.

来的不是别人,正是枚得孙小姐。只见这个妇人,满脸肃杀,发肤深色,和她兄弟一样,而且噪音,也都和她兄弟非常地像。两道眉毛非常地浓,在大鼻子上面几乎都连到一块儿了,好像因为她是女性,受了冤屈,天生地不能长胡子,所以才把胡子这笔帐,转到眉毛的帐上了。她带来了两个棱角峻嶒、非常坚硬的大黑箱子,用非常坚硬的铜钉,把她那姓名的字头,在箱子的盖儿上钉出来。她开发车钱的时候,她的钱是从一个非常坚硬的钢制钱包儿里拿出来的,而她这个钱包儿,又是装在一个和监狱似的手提包里,用一条粗链子挂在胳膊上,关上的时候像狠狠地咬了一口一样。我长到那个时候,还从来没见过别的妇人,有像枚得孙小姐那样完全如钢似铁的。

这段话描写的是枚得孙的姐姐兼管家初到考波菲尔家时的情况。狄更斯对这一人物显然是持否定态度的。张译深得作者意图,在遣词造句时处处注意反映作者精神、再现原文情境。如,"gloomy-looking"译为"满脸肃杀","uncompromising"译为"棱角峻嶒","like a bite"译为"像狠狠地咬了一口一样","metallic"译为"完全如钢似铁的"等。于是,这个人物的可怕形象跃然纸上,使译文读者产生如见其人的感觉。

再以黄源深翻译的夏洛特·勃朗蒂的长篇小说《简·爱》中的两段文字为例:

All John Reed's violent tyrannies, all his sisters' proud indifference, all his mother's aversion, all the servant's partiality, turned up in my disturbed mind like a dark deposit in a turbid well. I dared commit no fault; I strove to fulfil every duty; and I was termed naughty and tiresome, sullen and sneaking, from morning to noon, and from noon to night.

约翰·里德的专横霸道,他姐妹的高傲冷漠,他母亲的厌恶,仆人们的偏心,像一口混沌的水井中黑色的沉淀物,一古脑儿泛起在我烦恼不安的心头。我不敢有丝毫闪失,干什么都全力以赴,人家还是骂我淘气鬼、讨厌坯,骂我阴丝丝、贼溜溜,从早上骂到下午,从下午骂到晚上。

这段话描写的是简·爱在又一次遭到虐待之后心中的愤怒之

情。原文语气连贯，激越顺畅；译文选词准确，一气呵成。如，"naughty, tiresome, sullen, sneaking"译为"淘气鬼，讨厌坯，阴丝丝，贼溜溜"，生动传神，与上下文情境接合自然。

  Though rank and wealth sever us widely, I have something in my brain and heart, in my blood and nerves, that assimilates me mentally to him. Did I say, a few days since, that I had nothing to do with him but to receive my salary at his hands? Did I forbid myself to think of him in any other light than as a pay master? Blasphemy against nature! Every good, true, vigorous feeling I have gathers impulsively round him.

  虽然地位和财富把我们截然分开，但我的头脑里和心里，我的血液里和神经中，有着某种使我与他彼此心灵沟通的东西。难道几天前我不是说过，除了从他手里领取薪金，我同他没有关系吗？难道我除了把他看作雇主外，不是不允许自己对他有别的想法吗？这真是亵渎天性！我的每种善良、真实、生气勃勃的情感，都冲动地朝他涌去了。

  简·爱看着周旋在社会名流中的罗切斯特，内心不禁泛起阵阵感情的涟漪。原文对这段内心独白的刻画细致入微。译文同样真切感人。译者把"Blasphemy against nature!"译为"这真是亵渎天性！"把"gathers impulsively round him"译为"都冲动地朝他涌去了"，都是极符合语境的表达方法。

  又如萨克雷的长篇小说《名利场》中有这么一段话：

  Rebecca thought in her heart, 'Ah, mon beau monsieur! I think I have your gauge'——the little artful minx.

  杨必的译文是：

  利蓓加暗暗想道："哈，我的漂亮少爷，你是块什么材料可给我捉摸出来了。"这小姑娘是个诡计多端的狐媚子。

  《名利场》是萨克雷的代表作，小说的女主人公利蓓加·夏泼虽出身卑微,但她为跻身上流社会,谄媚阿谀,投机钻营,是个自私虚伪的人物。译文调整了句式,读来倍感顺畅。尤其是"artful"一词的翻译更是令人叫绝,因为"诡计多端"一词用在这里形容利蓓加的性格特征比其他的词都要贴切传神。

二、人物描绘的传译

人物描绘即人物刻画,它在小说中起着举足轻重的作用。人物描绘不仅包括人物的肖像和外貌,而且还包括人物的动作、语言、心理活动等等,以及与人物的性格发展有关的方方面面。在翻译时译者必须时刻注意与人物性格的一致性。什么样的人该说什么样的话,做什么样的事,对某件事情采取什么样的态度,这些都是译者应该加以考虑的。译者必须用心选词、寻找最恰当的表达方式,使小说中的人物通过译文在读者的心目中留下鲜明深刻的印象。

以黄怀仁、朱攸若两位合译的美国长篇小说《飘》的开篇段落为例:

Scarlett O'Hara was not beautiful, but men seldom realized it when caught by her charm as the Tarleton twins were. In her face were too sharply blended the delicate features of her mother, a Coast aristocrat of French descent, and the heavy ones of her florid Irish father. But it was an arresting face, pointed of chin, square of jaw. Her eyes were plae green without a touch of hazel, starred with brisitly black lashes and slightly titled at the ends. Above them, her thick black brows slanted upward, cutting a starting oblique line in her magnolia — white skin — that skin so prized by Southern women and so carefully guarded with bonnets, veils and mittens against hot Georgia suns.

Seated with Stuart and Brent Tarleton in the cool shade of the porch of Tara, her father's plantation, that bright April afternoon of 1861, she made a pretty picture. He new flowered—muslin dress spread its twelve yards of billowing material over her hopops and exactly matched the flat—heeled green morocco slippers her father had recently brought her from Atlanta. The dress set off to perfection the seventeen—inch waist, the smallest in three counties, and the tightly fitting basque showed breasts well matured for her sixteen years. But for all the modesty of her spreading skirts, the demureness of hair netted smoothly into a chignon and the quietness of small white hands folded in her lap, her true self was poorly concealed. The green eyes in the carefully sweet face were turbulent, willful, lusty with life, distinctly at variance with her decorous demeanor. Her manners had been imposed upon her by her mother's gentle admonitions and the sterner discipline of her mammy; her eyes were her own.

　　斯卡利特·奥哈拉长得不算美，但男人常常还来不及端详她的姿容，就被她的魅力所迷醉，比如塔尔顿家那对双胞胎兄弟，就正是如此。她脸上鲜明地糅杂着两种物质，一种是来自母方的纤细，一种是来自父系的粗犷。她母亲出身于法国血统的海岸贵族之家，父亲则是肤色红润的爱尔兰后裔。她的脸庞特别引人注目，尖尖的下巴，方方的牙床，一双浅绿色纯净的眸子，眼角微微翘起，长长的睫毛根根挺直，浓黑的眉毛成两条斜线，挂在木兰花般的白皙肌肤上——那是南方女人极为珍爱的玉肤，出门时要用面纱、软帽和手套保护起来，不让佐治亚州的灼热阳光把它晒黑。

　　1861年4月里的一天下午，阳光明媚。斯卡利特小姐在她爸爸那个叫作塔拉的庄园里，由塔尔顿家两兄弟，斯图尔特和布伦特陪着，坐在走廊的阴影处，显得颇为妩媚动人。她穿着一身簇新的绿色花布衣服，裙摆展开呈波浪形，脚上配着一双绿色平跟山羊皮鞋,那是她爸爸新近从亚特兰大给她买来的。这身衣服把她只有十七英寸的腰肢——邻近三个县里首屈一指的纤腰——衬托得格外窈窕。一件巴斯克紧身上衣贴着一对隆起的乳房,使这年方十六的妙龄少女,看起来相当丰满成熟。可是不管她那展开的长裙显得多么端庄,她那梳得平整的发髻多么严肃,她那交叠着放在膝盖上的雪白小手多么文静,却还是掩饰不了她的本性。在她可爱而正经的脸容上,那一双绿色的眼睛显得风骚、任性、充满活力,和她那淑静的举止丝毫不能相称。她的仪态是她母亲的谆谆教诲和嬷嬷的严厉管束强加于她的,那双眼睛才真正属于她自己。

  小说的开头详尽地描绘了女主人公斯卡利特·奥哈拉的形象,为以后刻画她的性格作了有力的铺垫。译者对原文仔细研究,融会贯通以后,用地道的汉语对原文进行了传译。使读者不像在读翻译作品,相反,倒像是作者在用汉语描写斯卡利特的外貌一样。译者把"But it was an arresting face, pointed of chin, square of jaw."译为"她的脸庞特别引人注目,尖尖的下巴,方方的牙床,……"把"The green eyes in the carefully sweet face were turbulent, willful, lusty with life, distinctly at variance with her decorous demeanor."译为"在她可爱而正经的脸容上,那一双绿色的眼睛显得风骚、任性、充满活力,和她那淑静的举止丝毫不能相称。"译文显得十分自然,将斯卡利特的形象描绘得栩栩如生。

  人物语言也是刻画人物形象的重要内容。在人物语言的翻译方面,黄源深翻译的《简·爱》是个很好的例子。

"Do you think I can stay to become nothing to you? Do you think I am an automation? —a machine without feelings? and can bear to have my morsel of bread snatched from my lips, and my drop of living water dashed from my cup? Do you think, because I am poor, obscure plain, and little, I am soulless and heartless? You think wrong! —I have as much soul as you—and full as much heart!"

"你难道认为,我会留下来甘愿做一个对你来说无足轻重的人?你以为我是一架机器?——一架没有感情的机器?能够容忍别人把一口面包从我嘴里抢走,把一滴生命之水从我杯子里泼掉?难道就因为我一贫如洗、默默无闻、长相平庸、个子瘦小,就没有灵魂没有心肠了?——你想错了!——我的心灵跟你一样丰富,我的心胸跟你一样充实!"

这段话呈现给读者的是一个自强自爱、要求平等的简·爱,她的精神和个性由此得到了充分的显示。译文在句子结构和语气上都极其忠实于原文,使女主人公的形象得到了准确生动的再现。

再如《简·爱》中男主人翁罗切斯特向简·爱诉说第一次婚姻时的一段话:

"The sea, which I could hear from thence, rumbled dull like an earthquake—black clouds were casting up over it; the moon was setting in the waves, broad and red, like a hot cannon—ball —she threw her last bloody glance over a world quivering with the ferment of tempest. I was physically influenced by the atmosphere and scene, and my ears were filled with the curses the maniac still shrieked out, wherein she momentarily mingled my name with such a tone of demon—hate, with such language! — no professed harlot ever had a fouler vocabulary than she: though two rooms off, I heard every word—the thin partitions of the West Indian house opposing but slight obstruction to her wolfish cries."

"在那儿我能听到大海之声,像地震一般沉闷地隆隆响着:黑云在大海上空集结,月亮沉落在宽阔的红色波浪上,像一个滚烫的炮弹——向颤抖着正酝酿风暴的海洋,投去血色的目光。我确实受这种气氛和景色的感染,而我的耳朵却充斥着疯子尖叫着的咒骂声,咒骂中夹杂着我的名字,语调里那么充满仇恨,语言又那么肮脏!——没有一个以卖淫为业的妓女,会使用比她更污秽的字眼,尽管隔了两个房间,我每个字都听得清清楚楚——西印度群岛房屋薄薄的隔板丝毫挡不住她狼一般的嚎叫。"

译文的读者在读了罗切斯特的这段倾诉之后,也会像原文的读者那样对他的不幸遭遇寄予深切的同情,因为译文同原文一样充满激情和诗意,一样令人产生惊心动魄之感。小说男主人公的形象变得更加丰满和鲜明。

又如张经浩先生翻译的英国女作家简·奥斯汀的《爱玛》,也是在人物描绘的传译上称得起是很出色的一部译作。现举两段译文为例:

"Emma Woodhouse, handsome, clever, and rich, with a comfortable home and happy disposition seemed to unite some of the best blessings of existence; and had lived nearly twenty—one years in the world with very little to distress or vex her."

爱玛·伍德豪斯简直是个得天独厚的人,又美丽,又聪明,又有钱,不但家里生活舒适,而且性情开朗。她快满二十一岁了,一直过着无忧无虑的生活。

原文用了一个长句来描写爱玛的形象,译文没有拘泥于原文的句式,用地道自然的汉语进行了传译,符合汉语语言"意合"的特点。译文不仅结构安排得好,而且选词造句极具匠心。如原文的"seemed to unite some of the best blessings of existence"译为"简直是个得天独厚的人";"handsome, clever, and rich"译为"又美丽,又聪明,又有钱"。于是,一个聪明美丽、家境富裕、快乐快乐的女主人公的形象立刻呈现在读者的面前。

They remained but a few minutes together, as Miss Woodhouse must not be kept waiting, and Harrit then came running to her with a smiling face, and in a flutter of spirits, which Miss

Woodhouse hoped very much to compose.

伍德豪斯小姐在等着，两人只站了一会儿。哈里特笑咪咪地跑过来，满脸高兴，伍德豪斯小姐一见马上就想泼一瓢凉水。

爱玛好管闲事，她觉得马丁配不上哈里特，因此她想让哈里特兴奋的心情"compose"下来。但如果译成"镇静下来"，在效果上就有些欠缺；译者用"泼一瓢凉水"来加以传译，可谓形象生动，爱玛那种富家小姐自以为是的性格尽现无遗。

事实上，人物刻画还可以通过很多其他途径加以体现，如行为动作、内心活动等等；译者能否将对人物的刻画准确生动地再现出来将直接影响到译作的效果。

三、风格的传译

小说的风格可以通过许多方面来体现，如小说的主题、人物形象、故事情节、使用的语言、创作的方法等等。译者不仅要忠实地再现原作的思想内容，而且还要再现原作的创作风格，只有同时做到了这两点，译文才能称得上是好的译文。

怎样才能再现原文的风格呢？译者首先必须把握作者的创作个性，其次要弄清作者的创作意图和创作方法。同时，译者也应了解作者的世界观、主要经历以及作品的创作情况。只有这样，译者才能更好地理解原作，也才能更好地再现原作的内容与语言特色。

萨克雷的《名利场》有这样一个片段：

... (her eyes) so attractive, that the Reverend Mr. Crisp, fresh from Oxford, and curate to the Vicar of Chiswick, the Reverend Mr. Flowerdew, fell in love with Miss Sharp, being shot dead by a glance of her eyes which was fired all the way across Chiswick Church from the schoolpew to the reading — desk. This infatuated young man used sometimes to take tea with Miss Pinkerton, to whom he had been presented by his mamma, and actually proposed something like marriage in an intercepted note, which the one—eyed applewoman was charged to deliver. Mrs. Crisp was summoned from Buxton, and abruptly carried off her darling boy, but the idea, even, of such an eagle in the Chiswick dovecot caused a great flutter in the breast of Miss Finkerton, who would have sent away Miss Sharp, but that she was bound to her under a forfeit, and who never could thoroughly believe the young lady's protestations that she had never exchanged a single word with mr. Crisp except under her own eyes on the two occasions when she had met him at tea.

杨必是这样翻译的：

契息克的弗拉沃丢牧师手下有一个副牧师，名叫克里斯泼，刚从牛津大学毕业，竟爱上了她。夏泼小姐的眼风穿过契息克教堂，从学校的包座直射到牧师的讲台上，一下子就把克里斯泼牧师射得灵魂出窍。这昏了头的小伙子本来是他妈妈介绍给平克顿小姐的，有时也来和平克顿小姐一块喝茶。他托那个独眼的卖苹果女人给她传递情书，被人发现，信里面的话简直等于向夏泼小姐求婚。克里斯泼太太得到消息，连忙从勒克登赶来，立刻把她的宝贝儿子带走了。平克顿小姐想到自己的鸽笼里藏了一只老鹰不由得心中忐忑不安，若不是有约在先，真想把夏泼小姐赶走。那女孩竭力辩白，说好只在平克顿小姐监视之下和克里斯泼先生在茶会上见过两面，说过两句话，此外从来没有跟他说过话。她虽然这么说，平克顿小姐仍旧将信将疑。

萨克雷创作的《名利场》揭露和讽刺了英国上流社会的堕落和虚伪。译者深刻领会作者的创作意图，用生动的笔触再现了原作那颇具讽刺味道的语言风格。译者将"…being shot dead by a glance of her eyes which was fired all the way across Chiswick Church from the schoolpew to the reading—desk."译为"夏泼小姐的眼风穿过契息克教堂,从学校的包座直射到牧师的讲台上,一下子就把克里斯泼牧师射得灵魂出窍。"其语言之形象与传神,实在令人叫绝。

又如海明威的《老人与海》中有这样一段话:

The boy went out. They had eaten with no light on the table and the old man took off his trousers and went to bed in the dark. He rolled his trousers up to make a pillow, putting the newspapers inside them. He rolled himself in the blanket and slept on the other old newspapers that covered the springs of the bed.

He was asleep in a short time and he dreamed of Africa when he was a boy and the long golden beaches and the white beaches, so white they hurt your eyes, and the high capes and the great brown mountains. He lived along that coast now every night and in his dreams heard the surf roar and saw the native boats come riding through it. He smelled the tar and oakum of the deck as he slept and he smelled the smell of Africa that the land breeze brought at morning.

孩子去了。他俩吃饭的时候,桌子上连个灯都没有。孩子走开以后,老头儿脱掉裤子,摸黑上了床。他把裤子卷成枕头,把那些报纸塞在里边,然后用军毯裹住身子,睡在破床弹簧上面的旧报纸上。

他不久就睡去,梦见了他儿童时代所看到的非洲,迤长的金黄色的海滩和白色的刺眼的海滩、高耸的海岬和褐色的大山。现在,他每晚住在海边,在梦中听到了海潮的怒号,看见了本地的小船从海潮中穿梭来去。睡着的时候,他闻到了甲板上柏油和填絮的味道,闻到了地面上的风在早晨送来的非洲的气息。　　(海观　译)

译文多用短句,简洁明快。这与海明威简洁的文风正好吻合。

除此而外,译文的遣词造句也切合原作朴实无华的语言特色,因而译文也较好地再现原文的总体效果。

再以马克·吐温的《百万英镑》中的一段话的原文及其译文为例:

"Let me just stand here a little and look my fill. Dear me! It's a palace — it's just a palace! And in it everything a body could desire, including cosy coal fire and supper standing ready. Henry, it doesn't merely make me realize how rich you are; it makes me realize to the bone, to the marrow, how poor I am — how poor I am, and how miserable, how defeated, routed, annihilated!"

让我在这儿站一会儿吧,我要看个够。好家伙!这简直是个皇宫——地道的皇宫!这里面一个人所能希望得到的,真是应有尽有,包括惬意的炉火,还有现成的晚饭。亨利,这不仅只叫我明白你有多么阔气;还叫我深入骨髓地看到我自己穷到了什么地步——我多么穷,多么倒霉,多么泄气,多么走投无路,真是一败涂地!

马克·吐温轻松幽默的文笔在上面这段原文中可见一斑,译文也相应地采用口语化的语言,读来轻松诙谐,较好地再现了原文的文风。

四、写作技巧的传译

细节描写是小说创作中常用的一种写作技巧。例如,约翰·高尔斯华绥的小说《开花的荒野》(*The Flowering Wildness*)中有这样一段文字:

She looked swiftly round the twilif room. His gun and sword lay ready on a chair! One supported disarmament, and armed children to the teeth! His other toys, mostly mechanized, would be in the schoolroom. No; there on the window still was the boat he had sailed with Ding, its sails still set; and there on a cushion in the corner was 'the silver dog', aware of her but too lazy to get up.

傅赵寰是这样翻译的:

她迅速环顾了一下那间灯光暗淡的房子。他的刀枪都在一张椅子上摆得好好的!人们支持裁军,却又把孩子全副武装起来!他的其他玩具,大部分是机械化的,一定都在书房里。不,窗台上不是放着他和丁妮玩过的那条船吗,帆篷都还没有收下来呢;墙角椅垫上也还躺着那条"银狗",明知她来了,却懒得起身。

原文的细节描写是为了揭示女主人公观察事物细致入微的性格。"No"后面用两个"there"引导两个分句,说明女主人公视线的转换。译者觉得直译难以表达原意,就把原来的句式改成了反问句和肯定句,收到了异曲同工的效果。

小说中的修辞手段的传译不是一件容易的事情。以《简·爱》中的一段为例:

When I saw my charmer thus come in accompanied by a cavalier, I seem to hear a hiss, and the green snake of jealousy, rising on undulating coils from the moonlit balcony, glided within my waistcoat, and ate its way in two minutes to my heart's core.

当我看见那个把我弄得神魂颠倒的女人,由一个好献殷勤的男人陪着进来时,我似乎听到了一阵嘶嘶声,绿色的妒嫉之蛇,从月光照耀下的阳台上呼地窜了出来,盘成了高低起伏的圈圈,钻进了我的背心,两分钟后一直咬啮到了我的内心深处。

小说把"嫉妒"比喻为"一条蛇",表达了罗切斯特对简·爱强烈的爱情。译文把原文的修辞直接移植了过来,并根据语境加了拟声词"呼地",使读者产生身临其境之感。

再如《简·爱》中的另一个例子:

"While such honeydew fell, such silence reigned, such

gloaming gathered, I felt as if I could haunt such shade for ever; …"

"在这种玉露徐降、悄无声息、夜色渐浓的时刻,我觉得仿佛会永远在这样的阴影里踯躅;……"

原文连续用了三个"such",语气连贯,富有文采;译文则用了"玉露徐降、悄无声息、夜色渐浓"三个汉语四字短语,文笔同样优美,语气也一样顺畅。

小说中有些具有民族特色或背景意义的表达方式在翻译时需要译者动一番脑筋。有时在没有办法的情况下,只好舍去不译,或者采用加注的办法加以弥补。

伊迪斯·华尔顿夫人(Mrs, Edith Wharton)的《伊坦·弗洛美》(*Ethan Frome*)中有这么一句话:

"No, I didn't forget; but it's as dark as Egypt outdoors. We might go tomorrow if there's a moon."

吕叔湘的译文为:

"没有,我倒没忘了;只是外头漆黑的。明儿个要是有月亮,明儿个去也成。"

原文中的词组"as dark as Egypt"出自圣经故事,讲的是以色列人逃出埃及时,摩西向天举手,埃及就三天三夜漆黑。译文中无法说明词组的来源,只能另外加注。

再如这部小说中的另一句话:

"… Where Mattie, encircled by facetions youths, and bright as a blackberry under her spreading hat, was brewing coffee over a gipsy fire."

原文中的"gipsy fire"原指像吉普赛人那样在野外点火烧饭,在这里宜直接译为"野火":

"玛蒂的身边围着一圈嘻嘻哈哈的年轻人,她头上戴着一顶阔边的帽子,漂亮得像一颗乌莓,正在一堆野火上煮咖啡。"

附：练习
　　将下列短文译成中文。

① The most important day I remember in all my life is the one on which my teacher, Anne Mansfield Sullivan, came to me. I am filled with wonder when I consider the immeasurable contrast between the two lives which it connects. It was the third of March. 1887, three months before I was seven years old.
　　On the afternoon of that eventful day, I stood on the porch, dumb, expectant. I guessed vaguely from my mother's signs and from the hurrying to and fro in the house that something unusual was about to happen, so I went to the door and waited on the steps. The afternoon sun penetrated the mass of honeysuckle that covered the porch, and fell on my upturned face. My fingers lingered almost unconsciously on the familiar leaves and blossoms which had just come forth to greet the sweet southern spring. I did not know what the future held of marvel or surprise for me. Anger and bitterness had preyed upon me continually for weeks and a deep languor had succeeded this passionate struggle. 　　　　　　　(*Ths Story of My Life*, by Helen Keller)

② On one of these occasions, when they had both been perfectly quiet for a long time, and Mr. Dombey only knew that the child was awake by occasionally glancing at his eyes where the bright fire was parkling like a jewel, little Paul broke silence thus:
　　"Papa! What's money?"
　　Mr Dombey was in a difficulty. He would have liked to give

him some explanation involving the terms circulating medium, currency, depreciations of currency, paper bullion, rates of exchange, values of precious metals in the market, and so forth; but looking down at the little chair, and seeing what a long way it was, he answered: "Gold and silver, and copper, guineas, shillings, half—pence. You know what they are."

"Oh, yes, I know what they are." said Paul, "I don't mean that, papa. I mean what's money after all?"

...

"What is money after all!" said Mr. Dombey backing his chair a little, that he might the better gaze in sheer amazement at the presumptuous atom that propounded such an inquery.

(*Donbay and Son*, by Charles Dickens)

③ Between the hounds and the horses and the twins there was a kinship deeper than that of their constant companionship. They were all healthy, thoughtless young animals, sleek, graceful, high—spirited, the boys as mettlesome as the horses they rode, mettlesome and dangerous but, withal, sweet — tempered to those who knew how to handle them.

(*Gone With the Wind*, by Margaret Michael)

④ Backstage the night of the performance, I felt nervous. A few minutes before the play, my teacher came over $ me. "Your mother asked me to give this to you," she said, handing me a dandelion. Its edges were already beginning to curl and it flopped lazily from its stem. But just looking at it, knowing my mother was out there and thinking of our lunchtime talk, made me proud.

After the play, I took home the flower I had stuffed in the apron of my costume. My mother pressed it between two sheets of paper toweling in a dictionary, laughing as she did it that we were perhaps the only people who would press such a sorry—looking weed.

(*My Mother's Gift*, by Suzanne Chazin)

第四节 戏 剧

英国是戏剧之邦。英语戏剧源远流长,其历史仅略短于诗歌,究竟起源于何时,实难确定。有证据证明在世纪初罗马人征服英格兰时就在当地建立了巨大的圆形剧场供戏剧表演之用。中世纪最早的纪录中所记载的表演都是由个人演出的,如弄臣、小丑、杂技演员、游吟诗人等,尤以游吟诗人起了最重要的作用。在10世纪时,教会在宗教仪式的基础上创造了宗教剧,接着又出现了奇迹剧、道德剧和娱乐观众的幕间短剧,他们仍属于宗教剧范畴。这些剧构成了中世纪主要的戏剧形式。16世纪中叶在文艺复兴运动的影响下,人文主义者利用戏剧来传播人文主义思想,在古希腊罗马戏剧的基础上创造了最初的英国喜剧和悲剧。到了伊丽莎白时代,最伟大的剧作家当属世界著名的戏剧大师莎士比亚(William Shakespeare 1564—1616)。1642年资产阶级革命开始以后,掌权的清教徒视戏剧为奢华堕落的享受,明令禁止戏剧演出。直到1660年查理二世王朝复辟后,英国戏剧才又兴旺起来。风俗喜剧在1688年以后发展至其顶峰。18世纪初英国戏剧的发展又处于低潮之中。18世纪下半叶仅出现了哥尔斯密(Oliver Goldsmith 1728—1774)和谢里丹(Richard Brinsley Sheridan 1751—1816)两位优秀的剧作家。而到19世纪末戏剧艺术的发展再一次处于停滞状态。其后出现了萧伯纳(George Bernard Shaw 1856—1950)的杰出的社会问题剧和王尔德(Oscar Wilde 1854—1900)的优秀风俗喜剧,推动了戏剧艺术的发展,迎来了20世纪上半叶英国戏剧的复兴。第二次世界大战后受各种现代主义和后现代主义思潮的影响,在英国产生了以贝克特(Samuel Beckett 1906—1989)、品特(Harold Pinter 1930—)为代表的荒诞派戏剧和奥斯本(John James Osborne 1929—)、奥顿(Joe Orton 1933—1967)为代表的愤怒派戏剧。而在美国,在20世纪20年代著名的剧作家奥尼尔(Eugene O'Neill 1888—1953)出现之前,几乎可以说美国戏剧在文学园地中不占什么地位。毫无疑问奥尼尔是美国最伟大的剧作家。第二次世界大战后著名的美国剧作家有米勒(Arthur Miller 1915—)、威廉斯(Tennessee Williams 1911—1983)、阿尔比(Edward Franklin Albee 1928—)等。

戏剧语言在戏剧中占有特殊的、绝对重要的地位。剧中人物的性格、故事情节,都通过人物自己的语言来表现。戏剧语言称为台词,有三种表现形式,第一种是对白,第二种是独白,第三种是旁白。这三种台词效用是各不相同的。对白是人物间的对话,这是主体;独白往往是人物内心的坦露;旁白则是背着剧中别的人物对观众的交待。

戏剧语言一方面来自生活,具有口语化的特点,保持着日常口语的活力与通俗易懂的长处,另一方面又是对日常语言加工提炼的结果,具有审美情趣。概括起来,戏剧语言有以下几个特点,在翻译中应特别引起注意。第一,性格化。在现实生活中人的性格、修养、趣味、感情等是多种多样的,说出的话也就各不相同。戏剧语言必须起到揭示人物各自不同的性格特征与内心世界的作用。第二,动作性。戏剧是在舞台上表演的艺术,人物的语言和动作密不可分。人物的语言必须具有动作性。第三,含蓄性。戏剧语言应精练而含蓄,富有潜台词。有限的台词却道出了无限的生活内容。戏剧语言的含蓄性对揭示剧中人物之间的关系与情节的进展有不可忽视的作用。在戏剧中常常使用象征和隐喻这一类修辞手段，使得语言的内涵更加丰富、形象，甚至整个戏都具有象征的意义。第四，优美性。戏剧语言经过剧作家加工提炼，又比日常口语具有更强的节奏感，甚至带有音乐般的韵律。有的语言更有诗一般的文采。这种更集中更优美的语言才会给人留下深刻的印象和回味的余地。但戏剧语言同时又必须准确明白、口语化，避免书卷习气，佶屈聱牙，否则观众无法接受。

译文中必须体现戏剧语言的这些特点，这给翻译带来了困难。现举几例：

Portia: A pound of that same merchant's flesh is thine:
　　The court awards it, and the law doth give it.
Shylock: Most rightful judge!
Portia: And you must cut this flesh from off his breast:
　　The law allows it, and the court awards it.
Shylock: Most learned judge! A sentence! Come, prepare!
Portia: Tarry a little; there is something else.
　　This bond doth give thee here no jot of blood;
　　The words expressly are a 'pound of flesh';
　　Take then thy bond, take thou thy pound of flesh;
　　But, in the cutting it, if thou dost shed
　　One drop of Christian blood, thy lands and goods
　　Are, by the laws of Venice, confiscate
　　Unto the state of Venice.
Gratiano: O upright judge! Mark, Jew! O learned judge!
Shylock: Is that the law?
Portia: Thyself shalt see the act;
　　For, as thou urgest justice, be assur'd

Thou shalt have justice, more than thou desir'st.

Gratiano: O learned judge! Mark, Jew: A learned judge!

Shylock: I take this offer, then; pay the bond thrice,
And let the Christian go.

Bassanio: Here is the money.

Portia: Soft! The Jew shall have all justice; soft! no haste:—
He shall have nothing but the penalty.

Gratiano: O Jew! an upright judge, a learned judge!

Portia: Therefore prepare thee to cut off the flesh.
Shed thou no blood; nor cut thou less, nor more,
But just a pound of flesh: if thou tak'st more,
Or less, than a just pound, be it so much
As makes it light or heavy in the substance,
Or the division of the twentieth part
Of one poor scruple, nay, if the scale do turn
But in the estimation of a hair,
Thu diest and all thy goods are confiscate.

(*Act* Ⅳ, *The Merchant of Venice*,
by William Shakespeare)

鲍西娅：那商人身上的一磅肉是你的；法庭判给你，法律许可你。

夏洛克：公平正直的法官！

鲍西娅：你必须从他的胸前割下这磅肉来；法律许可你，法庭判给你。

夏洛克：博学多才的法官！判得好！来，预备！

鲍西娅：且慢，还有别的话哩。这契约上并没有允许你取他的一滴血，只是写明着"一磅肉"；所以你可以照约拿一磅肉去，可是在割肉的时候，要是流下一滴基督徒的血，你的土地财产，按照威尼斯的法律，就要全部充公。

葛莱西安诺：啊，公平正值的法官！听着，犹太人；啊，博学多才的法官！

夏洛克：法律上是这样说吗？

鲍西娅：你自己可以去查查明白。既然你要求公道，我就给你公道，而且比你所要求的更公道。

葛莱西安诺：啊，博学多才的法官！听着，犹太人；好一个博学多才的法官！

夏洛克：那么我愿意接受还款；照契约上的数目三倍还我，放了那基督徒。

巴萨尼奥：钱在这儿。

鲍西娅：别忙！这犹太人必须得到绝对的公道。别忙！他除了照约处罚以外，不能接受其他的赔偿。

葛莱西安诺：啊，犹太人！一个公平正直的法官，一个博学多才的法官！

鲍西娅：所以你准备着动手割肉吧。不准流一滴血，也不准割得超过或是不足一磅的重量；要是你割下来的肉，比一磅略微轻一点或是重一点，即使相差只有一丝一毫，或者仅仅一根汗毛之微，就要把你抵命，你的财产全部充公。

（朱生豪　译）

《威尼斯商人》是莎士比亚著名的喜剧，第四幕法庭上的一场乃本戏高潮，充分表现了夏洛克的残忍，鲍西娅的机智和安东尼奥的忠实。莎士比亚通过生动的语言充分体现了三人各自不同的个性。朱生豪先生的译文将原作的语言特征完满地再现出来。例如将鲍西娅的话译为："那商人身上的一磅肉是你的；法庭判给你，法律许可你。"将她接着说的话又译为："你必须从他的胸前割下这磅肉来；法律许可你，法庭判给你。"不仅意思明确，语言工整，且原文深层的含蓄也藏进了译文。"必须"一词和原句中的"must"相对应，成了下文转折的关键。而莎士比亚优美简练的诗句"The court awards, and the law doth give it."的风韵也在译文的"法庭判给你,法律许可你"这两句中展现无遗。译者将"Tarry a little"译成"且慢",将"confiscate unto the state of Venice"译成"充公",将"division of the twentieth part of one poor scruple"译成"相差只有一丝一毫",将"if the scale do turn but in the estimation of a hair"译成"仅仅一根汗毛之微",译文既生动又简练,十分忠实地表达了原文的含义,而又紧随汉语习惯,朗朗上口,正符合戏剧语言的要求。同时译文又保持了原文的高雅用词和古朴风格,使读者体验到原作的诗意。这样的译文值得学习仿效。

Lady Bracknell: (*sitting down*) You can take a seat, Mr. Worthing. (*Looks in her pocket for note-book and pencil.*)

Jack: Thank you, Lady Bracknell, I prefer standing.

Lady Bracknell: (*pencil and note-book in hand*) I feel bound to tell you that you are not down on my list of eligible young men, although I have the same list as the dear Duchess of Bolton has. We work together, in fact. However, I am quite ready to enter your name, should your answers be what a really affectionate mother requires. Do you smoke?

Jack: Well, yes, I must admit I smoke.

Lady Bracknell: I am glad to hear it. A man should always have an occupation of some kind. There are far too many idle men in London as it is. How old are you?

Jack: Twenty-nine.

Lady Bracknell: A very good age to be married at. I have always been of opinion that a man who desires to get married should know either everything or nothing. Which do you know?

Jack (*after some hesitation*). I know nothing, Lady Bracknell.

Lady Bracknell: I am pleased to hear it. I do not approve of anything that tampers with natural ignorance. Ignorance is like a delicate exotic fruit; touch it and the bloom is gone. The whole theory of modern education is radically unsound. Fortunately in England, at any rate, education produces no effect whatsoever. If it did, it would prove a serious danger to the upper classes, and probably lead to acts of violence in Grosvenor Square. What is your income?

Jack: Between seven and eight thousand a year.

Lacy Bracknell: (*makes a note in her book*) In land, or in investments?

Jack: In investments, chiefly.

Lady Bracknell: That is satisfactory. What between the duties expected of one during one's life-time, and the duties exacted from one after one's death, land has ceased to be either a profit or a pleasure. It gives one position, and prevents one from keeping it up. That's all that can be said about land.

Jack: I have a country house with some land, of course, attached to it, about fifteen hundred acres, I believe; but I don't depend on that for my real income. In fact, as far as I can make out, the poachers are the only people who make anything out of it.

Lady Bracknell: A country house! How many bedrooms? Well, that point can be cleared up afterwards. You have a town house, I hope. A girl with a simple, unspoiled nature, like Gwendolen, could hardly be expected to reside in the country.

Jack: Well, I own a house in Belgrave Square, but it is let by the year to Lady Bloxham. Of course, I can get it back whenever I like, at six months' notice.

(Act I, The Importance of Being Earnest, by Oscar Wilde)

布雷克耐尔夫人：(坐下)你可以坐下,沃辛先生。(在口袋里找笔记本和铅笔。)

杰克：谢谢您,布雷克耐尔夫人,我喜欢站着。

布雷克耐尔夫人：(手拿着铅笔和笔记本)我觉得一定要告诉你,你不在我合格的年轻人的名单上,尽管我的名单和亲爱的勃尔顿公爵夫人的一样。事实上我们是在一起拟的。不过如果你的回答正是一个真正深爱子女的母亲所要求的话,我很乐意把你的名字登记进去。你抽烟吗？

杰克：嗯,是的,我必须承认我抽烟。

布雷克耐尔夫人：听你这样说我很高兴。一个男人总应该有点事干。事实上在伦敦游手好闲的人太多了。你多大年纪？

杰克：二十九岁。

布雷克耐尔夫人：正是结婚的好岁数。我一直认为一个想结婚的男人应该什么都懂或者什么都不懂。你是哪一种？

杰克：(犹豫一下)我什么都不懂,布雷克耐尔夫人。

布雷克耐尔夫人：听你这样说我很满意。减轻蒙昧无知的一切办法我都不赞成。无知就像是一种外国来的娇嫩水果,碰一下,就不鲜了。现代教育的整个理论根本就有毛病。好在,在英国教育没有产生任何效果。如果有的话,那对上层阶级就会是一大危险,可能会导致格罗斯文诺广场的暴力行为。你收入多少？

杰克：一年七千到八千英镑。

布雷克耐尔夫人：(记在笔记本上)土地还是投资？

杰克：主要是投资。

布雷克耐尔夫人：这很让人满意。土地活着要交税,死后还要交税,既生不了利也无乐趣可言。土地让人有地位,但又让人保不住地位。对土地所能说的就是这些。

杰克：我在乡下有幢房子,还有些地,当然紧靠房子,我想大约有一千五百英亩。但我的真正收入不靠它。事实上,就我所知,来偷猎的人才是唯一的受惠者。

布雷克耐尔夫人：乡下有幢房子！有多少间卧室？嗯,这一点以后能弄清楚。我希望你城里有幢房子。像格温多琳这样生性单纯朴质的姑娘总不能要她住在乡下。

杰克：嗯,我在贝尔格莱夫广场有一幢房子,不过按年租给了布洛克珊姆夫人。当然我什么时候想要,提前半年通知就可以收回来。

《贵在认真》是英国19世纪末著名的喜剧作家王尔德(Oscar Wilde)的代表作之一。该剧于1895年上演,被认为是王尔德事业的顶峰,迄今仍然是最受欢迎的英国戏剧之一。这是一出讽刺喜剧,情节荒诞可笑,讲的是两个花花公子的恋爱故事。剧名中"Earnest"一词是个双关语,既是人名又有原意"认真"的意思。而一位年轻的小姐爱的正是这个名字,于是也就爱上了叫这个名字的青年人而不管他是谁。这样的事情超出常理,然而这正反映了上层阶级生活的空虚无聊,追求刺激。从上面一段两个人物的生动对话中可看出所谓上流社会的择婿标准。

这一段对白不仅刻画了两个人物各自的性格,也揭示了不同的社会背景。布雷克耐尔夫人是一位典型的城里上流社会的有钱女人,势利、浅薄、傲慢、无知。她的眼睛只见钱不见人。她的择婿标准不在人品,甚至也不在地位,而在钱。她也不顾年轻人是否真正相爱,只要是有钱、有家产就可以成为她的女婿。她在提问和评论中毫不隐讳地公开宣布自己的主张。她的话有时荒唐得出人预料,但这正是这些阔太太们的真实写照。

杰克其实也是一位花花公子,有钱的少爷,不过却在乡下长大,毫无社会经验,在骄傲自大的布雷克耐尔夫人面前显得拘束而腼腆,几乎有些手足无措。他听着布雷克耐尔夫人的令人费解的评论不知说什么好,只得老老实实地回答问题,把自己的底细无保留地一一抖露出来。

两人的性格和背景形成了对照,相应地两人的语言也形成了对照。布雷克耐尔夫人占据对话的中心位置,不仅提问,还长篇大论地发表意见。句子长而复杂,跳动性大。杰克则似乎处于受审地位,只敢简单明了地回答问题。句子短而简单,大多只用短语。例如回答年龄的问话时只说了四个字:二十九岁。在回答一年有多少收入时只说了钱数:一年七千到八千英镑。关于收入来源也只用了五个字:主要是投资。

译文很注意保持原有对话的风格,较好地体现了人物的不同个性。语句的长短结构、用词的变化均与原文十分相称。如将"That is satisfactory, What between the duties expected of one during one's life-time, and the duties exacted from one after one's death, land has ceased to be either a profit or a pleasure."译成"这很让人满意。土地活着要交税,死后还要交税,既生不了利也毫无乐趣可言。"又如,将"Ignorance is like a delicate exotic fruit; touch it and the bloom is gone."译成"无知像一种外国来的娇嫩的水果,碰一下就不鲜了。"这不仅忠实地传达了原句的意思,其句子结构和言语节奏也与原句无异,用词又极符合汉语习惯,将"bloom"一词译成"鲜",十分传神。此外译文中有的词译法也颇具匠心。例如:将"enter your name"中的"enter"一词译为"登记",这既和布雷克耐尔夫人一手拿笔一手拿笔记本的形象相呼应,又与她说的长长"名单"这一用词统一起来,读者会深深感到其中的讽刺意味。这哪里是和未来的女婿谈话,这简直是在作人口调查。又如,将布雷克耐尔夫人自称的"affectionate mother"译成"深爱子女的母亲"和"idle men"译成"游手好闲的人",其中的幽默也展现无余。读者不禁会感到好笑,她居然也称得上"深爱子女的母亲",而抽烟的人却算有事可做,不在"游手好闲的人"之列,这真是天大的讽刺。

Liza: How do you do, Professor Higgins? Are you quite well?

Higgins: (*choking*) Am I — (*He can say no more*).

Liza: But of course you are: you are never ill. So glad to see you again, Colonel Pickering. (*He rises hastily; and they shake hands*). Quite chilly this morning, isnt it? (*She sits down on his left, he sits beside her.*)

Higgins: Dont you dare try this game on me. I taught it to you; and it doesn't take me in. Get up and come home; and don't be a fool.

Eliza takes a piece of needlework from her basket, and begins to stitch at it, without taking the least notice of this outburst.

Mrs Higgins: Very nicely put, indeed, Henry. No woman could resist such an invitation.

Higgins: You let her alone, mother. Let her speak for herself. You will jolly soon see whether she has an idea that I havnt put into her head or a word that I havnt put into her mouth. I tell you I have created this thing out of the squashed cabbage leaves of Covent Garden; and now she pretends to play the fine lady with me.

Mrs Higgins: (*placidly*) Yes, dear; but you'll sit down, won't you?

(*Higgins sits down again, savagely.*)

Liza: (*to Pickering, taking no apparent notice of Higgins, and working away deftly*) Will you drop me altogether now that the experiment is over, Colonel Pickering?

Pickering: Oh dont. You mustn't think of it as an experiment. It shocks me, somehow.

Liza: Oh, I'm only a squashed cabbage leaf—

Pickering: (*impulsively*) No.

Liza: (*continuing quietly*) — but I owe so much to you that I should be very unhappy if you forgot me.

Pickering: It's very kind of you to say so, Miss Doolittle.

Liza: It's not because you paid for my dresses. I know you are generous to everybody with money. But it was from you that I learnt really nice manners; and that is what makes one a lady, isn't it? You see it was so very difficult for me with the example of Professor Higgins always before me. I was brought up to be just like him, unable to control myself, and using bad language on the slightest provocation. And I should never have known that ladies and gentlemen didn't behave like that if you hadn't been there.

(Act V, *Pygmalion*, by George Bernrd Shaw)

莉莎:您好,希金斯教授。您身体好吗?

希金斯:(噎住了)我——(他再也说不出话来)

莉莎:您当然很好,从来不生病。很高兴又见到您,皮克林上校。(他赶快站起来,相互握手。)今天早晨很冷,是吗?(她在他的左边坐下,他坐在她身边。)

希金斯:你敢对我玩这一套把戏。是我教给你的,你骗不了我。起来,回家去,别犯傻。(莉莎从篮中拿出一件针线活,开始绣起来,全不理会他的发火。)

希金斯夫人:亨利,话说得真好。这样的请求没有哪个女人能不接受。

希金斯：妈妈，你别管她。让她自己说。你马上会看见她是不是有一个主意不是我塞进她脑子里去的，或者有一个字不是我塞进她嘴里的。告诉你，我把考文特花园的烂菜叶变成了这个玩艺，现在她倒跟我装起大小姐来了。

希金斯夫人：（平静地）是的，亲爱的，但是你先坐下来，好吗？

（希金斯又怒冲冲地坐下来。）

莉莎：（表面上不理希金斯，灵巧地做她的针线活，朝皮克林说）既然试验已经完了，您会全丢下我不管吗，皮克林上校？

皮克林：啊，别这样说。您不该把这看成是一种试验。这让我有些吃惊。

莉莎：啊，我只不过是片烂菜叶——

皮克林：（冲动地）不。

莉莎：（平静地接着说）——我欠您的情太多了，如果您忘记了我，我会很难过的。

皮克林：您这样说太客气了，杜里特尔小姐。

莉莎：不是因为您花钱替我买衣服。我知道您对大家花钱都很慷慨。是从您身上我学到了真正文雅的举止；正是这一点使人变成一位小姐，对不对？您看在我面前一直有希金斯教授这样一个榜样，要学到这点真难。原来我长大成人就像他一样。不能控制自己，遇到一点点刺激就说粗话。如果没有您在面前的话，我决不会知道小姐和先生们的举止不像那种样子。

《卖花女》是20世纪英国著名的现实主义戏剧大师萧伯纳的名剧，讲的是卖花女莉莎在语言学教授希金斯的教导下由一个出身低贱、满口污言秽语的粗俗少女变成一位姿态高贵、谈吐文雅、俨然大家闺秀的故事。除了其中饱含的幽默和讽刺之外，语言的运用十分巧妙，恰如其分地反映了剧中各个人物的身分、背景和性格。既有上层人士温文尔雅的文明语言，又有下层阶级缺乏教养的通俗口语，以至土语、方言、俚语、粗话等，给人留下深刻印象。萧伯纳的确不愧为一位杰出的语言大师。

具有讽刺意味的是，莉莎举止端庄，语言彬彬有礼，希金斯教授反而控制不住自己，情绪冲动，语言粗俗。两者形成鲜明的对照。而这一对照恰恰是戏剧开始时的反面。

译文较好地体现了原文的语言风格。莉莎的语言十分正规而有礼貌。她对别人说话都称呼"您"。见面就问"身体好吗？"并和客人皮克林上校握手。接着按上层社会的习惯客套，谈论起天气来。希金斯教授的答话却十分粗俗。译文将"try this game"，"Get up and come home; and don't be a fool."译成"玩这一套把戏"，"起来，回家去，别犯傻"。十分符合原文中说话人粗暴无礼的态度和粗俗的用词。在下文又将"put into her head"和"put into her mouth"中的"put into"译成"塞进"。这一动词十分传神，生动表明了希金斯当时说话的口气。希金斯骂莉莎是"squashed cabbage leaves"。译者将其简译成"烂菜叶"，既忠实于原文意思，又简练上口，符合汉语习惯。译者更将"created this thing"译成"变成了这个玩艺"，充分表明了希金斯对莉莎的厌恶与蔑视。莉莎的最后一段讲话暗含着对希金斯的指责与讽刺，借与皮克林的对比来衬托出希金斯恶劣专横的作风。译文较好地体现了原文含沙射影又措词温和的风格。如将最后一句"And I should never have known that ladies and gentlemen didn't behave like that if you hadn't been there."译成"如果没有您在面前的话，我决不会知道小姐和先生们的举止不像那种样子。"准确而恰当地表达了原句的含蓄语气。

附：练习

将下列戏剧片断译成中文。

① *Enter* portia, *dressed like a doctor of laws*, *with* NERISSA *and others*.

Duke: Give me your hand. Came you from old Bellario?
Portia: I did, my lord.
Duke: You are welcome: take your place.
    Are you acquainted with the difference
    That holds this present question in the court?
Portia: I am informed throughly of the cause. Which is the merchant here, and which the Jew?
Duke: Antonio and old Shylock, both stand forth.
Portia: Is your name Shylock?
Shylock: Shylock is my name.
Portia: Of a strange nature is the suit you follow;
    Yet in such rule that the Venetian law
    Cannot impugn you as you do proceed. (*To* Antonio)
    You stand within his danger, do you not?
Antonio: Ay, so he says.
Portia: Do you confess the bond?
Antonio: I do.
Portia: Then must the Jew be merciful.
Shylock: On what compulsion must I? Tell me that.
Portia: The quality of mercy is not strain'd.
    It droppeth like the gentle rain from heaven
    Upon the place beneath. It is twice bless'd;
    It blesseth him that gives and him that takes:
    'Tis mightiest in the mightiest: it becomes
    The throned monarch better than his crown.
    His sceptre shows the force of temporal power,
    The attribute to awe and majesty,
    Wherein doth sit the dread and fear of kings;

But mercy is above this sceptred sway;
It is enthroned in the hearts of kings,
It is an attribute to God himself;
And earthly power doth then show likest God's
When mercy seasons justice. Therefore, Jew,
Though justice be thy plea, consider this, —
That, in the course of justice, none of us
Should see salvation: we do pray for mercy,
And that same prayer doth teach us all to render
The deeds of mercy. I have spoke thus much
To mitigate the justice of thy plea,
Which if thou follow, this strict court of Venice
Must needs give sentence 'gainst the merchant there.
Shylock: My deeds upon my head! I crave the Law: —
The penalty and forfeit of my bond.
Portia: Is he not able to discharge the money?
Bassanio: Yes, here I tender it for him in the court;
Yea, twice the sum: if that will not suffice,
I will be bound to pay it ten times o'er
On forfeit of my hands, my head, my heart;
If this will not suffice, it must appear
That malice bears down truth. And, I beseech you,
Wrest once the law to your authority:
To do a great right, do a little wrong,
And curb this cruel devil of his will.
Portia: It must not be; there is no power in Venice
Can alter a decree established;
'Twill be recorded for a precedent,

>   And many an error by the same example
>   Will rush into the state. It cannot be.
> Shylock: A Daniel come to judgment! Yea, a Daniel!
>   O wise young judge, how do I honour thee!
> Portia: I pray you, let me look upon the bond.
> Shylock: Here 'tis, most reverend doctor, here it is.
> Portia: Shylock, there's thrice thy money offer'd thee.
> Shylock: An oath, an oath, I have an oath in heaven:
>   Shall I lay perjury upon my soul?
>   No, not for Venice.
> Portia: Why, this bond is forfeit;
>   And lawfully by this the Jew may claim
>   A pound of flesh, to be by him cut off
>   Nearest the merchant's heart. Be merciful:
>   Take thrice thy money, bid me tear the bond.
> Shylock: When it is paid according to the tenour.
>   It doth appear you are a worthy judge;
>   You know the law: your exposition
>   Hath been most sound. I charge you by the law,
>   Whereof you are a well-deserving pillar,
>   Proceed to judgment: by my soul I swear
>   There is no power in the tongue of man
>   To alter me. I stay here on my bond.
>   (*Act* IV *The Merchant of Venice*,
>   by William Shakespeare)

② Jack: Charming day it has been, Miss Fairfax.
Gwendolen: Whenever people talk to me about the weather, I al-

ways feel quite certain that they mean something else. And that makes me so nervous.

Jack: I do mean something else.

Gwendolen: I thought so. In fact, I am never wrong.

Jack: And I would like to be allowed to take advantage of Lady Bracknell's temporary absence ...

Gwendolen: I would certainly advise you to do so. Mamma has a way of coming back suddenly into a room that I have often had to speak to her about.

Jack: (*nervously*) Miss Fairfax, ever since I met you I have admired you more than any girl ... I have ever met since ... I met you.

Gwendolen: Yes, I am quite aware of the fact. And I often wish that in public, at any rate, you had been more demonstrative. For me you have always had an irresistible fascination. Even before I met you I was far from indifferent to you. (*JACK looks at her in amazement.*) We live, as I hope you know, Mr. Worthing, in an age of ideals. The fact is constantly mentioned in the more expensive monthly magazines, and has reached the provincial pulpits I am told: and my ideal has always been to love some one of the name of Ernest. There is something in that name that inspires absolute confidence. The moment Algernon first mentioned to me that he had a friend called Ernest, I knew I was destined to love you.

Jack: You really love me, Gwendolen?

Gwendolen: Passionately!

Jack: Darling! You don't know how happy you've made me.

Gwendolen: My own Ernest!

Jack: But you don't really mean to say that you couldn't love me if my name wasn't Ernest?

Gwendolen: But your name is Ernest.

Jack: Yes, I know it is. But supposing it was something else? Do you mean to say you couldn't love me then?

Gwendolen: (*glibly*) Ah! that is clearly a metaphysical speculation, and like most metaphysical speculations has very little reference at all to the actual facts of real life, as we know them.

Jack: Personally, darling, to speak quite candidly, I don't much care about the name of Ernest ... I don't think that name suits me at all.

Gwendolen: It suits you perfectly. It is a divine name. It has a music of its own. It produces vibrations.

Jack: Well, really, Gwendolen, I must say that I think there are lots of other much nicer names. I think, Jack, for instance, a charming name.

Gwendolen: Jack? ... No, there is very little music in the name Jack, if any at all, indeed. It does not thrill. It produces absolutely no vibrations ... I have known several Jacks, and they all, without exception, were more than usually plain. Besides, Jack is a notorious domesticity for John! And I pity any woman who is married to a man called John. She would probably never be allowed to know the entrancing pleasure of a single moment's solitude. The only really safe name is Ernest.

(*Act I, The Importance of Being Earnest*, by Oscar Wilde)

③ Higgins: Come back to business. How much do you propose to pay me for the lessons?

Liza: Oh, I know whats right. A lady friend of mine gets French lessons for eighteen-pence an hour from a real French gentleman. Well, you wouldn't have the face to ask me the same for teaching me my own language as you would for French; so I wont give more than a shilling. Take it or leave it.

Higgins: (*walking up and down the room, rattling his keys and his cash in his pockets*) You know, Pickering, if you consider a shilling, not as a simple shilling, but as a percentage of this girl's income, it works out as fully equivalent to sixty or seventy guineas from a millionaire.

Pickering: How so?

Higgins: Figure it out. A millionaire has about £150 a day. She earns about half-a-crown.

Liza: (*haughtily*) Who told you I only—

Higgins: (*continuing*) She offers me two fifths of her day's income for a lesson. Two fifths of a millionaire's income for a day would be somewhere about £60. It's handsome. By George, it's enormous! It's the biggest offer I ever had.

Liza: (*rising, terrified*) Sixty pounds! What are you talking about? I never offered you sixty pounds. Where would I get —

Higgins: Hold your tongue.

Liza: (*weeping*) But I ain't got sixty pounds. Oh—

Mrs Pearce: Don't cry, you silly girl. Sit down. Nobody is going to touch your money.

Higgins: Somebody is going to touch you, with a broomstick, if you don't stop snivelling. Sit down.

Liza: (*obeying slowly*) Ah—ah—ah—ow—oo—o! One would think you was my father.

Higgins: If I decide to teach you, I'll be worse than two fathers to you. Here (*he offers her his silk handkerchief*)!

Liza: What's this for?

Higgins: To wipe your eyes. To wipe any part of your face that feels moist. Remember: that's your sleeve. Don't mistake the one for the other if you wish to become a lady in a shop.

Liza, utterly bewildered, stares helplessly at him.

Mrs Pearce: It's no use talking to her like that, Mr. Higgins: she doesn't understand you, besides, you're quite wrong: she doesnt do it that way at all (*she takes the handkerchief.*)

Liza: (*snatching it*) Here! You give me that handkerchief. He gave it to me, not to you.

(*Act* II, *Pygmalion*, by George Bernard Shaw)

④ *The* Inspector *is watching* Birling *and now* Birling *notices him.*

Inspector: I think you remember Eva Smith now, don't you, Mr. Birling?

Birling: Yes, I do. She was one of my employees and then I discharged her.

Eric: Is that why she committed suicide? When was this, Father?

Birling: Just keep quiet, Eric, and don't get excited. This girl left us nearly two years ago. Let me see — it must have been in the early autumn of nineteen-ten.

Inspector: Yes. End of September, nineteen-ten.

Birling: That's right.

Gerald: Look here, sir. Wouldn't you rather I was out of this?

Birling: I don't mind your being here, Gerald. And I'm sure you've no objection, have you, Inspector? Perhaps I ought to explain first that this is Mr. Gerald Croft — the son of Sir George Croft — you know, Crofts Limited.

Inspector: Mr. Gerald Croft, eh?

Birling: Yes. Incidentally we've been modestly celebrating his engagement to my daughter, Sheila.

Inspector: I see. Mr. Croft is going to marry Miss Sheila Birling?

Gerald (*smiling*): I hope so.

Inspector (*gravely*): Then I'd prefer you to stay.

Gerald (*surprised*): Oh — all right.

Birling (*somewhat impatiently*): Look — there's nothing mysterious — or scandalous — about this business — at least not so far as I'm concerned. It's a perfectly straightforward case, and as it happened more than eighteen months ago — nearly two years ago — obviously it has nothing whatever to do with the wretched girl's suicide. Eh, Inspector?

Inspector: No, sir. I can't agree with you there.

Birling: Why not?

Inspector: Because what happened to her then may have determined what happened to her afterwards, and what happened to her afterwards may have driven her to suicide. A chain of events.

Birling: Oh well-put like that, there's something in what you say. Still, I can't accept any responsibility. If we were all responsible for everything that happened to everybody we'd had anything to do with, it would be very awkward, wouldn't it?

Inspector: Very awkward.

Birling: We'd all be in an impossible position, wouldn't we?

Eric: By Jove, yes. And as you were saying, Dad, a man has to look after himself—

Birling: Yes, well, we needn't go into all that.

Inspector: Go into what?

Birling: Oh—just before you came—I'd been giving these young men a little good advice. Now — about this girl, Eva Smith. I remember her quite well now. She was a lively, good-looking girl—country-bred, I fancy—and she'd been working in one of our machine shops for over a year. A good worker too. In fact, the foreman there told me he was ready to promote her into what we call a leading operator — head of a small group of girls. But after they came back from their holidays that August, they were all rather restless, and they suddenly decided to ask for more money. They were averaging about twenty-two and six, which was neither more nor less than is paid generally in our industry. They wanted the rates raised so that they could average about twenty-five shillings a week. I refused, of course.

Inspector: Why?

Birling (*surprised*): Did you say "Why?"?

Inspector: Yes. Why did you refuse?

Birling: Well, Inspector, I don't see that it's any concern of yours how I choose to run my business. Is it now?

Inspector: It might be, you know.

Birling: I don't like that tone.

Inspector: I'm sorry. But you asked me a question.

Birling: And you asked me a question before that, a quite unnecessary question too.

Inspector: It's my duty to ask questions.

Birling: Well, it's my duty to keep labour costs down, and if I'd agreed to this demand for a new rate we'd have added about twelve per cent to our labour costs. Does that satisfy you? So I refused. Said I couldn't consider it. We were paying the usual rates and if they didn't like those rates, they could go and work somewhere else. It's a free country, I told them.

Eric: It isn't if you can't go and work somewhere else.

Inspector: Quite so.

Birling (*to* Eric): Look—just you keep out of this. You hadn't even started in the works when this happened. So they went on strike. That didn't last long, of course.

Gerald: Not if it was just after the holidays. They'd be all broke —if I know them.

Birling: Right, Gerald. They mostly were. And so was the strike, after a week or two. Pitiful affair. Well, we let them all come back—at the old rates—except the four or five ringleaders, who'd started the trouble. I went down myself and told them to clear out. And this girl, Eva Smith, was one of them. She'd had a lot to say—far too much—so she had to go.

(Act I, *An Inspector Calls*,
by John Boynton Priestley)

⑤ Alison: Did you manage all right?
Helena: Of course. I've prepared most of the meals in the last week, you know.
Alison: Yes, you have. It's been wonderful having someone to help. Another woman, I mean.
Helena: (*Crossing down L.*) I'm enjoying it. Although I don't think I shall ever get used to having to go down to the bathroom every time I want some water for something.
Alison: It is primitive, isn't it?
Helena: Yes. It is rather. (*She starts tearing up green salad on to four plates, which she takes from the food cupboard.*) Looking after one man is really enough, but two is rather an undertaking.
Alison: Oh, Cliff looks after himself, more or less. In fact, he helps me quite a lot.
Helena: Can't say I'd noticed it.
Alison: You've been doing it instead, I suppose.
Helena: I see.
Alison: You've settled in so easily somehow.
Helena: Why shouldn't I?
Alison: It's not exactly what you're used to, is it?
Helena: And are you used to it?

Alison: Everything seems very different here now — with you here.

Helena: Does it?

Alison: Yes. I was on my own before—

Helena: Now you've got me. So you're not sorry you asked me to stay?

Alison: Of course not. Did you tell him his tea was ready?

Helena: I banged on the door of Cliff's room, and yelled. He didn't answer, but he must have heard. I don't know where Cliff is.

Alison: (*Leaning back in her chair*) I thought I'd feel cooler after a bath, but I feel hot again already. God, I wish he'd lose that damned trumpet.

Helena: I imagine that's for my benefit.

Alison: Miss Drury will ask us to go soon, I know it. Thank goodness, she isn't in. Listen to him.

Helena: Does he drink?

Alison: Drink? (*Rather startled*) He's not an alcoholic, if that's what you mean. (*They both pause, listening to the trumpet*) He'll have the rest of the street banging on the door next.

Helena: (*Pondering*) It's almost as if he wanted to kill someone with it. And me in particular. I've never seen such hatred in someone's eyes before. It's slightly horrifying. Horrifying (*Crossing to food cupboard for tomatoes, beetroot, and cucumber*) and oddly exciting.

(Act II, *Look Back in Anger*, by John Osborne)

第五节　诗　歌

英语诗歌和汉语诗歌一样,同是最古老的文学体裁,源远流长,浩如烟海,常盛不衰,丰富多采。英语诗歌如果从 8 世纪长达 3,000 余行的史诗《贝奥伍尔夫》("Beowulf")算起,迄今已有一千二百余年的历史。但这部史诗只属于口头文学,由游吟诗人传唱下来,后来才用文字记录,流传至今。

诗不同于散文,不仅形式大异,诗更有其内在的特点。文学语言是民族语言的精华,而诗的语言则是精华中的精华。诗能陶冶性情,涵养道德,对人的精神起潜移默化的作用。

诗在音韵(rhyme)、节奏(rhythm)、格式(form)等方面都有一定的规律和要求,不能随意更改。以音韵而论,英诗中的押韵(rhyme)指句尾一词的重读音节元音应相同,而前面的辅音却不同,后面如有辅音,也应相同,如后面还有轻读音节,同样也应相同。最后音节如为重读音节,则称阳性韵(masculine rhyme),如 why—sigh, hate—late。重读音节后如尚有轻读音节,则称为阴性韵(feminine rhyme),如 ending—bending, expression—confession。此外还有①头韵(alliteration)。头韵指诗句中相邻的词的起首字母(元音或辅音)发音相同,如 The fair breeze blew, the white foam flew,又如 with bloody blameful blade。②元音迭韵,亦称半谐韵(assonance)。即指相同或相似的元音在诗行中重复出现,如 The rain in Spain Stays mainly in the plain;又如 late—fake, boat—hope 等。③和声(consonance)。和声指的是两个或两个以上词的词尾辅音完全一致,如 dash—fish, add—read, born—burn 等。④反韵(reverse rhyme)。反韵指两个或两个以上词的词首重读音节均由相同的辅音加上相同的元音构成,如 great—graze, student—studio 等。⑤旁韵(pararhyme)。旁韵指两个或两个以上词的词首辅音和词尾辅音均相同,如 great—groat,spit—spat 等。

以节奏论,一首英诗往往包含若干诗节(stanza),每一节又分成若干诗行(line),每一行又可分成若干音步(foot)。音步是由重读音节和非重读音节按照一定的规则排列而成,由此产生诗的格律(metre 或 measure)。一般说来,英诗的格律有以下几种:①抑扬格(Iambus),即每个音步由一个非重读音节加上一个重读音节构成(˘ ¯),如:Ĭ wān/der'd l ō nd/lȳ ās/ă cloūd。② 扬抑格(Trochee),即每个音步由一个重读音节加上一个非重读音节构成(¯ ˘),如:Art is/long and/Time is/fleeting。③ 扬抑抑格(Dactyl),即一个重读音节加上两个非重读音节(¯ ˘ ˘),如:mērrĭlў/mērrĭlў/shāll Ĭ līve。④抑抑扬格(Anapaest),即两个非重读音节加上一个重读音节,如:Like ă chĭld/frŏm thē wōmb/lĭke ă ghōst/frŏm thē tōmb。以上四种为英诗最基本最常见的格律。还有三种较少见的格律:⑤抑扬抑格(Amphibrach),⑥扬扬格(spondee),⑦抑抑格(Pyrrhic)。

根据诗行含有的音步数目,可分成以下八种音步:一音步(monometer),二音步(dimeter),三音步(trimeter),四音步(tetrameter),五音步(pentameter),六音步(hexameter),七音步(heptameter)和八音步(octameter)。最后两种比较罕见。

英诗可分成不同的种类。(一)史诗(epic)。这是有关重大历史题材的严肃的长篇巨著,如弥尔顿(John milton)的《失乐园》(*Paradise Lost*)。(二)戏剧诗(dramatic poems)。这是用诗写成的戏剧,最著名的当数莎士比亚的戏剧。(三)故事诗(metrical tale)。即用诗写成的故事,一般比史诗短小,如乔叟写的《坎特伯雷故事集》。(四)民谣(ballad)。大多数民谣是无名诗人留下、当初由艺人吟唱的故事诗。后来有些诗人模仿民谣体写的故事诗,称为文学民谣(literary ballad)。以上四种均属叙事诗。(五)抒情诗(lyric)。这是最常见的一类诗,一般较短小,从几行到几十行不等,也有更长一些的,用来抒发感情,叙述心怀,描写景物,发表议论等,又可分为颂诗(ode),悼念诗(elegy),田园诗(idyll),爱情诗(love poem)等几种。(六)说理诗(didactic poem)。可以说这是用诗的形式写出的论文。

从诗的行数上来分,则有英雄双行体(heroic couplet),三行体(tercet),四行节(quatrain),斯宾塞式的九行节(Spenserian stanza),和十四行诗(sonnet)等。

诗歌的语言是形象性的语言,富有艺术魅力。为了增强诗的形象性和艺术性,修辞手段的运用在诗歌中起着重要作用,如明喻(simile)、暗喻(metaphor)、换喻(metonymy)、提喻(synecdoche)、拟人(personification)、夸张(hyperbole)、含蓄或淡化(understatement)等。

译诗大概只有通过再创造的方式才能成功。译诗的忠实不能只着眼于词语、韵律、形式。更重要的是诗的内涵、诗的意境。在译诗时要掌握以下四个要点:第一,了解诗的大意和内涵,抓住诗中的意象及其所暗示的意义。这是最根本的一个步骤。只有深入地理解原作,才能在翻译中正确、忠实、深入地传达原作的意蕴。第二,要有丰富的想象力。诗人的创作是想象力的结晶,所用的语言是形象性的语言。只有发挥想象力才能进入诗人的想象世界,领会诗的意境,也才能用同样形象的语言译出原诗的意象。第三,诗的语言是富有感情的语言。诗人通过生动激越的语言抒发心中的情感,以情感人。只有译者受了感动,怀着同样的感情,才能选择动情的语言,在译作中忠实而热烈地传达原作的情感。第四,分析原诗的形式和语言特征,包括词法、句法、诗节、诗篇的结构和使用的修辞手段等。诗的形式与思想内容是密不可分的。诗人选择何种形式为的是最好地表达自己的思想感情。因此在翻译时应尽可能采用相应或近似的形式,以求保持原作的韵味。但也不能完全受原作形式的束缚,否则保持了躯壳而丢了灵魂,得不偿失。事实上英诗与汉诗在形式上差异极大,在翻译中完全保持原诗的形式几乎是不可能的。适当的改变不仅允许,也是实践中不可避免的结果。

现举几首英诗的翻译为例:

SONNET 18

Shall I compare thee to a summer's day?
Thou art more lovely and more temperate:
Rough winds do shake the darling buds of May,
And summer's lease hath all too short a date.

Sometime too hot the eye of heaven shines,
And often is his gold complexion dimmed:
And every fair from fair sometime declines,
By chance, or nature's changing course, untrimm'd:

But thy eternal summer shall not fade
Nor lose possession of that fair thou ow'st;
Nor shall Death brag thou wander'st in his shade,
When in eternal lines to time thou grow'st:

  So long as men can breathe or eyes can see,
  So long lives this, and this gives life to thee.

(William Shakespeare)

十四行诗 第18首

我能不能拿夏天来同你相比?
你呀比夏天来得可爱和温煦:
娇宠的蓓蕾经不起五月风急,
而夏天又是多么短促的季节。

有时那天上的眼睛照得太热,
它金色的脸庞又常黯淡无光:

任凭哪一种美也难永葆颜色——
　　机遇或自然进程剥去它盛装。

　　可是你永恒的夏天不会变化，
　　不会失去你享有的美丽姿容；
　　死神不能吹嘘你落在他影下——
　　在不朽的诗中你像时间无穷：

　　　只要人还能呼吸，眼睛能看清，
　　　我的诗就将流传并给你生命。

（黄杲　译）

　　这是莎士比亚一首著名的十四行诗，每行五个音步，抑扬格，韵脚的安排是 abab, cdcd, efef, gg。十四行共分为四节，即前四行，中四行，后四行和最后两行各成一节。前四行是"起"，中四行是"承"，都是讲岁月无常、青春难再。后四行可以说是"转"，诗意一变，诗人宣告虽然别人美貌难存，他所爱的朋友则将靠他的诗笔而永葆颜色。最后两行是音韵铿锵的小结，亦即是"合"。结论是"只要人还能呼吸，眼睛能看清，我的诗就将流传并给你生命"。

　　译文不仅忠实地传达了莎士比亚诗中的原意，并尽可能地保持了原诗的形式。每一行、每一小节都与原诗相对应，甚至连标点符号也尽可能不作改变。原诗通篇用五音步写成，在汉语中不存在音步问题，译者就用每行十二个字亦即十二个音来表示这一固定的声音组合模式。在用词上译者使用了含义与原文对等的词，同时又注意使这些词包含英语原词的感情色彩与高雅风格。如将"temperate"译成"温煦"，将"short"译成"短促"，将"dimmed"译成"黯淡无光"等。原诗中的形象化的比喻均在译文中保留了下来。例如将"winds"，"buds"，"complexion"，"Death"分别译成"风"、"蓓蕾"、"脸庞"、"死神"。在必要时译者也作了一些变化，例如将"Rough winds do shake the darling buds of May"一句译成"娇宠的蓓蕾经不起五月风急",改变了原句中"of May"的形容关系,但又不失原意,因为"rough winds"显然也是在五月中吹来的。这样译法,汉语更为通顺,更具诗意。使人不禁想起了南宋女词人李清照的诗句:"三杯两盏淡酒,怎敌他,晚来风急。"又如将正面描述的原句"And every fair from fair sometime declines"改从反面来说明,译成"任凭哪一种美也难永葆颜色",这更符合汉语表达习惯。有时为了汉语诗行的字数,译者在译文里也故意省略了原句的某些词意或增添汉语的词语。上句中"也难永葆颜色"就是一种改变和增添。而在"死神不能吹嘘你落在他影下",就省略了原句中"wanderest"一词,改用一个"落"字来代替,既规范了字数,又不失原句的意蕴。

  A Red, Red Rose
O, my Luve's like a red, red rose,
That's newly sprung in June;
O, my Luve's like the melodie
That's sweetly play'd in tune.

As fair art thou, my bonnie lass,
 So deep in luve am I,
And I will luve thee still, my dear,
Till a' the seas gang dry.

Till a' the seas gang dry, my dear,
 And the rocks melt wi' the sun!
And I will luve thee still, my dear,
 While the sands o' life shall run.

And fare thee weel, my only Luve,
And fare thee weel, a while!
And I will come again, my Luve,

Tho' it were ten thousand mile!

(Robert Burns)

红玫瑰

吾爱吾爱玫瑰红,
六月初开韵晓风;
吾爱吾爱如管弦,
其声修扬而玲珑。

吾爱吾爱美而殊,
我心爱你永不渝,
我心爱你永不渝,
直到四海海水枯;

直到四海海水枯,
岩石融化变成泥,
只要我还有口气,
我心爱你永不渝。

暂时告别我心肝,
请你不要把心耽!
纵使相隔十万里,
踏穿地皮也要还。

(郭沫若 译)

　　这首著名的抒情诗是用民歌体写成,是诗人献给爱人的情诗。全诗分成四节,每节的第一行与第三行为四音步,第二行与第四行为三音步,并相互押韵,其韵脚为 abcb,属抑扬格。后两节第一行与第三行结尾用了同一个词,这一重复增强了韵律感,使诗更朗朗上口,同时也起到强调的作用。

　　郭沫若先生以汉语诗中常见的七言诗,用非常规范的形式译出,颇似李白的清平调,但不是三节而是四节。语言虽较古雅,但将原诗动人的情思与美丽的喻象十分忠实而深刻地传达出来。由于原诗中有不少古老的苏格兰词汇,译文中相应出现一些古汉语词汇也就显得比较自然,并不使人感到过时或不当。译文的每一行都与原诗的诗行相对应,可谓从内容到形式都完全忠实于原作。但由于诗行字数所限,也为了押韵,译文有时不得不作些变化,或者改变词性,或者压缩用词,或者增添词汇。如第一行就将"a red, red rose"改译成"玫瑰红",缩减了原词,并将"红"字置于尾部以便与第二行的尾词"风"押韵。第四行却将"sweetly"一词在汉语中扩张为"悠扬而玲珑",以符合字数与韵脚的需要。至于某些改变是否十全十美,仍可商榷。如最后一句"踏穿地皮也要还",似乎与原文相去甚远,若改成"天涯海角定回还"是否更符合原诗的意境一些?而第三节中的"只要我还有口气"一句显得太口语化,第四节的第一句"暂时告别我心肝"又未免太俗气一点,与全诗古雅的文风有些相左。

　　台湾陈美月先生的译法却完全不同:

　　红红的蔷薇

　啊,我的爱人像是朵红红的蔷薇,
　在仲夏之月焕然初绽;
　啊,我的爱人像是首甜美的旋律,
　在和谐之中轻盈流转。

　如花之妍姿,我美丽的女孩,
　我沉醉于"爱"的深情;
　愿爱你逾恒,我的爱,
　直到海枯。

　直到海枯,我的爱,
　而且石烂;
　愿爱你逾恒,我的爱,

只要生命的流沙不停歇。

再会啦,我唯一的爱!
暂时与你别!
我会再寻来,我的爱,
纵它是万里之遥!

(陈美月　译)

  这一译文十分平易流畅,体现了原文"明白如话"的文风。每一诗行都与原诗行相对应,连标点符号都无丝毫改变。词汇、短语、句式都忠实于原文。在这一点上似优于前一译文。如第一句"啊,我的爱人像是朵红红的蔷薇,"将原句中的两个"red"译成"红红的",十分生动而又符合汉语习惯。汉语中这种重复结构十分普通,如"高高的"、"远远的"等。第二句"在仲夏之月焕然初绽"诗意盎然。如果完全按原词译成六月,则不如"仲夏之月"给人以引起遐想的形象,同时也是为了增加字数,达到句式长短平衡的目的。但有的诗句如果完全直译,其效果反不尽人意。如第三节的第四句,译者完全按原文译成"只要生命的流沙不停歇",中国读者很难理解什么是"生命的流沙",其实这指的是古代计时的沙漏,因此"sands o' life"无非是诗人用形象的语言来表达一生的时间。从整体看,诗的译文在形式上也不够规整,如第二节的第四句"直到海枯",第三节的第二句"而且石烂",第四节的第二句"暂时与你别",都嫌过短,显得不够协调,尤其第四句为节尾,不宜过于突兀。在韵脚的使用上也不够严格,如第二节就几乎未押韵。第三节与第四节的韵律也不规范。和郭沫若先生的译文比来,这一译文在形式上要自由得多,并未完全拘于原诗的格式。可见两种译本各有所长,也各有所短。

THE DAFFODILS

I wander'd lonely as a cloud
That floats on high o'er vales and hills,
When all at once I saw a crowd,
A host, of golden daffodils,
Beside the lake, beneath the trees,
Fluttering and dancing in the breeze.

Continuous as the stars that shine
And twinkle on the milky way,
They stretch'd in never-ending line
Along the margin of a bay:
Ten thousand saw I at a glance
Tossing their heads in sprightly dance.

The waves beside them danced, but they
Out-did the sparkling waves in glee:—
A poet could not but be gay
In such a jocund company!
I gazed—and gazed—but little thought
What wealth the show to me had brought;

For oft, when on my couch I lie
In vacant or in pensive mood,
They flash upon that inward eye
Which is the bliss of solitude;
And then my heart with pleasure fills,
And dances with the daffodils.

(William Wordsworth)

水　仙

我独自漫游,像山谷上空
高高飘过的一朵云彩,
我突然望见,望见一大丛
金黄的水仙,纷纷绽开;
在湖水之滨,树荫之下
正迎风摇曳,舞姿潇洒。

连绵密布,像繁星万点
在银河上下闪烁明灭,
这一片水仙,沿着湖湾
排成延续无尽的行列:
我一眼就看见万朵千株,
摇动着花冠,轻盈飘舞。

湖面的涟漪也迎风起舞,
水仙的欢乐却胜过涟漪:
有了这样愉快的伴侣,
诗人怎能不心旷神怡!
我望了又望,却未曾想到
这美景给了我怎样的珍宝。

因为,每当我倚榻而卧,
或情怀抑郁,或心境茫然,
水仙呵,便在心目中闪烁——
那是我孤寂时分的乐园;
于是我的心便欢情洋溢,
和水仙一道,舞蹈不息。

(杨德豫　译)

华兹华斯是著名的英国浪漫主义诗人，位居"湖畔派"(the Lake Poets)诗人之首，以其歌颂大自然的诗篇见长。《水仙》是他著名的抒情诗。诗人在独自漫游时忽然发现湖边一大片金黄色的水仙在微风中摇曳起舞。大自然的这一奇妙美景令诗人心旷神怡，始终留在他的记忆中。水仙成了大自然的化身，他联想到夜空中闪烁的繁星，翩翩舞蹈的花儿胜过湖面上迎风起舞的水波。诗人不再感到孤独，而融入了水、土、空气等大自然的元素之中，感到欢乐与和谐。这一领悟将永远充实着他的生活。这首诗可说是他的存在和宇宙生命气息相互撞击所引起的灵感的具体体现。

诗的形式比较单纯，共分四个诗节，每节六行，每行四音步，属抑扬格，偶有变化，如第六行的第一个字 Fluttering 则为扬抑抑调。韵脚结构为 ababcc。每节的最后两行为对句。杨德豫先生的译文比较自由，只求意义与语言的忠实，并未拘泥于原诗的句型与形式，也未完全遵循汉语诗的格式习惯。他使用的句式结构明显带着受英诗体式影响的痕迹。如第一句"我独自漫游，像山谷上空"，译者不仅中间用逗点隔开了后一短语，并在句子中间断掉，第三句"我突然望见，望见一大丛"与第一句完全一样，也中间点开，句尾断掉。这是传统汉语诗歌中少见的，现代新诗中却常有，那正是受西方诗歌影响的结果。这使汉语诗歌摆脱了严格的格式，变得自由而随意得多。为了增强译文的诗意，译者有意在原文的基础上添加了一些词语。如第一节的第四行，译者加上"纷纷绽开"四个字，使水仙花的形象格外具体丰富。第四节的第三行，译者在句首加上了感叹词"水仙呵，"用来代替原诗中的"they"一词，使诗行更加生动，主语也分外明确。译诗与原诗的最大不同之处是在押韵上。原诗的韵脚十分规范，而译者似乎对译文诗行的押韵与否并不太在意，只求意到，不求声同。这也是自由新诗的特点，如译时过分求全，反会使译文刻板呆滞，甚至有损诗的意境。

译诗是翻译活动中最困难的工作，要求译者具有两种语言的深厚根基和高度的文学修养。对初学者不宜期待过高,仅举几首简单的小诗,以兹练习。

附:练习

将下列诗歌译成中文。

①   The Example
Here's an example from
    A butterfly;
That on a rough hard rock
    Happy can lie;
Friendless and all alone
On this unsweetened stone.

Now let my bed be hard
    No care take I;
I'll make my joy like this
    Small butterfly;
Whose happy heart has power
To make a stone a flower.
                (William Henry Davies)

②   REQUIESCAT
Tread lightly, she is near
    Under the snow,
Speak gently, she can hear
    The daisies grow.

All her bright golden hair

    Tarnished with rust,
She that was young and fair
    Fallen to dust.

Lily-like, white as snow,
    She hardly knew
She was a woman, so
    Sweetly she grew.

Coffin-board, heavy stone
    Lie on her breast,
I vex my heart alone,
    She is at rest.

Peace, Peace, she cannot hear
    Lyre or sonnet,
All my life's buried here,
    Heap earth upon it.

                (Oscar Wilde)

③   Requiem

Under the wide and starry sky,
Dig the grave and let me lie.
Glad did I live and gladly die,
And I laid me down with a will.

This *be* the verse you grave for me:
Here he lies where he longed to be,
Home is the sailor, home from sea,
And the hunter home from the hill.
            (Robert Louis Stevenson)

④ THE YEAR'S AT THE SPRING
The year's at the spring,
And day's at the morn;
Morning's at seven;
The hill-side's *dew-pearled*;

The lark's on the wing;
The snail's on the thorn:
God's in his heaven—
All's right with the world!
(Robert Browning)

⑤ A Widow Bird Sate Mourning For Her Love
A widow bird sate mourning for her love
Upon a wintry bough;
The frozen wind crept on above,
The freezing stream below.

There was no leaf upon the forest bare,
No flower upon the ground,
And little motion in the air
Except the mill-wheel's sound.
(Percy Bysshe Shelley)

⑥ Love's Secret
Never seek to tell thy love,
Love that never told can be;
For the gentle wind doth move
Silently, invisibly.

I told *my love*, I told my love,
I told her all my heart,
Tembling, cold, in ghastly fears —
Ah! she did depart!

Soon after she was gone from me,
A traveller came by,
Silently, invisibly:
He took her with a sigh.

      (William Blake)

⑦   The Arrow and the Song
I shot an arrow into the air,
It fell to earth, I know not where;
For, so swiftly it flew, the sight
Could not follow it in its flight.

I breathed a song into the air,
It fell to earth, I knew not where,
For who has sight so keen and strong,
That it can follow the flight of song?

Long, long afterward, in an oak
I found the arrow, still unbroke;
And the song, from beginning to end,
I found again in the heart of a friend.
    (Henry Wadsworth Longfellow)

⑧ Stopping by Woods on a Snowy Evening
Whose woods these are I think I know.

His house is in the village, though;
He will not see me stopping here
To watch his woods fill up with snow.

My little horse must think it queer
To stop without a farmhouse near
Between the woods and frozen lake
The darkest evening of the year.

He gives his harness bells a shake
To ask if there is some mistake.
The only other sound's the sweep
Of easy wind and downy flake.

The woods are lovely, dark, and deep,
But I have promises to keep,
And miles to go before I sleep,
And miles to go before I sleep.

(Robert Frost)

翻译练习参考译文

第二章　应用文文体的翻译

第二节　信　函

二、社交信函

1. 请柬及邀请信

① 兹订于 6 月 8 日（星期五）下午四点至六点在公园路 250 号舍下举行鸡尾酒会，敬请光临。

托马斯·马太·本顿博士及夫人谨订

② 兹订于六月十六日（星期一）下午五时于纽约威廉街十四号举行小女珍妮同约翰·阿特瓦特先生的婚礼。
敬请光临。

阿尔弗雷特·肯特先生及夫人谨订

③ 兹订于 11 月 8 日（星期日）10 时在优伊广场举行舞会，敬请光临，恭候回音。

托马斯·马太·本顿博士及夫人谨订

回函请寄　公园路 250 号

④ 亲爱的朱丽叶：

我从今日报纸上得知，公园内举办的一个美术展览将于本月十日开幕，届时将展出许多名画。此外，我还听说公园里正值牡丹盛开。下周日如果天气好的话，我打算到公园去走走看看。

趁此好季节，工作之余消遣一下。如果你那天没有别的安排的话，请与我同行。

下周日和我一起去,好吗?我们上午十点在公园门口碰头如何? 祝
　　好

　　　　　　　　　　　　　　　　　　　　　　　　　　安妮塔

⑤　亲爱的哈里斯夫人:
　　我和弗兰克·彼德斯订于10月4日(星期二)晚八时在寒舍举行婚礼。弗兰克和哈里斯先生长期融洽共事,婚礼倘若没有他参加,将是一个缺憾!希望贤夫妇都来,并参加仪式后举行的小型招待会。

　　　　　　　　　　　　　　　　　　　　　　您真诚的
　　　　　　　　　　　　　　　　　　　　　　凯瑟琳·米勒

⑥　亲爱的杰克:
　　久未见面,近况如何?我时刻想念您。现在天气很好,我和艾丽丝、鲍勃打算作一次郊游。张萍建议我们大家都骑自行车去,每人都带点吃的东西,在山坡野餐。农村风光秀丽,草木丰茂,花儿盛开。大地一片葱绿,阳光灿烂,任由我们尽情观赏。我们希望你带上你的新照相机,拍摄几张照片,留影纪念。我们可否早上7点在渡口集合?我想我们一定会玩个痛快的。请你千万来啊!

　　　　　　　　　　　　　　　　　　　　　　挚友
　　　　　　　　　　　　　　　　　　　　　　比尔

2. 祝贺信

①　亲爱的泰勒夫人:
　　得知令郎保罗以优异的成绩已从著名的麻省理工学院毕业,你对他的卓越成就一定感到快慰。他无疑是你全家的骄傲。
　　我们为你高兴,并向你表示最热烈的祝贺。我相信,他所获得的知识将使他今后无论从事什么工作都能取得成功。
　　谨祝他成功、幸福。

　　　　　　　　　　　　　　　　　　　　　　真诚的
　　　　　　　　　　　　　　　　　　　　　　玛拉·特·克拉克

② 亲爱的安妮和杰里：

圣诞快乐！新年幸福！在光辉美好、繁荣昌盛的新的一年到来之际，请允许我向你们表示节日的祝贺。深信节日里你们阖家欢乐、身体健康。

我们全家人都健康快乐，共同表示对你们的美好祝愿。愿年年岁岁我们的心连得更紧。

你真诚的
芭芭拉

③我亲爱的卡特：

你下星期六就要和格林伍德小姐结婚了，这真是一个大好消息！在这幸福时刻，我最热烈地祝贺你们。

我和汤姆向你们俩表示真挚的问候和良好的祝愿，祝你们生活幸福美满。我们高兴地给你们另外寄上一件小礼物来表示我们的良好祝愿。

愿你们永远幸福愉快。

真诚的
玛拉·菲利浦

3. 感谢信

① 亲爱的穆丽尔：

真不可思议！那套有你亲手绣上我们名字的浴巾真美极了。谢谢你的珍贵礼物。手工制的礼品总是很特别，因为其中凝聚着时间、智慧，尤其是爱。

泰德看到终于有了一件上面绣有"他的"名字的东西，高兴极了。他嘱我千万代他向你致谢。　　　　　　祝

好！　　　　　　　　　　　　　　　　　　　　　　　劳拉

② 亲爱的彼特森

当我收到你寄来的《现代英语》一书时，我格外欣喜。这确实是一本好书，真正有助于英语学习。一本多么难得的宝书啊！多谢你的关怀和慷慨的帮助。

我的许多同事常提到这本书的优点。我要说的是，这是唯一一本可以使中国学生获益很多，了解如何读、写、说英语的书。事实上，它是掌握道地英语的一个诀窍。

我们夫妇二人再次致谢。

您真诚的
安东尼·斯图尔特

③ 亲爱的安妮：

　　昨天下午我安全抵达家中。现在我写此信衷心感谢你和伯父母对我的盛情款待。我将把这次对你的拜访看作我一生中最愉快的一周而牢记心头。

　　我想我的逗留给你们添了许多麻烦，但我明白，伯父母都很客气，会原谅我的打扰的。

　　我父母非常感谢你们的殷勤周到。很希望下次，我们能有机会答谢你。多谢你对我的慷慨招待。请问候伯父母。

你真诚的
卡洛

4. 慰问信和吊唁信

① 亲爱的汤普森先生：

　　听说你邻居家失火，殃及你那所漂亮的房子，我很难过。真是太不幸了！这是多么可怕的事啊！你们全家一定感到很难过。在此，我深表同情，希望你们都安然无恙。

　　如欲有用到我们之处，请尽管吩咐。希望听到你们平安的消息，但愿不久能见到你。

真诚的
罗杰·惠特尼

② 亲爱的汤姆

　　听到车祸的消息，我们感到万分震惊和不安。谢天谢地，你受的伤不太重。你家里人告诉我们，你的身体日渐好转，大约十天左右就可出院。听到这话，我们都放心了。

　　现给你寄上一些你准感兴趣的书。希望不久听到你完全康复的消息。

忠实的
鲍勃

③ 亲爱的比尔:
听说你必须住院,我真感到难过。不过幸好你选的那家医院离我们很近,这样,中午我们可以来看你。你病假期间,我们会把工资交给杰克逊夫人的。如果需要什么而又不告诉我们,你就立刻会被炒鱿鱼。记住我的警告。
祝早日康复。

真诚的
安塞姆

④ 亲爱的鲍勃和朱丽叶:
任何言词在此刻都显得苍白无力,但我必须让你们知道我多么牵挂你们,同你们一样悲伤。
迈克这样的孩子,任何父母都会为之骄傲。他那么自信,风度迷人,使人一看便知亲人们都深深地爱着他。
我非常愿意随时帮忙。请到我家来吧。

真诚的
德克斯特

⑤ 亲爱的杰里:
伊夫琳的死讯使我极为震惊。虽然没有任何语言能减轻你丧偶之痛,但我想让你知道,在这悲痛的时刻,我的心和你在一起。
艾丽斯四年前去世时,我也觉得好像天一下子塌下来了。但是除了从绝望的深渊里挣脱出来之外,别无它途。渐渐地,你就会发现,时间已开始治愈你的悲伤。
请接受我最深切的慰问。

你的朋友
迪安

⑥ 亲爱的爱德华:
今天上午我们获悉你父亲去世的噩耗,感到十分震惊,当时我们都难以相信这会是真的。你们全家一定非常悲痛,我难以找到恰当的语言来减轻你的悲伤。谨致深切哀悼。我将立即亲来吊唁,在令尊的灵前致哀。

我妻子也向你表示最沉痛的哀悼和深切问候。

你真诚的
康拉德·埃利斯

5. 道歉信

① 亲爱的伍德先生：

你上月二十号的来函，我迟迟未复，请原谅。耽搁的原因是，当你来信时，我因任务紧急出差在外，历时约一个月。所以那封信一直放在我的桌子上。现在我立即做的头件事便是给你回这封短信，以致歉意。

下星期我将登门拜访，到时我们可以商讨你信中所提到的我们的论文。谨致亲切的问候。

真诚的
爱德华·戴维

② 亲爱的本顿夫人：

请原谅，我还书迟了一点。这本书我通读了一遍，感到很有趣味。当我读完之后，正准备奉还时，我的一位挚友来看我。他对此书亦很感兴趣，求我让他也看看这本书。于是我就冒昧地推迟了还书的时间。

我相信你会原谅我的过失的。我们俩都很感谢你，并且随时准备报答你的好意。

忠实的
玛塔·兰思

③ 亲爱的琼：

我们都别为一点小小的误会而影响了我们的关系。我确实记得你说过要为霍莉买件礼物，你认为我会办妥此事。所以，当我们俩分别去参加为新娘举行的送礼会而又都没带礼物时，我们都非常尴尬。

我十分抱歉没有在这之前与你敲定一下。霍莉很体谅人，但我却急于想早点给她买件礼物。我建议这次咱们各自买各自的，以免再出乱子。

真诚的
基蒂

三、事务信函

1. 私人事务信函
(1)索要信与申请信
① 亲爱的先生:

我打算申请史密斯学院1995年秋季入学。请寄给我一份贵校的简章,入学申请表以及有关入学条件的资料。

真诚的
托马斯·爱德华

② 先生:

我很想得到贵校的入学申请表。

目前我正在北京第四中学高中二年级读书。请告知我贵校的入学条件和考试日期。

真诚的
杨华

③ 亲爱的先生:

我现在佛罗里达州盖恩斯维尔佛罗里达大学攻读工商管理硕士学位,希望1990年秋季转到贵校去读相同的学位。现在我已读完了12个学分的课程,到6月底我将再学完8个学分的课程。我的成绩都在B以上。

来佛罗里达大学之前,我在武汉大学获工商管理学士学位,并曾在一家国营工厂工作了一年。我在本科和研究生学习期间的成绩单可以寄来。

望能尽快寄给我申请表格。不胜感谢。

忠实的
李林

④ 美国马萨诸塞州(02139)坎布里奇
马萨诸塞理工学院工程研究生院
招生办公室负责人

中华人民共和国湖南省长沙市
湖南工业大学电机工程系
1984年4月2日

亲爱的先生：

　　我于1981年8月毕业于XX大学电机工程系，目前在湖南工业大学电机工程系工作，担任助教兼实验员。为了进一步深造，我希望能入马萨诸塞理工学院工程研究生院攻读理学硕士学位。贵院有着悠久的历史和优良的学风，师资力量雄厚，教学设备精良，享有国际声誉。能在这样一所理想的高等学府深造，实为一件无尚光荣的幸事。很久以来我一直希望有幸进贵校学习。

　　我很想知道贵院招收研究生的条件。烦请给我寄一份入学申请表和有关材料。不胜感激。

　　盼能早日收到您的复信。

您的恭敬的
李锋生

⑤　亲爱的先生：

　　我高兴地听说，贵会自成立以来工作成绩卓著，在国内外享有盛名。因此，我将能成为贵会的会员看成是莫大的荣誉。

　　本人于1958年毕业于XX大学物理系，后受聘于XX实验室，担任助理。1964年进XX高能物理研究所，从事研究工作，现仍在该所任职。毕业后25年来，我先后撰写了两本有关高能物理的专著和五篇论述原子物理和其它题目的论文。我一向觉得，在许多情况下靠我个人的努力难于克服研究工作中的困难。我经常请求其他人帮助和支援。为了向前辈学习，取得他们的指导，合作和配合，跟上物理学飞速发展的形势，如果合格，我希望能加入贵会，成为会员。

　　如您回信寄来一份有关规定和入会申请表，我将感谢之至。

　　敬候您及早回复。

诚挚的
布莱尔·阿登

(2)推荐信与谋职信

① 亲爱的科顿先生：

我怀着极为喜悦的心情向你推荐我的一位老同学豪斯小姐。她是一位德才兼备的女士，曾在打字方面受过专门训练。她的人品和习惯是值得称赞的。她一向严守时间，兢兢业业地做好本职工作，谨慎而务实地处理每件事情。总之，她特别胜任秘书工作。

如果你能帮她在你公司安排一个职位，我相信，她今后的表现会证明她是值得你信任的。

真诚的

罗伊·福勒

② 亲爱的里德先生：

关于您六月二十七日之信，谨回复如下：我高兴地告诉你，我可郑重地推荐高小姐为令郎的家庭教师。我和内人都觉得她聪明颖悟，诚实爽朗，小女和小儿均极喜欢她。在雇用她三年期间，我们从未见过她心情不快。如果对她有什么可评论之处的话，那就是她显得有点太过男性化，但这点对令郎来说，毋宁是好事。

她跟我们在一起的这段时间，已学会并掌握了近乎完美的英语。至于母语方面，我知道她说一口好汉语，且精通中国文学。我们辞退她，仅仅是因为我们的孩子都已长大。总之，我相信你们雇用她是决不会错的。

真诚的

J.P.豪斯尔

③ 亲爱的××教授：

我写信向您推荐××医学院传染病研究室的××医生。他于1983年毕业于××医学院，尔后考取研究生，从事传染病研究，并于1986年获硕士学位。

××医生是一位出色的学生，又是一位极有培养前途的医生。我相信，如果您能接受他的话，他会成为贵系最好的学生之一。他的英语不错，并通过了我国政府的官方英语考试，已取得政府资助出国学习和研究的资格。换言之，中国政府将为他提供奖学金和来往旅费。如您能接受他作为贵系的访问学者，我将感激不尽。

盼望您尽早答复。　　　　　谨致
　　　　　敬意

　　　　　　　　　　　　　　　　　　　　　　　　（签名）

④　先生：
　　看到《晨邮报》上有贵公司招聘口译人员的广告，我甚愿应聘，谋此职位。
　　我于1952年生于日本，1977年毕业于一所外国语学院。1977年至1981年在国际旅行社任译员。1980年结婚，1981年辞去该社职务来美国。我会讲流利的英语，并通晓日语和俄语。因而我自信能胜任口译工作。
　　至于我的人品和习惯，请向贵友乔治·布来克先生了解。
　　希望你们抽时间予以接见并惠赐佳音。

　　　　　　　　　　　　　　　　　　　　　　　　哈里·格林伍德

⑤　亲爱的先生：
　　从友人处获悉，罗街初级中学有教职空缺，我拟申请此职位。
　　我是林肯高中和州立师范学院(八六级)毕业生。最近两年在本市瓦登中学教化学。
　　随函寄上瓦登中学威斯特校长和州立师范学院里昂斯博士的介绍信。我也征得同意，请师范学院教育系鲍尔教授作证明人。
　　盼望在您方便的时候面谈。

　　　　　　　　　　　　　　　　　　　　　　　　您真诚的
　　　　　　　　　　　　　　　　　　　　　　　　伯特·米勒

⑥　亲爱的先生：
　　得知您办公室需要一名打字员兼速记员，我立即写此信申请这一职位。
　　我生于1964年，1968年毕业于芝加哥的一所商业学校。嗣后受打字和速记专门训练一年。自1984年到1992年在旧金山一家轮船公司担任经理的私人秘书。1991年结婚。由于患病辞去该项工作。
　　我丈夫在伊利诺伊大学任教。我们有一个六岁的儿子和一个四岁的女儿。他们已长大而且天真可爱，我外出时可请我的婆母看管，因此我极愿再度在办公室工作。

我过去工作的速度是：速记每分钟100个字，打字每分钟60个字。我过去常受命代经理拟信稿。在大多数情况下，那些信稿不经修改就被采用。当然，我很久没有练习了，但我自信在短期内即可恢复原有的能力。

如蒙给以面谈的机会，我当非常感激。

您真诚的

海伦·普金斯

2. 公务信函

① 费城 PA 19104

宾夕法尼亚大学

口腔系

系主任

亲爱的普金斯先生：

收到了您填好的申请表，并从其他渠道收到了全部必要的文件和材料。

对材料的初审结果表明，在学业上您符合录取条件。谨通知你于1989年秋季来参加医学院研究生的课程学习，攻读医学。

我们真诚地欢迎您来我校学习。

你的真诚的，

（签名）

1989年9月2日

② 加拿大 N6A 5A5，伦敦

西安大略大学

麻醉系

系主任，教授

亲爱的泰勒博士：

柯特兰博士已和我谈了您的来信。我完全赞同您想在××医学院和西安大略大学间促进教师交流的计划。

毫无疑问，我们非常欢迎贵校的交流人员来我院，并为他们承担在此地的生活费用。我也鼓励我院教师接受您的邀请去伦敦。

您请我作为两校的外交联络人员去访问贵校，您的好意我特别感激。

致以良好的问候和祝愿。

　　　　　　　　　　　　　　　　　　您真诚的
　　　　　　　　　　　　　　　　　　（签名）
　　　　　　　　　　　　　　　　　　1995年1月29日

③　北京
　　××国驻华特命全权大使×××先生阁下：
　　我荣幸地收到您1983年5月18日的来函，承蒙告知您于昨天向中华人民共和国全国人民代表大会常务委员会委员长×××先生阁下递交了委派您为××国驻中华人民共和国特命全权大使的国书一事，深表感谢。
　　我非常高兴地与阁下建立公务和私人的关系，并保证永远努力维护和进一步发展我们两国使团之间的亲密合作，因为这种合作非常融洽地体现了我们两国之间日益增进的友好关系。顺致
　　崇高的敬意。

　　　　　　　　　　　　　　　　　　××国驻华特命全权公使
　　　　　　　　　　　　　　　　　　（签署全名）
　　　　　　　　　　　　　　　　　　1983年5月19日

④　北京
　　中华人民共和国外交部长×××先生阁下：
　　我荣幸地通知阁下，我于1988年2月20日返回北京，并于即日主持馆务。此达。顺致
　　崇高敬意。

　　　　　　　　　　　　　　　　　　XX国驻华特命全权公使
　　　　　　　　　　　　　　　　　　（签署全名）
　　　　　　　　　　　　　　　　　　1988年2月24日

⑤　北京
　　中华人民共和国外交部礼宾司司长阁下：
　　前些日子，我大使馆有一位工作人员请领护照，前往西藏旅游。他于三天前返回北京并交还了护照。他说，他此次旅行所到之处，受到地方政府的妥善

照料。对此他深表感谢。兹将前领护照一份送上,敬希阁下查照核销。此达。
顺致
敬意

美利坚合众国大使馆
文化参赞
(签署全名)
1984年2月16日

四、商业信函

① 诸位先生:

七月二十三日来信已收到,得悉贵方对我公司的建筑用钉很有兴趣,我们感到非常高兴。

遗憾的是,目前由于订货量大,几无存货,实难满足贵方需要。然而,我们现在在设法补进,预计一两个月内新货即可到达。

我们会记住贵方的询价,一旦到货,定立刻向贵方报价。特此奉复。
此致
敬礼

真诚的
哈里·史密斯

② 诸位先生:

我们在前函里曾向贵方询问我们订购货物的装运情况,遗憾的是迄今没有收到贵方任何消息。

我们初次询价时就曾指出急需此货。贵方应清楚地记得正是贵方答应及早装运,才促成我们向贵方订货的。我们已将信用证延期一次,恐怕不能再延了。请注意该信用证于五月三十一日满期。

希望贵方对此事立即予以重视并望早日接到贵方装运通知,勿再延误。
顺致
敬礼

约翰·克拉克

③ 诸位先生：

　　已接到十二月十四日贵方来信,获悉我方发出的货箱内装的钢笔并非贵方所定的型号,甚为抱歉。

　　经查核,发现因号码弄混而造成了装箱错误。我们已换好货品立即发运给贵方。请将那箱错装货品退还我们,不胜感激。所需一切费用由我方支付。

　　由于错误给贵方造成麻烦,我们深表歉意。今后将尽力防止类似错误再次发生。　　　　　　　　　　　　　　　　　　　　　　此致

　　　敬礼

　　　　　　　　　　　　　　　　　　　　　　　　　　凯瑟琳·哈里斯

第三节　电报

① 恭祝寿诞,并致良好祝愿。
② 祝旅途平安愉快。
③ 惊闻违和,祝早日康复。
④ 唐于11月11日乘471班机抵京,请林机场迎接。
⑤ 上述问题如接受,请电告。
⑥ 有关222和333电,下月再谈。
⑦ 如欲报价,再作联系。
⑧ 十月底前不能再接订单,憾甚。

第四节　便条、通知、启事、海报

一、便条

① 亲爱的先生：

　　很抱歉,我不能参加下午的会议。兹附上证明一张。医生说,我必须卧床休息几日后才能上班。希望我的病假不会给您造成太大不便。　　此致

　　　敬礼

　　　　　　　　　　　　　　　　　　　　　　你的真诚的
　　　　　　　　　　　　　　　　　　　　　　（签名）
　　　　　　　　　　　　　　　　　　　　　　星期一

② 亲爱的史密斯先生：
因家中有要事，今天不能来上课，特此请假。若能获准，不胜感激。
$\qquad$ 此致

　　敬礼

$\qquad\qquad\qquad\qquad\qquad$你的真诚的
$\qquad\qquad\qquad\qquad\qquad$（签名）
$\qquad\qquad\qquad\qquad\qquad$1996.5.12

③ 布朗医生：
见条请即来外宾宾馆202房间。大卫·贝克尔患重病，需您照管。必须立即治疗，务请速来。多谢。

$\qquad\qquad\qquad\qquad\qquad$杰克

④ 琳达：
请告诉我，本周什么时候一起讨论今年的教学和科研工作为宜？本次会议由您主持，谨此提醒。

$\qquad\qquad\qquad\qquad\qquad$爱丽丝

二、通知：

① 亲爱的艾利斯夫妇：
我怀着十分悲痛和遗憾的心情告诉你们：我的妻子玛丽·安由于心力衰竭，突于4月16日晚去世。这一打击犹如晴天霹雳。我妻虽血压偏高，却从未闹过心脏病。

告别仪式已于昨日在香港圣彼得教堂举行。忽遭爱妻逝世之巨变，令人难以自处。但时间会逐渐医治我的悲痛，使我适应独居生活。　谨祝
　　健康愉快

$\qquad\qquad\qquad\qquad\qquad$爱德华·R·史密斯
$\qquad\qquad\qquad\qquad\qquad$1995年4月23日
$\qquad\qquad\qquad\qquad\qquad$于香港

② <center>免 职 通 知</center>

经董事会投票一致通过，免去×××先生校长办公室主任职务，现予公布。

主任办公室
1988年5月20日

③ <center>通　　知</center>

接外事办公室通知，托马斯·杰弗逊大学副校长兼杰弗逊医学院院长约瑟夫·冈纳拉博士不能按期来中国访问。他关于医学教育的报告将推迟到1994年4月22日（下星期四）下午2时在学校礼堂举行。

教务处
1994年4月10日

三、启事

① <center>遗 失 启 事</center>

遗失现金，拾者请与我室联系。
电话：577577转2202

化学系办公室
1996年7月10日

② <center>订 婚 启 事</center>

小女露西与塞穆尔·罗素先生订于一九九六年八月十七日（星期六）订婚，特敬告亲友。

荷兰德·沃尔什曼夫妇鞠躬

③ <center>招领公文包</center>

拾得公文包一只，内有现金及其他东西。失者请到办公楼107房间失物招领处认领。办公时间：上午8至11点，下午2至5点。

1995年12月6日

四、海报

①

欢迎参观

针刺麻醉外科手术
真正的中国奇迹

时间：五月五日（星期五）上午八时半
地点：广州中山医学院第二附属医院

名额有限　赶快登记！

②

广交会国际足球比赛

"英国"

"西德"

地点：中山大学体育场
时间：1975年4月28日下午三时半
下午二点至二点半从东方宾馆开车（约三十个座位）
其余的人可乘出租车自行前往

欢迎前往助兴！

③

> **上海杂技团演出**
>
> **杂　技**
>
> （五十名优秀杂技演员）
>
> **丰富多彩的节目　扣人心弦的表演**
>
> ·绝·技·健·美·
>
> 四月十六日下午七时半
>
> 友谊剧场
>
> ————————————
>
> 中国出口商品交易会主办
>
> 在 406 号房间领票

第五节　合　同

①
聘　约　合　同

　　××医学院药理系（聘方）聘请×××博士（受聘方）为药理教师。双方本着友好合作的精神，同意签定并遵守下列条件：

　　1. 聘期为一年，自 1988 年 9 月 1 日起至 1989 年 8 月 31 日止。

　　2. 受聘方的工作任务，经双方确定如下：

　　　(1) 担任药理教研室师资和进修生的培训工作；

　　　(2) 从事药理学课程教学工作，指导学生和教师开展药理学术活动；

　　　(3) 编写药理学教材和补充读物以及进行其他与药理学有关的工作。

　　　(4) 每周工作量为 18～20 课时。

　　　(5) 受聘方每周工作 5 天，每天 8 小时。受聘方按照中国政府规定的节、假日放假，按照学校规定的寒暑假休假。

　　3. 聘方每月支付给受聘方工资人民币 900 元，并为受聘方提供各种福利待遇。

4.受聘方入境、离境或过境时必须遵守中国政府有关外国人居住、工资福利及旅行的管理规定,并遵守聘方的工作制度。

5.聘方欢迎受聘方在工作中提出意见,并在条件允许时予以采纳。受聘方遵守聘方决定,积极工作,努力合作完成工作任务。

6.双方均不得无故解除合同。聘方如果要求中途结束合同,除按照待遇条件承担受聘方的有关费用外,须给受聘方增发一个月的工资作为补偿金并于一个月以内安排受聘方及其家属回国。如果受聘方中途提出辞职,聘方自同意之日起即停发工资,受聘方不再享受各种待遇条件。受聘方及其家属回国的一切费用均由本人自理。

7.本合同自受聘方到职之日起生效,聘期届满,即自行失效。如一方要求延长聘期,必须在合同期满前向对方提出,经双方协商确认后,可另行签定新合同。

8.本合同在执行中如有争议,由双方协商解决。

9.本合同的中文版应与英文版完全一致,对双方均具约束力。

....
聘　　方　　　　受　聘　方

② 商 业 合 同

编号_____
日期_____
买方_____
卖方_____

本合同由买方和卖方订立,据此,买方同意购买,卖方同意出售下列商品:

品名:
规格:
数量:
价格:
包装:

交货日期：
目的地：
付款条件：

　　……………　　　　　……………
　（买　　方）　　　（卖　　方）

第六节　规则、指南、说明

① <center>阅览室规则</center>

① 认真看书学习,关心天下大事。
② 保持室内安静,注意清洁卫生。
③ 室内不得高声谈笑,不准吃零食,不准吸烟,不得在地上乱扔纸屑。
④ 不准随地吐痰。
⑤ 借书时出示学生证或身分证,每次限借一本。
⑥ 爱护公共财物,不准在图书上乱涂乱画。不得撕毁书页。如有任何损毁,照价赔偿。
⑦ 不得随便搬动桌椅,离室时关好窗户。
⑧ 读者和管理员互相帮助,共同管好阅览室。

1984年4月1日

② <center>电视机保养须知</center>

① 本机灵敏度极高,务必小心轻放。
② 本机不得放在暖气管、炉灶等热源旁边和满布灰尘的地方,或机器震动、冲撞之处。
③ 本机不得放在阳光直射之处或潮湿的地方。
④ 注意本机四周应保持通风,以防机内积热,无处散发。
⑤ 勿把本机放在地毯,毛毯等软东西上,或靠近窗帘、帷幕处,以免空气流动受到阻塞。
⑥ 本机内装有危险的高电压,使用时切勿打开机箱,以防触电。
⑦ 保存装放本机的厚纸箱和捆包填塞物,便于日后需要重新包装运送

时使用。捆包机器时,最好按照出厂时的原捆包形式。
⑧ 为了保持机器外表的新鲜色泽,应时常用柔软的抹布擦拭。
⑨ 如遇污秽沾粘,不易脱落,可用抹布沾上一点中性洗涤剂擦拭。切勿使用松脂油、挥发性汽油等烈性溶剂或摩擦粉,以免机体外部受损。
⑩ 若长期不使用,应拔下墙上插座上的插头。拔电线时,应拉住插头拔出,切勿抽拉电线,以免折断。

③ 安替司丁使用说明书
治疗过敏性病症的抗组胺剂

〔性质〕

安替司丁可减弱或抑制组胺作用,组胺在激发过敏性病症中起重要作用。本品的适应症正是根据这种实验证明的抗组胺作用来确定的。

〔适应症〕

荨麻疹、食物过敏、枯草热、血管舒缩性鼻炎;由皮肤炎症引起的搔痒(包括湿疹);搔痒病和血清病。

〔服法与剂量〕

片剂

成年人:每次1片,1日3～4次。

小儿:每次1/2片,1日1次。

学龄儿童:每次1/2片,1日2～3次。

本片剂应在用餐时服用,用少量的水吞服。

针剂

每次1瓶,1日2～3次,肌注或缓慢静注。儿童剂量相应减少。

〔注意事项〕

本品可引起暂时性倦怠,使用时要严加注意。例如,司机服用就要慎重。正如其他抗组胺药物一样,本品也可能引起过敏性反应。如遇这种情况,应停止使用。

〔成分和包装〕

2—(苯基—苄基—氨钾基)—咪唑啉(＝安塔唑啉):每片含100mg;2ml装的安瓿含100mg。 瑞士制造

第七节 演 讲

① 美国商业部长的祝酒词

主任先生,

女士们,先生们,

我们很高兴来到你们可爱的城市——广州。在这里我们将结束我们对这个伟大国家的难忘的访问。

我们访问了你们的历史名城、英雄的首都——北京。

我们访问了繁忙的工业和海港城市上海,我们两国间日益增长的贸易的相当一部分要通过这个港口吞吐的。我们游览了仙境般的、景色迷人的桂林,这是个非常安静的城市。

现在我们来到广州参加广交会的闭幕式,这是我们两国间关系日益密切的又一个象征。

可以肯定地说,在我们短暂的逗留期间我们已经取得了丰硕的成果。

我们已经签订了六个协议,两倍于我们两国政府过去签订的协议数字的总和。更重要的是,我们看到了你们的人民,并和他们进行了接触。我们和你们在同一张桌子上进餐、饮酒,在同一张桌子上谈判,一起分享忧虑和欢乐。这一切使我们之间的相互尊重得到了增强,使我们之间的友谊得到了巩固。

现在我提议

为我们的主人及中国人民的健康,

为我们个人间的关系以及商务往来的增强,

为我们下次访问你们美丽的国家及你们的回访干杯!

② 现在,回头看看我们刚才的所做的实验。

首先,我们在软木塞上开一个孔,然后插进一根细长的玻璃管,再把塞子塞进一个盛满有色水瓶子的瓶颈。塞子一塞进去,有色水就沿试管上升。然后将瓶子放入一个盛着热水的盆里。

这时,试管中的水位马上有所下降,但随即又开始上升,直至水从试管口溢出。

这是由于水受热体积膨胀的缘故。开始液面降低的原因是,瓶子先受热,受热后,瓶子的体积稍稍增大。然后水受热,受热后水的体积膨胀。几乎所有液体和固体受热时都会膨胀。

接着,把瓶内的水倒空,试管内留下少许有色水,将塞子重新塞上,把瓶子再放进热水之中。这时,试管内的水马上由管口喷出,这是因为瓶内空气受热后体积急剧膨胀的缘故

③ 热血、辛劳、汗水与眼泪
——温斯顿·丘吉尔

星期五晚我奉国王陛下之命组织新内阁。

国会与国民显然希望这一内阁在最广泛的基础上组成,包括所有党派在内。

迄今我已完成此项任务中的最重要部分。一个五人战时内阁已经组成,其中包括反对党工党和自由党,代表了国家的统一。

……

现在我提请议院作出决议,认可已采取的各项步骤,记录在案,并宣布对新政府的信任。决议全文如下:

"本议院欢迎新政府成立。新政府代表了全国团结一致、坚定不移的决心:对德作战,直到最后胜利。"

组织如此复杂并具有如此规模的内阁,本身就是一项严肃的任务。但我们目前正处于有史以来一次规模最大的战役的最初阶段。我们正在其他许多地方作战,例如挪威与荷兰。我们在地中海也要准备战斗。空战正在继续进行,我们在国内需要做许多准备工作。

在此非常时期,我相信议院将原谅我今天发言简短,我还希望我的朋友、同事或受到这次政治改组影响的前任同事们,能体谅省去一般情况下必需的仪式。

我已告诉过组成新政府的各位大臣,在此再告诉诸位议员:我所能奉献的,只有热血、辛劳、汗水与眼泪。我们还要经受极其严峻的考验,我们面临着漫长而艰苦卓绝的斗争。

要问我们的政策是什么?我的回答是:在海、陆、空作战,尽我们所能、以上帝赐予我们的一切力量作战。我们的敌人是人类黑暗可悲犯罪史上空前暴虐凶残的暴君,我们要和敌人决一死战,这就是我们的政策。

要问我们的目的是什么？我可以用两个字回答,那就是:胜利。不惜一切代价夺取胜利,不顾一切流血恐怖夺取胜利。不论道路多么漫长,多么崎岖,一定要夺取胜利! 因为没有胜利就不能生存。

希望大家认识到这一点:没有胜利,英帝国将不能生存,英帝国所代表的一切将不再存在,推动人类历史不断朝着其目标前进的动力将不再存在。

我满怀希望地接受我的任务,我确信人们不会听任我们的事业遭到失败。

此时此际,我认为我有权要求所有人的支持,我要说:"让我们团结一致,共赴国难吧。"

④ 火炬已经传给新一代美国人
—— 约翰·肯尼迪

今天我们庆祝的不是政党的胜任,而是自由的胜利。这象征着一个结束,也象征着一个开端,表示了一种更新,也表示了一种变革。因为我已经在你们和全能的上帝面前,宣读了我们的先辈在170多年前拟定的庄严誓言。

现在的世界已大不相同。人类的巨手掌握着既能消灭人间的各种贫困,又能毁灭人间一切生命的力量。但我们的先辈为之奋斗的那些革命信念在世界各地仍然有着争论。这个信念就是:人的权利并非来自国家的慷慨,而是来自上帝的恩赐。

今天,我们不敢忘记我们是那第一次革命的继承者。让我们的朋友和敌人同样听见我此时此地的讲话:火炬已经传给新一代美国人。这一代人诞生在本世纪,受过战争的锻炼和艰苦和平的磨砺。他们为我国悠久的传统感到自豪,他们不愿目睹或听任我国一向保证的,今天仍在国内外作出保证的那些人权渐趋毁灭。

让每个国家都知道——不论它希望我们繁荣还是希望我们衰落——为确保自由的存在和自由的胜利,我们将付出任何代价,承受任何负担,应付任何艰难、支持任何朋友、反抗任何敌人。

……

在漫长的世界历史中,只有少数几代人在自由处于最危急的时刻被赋予保卫自由的责任。我不会推卸这一责任,我欢迎这一责任。我相信我们中间没有人愿意同其他人或其他时代人交换位置。我们为这一努力所奉献的精力、信念和忠诚,将照亮我们的国家和所有为国效劳的人,而这火焰发出的光芒定能真正照亮全世界。

因此,同胞们,不要问国家能为你们做些什么,而要问你们能为国家做些什么。

全世界的公民们,不要问美国将为你们做些什么,而要问我们能共同为人类的自由做些什么。

最后,不论你们是美国公民还是其他国家的公民,你们有权要求我们献出我们同样要求你们的高度力量和牺牲。问心无愧是我们唯一可靠的赞赏,历史是我们行动的最终裁判。让我们走向前去,引导我们所热爱的国家。我们乞求上帝的祝福和帮助,但我们知道,上帝在人世的工作一定是我们自己的工作。

第三章 新闻文体的翻译

第二节 各类体裁新闻的翻译

一、硬新闻

① 英国失业率四月份达百分之十点二

伦敦——四月份英国劳动力失业率超过10%,引起了英国工人和资方的苦恼与抱怨。

四月份的数据表明,失业人数已从上一年的1,456,200人和上个月的2,380,800人季节性地增加到目前的2,466,000人。劳工部称,失业率从一年前的6%和三月份的9.9升至10.1%。英国劳工联合组织工会代表大会总书记冷·莫里说:"这些数字创下了第二次世界大战后又一个令人惊恐与沮丧的记录。"

英国工业联合会,一个主要的雇主团体,将失业率的上升说成是一件"既令人遗憾又令人担心的事。"它说预计到年底,失业人数将达到三百万。

② 发展中国家确定目标

新华社转发路透社加拉加斯 5 月 18 日电——来自 122 个发展中国家的外长和高级代表于今日开会,确定与工业化国家的关系及拟订国际合作的方案。

35 位来自 77 国集团的发展中国家的外长将出席会议,其它成员国预计也将派部长级的高级代表团出席这次为期两天的会议。

过去一周里,该集团的各工作委员会已分析了在原材料、能源、贸易、开发、金融、技术交流和工业化方面的共同目标。

77 国集团是 1964 年在联合国范围内成立的一个非正式集团。它与联合国贸易与发展会议理事会密切合作,促进贸易。此后成员国的数目有所增加。

这些委员会同意明年在维也纳举行一次各国有能源公司的会议。委员会的成员包括石油输出国组织(欧佩克)中的国家。

77 国集团赞同建立自己的多国能源公司。

这次在加拉加斯附近的卡拉巴列达召开的为期两天的会议,将由委内瑞拉总统路易斯·埃雷拉·坎平斯宣布开幕。

③ 法国教授说:疟疾仍威胁四分之一人类

新华社拉巴特四月十二日电——据当地报纸报道,法国教授马克·让蒂里尼在阿加迪尔说,今天世界上大约 10 亿人仍受到疟疾的威胁,每年近两百万人死于此病。

这项声明是在本周于摩洛哥的阿加迪尔召开的第一届法语国家热带医学会议上提出的。

让蒂里尼教授指出,更严重的是寄生虫病常与营养不良以及细菌性和病毒性疾病相关。

④ 世界首例试管双胞胎在墨尔本诞生

新华社转发路透社墨尔本 6 月 8 日电——世界首例试管双胞胎上周末在墨尔本的维多利亚女王医院诞生。此消息是在当地发布的。

一份由院方发布的简要声明称:医生刚开始引产不久,母亲就分娩了,生出一对双胞胎,一男一女。

她已怀孕37周,两周后将进入预产期。

医生说由于对母亲的特殊要求,双胞胎婴儿早产并不少见。

双胞胎中的男婴经过精细的心脏外科手术,存活下来了。医生说他已脱离危险并且"进步很大"。

这对双胞胎的诞生使墨尔本的试管婴儿出生数升至六名。

《中国日报》1981

二、中间类新闻

1. 通讯

① 从底特律看到的两个美国

同这座饭店隔几条街的地方是另外一个美国。

他们是劳工阶级,没有种族界限,靠抵押度日,整天为生活操心。这个阶级中挣工资的人没有工作可干。全国有千百万人失业,但是底特律的失业率却相当于全国平均失业率的两倍。被解雇的人很多,因此不得不增设许许多多失业人员救济办事处。

前几天,我走过失业人员排成的长队,和这个美国里的人谈话。他们垂头丧气,内心痛苦,不知如何是好。但是,他们并不自怜自叹。

一位三十岁上下的黑人妇女对我说:"我只要求恢复工作。我要离开这个长队,回到装配线上去。"她原来是在福特汽车厂上班的,将近九个月前失了业。她曾经二十五次申请别的工作,都没有成功。

一位五十多岁的白人妇女已经排了一个小时的队,手里还牵着十岁的孙子。她说:"我干了一辈子活。这是我第一次被解雇。我不愿意领政府的救济。我要工作。"

站在他背后的是一对夫妇。他们都是汽车工人,都失了业,而且都是五十多岁的人了。女的说:"我们的情况还不算很坏。除了领救济金以外,我的丈夫还能够在附近干一点修修补补的零活,挣几块钱。可是我的两个儿子就苦了。一个已经被解雇,另外一个就要被解雇。"

还有一些人遭遇更惨:有一些汽车工人失业以后,妻子为环境所迫,流了产,或者离开了家。有一个失业工人,年龄在二十五岁上下,老婆孩子都离开了他。他对《华盛顿邮报》的记者说:"我已经节省到极点。我遇到这么多头疼的事情,这么多困难。我对妻子说,我们的问题不是我们自己造成的,是制度造成的。可是,她却带着儿子回娘家去住了。"

在另外一个失业人员救济办事处里,我遇到一个黑人青年。他去年从陆军中退役,至今还没有找到工作。他说:"老兄,我过去为国家服过役,可是,我现在却找不到工作。我来到这里,排这个队领支票,再排那个队换现金。老兄,我一直在想.难道我服役就是为了这个吗?难道这就是我应有的结局吗?"

确实有两个美国。它们是邻居,却又相距遥远。

② <center>警察遭枪击</center>

这是个雾气蒙蒙的周四夜晚,在达拉斯中心区,警官约翰·韦士和杰伊·詹姆士让六个小时令人恼火的例行公事缠得苦不堪言,这类工作与电视上充满戏剧色彩的警察形象全然不同。他们沉闷地处理了一些小事,有人撞弯了汽车挡板,有人报告汽车失窃了,有人假报受盗,有人未受骚扰而说受骚扰。终于他们打了一个小胜仗,抓了一名头戴棒球帽的男子,身上带着0.2克强效混杂可卡因。他们离开街区一个多小时,为这位倒霉的犯人登记办理关进县监狱的手续。但是晚上十点,无线电响起急促的声音,报告一起驾车枪击事件。就在詹姆士和韦士赶到,停下车向一名嚎啕大哭的西班牙妇女和愤怒的旁观者了解情况时,那辆开枪歹徒的红色卡车疾驶而过。

追逐开始了。詹姆士急忙倒转巡逻车,变速器发出嘎嘎响声。汽车轮子飞转,冒出黑烟。不一会詹姆士和韦士便飞驶在小街上,见到红灯猛地刹住。当汽车急速驶入拥挤的大街时,车子留下轮胎橡胶的痕迹。不一会他们的车子以80英里高速歪歪斜斜地在行驶的汽车中穿来穿去,后来又猛地刹车,向前滑去,停在一个停车场上。当另外两部警车与他们会合时,韦士与詹姆士纵身跳下汽车,推开车门掩护自己,一面拔枪瞄准,动作一气呵成,同时令他们吃惊的是其他警官径直跑到这辆卡车旁,从车里猛地拉出一个矮胖的年青人,使劲地将他摔倒在地面上,用枪对准了他的头部。后来詹姆士称这辆卡车为"老约翰·韦恩理学士"。这就是达拉斯中心区典型的平日晚班情况。周末当然就更危险了。

2.特写

① 苏联沙德林斯克见闻

　　这个城市是一个铁路工人城。市内有许多小工厂。街道上满是尘土,沿街整齐划一地排列着战后兴建而又缺乏个性特点的公寓建筑;楼房旁边是一座座用木板或圆木搭成的屋子,由于风雨的剥蚀而摇摇欲坠。市长尼古拉·伊里奇·瓦尔拉科夫说:"这是一座典型的古老的俄罗斯城市。"

　　这个城市不仅古老,而且友好,只是对外国人有些多疑。我和一位同仁是第一批访问沙德林斯克的西方记者,谁也不记得有别人来过。所以,当地人对我们都十分好奇,就像我们对他们一样。市民们显然决心给我们一个好印象。我们下榻在市内唯一的旅馆——乌拉尔饭店。我们住的房间散发着新油漆的气味。当地一位年轻的商店售货员说,她事先接到通知,有两位西方记者要来沙德林斯克,必须多加注意,并且要把最好的商品摆在货架前面。

　　看来,美国的粮食禁运一类的经济制裁是不会使沙德林斯克人感到惊慌的,因为物资短缺是这里日常生活中司空见惯的现象。易腐的奶制品和其他食品一直供应不足;在国营食品商店里我们所见到的肉食品只有猪蹄、猪头肉和香肠。我们在城里看到的新鲜农产品也只有小萝卜和洋葱。

　　在市中心附近,常常可以见到妇女们从街头机井打水,然后提着水桶回去,或者推着用手工制成的,装满要洗的衣物的推车,吃力地朝泥泞的河岸走去。当东驰的列车在西伯利亚大铁路线上穿越俄罗斯原野时,那不时闪现出来的一座座小村落更叫人吃惊。那是一些东倒西歪的小木屋坐落在满布车辙的土路间,构成小小的居民点。列车在这些地方附近一停下来,一些身穿四季如一的肥大衣裙,头裹披巾的老妇就拥挤在餐车周围,兜售食品和农产品。

② 心力交瘁的金敦促公众停止暴力行动

　　路透社洛杉矶五月三日电:摇摇晃晃、情感濒临崩溃的罗德尼·金先生恳求人们停止暴乱。

　　看上去被此事搞得焦头烂额的金先生周五出现在传媒上,这是自陪审团宣布四名被指控殴打他的洛城警官无罪的裁决后,金第一次公开发表讲话。

　　公开发表声明对金先生来说异常困难,因为他与美国现代史上最严重的骚乱之一联系在一起了,而他的律师斯蒂夫·赫尔曼却说:这与他"毫不相干"。

金先生是一位腼腆而不善言辞的二十六岁的年轻人。他面对传媒说话前深深地吸了几口气。别人要他讲慢点。

金先生边说边想,在他三分钟的讲话过程中,他几次说不下去,几乎要哭出来了。

但他的意思很明确,就是停止抢劫,停止纵火,停止暴力行为。

3. 新闻评论

① 华盛顿是国父,还是可耻的叛臣逆子?

怎样教养儿童,才能使他长大成人以后不致惹事生非,叫人讨厌?关于这个问题,概括起来,有两种截然不同的理论。

第一种是比较古老的理论。这种理论侧重训练,认为要对儿童进行训练。要把儿童训练得长大以后有一套现成的价值观念,处世态度,以至生活习惯。按照人们训练他或教导他的那一套去待人接物。

第二种是比较现代的理论。这种理论转而侧重教育。要把儿童教育得长大以后可以独立思考和形成一套在迅速变化的环境中对他最有用的价值观念、处世态度和生活习惯。

这两种学说只有格式上的差别,在实践中显然并无二致。其选择并不是"非此即彼"。而我们只要从有关教科书的争论中举出一个例子,就足以说明这场关于侧重点之争的意义了。

大多数美国人自幼受到教诲,习惯于把爱国主义看作是他们生为美国公民和十分幸运的标志。他们是在这种价值观念的熏陶下成长起来的,或者说训练出来的,因为他们的家长和老师都希望这样。他们都希望把下一代美国人训练得忠于祖国,克尽职守。而不希望把下一代教育得在爱国和叛逆这两种相互冲突的价值观上随心所欲,以致误入叛国的歧途。

教导的方法是人人都熟悉的——效忠宣誓、国歌、向国旗致敬。对于这一命令式的决定,人们并不教育学生去进行彻底的思考,去自行判断乔治·华盛顿究竟真是美国国父,还是像千百万忠诚的英国人认为的那样,是奥利弗·克伦威尔以来英国王室最可恶的叛臣逆子。他们在到达学会思考这个问题的年龄之前,就知道了这一问题的答案。

教科书争端所涉及的问题归根到底就是这样一个问题。如果我们不用家长们奉为传世圭臬的价值观念训练儿童的话,那就是对儿童疏于管教。如果我们不对儿童进行教育的话,那就要使儿童沦入世世代代的愚昧状态。

问题在于怎样把这两种办法恰当地结合起来。现在需要大家在这个问题上取得一致意见。一旦大家的意见趋于一致,教科书之争就会烟消云散。

② 摇摆不定的美国对外政策

现实情况:阐述一项不偏不倚的政策是乏味的,执行这项政策更为复杂。但是唯有这条路线能使我们积聚一切资源,面对世界现实并保持国内的和谐一致。二次大战以来,我们的重大成就都是靠中间路线创建的。美国的对外政策必须兼备力量和原则二要素,以达到促进安全与正义这一双重目的。

跟敌对国家,我们既要坚定,不妥协,也要跟他们谈判。与盟国相处,我们不仅要领导,还要敦促他们更多出力。为了国家安全,我们必须加强防务,同时寻求军备控制。在发展中国家,我们在顾及东西方关系这个领域的同时,也要着手解决造成不安定形势的更为深刻的根源。

我们的长远利益并非每隔四年就变一次。不管下届政府是民主党还是共和党主持,都应当从一开始就奉行平衡的政策。它必须承认,有些时候,它的前任还是对的;它应当任命几名反对党的成员;有选择地套用斯考克罗夫特委员会的模式,努力求得各方面机构的协调一致——总之,在执行对外政策时不带任何党派色彩。辩论肯定不会停息。不过,在辩论中人人要认识到全体美国人民都在从事一项共同的事业。

这样,美国将向世人表明:纵使我们已不再年轻,也尚未衰老;如果我们不像过去那样天真无邪,也还没腐败堕落;尽管我们不再是凌驾一切的主宰,也决不是可以任凭命运摆布的小卒。

③ 毒品应合法化吗?

我看不出合法化有何好处。事情很简单,吸毒是错误的。道德上的理由终究是最无可争辩的。一个人沉迷于毒品,昏昏噩噩,无论是在自家后院的地上,还是在贫民窟毒品馆的床垫上,都决不是开国的先辈们所指的"幸福的追求"。尽管妄图使吸毒合法化的人争辩说吸毒纯属"个人自由",但我们民族对自由的概念是扎根于全体公民自强自立的理想中。戒毒所里无用的废物,被可卡因牵着鼻子走的人——这些人是奴隶。

试想一下,在1940年最黑暗的日子里,如果温斯顿·丘吉尔用这样的话来团结西方说:"这场战争看来没有希望了,而且花费也会太大。希特勒不会那么坏,让我们投降吧,看看情况会怎样。"那将如何。从本质上说,我们从妄图让毒品合法化者口中听到的正是如此。

这场战争能够取胜。有迹象表明教育和公众的反感正对吸毒产生影响,我倍感振奋。国家毒瘾研究所对目前吸毒者的最新调查表明,吸毒量自1985年以来降低了37%,可卡因减少了50%,年轻人中大麻吸食率降至1972年以来的最低点。我在各地旅行,看到种种迹象表明美国人正在向毒品展开反击,我很受鼓舞。

我不存幻想,无论这些进展多么充满希望,并不意味着战争已经结束。我们还需动员更多的人投入战斗,向毒品罪犯增加压力,开展各种已被证明有效的反毒活动。这不会很容易,但是投降给道德和社会造成的损失实在太大,决无考虑余地。

④ 向违法者亮红灯

法律和秩序,可以说是美国历史上历时最久,或许还是人们最爱谈论的政治问题。然而说来痛心,显然成百上千万美国人从来没有想过自己会违法,更不用说犯罪了,却放任自己愈来愈随意对待那些旨在保护和培育他们的社会的法律条文。今天,乱扔的垃圾,逃税,违禁的噪音,汽车的横冲直撞,比比皆是;有时简直让人觉得:违法者代表了未来的潮流了。哈佛大学的社会学家戴维·里斯曼认为:大多数美国人都轻率地把犯点所谓"小过失"看成理所当然。里斯曼说:美国社会的道德规范已差不多快变成"谁守法谁就是傻瓜了"。

里斯曼这句话的证据有目共睹,再明显不过了。违法者形形色色,多得令人吃惊。喜欢到处乱涂乱写的人,把公共场所的墙面地面变成了视觉的垃圾场。骑自行车者无拘无束,仿佛两轮车就可以不遵守交通规则似的。随地乱扔垃圾的人,把他们的居住区变成了垃圾堆。到处张帖着的禁令,也未能使公共场所免受手提收音机的高分贝噪音的污染,正如以前的法令未能消除啤酒灌得烂醉的流氓在公园中闹事一样。瘾君子对那些"禁止吸烟"的布告牌视若无睹。衣冠楚楚的大麻烟客出入烟馆不再藏头缩尾,怕人发现。可卡因毒品泛滥,是中上层社会中愈来愈恼人的丑闻。当然,还有对来往车辆高喊"喂,大家小心我"的那些乱穿马路的行人。

三、软新闻类

① <center>电子邮件——新时代的交际手段</center>

朋友和家人如同干黄的树叶一样,散布各地,漂移到不同的城市和国家。"我会写信的,"我信誓旦旦地许诺。唉,我的这些良好愿望只停留在想象中。这些信从未付诸笔端,更未贴过邮票。

啊,但电子邮件改变了我的习惯。我的计算机成了书信的平纳吐波火山,喷出大量信件、公文和便函,以飞快的速度传向世界各地。我与新西兰的笔友,在孟买提出问题的陌生人和曼哈顿辩论术士进行思想交流。

以前从没试过电子邮件,我曾瞧不起它,把它看成是枯燥无味的高科技,用于商业交往的东西。后来一个朋友坚持要我探索一下这个被他称作"看不见的世界",声称它正以指数的比例在扩展。我登记上了一家名叫"康普瑟弗"的全国联网信息服务网络,就上瘾了。

……

不眠之夜。然而正是电子邮件这种引人入胜的特点使人卷入读写电子邮件的旋涡,它吞没了空余时间,害我许多夜头昏眼花。只要你不上瘾,这种几乎即刻就获得的满足使写信变得非常有趣,我的通讯圈好似成几何级数般地扩大,从我的计算机键盘上不断涌出电子邮件。我以为我可以只与几个朋友交谈来限制住我的邮件量。但电子邮件实在是太诱人了,因为它驱使我去探索未知领域,提出更多问题,并且与半个世界以外的人建立联系。

丽塔·莱文,一位住在匹兹堡的母亲说,这种长距离的接触也能使家人更加亲近。她每天与她女儿爱琳交换电子信件,她女儿是特拉华大学一年级学生,那里的所有学生都有互联网地址。在开学头两个月里,莱文收到爱琳53封电子信件,只要她走近终端,她就会给妈妈发几行闲聊的话。"真有意思,"莱文说,"我们现在比爱琳住在楼上时谈得更多。"

② <center>简朴生活重返美国</center>

告别拥有一切。由于厌倦追求时髦和实利主义,美国人重新发现家庭生活的乐趣、基本价值和经久不衰的东西。

经过一场为期十年华而不实的美梦和罪恶的消费之后美国人正开始转向低消费。他们想减少对地位的象征、快节奏的职业和拥有一切的期望等的仰慕。高消费已过时,低消费正得势。雅皮士已成为古文化。夸耀钱财被视为粗俗:如果你有钱,请自己留着——或者干脆捐点出来。

许多美国人正在信奉较质朴的享受和家庭亲情的价值观,而不再信奉实利主义。他们正在努力思索着什么是生活中真正重要的东西,并且已经决定要有所改变。真正重要的是有时间与家人和朋友在一起,有时间休息和娱乐,有时间做好事和得到精神上的享受。对有些人来说,这是根本性的一步:改变了人的生涯,生活得更简朴,或者收拾行李搬到一个更安静的地方。对另一些人来说,这只是一种细微的变化,就像选一种较便宜品牌的跑鞋或早些下班去看孩子的足球赛一样微不足道。

③ 从生活中获取您想得到的

在卢·霍尔茨成为国家级的圣母玛丽亚大学橄榄球队教练,在全国出名的好多年前,他就列出了在"死之前要干的"107件事。包括各个方面,从参加白宫宴会到延缓开伞的高空运动。

迄今为止,霍尔茨已实现了第91个目标——看着他的四个孩子全部大学毕业,他说:"确定目标,并坚持努力实现目标。你就把自己从生活的旁观者转变成真正的参与者。"

我们都有梦想和愿望,但只有比较少数的人有目标。强烈的愿望,诸如"我要有钱",或"我想瘦一些"都不算数。尽管目标一开始和梦想一样,但目标是一些具体的目的,只有通过具体行动才能达到。一位新奥尔良的商务顾问麦克尔·利波夫说:"如果你不能衡量它,评估它或描述它,那就可能不是目标。"

霍尔茨教练亲身体验到这一点。几乎每一个大学一年级的球员都梦想成为职业球员。他向他们解释了目标与空想之间的区别。"我告诉他们从集训队打球到参加全国橄榄球联盟赛,这中间有很多小的目标。首先他们必须打进校队,然后一步一步地扫除障碍。实现每个预定的目标都必须如此。"

正如霍尔茨所说,取得巨大成功的人清楚地知道他们想达到的目标。以下是他和其他人为实现梦想所采取的步骤。

明确自己的目标。

把它写在纸上。一旦确定了目标,就写下来。取得巨大成功的人把他们的成就回溯到在纸上写下自己目标的时刻。

制订出策略。把一个目标分成一些可以一口口咽下的小块,使完成这个目标显得不大令人望而生畏。有一种称为前推设计的技巧,就是定下一个目标后,就一步一步往前推出需用来完成目标的步骤。

规定截止时间。动机研究专家齐格·齐格勒说:"目标就是带有截止时间的梦想。最后期限提供了行动的时间框架并启动我们去追求梦想。"

全力以赴。

不惧失败。

坚持,再坚持。在实现目标的过程中,你会遇到各种障碍。自信心能消除遭受挫折的痛苦。

永不言迟。年龄不是事业成就的障碍。我们年龄越大,学得越多,就越有信心接受新的挑战。

④ 　　　　　　　整洁之风的衰退

服饰、语言和情感的不洁与人际关系息息相关。电影中如此流行的两性关系随便的问题,并非会激起性欲而会使感情麻木,隐私无存。这种危险并不在于性宣传会产生色狼,而在于可能造成丧失性功能。那些习惯于什么都看,什么都干的人有失去感觉的危险。

我说这些话的目的不是提倡维多利亚式的礼仪,不是要大家多愁善感。我反对的是衣冠不整,行为不端,言语不当和人际关系的不和谐。只能希望这种有意的邋遢之风自然减退。谁知道呢,也许有些时装设计师会发现他们可以通过设计出没有磨损,又可增加身材美感的流行款式来发财。同样,电影和电视制片商和放映商也许会意识到有大批观众更爱看给人视觉美感和精神美感的东西,而不是看一个人被从铺店临街的橱窗里摔出来或从楼顶房屋的平台上推下去的场面。而观众甚至会对那些敢于用更加令人信服的方式表现人们真心相爱和相互尊重的电影表示欢迎和敬意,而不是那些尽演一些莫名其妙的相互搂抱和打闹的影片。

最后,我们的学校应该提倡这样的概念:无论在服饰上,交际方式上,人际关系的培养上,还是在如何发现自身长处和发挥其作用方面,没有什么比真正的创造力更有价值了。

第四章 广告文体的翻译

第二节 不同类型广告的翻译

一、硬卖类

① <center>按下揿钮</center>

照相机自动聚焦,自动曝光,自动拍摄,自动送出印好的照片。

拍立得 SX-70 声纳单步照相机。

要获得一张聚焦精确,曝光恰当的照片,只需按下拍立得 SX-70 声纳单步照相机上的揿钮即可。这是世界上最好的即刻显影照相机。

声纳自动测距。四元镜头旋至焦点,近到 10.4 英寸,远至无限。单镜反射取景器预现目标。自动曝光控制系统完成曝光。内设的小电机将印好的照片送出。整个过程在 1 秒半内完成。照相如此简便精美,以前何曾有过!

② <center>住宅汽车像一个四处为家的家。</center>

住宅汽车有两大特点:开得动,住得好。

GMC 住宅汽车就具有这两大特点。

GMC 用前轮驱动,无从前到后的传动轴,重心稳定,驾驶安全。

后轮皆为前后纵排而非横排。优点为:第一,当与 GMC 空气悬浮系统联用时,有助于平稳驾驶;第二,有六个而不只是四个制动器,每个轮子一个;第三,汽车内部更宽敞,因后轮纵向排列,内部空间占用较少。

GMC 式样美观,居住舒适。内部布置整齐,设备完善。包括一只 $7\frac{1}{2}$ 立方英尺的冰箱,方便高效的炉灶,两个相连的不锈钢水池。

座位舒服漂亮,颜色和质地与地板图案十分协调。

③ 　　　　　　　　保健办公椅

专为防止和缓解背疼而设计定制。
　具有矫形功能。
· 可前倾的斜度
· 可调节的颈枕
· 内有可调节的腰垫
全新设计！
身高 1.58m—1.98m 均宜
背舒尔

④ 　　　　　　火灾保险——农民保险公司
　　　　　　　　赔偿火灾高额损失

价格在上涨,火灾后重建家园的费用太高,您难以承受。我公司愿为您服务。农民保险公司关心每一家。

我们会查对您当前的保险范围,设法让您得到妥善的保险,为您负担高涨的费用。根据我公司的保值规定,将来会自动为您提供充分的赔偿。

此外,我公司还开展抵押保护保险,如果家庭生计的主要担负者去世,我公司将偿付抵押金。

为您提供快速、公平、友好的服务。
农民保险公司
家庭的守护神
始终关心您

⑤ 　　　　　　治疗关节疼痛、关节炎有良药

服用巴啡啉,很快就能解除轻微关节疼痛。它能直接作用于疼痛部位,并迅速解除关节疼痛。用后几小时内,您能感到轻松自在。

服用巴啡啉可消除炎症。泰勒农无此效果。尽管许多患者关节疼痛、肿胀或麻木僵硬,但他们并没有认识到这些痛苦的根源是炎症。泰勒农止疼,却不消炎;而巴啡啉既止痛又消炎。按时服用巴啡啉,可消除炎症,数日后,您定会开始从关节肿胀和压迫的病痛中解脱出来。

关节炎危害性很大。如果疼痛持续 10 天以上,或出现红肿,务必立即就医。

巴啡啉止痛又消炎。

服用时,请遵医嘱。

布里斯多—美亚有限公司

二、软卖类

① <center>澳大利亚——神奇的地方</center>

土著人深信整个澳大利亚是神唱出来的。来听听这种音乐吧。

听听翠鸟在原始森林中的欢笑。听听土著人反映世界创始的古老庆典上强节奏的原始音乐的喧嚣。听听内地酒馆中的高谈阔论。听听波涛拍岸低沉的轰隆声。最后再听听那种据说在万籁俱寂时还能听见的音乐。

② <center>音像协奏曲</center>

看一眼,您就会心满意足。这就是富有创意的革新。在此,感受与体验融合在音乐的海洋中,似清澈的声波,似美丽的风光,美妙动人,任君欣赏。现在,请注意听。开始,您就像是在爵士音乐俱乐部里,而后又像是在教堂内,又像是在电影院中,随后又到了……?

弹指之间,按动 UD-90 摇控器上的六个选择按钮,音乐画面立刻跃然眼前。

康　伍
音像美妙的结合

③ 最近,我得去圣路易斯开会。四年来我一直是乘飞机,但这次我决定乘夜车的卧铺。我走时正巧下雨,但不妨事,火车准点。而且我上车前未遭雨淋。

我走进包间时,手提箱已放在那里了。我将衣服挂在衣橱里,换了一条便裤,然后靠在宽大而又舒适的座位上,开始在宁静的包间里办公。一个小时干完的工作比我在办公室里要花半天时间才能完成的还要多。

不用说我睡得有多香!

火车提前半分钟到达了圣路易斯车站。下车前,我饱吃了一顿早餐,穿上了笔挺的衣服和闪亮的皮鞋,神气十足。转眼出租车就把我带到了约会的地点。这一切表明:过去我总以为是受罪的旅行,现在已变成愉快的享受了。我期待乘卧铺车作更多的旅行。

④ 美能达照相机:它将人们连在一起

我们在拂晓开始充气,准备静静地随风飘流,飞过童话般的美丽景色,这是最令人难忘的时刻。

照相把人们连在一起,让世界欢笑、思念和哭泣。美能达照相机最懂得这一点,因为50多年来,它照出了全世界。

⑤ 果 味 奇 珍

这是梦寐以求的松饼。松软的黄饼裹着一层殷红的草莓糖浆。糕上的点缀呢?糕面上的奶油闪耀着珍珠般的光泽。

当您品尝每一口时,请想想裹着椰仁和杏仁糖衣的德国巧克力饼和草莓奶酪饼——光滑,柔软,美味。

甜蜜的梦想。维娃奇公司制作的点心是您的生活乐趣。无论有无果味,您都会喜欢它。

维 娃 奇
维娃奇国际食品公司

第五章 科技文体的翻译

第二节 科技报道

① 臭 氧 问 题

31个国家为保护地球的大气层向达成一项国际协定迈出了第一步。它们对破坏臭氧的化学品的生产和使用提出了一些限制。埃及的马斯塔发·托尔巴博士是联合国环境规划署的主任。他的小组最近在瑞士的日内瓦召开了一个关于臭氧问题的会议。他说,在9月前可能签署一项关于保护大气层的最后协定。

业已提出的这项协定要求限制含氯氟烃化学品的生产。这些化学品俗称 CFCs。签署这项协定的国家 CFCs 产量将不超过其 1986 年的水平。这项规定将于 1990 年开始实施。几年后，CFCs 的生产和使用量将会削减 20%。托尔巴博士说，出席日内瓦会议的代表们一致认为世界正面临一个丧失防护性臭氧的严重问题。可是，他说，他们也共同感到工业变革需要时间。

臭氧是氧的一种，主要见于高层大气。它阻止大量的太阳紫外线到达地球。大量的紫外线会损坏农作物并能引起皮肤癌。所以，我们需要臭氧来起防护作用。

科学家们说，用于许多工业产品中的 CFCs 和其他化学品能破坏臭氧。在 70 年代后期，加拿大、芬兰、挪威、瑞典和美国曾禁止在雾化器内使用 CFCs。但是，在其他国家和其他产品中 CFCs 的使用并没有停止。美国国务院的一位官员说，业已提出的关于臭氧问题的国际协定十分重要。他说，它表明能够进行国际合作来保护环境，防患于未然。

② 温 室 效 应

一个环境保护团体——世界资源协会，最近发表一份部分关于日内瓦所讨论的这一问题的报告。这篇报告对大气变化的后果提出警告。它说，全世界必须立即行动起来，制止这些变化。否则，地球温度将上升到危险的程度。世界资源协会的一位科学家，欧文·明策尔，使用计算机研究了人们称作温室效应的大气的变化。

温室是一座能捕获热量、在寒冷的天气也能在里面种植植物的玻璃建筑物。含氯氟烃、二氧化碳以及大气层中的其他气体起着像温室一样的作用。它们允许太阳的热量到达地球，却能将热量扣住，不许其逃回宇宙空间去。

明策尔先生的研究表明，倘若当今的工业政策不予改变，平均气温可能会上升 4 摄氏度以上。他说，这种温升可能在 45 年以内就会出现。升高的温度会使南北两极的冰块溶化。海平面平均可能会升高 1 米之多，使沿海地区发生严重的洪水灾害。

明策尔先生说，如果各国政府赞同采取强硬措施来限制温室效应，那么，问题不会那么严重，这些措施包括减少含氯氟烃的使用量，减少石油和煤气的燃烧量以便减少二氧化碳的产生以及重新种植有助于消除大气中二氧化碳成分的雨林。

③ 废 水 处 理

一位美国研究人员已试验成功一种不用化学品净化废水的方法。这种技术采用绿色植物。研究员威廉·朱厄尔是纽约州科内尔大学的一名农业工程师。他称他的净化方法为"滋养膜法"。他说,这种方法非常简单,其原理是废水是植物的极好肥料。

美国环境保护署正在支持朱厄尔教授的试验。试验是在东北部的新罕布什尔州的一座现存废水处理中心进行的。科学家们把植物放入玻璃暖房中狭窄的容器内。每个容器的一端都比另一端高出一些。废水流过这些容器,穿过植物厚密的根须。正如预期的那样,根须抓住水中的废物,用作肥料。同时,这些植物还产生天然气。这种气体可以收集起来,作为燃料出售。

朱厄尔教授说,他的滋养膜法比大多数化学方法更有效。他还说,这种方法能以大约一半的成本生产出清水。这种技术可以用于以太阳能为燃料的废水处理中心。佛罗里达州已有4个地方在利用绿色植物来净化废水。

④ 焦油不一定是香烟中的致命物质

美国开展的研究工作获得了新证据表明,低焦油香烟不一定危害较小。肯塔基大学的科学家曾把老鼠的细胞暴露于香烟冒出的烟中。这些科学家说,普通过滤嘴能减少吸烟者吸入的焦油量,却不能减少香烟的烟对细胞的毒害。肯塔基大学药理学院的罗伯特·格里菲思说:"这些见解对设计香烟具有重大潜在意义。人们一直只过分强调了焦油的重要性。"

用醋酸纤维制做的标准过滤嘴能有效地减少香烟的烟中某种特殊物质,比如焦油的含量,却不能有效地滤掉各种气体,这是大家公认的事实,也正是问题的核心。英国烟草顾问委员会说,一般的过滤嘴可使吸烟者吸入的焦油量减少40%到75%。

人们曾普遍认为,焦油含有多种致癌化学物质,是香烟的烟中最致命的成分。政府鼓励香烟公司降低人们吸每一口烟时吸入的焦油量就是考虑到这个因素。政府公布的焦油含量表暗示低焦油香烟危害较小。但是美国的研究成果根本否定了这种做法。

以格里菲思为首的科学家们把培养的老鼠细胞暴露在不同种类香烟冒出的烟中。他们在《毒物学志》(第58期,120页)报道说:"使用醋酸纤维过滤嘴对细胞死亡率没有什么改变。实验结果表明,烟中的气体情况可能对造成所说的中毒现象起重要的作用。"

　　不过,当代一些焦油释放量不足10毫克的最低焦油香烟可能略微有助于减轻香烟的实际毒害。

　　卷这些香烟用的是多气孔低,有时过滤嘴的卷纸还经激光处理,打上了许多微孔。英国科学家温德尔·穆尔说,香烟采取这种通气措施,为的是使用质地较密的过滤嘴而不会给吸烟者在吸烟时造成太大的困难。过滤嘴采取通气措施后,每吸一口烟,其中三分之一将是新鲜空气。他说:"焦油含量低于10毫克的各种牌号香烟都采用了这些技术措施。"格里菲思在研究中发现,降低吸入烟的浓度,确实减少了烟的毒性。但存在一个问题,很多人吸低焦油香烟时,吸的口数增多,于是抵消了降低烟的浓度的益处。

第三节　科技论文

Stabdump——一种用来帮助调试的转储解释程序

(英国)苏格兰格拉斯哥市斯特拉斯

克莱德大学计算机科学系

D.R.麦格列高和J.R.马隆

[摘　要]

　　采用一种转储分析程序能够大大地加速程序开发,这种转储分析程序可以使程序员更清楚地看见一个程序的状态。现已证明,一种以尽量简明的方式提供尽量多的有关材料的单一的综合性分析,在使用方面要比另一种一次一项的交互分析优越。本文叙述了在STAB用法中所采用的几种方法,采用这些方法的目的在于实现综合性的而又简明的输出。还讨论了这种系统以及为保障这种类型的系统所需的编译程序修改问题。

关键词:程序开发　示差转储　调试辅助程度

[引　言]

　　本文描述了一种程序设计工具。我们使用这种工具已将近两年。这种工具,对于寻找"故障"和检验程序的确实正常运行,都是很有效的。这种工具结合我们的STAB—1程序编制系统一起工作(STAB—1是一种最初从BCPL派生出来的软件书写语言)。可以制成一种类似的工具,实际上可供任何语言或程序编制系统使用。这里,我们想把重点放在我们所认为的、这种工具的主要优点上,并指出哪些特征是最成功的,以及有哪些特征是我们认为值得引进到其他类似系统中去的。

[程序原理]

由于程序员试图在证据不足的情况下进行工作,在寻找程序中的错误时,常会遇到巨大困难。等到检测出一个错误——或者一个程序非法进入时,计算机很可能早已执行了许多个语句。原始错误的寻找很可能大大超出程序员的推断论证能力。如果他的开发系统能够使他的程序的工作变得更加清楚可见,日子就会好过很多。我们所需要的是为程序员提供最大的洞察力。传统的调试方法之一是让程序员获取(并浪费很多时间去分析)一个大型的、粗糙的存储转储(十六进制或者八进制)。这种方法的主要缺点是,信息不是用源语言程序来表示的,提供了大量无关的细节,以及数据格式可能没有什么用处,却要求程序员将它们转换成其它表示法。

现假定我们希望能够用源程序术语(即用符号名称)来检验转储,那么,应该提供多少细节呢?应该交互地一次一项提供细节呢?还是我们应该设法提出一份综合性报告呢?有若干种系统提供了符号名称,用以从转储中提取信息,但是只有一个相当小的可见度"窗口"。

能够做到这点的三种交互系统是:Unix系统中的"程序错误排除器"、近期介绍的供BCPL使用的系统以及一种较早形式的STAB系统。我们的经验是,这类系统提供的可见度有限,而使它们难以应用。然而,我们并不希望程序员被大量的不相关细节纠缠得难以脱身。理想的系统只显示所有的那些重要的和相关的细节。

[系统要求]

我们现在描述的工具是一种符号转储解释程序,它能充分地叙述采用转储时的程序状态。首先叙述的是转储本身。

在STAB系统的所有操作环境中,程序故障的检测(由操作系统、程序库程序或用户程序进行检测)结果,会产生正被转储到后备存储文件中去的那个程序的存储图像。能够在随后不终止运行的情况下,根据来自该程序的调用自动地产生这个存储图像,同样也很方便。在一些操作系统中已经装有这种自动转储设备。(我们所了解的最早的系统,是大约十年前利弗摩尔科学研究中心的一个系统。其它的系统包括斯特拉斯克莱德的前端处理机和贝尔公司著名的 Unix 系统。)我们将把它作为一种任何系统的程序开发的基本工具而大力加以推荐。在大多数系统上,获得所希望的效果并不困难。

这种获得程序故障信息的方法的主要优点是,在空间或速度方面实际上没有运行时间辅助操作。不需要另外的跟踪程序,而且转储解释软件是一个独立的系统设备,只在需要时使用。这样一种设备,在程序已经进入生产使用时仍然有效,而且在"说明"生产环境中的那些偶然故障方面极为有效。

[编译程序要求]

编译程序符号表的内容必须以某种方便的机器可读形式保存起来,从而使独立的转储分析器能够利用它们来解释二进制存储图像。

[STABDUMP 程序]

STABDUMP 转储分析程序获得该程序的符号表信息(系由编译程序为其保存)——存储图象,并送回包括诸如阵列和记录之类的数据结构内容在内的所有变量的转储值。STAB 语言具有全程变量以及固有(静态)变量和局部(以栈为基础的)变量,而且 STABDUMP 程序还有相应的节,这些节中的每一个节执行转储文件的一个分析步骤。第一步是栈解释程序,它"展开"这个栈,打印出现行的例行程序调入序列以及所有局部变量的内容和调用参数值。第二步是处理 STAB 语言全程变量和固有变量。程序将为每个全程变量打印出名称、地址和内容(简单变量为十进制和八进制。阵列则为十进制和字符)。这种显示程度同其它系统相比,大得异乎寻常。然而,我们要强调的是,把所有信息用这类方法表示出来是很有价值的。只要对转储报告加以粗略的检验,就可以使许多问题得到解决,而且程序员也不需要把信息从一种形式转换到另一种形式。然而,要想提出这种详细程度的简明而又能理解的报告,我们还得采取步骤来减少正在输出的无关信息量。

首先,仅将动态记录的初始节——为指示字变量访问过——打印出来。总之,这些初始节所驻留的阵列本身被转储时,它们就会全部被打印出来。其次,转储上的复制行不予打印。打印输出仅打印一行,并且指出它被重复了多少次。第三(也是最重要的),我们使转储成为"示差"的。这就是说,将正被分析的转储同正在较早运行状态下的程序转储加以比较。只有在后一转储同正在较早运行状态下的程序转储加以比较。只有在后一转储出现差异的场合，才把所有信息打印出来，供程序员检验。在最简单和最常用的使用方式中，将要求转储程序对算后检查或检验点与初始存入时的程序图像加以比较。我们已经发现，这种示差原理在减少信息量以及将程序员的注意力引向会有错误出现的那些领域等方面，都是非常有益的。在程序的初始检测期间，它最为有效。发现 15～20 页的整个转储被示差转储减少到只有 2～3 页，这种情况并不希罕。尽管减少了这么多，但是示差输出是如此完整，以致再也不需要使用整个转储了。

也有一些专用节，能解释存储图像中的许多指定的缓冲寄存作用。只有在各种跟踪或监督程序包已被编译成源程序时，才出现这些缓冲寄存作用。这是一种用于组织这类信息输出的有用而方便的方法。一节解释一个含有追溯的跟踪信息的缓冲寄存(当程序中出现跟踪程序包时)。另一节解释一个含有执行特定例行程序和语句时的次数计数的缓冲寄存，从而产生直方图和计数表。

[结　论]

我们的经验总结如下：

①系统的设计应该是，在后备存储文件中如果没有产生存储图像，就不可能使程序错误地结束。越是自动越好。辅助操作较少，如有必要的转储分析辅助设备可以利用的话，这种辅助操作还是值得承担的。②综合性的算后检查分析要比交互的一次一项分析更为方便和更为有效。③打印输出应该表明所有变量的内容——不仅限于简单的(标量)变量。④用"示差转储"原理和压缩重复信息的方法进行数据选择是值得去做的。⑤即使在那些没有全程变量的系统中，也可以通过在变量被预置以后进行程序抽点检验的办法来获得所需的效果。在我们大学的系里，最近已将这种示差转储原理推广到我们的微处理机研制站；在这些研制站中，可以将微处理机的存储内容转储回到主研制机中，以便与装入的初始内容加以比较。

[致　谢]

在过去的七年中，许多人对 STAB—1 系统的研制作出了贡献。我们愿对计算机科学系同事们的建议和有益讨论表示感谢。

第四节 专利文献

把套筒贮存在手柄中的套筒扳手

[发明背景]

套筒扳手是一种很普通、很有用的扳手,它由手柄、扳头、一组不同尺寸的套筒构成。扳头在手柄的一端,它含有一方键。套筒可以分别装在方键上。套筒放在一个盒子里,盒子有一个放手柄的格子,还在许多放套筒的格子,通常称为"套筒扳手组"。此外,这种扳手通常有一个连接杆,它的一端有一方键,另一端也有一个方键,用于装入各种套筒。

套筒扳手通常用于机器或车辆的维修工作。操作者经常有这样的体会,当需要更换套筒时,发现放着各种套筒的盒子不在身边,这造成不必要的延误,有时很叫人着急。

许多套筒由于没有及时放回盒子而丢失。特别当操作者从盒子里取出所需的二、三个套筒去干活,然后随手一放,最易丢失。

[发明概述]

本发明的主要目的是提供一种改进的套筒扳手,把套筒放在手柄中,其结构是:把手柄做成槽形断面,沿轴向做成空腔。手柄的一侧有开口,通过开口可以把套筒装入空腔。空腔各部分的尺寸不同,每个间隔的槽靠摩擦力夹住一个套筒。

上述手柄上的开口与空腔内每个间隔相连,可由此用力取出每个套筒。

[图　例]

图 1 是本发明第一种类型的套筒扳手的立体图,贮存腔开口向上。

图 2 是图 1 中的扳手的立体图,开口向下。

图 3 是图 1 中 3—3 截面的纵向剖视。

图 4 是图 3 中 4—4 截面的剖视。

图 5 是图 3 中 5—5 截面的剖视。

图 6 是本发明第二种类型的套筒扳手的立体图,类似于图 1。

图 7 是图 6 中 7—7 截面的横断面图。

图 8 是本发明第三种类型的套筒扳手的立体图,类似于图 2。

[发明详述]

参阅本发明附图,首先看图 1 至图 5。套筒扳手 10 包括:手柄 11、扳头 12、方键 13、套筒 14 至 20、连接杆 21。扳头 12 装在手柄的一端上,方键 13 装在扳头上,套筒 14 至 20 具有不同的尺寸,可分别装在方键 13 上。连接杆 21 的一端为 22,装在方键 13 上,另一端为 23,含有一方键用来装 14 至 20 的任一个套筒。

手柄 11 上的槽形套管 24 形成一个带有开口 26 的空腔 25,24 由大端 27 逐渐变小,到小端 29 为止。大端 27 有端板 28,颈缩处 29 紧靠扳头 12。

空腔 25 中有多个间隔 30 至 36(图2),它们分别用来存放并夹紧套筒 14 到 20。此外,空腔 25 还包括颈部 37,它紧紧夹住连接杆 21。空腔 25 中用横向筋板来确定 30 至 37 各部分的尺寸,如图 3 和图 4 中的 38 和 39 所示,它们的作用是把 14 至 21 隔开,以便放置套筒。当然,套筒 20 的格子由筋板 39 和手柄端壁 28 构成。筋板的锐边经过倒角或倒圆,以便于装入套筒。

30 至 37 各个间隔都钻有孔,分别标为 40 至 47,位于槽形套管 24 的纵向轴线上。可以通过每个孔把力加在筋板间的套筒上,从而由开口 26 取出套筒。如图 3 中的 45 和 46 的放大截面图所示,孔的边缘经倒角圆呈圆弧形,因此用手指推出套筒时,不会划伤,套筒不会自己掉出,也不会取不出。

间隔 30 至 37 作得有回弹力,如图所示,它是一对用弹性材料做成的软镶条 48,紧靠在套管 24 的上边缘 49 上。由它确定开口 26 的尺寸。

如图 4 和图 5 所示,在间隔 30 至 37 区域内,套管 24 的半径比所要存放的套筒的半径大一些,不过套管 24 的上口 49 比所存放的套筒的水平中心线高,并且内曲线也高于套筒的直径,因此套管的截面是一个大于 180°的弧形。弹性镶条 48 稍微高于每个套筒的水平直径,以便能夹紧每一个套筒。每个套筒按其各自的直径自弹性镶条 48 的最小开口处挤入。显而易见,可以仅在空腔的一侧装有弹性镶条,另一侧由套管的边缘紧紧卡住。大家都清楚,通过选择适当的套管材料和壁厚,套筒也可被卡入、定位,而不用专门的弹性镶条。

套筒 14 至 20 都是标准型号的。每一个套筒的一端有一方孔,如图 4 中 19_a 所示。套筒的另一端有一个六方孔,如图 5 中 20_b 所示。用方孔把套筒装入方键 13 或连接杆的方键 23 上。

图 6 和图 7 是本发明第二种类型的套筒扳手,类似于第一种。所不同的是,手柄套管 24 的中线上没有径向孔。手柄套管 124 上有许多槽,例如 149

上的弓形槽。在图6和图7中,弓形槽的号码标为140至147,相当于第一种类型的开口40至47。如图7所示,凹槽的边缘倒为圆角,以免手指划伤。凹槽便于对套筒加力,用手指夹紧套筒。凹槽把套筒从空腔中取出,情况与第一种类型相同。

第一种类型的套筒扳手与第二种唯一不同的地方是,第二种扳手的弓形槽使得弹性镶条148必须以单个的垫片的形式连接在弓形套管124上,且位于各凹口之间。第一种类型的扳手则采用整条的垫片。

图8是本发明的第三种类型的套筒扳手。它的手柄套管224很像第一种类型的套管24,都是利用侧面上的开口来确定贮存腔尺寸,套管的孔的轴线在套管224的轴线上。在第三种类型的扳手中,套筒14至20、连接杆21,连同各自的旋转轴均在开口的纵向中平面上。孔240至247的尺寸不同。因此每一个孔适于存放一种尺寸的套筒。这种套筒扳手与第一种和第二种类型的套筒扳手一样,横向筋板(未示出)把贮存腔分隔成若干部分,各部分分别存放套筒14至21,并紧紧夹住。因此,当需要从贮存腔通过开口取出14至21中任一个套筒时,可以把力加在套筒的凸出部分。

必要的话,弓形套管224可以更改,把管壁做得厚一些,这时,套筒14至21可以完全密封在空腔内,因而这种扳手的开口与第一种类型的扳手的开口40至47相同。

为使人们了解本发明,上面已作详细描述。应当懂得本发明所包括的范围。因为对于技术熟练的人,进行各种改进并不难。

[专利权利要求范围]

1. 本发明的套筒扳手由手柄、扳头和套筒构成。扳头在手柄的一端,带有一个能装套筒的方键。套筒有若干个,尺寸不同,但可互相更换,适于分别装在方键上。本发明的改进措施包括:

手柄是一弓形套管,由它确定空腔的尺寸,在套管一侧开口。

套管部位不同,尺寸也不同,因而能紧紧卡住每一个套筒。

通过弓形套管上的孔可以对放置在空腔中的套筒加力,从而通过开口取出。

2. 权利要求1中的改进范围包括开孔位于弓形套管的纵向中心线上。

3. 权利要求2的改进范围也包括开孔为棱角倒圆的椭圆孔,其大小足以容纳手指头,以便对套筒加力。

4. 权利要求 3 的改进范围也包括,空腔中每个部位均能放置套筒,并紧紧将其夹住。套筒的轴线与手柄的轴线相一致。

5. 权利要求 2 中的改进范围也包括,空腔中每一个部位适于放置套筒并将其夹住,套筒的旋转轴实际上被置于开口正中。

6. 权利要求 5 中的改进范围也包括,每个开口适合于套筒的端部突出,以便对套筒加力。

7. 权利要求 1 的改进范围也包括,开口位于套筒每一边的弧形壁龛,因而可以用两个手指夹住套筒,对其加力。

8. 上述各权利要求的改进范围包括空腔有一颈部,颈部与扳头连接,扳头能卡住连接杆,连接杆一端接在方键上,另一端含有一个能装入各种套筒的方键。

9. 上述各权利要求的改进范围包括手柄的尺寸由靠近扳头的颈部到外端从小到大顺序排列。

10. 上述各权利要求的改进范围包括,在空腔中设置完整的横向筋板,把空腔分隔成若干部分,从而确定每一部分的尺寸。

第五节 科普读物

① 能 量 转 换

机械能转换为热能对我们一点也不生疏。我们也熟悉其他的能量转换。燃料燃烧时,化学能就转换成热能。在电灯及电炉中,电能转换为光能和热能。太阳光照到吸收光的物体上时,辐射能就转换为热能。"一切矛盾着的东西,互相联系着,不但在一定的条件之下共处于一个统一体中,而且在一定条件之下互相转化。"总而言之,一切能都可以从一种形式转换成另一种形式,并且它们自己都能转换成热能。热能是物质微粒无规则运动的能量,在常温下它比其他各种能的用处都小。

然而在高温下,热能可转换成更有用的能量。人们已经制造出一些把热能转换为机械能的各种机器。柴油发动机和汽油发动机把燃烧燃料产生的热能转换成机械能,用来开动拖拉机、卡车和汽车。蒸汽涡轮机把热能转换为机械能,使发电机运转。而发电机又把机械能转换为电能。这些能量转换在我们的日常生活和生产中时时处处都在发生着。

② 在各门科学之中,生物学对于了解人类关系最大。1859年,也就是稍多于一个世纪以前,达尔文提出了本书所涉及的革命思想——人类以及所有其他生命体,乃是进化发展过程的产物。但是,人类不仅已经进化,而且依然在不断进化。人类的进化不完全是过去的事情,它同时也是现实,而且关系着未来。人类由于处在辐射威胁之下,其中包括原子武器试验产生的放射性散落物所造成的辐射威胁之下,很可能遭到基因损伤。这一问题近年来已经理所当然地引起了人们的广泛重视。

③ 上面作为有机化合物的例子列举的许多物质,曾一度被认为是有生命的生物的产物,所以称作有机的。然而,在进行了许多实验室实验以后,化学家们能够证明,以前认为是生命过程产物的某些物品,却是可以在实验室制造出来的。这类工作的一个最典型的例子,就是韦勒所合成的尿素。1828年,德国化学家韦勒用对原来属于无机化合物的氰酸铵盐加热的方法,制造出了蛋白质的一种分解物——尿素:$NH_4CNO-CO(NH_2)_2$。

这就开创了一个新纪元:科学家以前认为不可能在实验室里制取的碳化合物,可以人工合成了。那种认为是生命过程的观点从此被抛弃。今天,在制取糖、维生素以及有关的化合物方面正在取得迅速的进展。有机合成化学家们每天都在实验室里制造新的化合物,其中许多与我们的日常生活有着重要的关系。

在谈到酸、碱、盐的水溶液的导电性时,人们指出,它们这一类是电流的较好的导体。

与此形成鲜明对比的是,酒精、糖、甘油之类的水溶液是极差的导体。这些事实表明,有机化合物几乎没有或者根本没有电离作用。因此,虽然无机的离子反应几乎在一瞬间就发生,而有机反应,甚至在最有利的情况下往往需要相当长的时间才能接近完成。

第六节 科幻小说

① 赛厄蒙若有所思地点点头,伸出杯子再接些水。谢林吝啬地从瓶子里滴出几滴红色液体。

"直到二十年前,"他润了润喉咙,接下去说,"才最终证明,正是万有引力定律造成了六个太阳按轨道运行。这是一大成功。"

谢林站起身来,走到窗前,手里还紧紧抓着瓶子。他说:"现在,我们谈到要害了。在过去的十年里,人们根据万有引力计算出了雷盖什星球绕着 α 星的运动。但这还不能解释已观察到的轨道。即使把其它太阳引起的摄动算在内,也不能解释这一点。不是定律不对,就是另有别的目前尚不知道的因素。"

赛厄蒙也走到窗前,站在谢林身边,凝视着窗外。他的目光掠过林木葱葱的山坡,移到远方萨罗市闪着红光的高楼大厦的屋顶。记者看了一眼 β 星,感到心中升起一股不安与紧张。β 星在天顶闪着红光,显得渺小而又充满不祥之兆。

"说下去,先生!"他轻轻地说。

谢林回答说,"多年来,天文学家们一直踌躇不决。每个人所提出的理论都不如前一个站得住脚——直到安东突然来了灵感,引进了宗教崇拜。宗教首领索 5 能得到某些资料,使这个问题大大简化。安东另辟新径,开始工作。"

"要是有另一个像雷盖什这样不发光的星体呢?如果有,你知道,它只能靠反射其他天体的光而发光。如它是由青色的岩石构成,就像雷盖什大体上一样,那么在鲜红的天空下,太阳永恒的强光就会使人看不见它——完全将它淹没。"

赛厄蒙吹了声口哨,"真是希奇古怪的念头。"

"你认为它希奇古怪吗?听着,假设这个天体在这样的距离,沿着这样的轨道,绕着雷盖什运转,并且具有这样大的质量,其引力恰恰造成雷盖什轨道的偏差,与理论不一致——你知道结果会怎么样?"

记者摇摇头。

"嗯,这一星体有时会挡住一个太阳的路。"谢林将瓶中剩下的水一饮而尽。

② 汤米·多特拿着最后两张立体照片走进机长室,说:

"我干完了,先生。这是我所能拍到的最后两张照片。"

他把照片递过来,带着职业性的兴趣看着视屏,上面显示出飞船外面的整个太空。柔和的深红色亮光显示出控制器,以及当班领航员为"莱弗邦"飞船导航所必须的那些仪器。有一个垫着厚垫子的控制椅,一个带有各种奇怪角度的镜子的小装置——从遥远的二十世纪摩托车手的后视镜发展演变而来——通过这种镜子,不用回头便能看到所有视屏。还有一些大的视屏,更为方便,可直接观看太空。

"莱弗邦"离家已经很远了。视屏上显示出每一颗其光度为肉眼看得见的星体,并可根据需要无限放大。视屏再现出大气层以外各种不同亮度的星星。它们色彩缤纷,令人惊叹。但每一颗星都是从未见过的。只有两个星座可以认得出,同在地球上看到的一样。这两个星座缩小而且变了形。银河似乎有点不得其位。但即使是如此新奇的景象,和朝着前方的视屏上所显出的景象相比,却如小巫见大巫。

前方有一片很大很大的雾状物,一团发光的雾气,似乎静止不动。虽然航速表表明飞船正以不可思议的高速度飞行,但仍然需要很长时间才能从视屏上看到飞船有一点点接近雾状物。这雾状物正是蟹星云。长6光年,厚3.5光年。从地球上望远镜所观测到的向外伸展部分,恰像一只螃蟹,故以此命名。它是一团气体,无比稀薄,其伸延的长度为太阳与其最邻近的恒星之间距离的一倍半。在其深处有两颗星在发光,一种双星。一部分显出人们熟悉的太阳的黄色,另一部分则呈邪恶的白色。

③　他得出了结果。一开始,他就很走运,后来则更走运了,因为他把概率律化成公式,达到极其简单的程度,几乎能确切地知道什么试验可以免除。当玻璃小碟上含混不清的云状带粘性的半流体开始流动时,他知道路子走对了。当它开始自动寻找食物时,他开始兴奋起来。当它分裂,几小时后再分裂,而分裂出的每一部分都在增长,并又一次分裂时,他成功了,因为他创造了生命。

他护理着自己脑力劳动的产物,呕心沥血地照顾它们,为它们设计出作各种各样震动的浴盆,给它们打针,吃药、喷雾。他所走的每一步又教会他下一步该怎么做。从他的容器里,试管里,细菌培养器里诞生的首先是阿米巴变形虫一样的生物,接着是有纤毛的微生动物。再后来,速度越来越快地产生出有眼点和神经胞囊的动物。最后,最为成功的是——一个真正的胚孔,具有多个细胞而不是单细胞。他比较缓慢地培育出了一个腹足类软体动物,一旦有了它,给它器官就不太难了,每个器官都有一种特殊的功能,每个器官都具有遗传性。

接下来就是人工培育的软体动物类的东西,和其鳃越来越完美的动物。那天,一个无法描绘的东西蠕动着爬上一斜板,爬出了容器,用鳃盖盖住了鳃,轻轻地呼吸起空气。基德放下了工作,跑到岛的另一头,喝得酩酊大醉。尽管酒后身体难受,他还是很快就回到了实验室,废寝忘食地投入他的课题。

他转入一条科学的蹊径,获得又一项巨大胜利:加速新陈代谢。他从酒精、可可、海洛因以及大自然母亲的高级麻醉品——长纳比斯因迪卡中提取并炼制出各种激素。就像有位科学家一样,他在分析用于治疗血液病的各种凝固剂的过程中,发现草酸,只有草酸才是活跃的基因。基德从有损人的道德和(或)导致"高尚实验"的各种物质中,把加速剂和减速剂分离出来,把兴奋剂与催眠剂分离出来。在这一过程中,他发现了自己迫切需要的东西:一种无色的灵丹妙药,使睡眠成为多余,这种时间的浪费本可以而且应该避免。从那时起,他就开始二十四小时昼夜不停地工作。

第六章 文学文体的翻译

第二节 散 文

一、记叙文

① 我第一次上学时才七岁。一个身材高大的十五岁女孩穿着普通的印花布衣服,戴着遮阳帽,她问我是否"吃烟"——意思是说我是否用嘴嚼烟。我说不。这使她很蔑视我。她把这件事告诉大家说:"一个七岁的男娃不会嚼烟。"

从这句话引起大家的表情和议论来看,我知道自己成了一个被人看不起的人。我为自己感到十分羞耻。我决心要改善一下。但这样做只让我感到恶心想吐。我没法学会嚼烟。抽烟我学得很不错,但是讨好不了别人,我仍然是个可怜虫,没有气概。我渴望受人尊重,但却无法提高声望。孩子们对相互的缺点是很少宽容的。

② 我长到十二岁时就永远离开了学校,找到了第一份正式工作,在杂货铺当伙计。我整天扛沉重的货物,但干得很起劲。要不是因为能干重活,我早就被辞退了,因为老板认为我跟那些"高我一等"的人说话时应毕恭毕敬,我却

受不了。

有一天是星期二,正是我歇半天班的日子,事情发展到了顶点。我总在星期二回家的路上捎一大篮子食物送到老板的嫂子家。因为她的家顺路,我从来没有说过不肯。

可是就在这个星期二,我们正关门上板时,一大包熏火腿送到店里来了。老板对我说:"等一下。"他打开包,拿出一只火腿,开始剔去骨头,然后用绳子扎好。

我想动身回家,越等越不耐烦,哪里是一会儿,一等就是半天。老板弄完时都快两点半钟了。他拿着火腿走到我面前,把它放在我身边的篮子里,叫我给一个订货的顾客送去。

这意味着我回家要绕一大段路,于是我抬头对老板说:"你知道星期二我两点钟下班吗?"我还从没见过一个人像他当时一样吃惊。他气都喘不过来地说:"你这是什么意思?"我告诉他我的意思是像平常那样捎点吃的东西还可以,但送那只火腿,不行。

他望着我好像我是一种希奇古怪的小虫,然后暴跳如雷,破口大骂起来。但我决不让步。他拿我毫无办法,就采取新的策略。他对一个店员大喊道:"出去再找一个伙计来。"

老板转过身来用威胁的口吻问我:"你送还是不送?"我把说过的话再说了一遍。他吼道:"从这里滚出去。"我就走了出去。

这是第一次我和一个老板真正翻了脸。

③ 我最初听到这个故事是在印度,那里的人们讲起来像真有其事似的,尽管任何博物学家都会知道这不可能。后来我得知在第一次世界大战之前不久,有一家杂志也刊登过这个故事的一个版本。至于这个故事的来源和作者,我至今也未能查出来。

故事讲的国家是印度。有位殖民官员和他的夫人举行了一次盛大的宴会。他们和客人们一起坐在宽敞的饭厅里,有军官、政府官员和他们的夫人,还有一个来访的美国博物学家。饭厅地板是大理石的,未铺地毯。房顶椽子露在外面,宽大的玻璃门开向外面的游廊。

席间一位年轻的小姐和一位上校之间发生了一场热烈的争辩。小姐坚持认为现在的妇女已不再是一见到老鼠就吓得跳上椅子的那种时代的人了,而上校却说毫无变化。

上校说:"女人一遇到危急情况必然的反应就是尖叫起来。而男人也许会有同样的感觉,但比女人要多一点自我控制的力量,而多的这一点点就很重要。"

美国学者未参加争论而是注意观察其他客人。在他环顾四周时,他看见女主人的脸上显出一种奇怪的表情。她两眼直盯着前方,脸上的肌肉有点抽搐。她微微做了个手势,叫站在她背后的土著仆人附耳过来。她轻轻说了几句话。仆人睁大了眼睛,匆匆离去。

在座的客人中除了美国人外没有人注意到这件事,也未看见那个仆人把一碗牛奶就放在开着的门外的游廊上。

美国人猛然一惊,醒悟过来。在印度,碗里放牛奶只意味着一件事,引诱蛇。他意识到室内一定有条眼镜蛇。他抬头看看椽子,这是蛇最可能藏身的地方,但椽子光光地。房间的三个角落也都是空的,仆人们等在第四个角落里,准备上下一道菜。那末只剩下一个地方——桌子底下。

他的第一个冲动就是想往后一跳,并警告别人。但是他知道人们的慌乱会惊动眼镜蛇,它会咬人。他马上说起话来,声音非常引人注意,大家都冷静下来。

"我想知道在座的诸位有多少自制力。我数到三百,要用五分钟。大家谁都不许动一下。一动就罚五十卢比。准备好!"

他数数时全体二十人坐着像石像一样。他数到:"……二百八十……"就在这时,他的眼角瞄见一条眼镜蛇出来了,向那碗牛奶游了过去。他跳起来把游廊的门关好,室内一片尖叫声。

主人叹道:"上校,你的话真对!有个男人向我们大家表明他就是一个能完全控制自己的榜样。"

"等一下,"美国人转身对女主人说:"威妮斯夫人,你怎么知道那条眼镜蛇在室内的呢?"

女人的脸上露出一丝微笑。她回答说:"因为它正从我的脚上游过。"

④ 我出身于工人阶级。很早我就发现自己满怀热情、抱负和理想,而实现这一切成了我童年生活的问题。我的环境野蛮、粗暴而严酷。我没有别的前景,只有向上爬。我处在社会的底层。在这里,生活提供给人的只有肉体上和精神

上的贫瘠与不幸,因为在这里肉体和精神都同样遭受到饥饿与折磨。

我的头上高耸着宏伟的社会大厦。在我看来唯一的出路是向上爬。我早就决心爬进这个大厦。在上面,男人们穿着黑西装和挺刮的衬衫,女人们则穿着漂亮的衣裙。还有,他们吃得好,吃得丰盛。这些是肉体上的享受。更有精神上的享受。我知道在我上面有无私的精神、圣洁的思想和敏锐的智力。我知道这一切,因为我读过"海滨图书馆"的小说。在小说中,除了坏蛋和下流的女人外,所有的男人和女人都思想纯洁,谈吐优雅,举止端庄。总之,就像我深信旭日东升一样,我深信在我的上面一切都美好、高尚与潇洒,一切都会使生活变得规矩而庄严,一切都会让生活变得有价值,都会使人所遭受过的轻视与痛苦得到报偿。

但是从工人阶级的地位爬上去并不十分容易。如果一个人受到满脑子的理想和梦幻的妨碍,那就尤其不容易。我住在加利福尼亚州的一个牧场上,很难找到一个往上爬的梯子。我早就打听到了用钱投资的利率,我绞痛我的幼小脑袋来弄懂那个人类了不起的发明——复利的好处和优点。此外我还搞清楚了各种年岁工人通常的工资率和生活费用。从这些资料中我得出结论,如果我立刻开始一边工作一边存钱,到五十岁时我就可以不再工作,享受到相当大一份欢乐和美好。这是那时我社会地位提高了所该得到的。当然我下定决心不结婚,但我还是完全忘记考虑工人阶级世界中的那个危险的大灾难——生了病该怎么办。

⑤ 白宫的生活是活跃而紧张的。首先,这是一个城市的家,总会感到和听到外面往来的车辆和行人。有时也听到游行示威的声音。屋子里往往使人觉得似乎绝不会有什么真正的幽静。因为屋里的管理服务人员进进出出忙于工作,而地下室的厨房里总是乱哄哄地准备着川流不息的早餐、午饭、下午茶、招待会和正式宴会。

起初我们想减掉一些排场。我和帕特都认为应该减少到处簇拥着总统的管事人员和随从的数目。我叫霍尔德曼将两位整天当总统按摩师的海军医生辞退去做更有用的工作。原来有一种几乎令我难以置信的惯例:总统只要一出华盛顿,他的床就先用飞机从白宫运走,好让总统永远不必睡陌生的床。我立刻停止了这种做法。我说到戴维营或比斯坎岛去度周末,在那里工作,只要马诺洛,或许再加一个管事来照料我的衣食就行了。我们下令让两艘备总统专用的海军大游艇退出服役。我们也设法削减常跟随着我们的特工人员的数目和保安措施。

即使如此,白宫里的生活仍然使人有受禁锢之感,这使得我们于1969年夏天在圣克利门蒂以退休后买的房子更具有特别意义。这是一幢西班牙式的旧屋,坐落在一个直接俯视海滩的美丽的制高点上。不停的海浪声使它显得宁静,周围的棕榈树和桉树成了天然的屏障,散步时至少可以将我们部分地隐蔽起来。我们将房子取名为和平居。在隔壁的海岸警备队的站点里盖起了一小片办公室。这里就成了西部白宫。

由于距离远,我们一年只能去圣克利门蒂几次,更多地是到比斯坎岛或戴维营去度周末。从某些方面说,帕特管理着三处家,华盛顿、加利福尼亚和佛罗里达各一处。哪怕我们只在那里住几天,她也把每处都安排得成个家的样子。

二、描写文

① 他是一位身材矮小的人,头和身体相比显得太大——一位病态的小个子。他的神经不好。皮肤有病。穿的内衣若比丝绸粗糙就会引起疼痛。他满怀宏伟的幻想。

他是一个自负的怪物。看人或世界没有一刻不从自己出发。他把自己看成不仅是世界上最重要的人,而且在他自己的眼中他是有史以来唯一的一个。他认为自己是世界上最伟大的戏剧家,最伟大的思想家,最伟大的作曲家中的一个。听他说起话来,他就是莎士比亚、贝多芬和柏拉图并成一体。听他说话的机会常有,毫不困难。他是人世间最令人忍受不了的饶舌者。晚上和他在一起就意味着整晚听他独白。有时他颇有才气,有时却令人讨厌到了极点。但不论他是否才气横溢还是索然无味,他讲的唯一题目就是他自己。他怎么想,他怎么做。

他发疯地想永远正确。任何人哪怕在最无关紧要的地方露出一点点不同的看法,就足可使他高谈阔论好几个小时。他想方设法来证明自己正确,令人不堪忍受地滔滔不绝地说下去。最后,听他讲话的人变得目瞪口呆,耳朵都起茧了,为了息事宁人起见,只好表示同意。

② 座中有一个古怪的人,他的幽默使大家更加快乐不已。布雷斯柏里奇先

生总是对他用一种古老有趣的称呼,称他为西蒙少爷。他是一个穿着整洁、生性活泼、身材矮小的人,带着一副老单身汉的神气。他的鼻子弯得像鹦鹉的嘴,他的脸上有一些麻子,像秋天霜打的叶子一样带着永久不变的干枯的红色。他的眼神机敏活泼,含有一种极为动人的滑稽可笑与暗藏讥讽的表情。显然他是全家人的才子,专门和太太小姐们开狡诈的玩笑、含沙射影,讲些陈年老话让大家异常高兴。遗憾的是我不了解其家史,无法分享这一快乐。在晚餐过程中,似乎他的最大乐趣就是让坐在身边的年轻姑娘一直忍俊不禁,苦不堪言,不敢看坐在对面的母亲的责备目光。他的确是在座的年轻人崇拜的偶像,他说的每句话,做的每个动作,脸上的每一个表情都会让他们大笑不已。我丝毫不感到奇怪,因为他在他们眼中一定是个多才多艺、奇迹般的人物。

弗朗克·布雷斯柏里奇简短地对我讲了他的历史。他是一个老光棍,有一份不多的独立的收入,小心地使用足敷他的需要。他像一颗游移不定的彗星,沿着自己的轨道在家族的体系中转来转去,有时拜访这一支亲戚,有时又去看望更远的另一支。在英格兰,财产有限而亲戚却极多的绅士们常常就是这样生活。他生性活泼,爱讲爱唱,总是只顾当前的快活。由于他常常东奔西跑,和不同的人作伴,这使他避免了老光棍们受人十分无情指责的那些迂腐而不合人意的习惯。他是一部完整的家史,对布雷斯柏里奇全家的宗谱、历史和通婚状况都了如指掌,这使他受到老人们的宠爱。他向所有年长的太太和已过退休年龄的老处女们献殷勤,她们通常把他看成还是一个年轻的家伙。在孩子们中间他却是一个嬉闹的专家。因此在他活动的范围内,西蒙·布雷斯柏里奇先生是一位谁也比不上的最受欢迎的人。

③ 他将球轻轻滚过草地。小猫望着球,着了迷。它俯伏在草地上,伸长颈子,竖起耳朵,张大眼睛,摇着尾巴,紧张地期待着。然后它向球冲了过去,一到面前又弓着背向旁一跳,躲开球。它坐下来,开始用舌头从膝盖往下舔舔右小腿,似乎完全忘记了球。我的朋友自满地说:"喂,你觉得奥利弗·克伦威尔怎么样?他是不是妙极了?"我同意说是的。他的妻子打断了我们的话说:"看,看。"这时小猫又开始俯下身子准备再对球冲过去。她咯咯地笑着好像对自己说:"啊,他真是一个小宝贝!他真是一个小宝贝!"这一次小猫真地向球跳过去,用前爪抓住球,高高捧起,抱着球倒翻了一个跟头,在草地上打着滚,然后好像害怕起来,拼命地逃进花坛内六角星形的花圃中去,躲在草茎里,像一头

老虎藏在丛林里一样,向外张望着刚刚被它捕来的动物。

④ 当我们仍在很高的山上,还未开始下山向阿根梯尔走去之前,我们抬头向一个邻近的山头望去,看见几朵白云纤巧得几乎就像蜘蛛织成的网一样,四周晴光闪烁,七彩缤纷。淡红色调和淡绿色调特别美。没有一种颜色是深色的,全都是最淡的色度,令人赏心悦目地混合在一起。我们坐下来仔细观察和欣赏这一奇景。色彩保持了几分钟——飘忽,变化,相互融合,一下子几乎淡到消失不见的程度,接着又闪出光彩——一连串变化万端、飘忽不定的柔和的乳白色光芒映照着那薄膜似的白云,将其变成一幅足可以让天使披在身上的精美纱巾。

不一会,我们看出这些最优美的色彩及其不断的闪烁和变化让我们想到了什么。这正是人们从飘来飘去的肥皂泡上所看到的一切。它飘过物体时就反射出变化的色调。肥皂泡在质地上是最美丽最精致的东西。天空中那片可爱的幻影般的纱巾使人联想起肥皂泡在阳光下破裂后舒张开来的景象。

三、说明文

① 诗歌不言自明。而诗人,却很奇怪,并非如此。因此该是由别人出来为他们讲话的时候了,讲出他们在使用散文体时会说的话。也该是维护他们免遭那种无声责备的时候了。正因为这种责备是无声的,因而更令人无法辩解。大家责怪他们是一类特别的男女人物,不同于人类的其他人,才气横溢。即使我们认识他们,这种才气也会使人因感到太不可思议而无法与他们生活在一起,更不用说会让人感到太局促不安了。我愿意帮助他们摆脱这种令人感到不舒服的负担。诗人被人看成是一种受苦受难的人,但他们遭受的唯一痛苦是被人误解为天生怀有一套奇特思想和感情的人——特别是感情。这种天赋是一种浪漫式的天赋。现在先从历史上来看,这种误解就在于认为几百年来诗人是什么形象,那他就总是或必须总是这样的形象。大家都期待他是一个雪莱、济慈、拜伦、波、魏尔伦、斯温伯恩、道森。当然,也许他是这样的一个诗人,但他同时也会是世上的任何一种人。我对诗人的唯一看法为他是一个写诗的人。这听上去简单得荒唐可笑。但这个结论是经过对诗人所写的数不清的各种各样的诗的研究后才得出的,是经过对诗人显露出的令人困惑不解的各种各样气质的思考后才得出的。

② 我能看出音乐史上有三类不同的作曲家。每一类都用颇为不同的方式来构思音乐。

最激发公众想象力的是有自然灵感的作曲家——换句话说,即舒伯特这一类型。当然所有的作曲家都有灵感,但这类作曲家却有更加自然的灵感。音乐从他心中涌出。他在纸上写都写不及。从丰富的产量中几乎就可分辨出这类作曲家来。在某几个月中,舒伯特一天写一首歌。雨果·沃尔夫也一样。

贝多芬代表第二类——也许可称为构思类。这一类比其他类更能证实我有关音乐的创造过程的理论,因为这一类作曲家的确从一开始就有一个音乐主题。毫无疑问贝多芬的情况就是如此,因为我们有他写下这些主题的笔记本。从他的笔记本中我们可看出他是如何构筑主题的——如何一直等到尽可能地使其完美无缺后他才罢手。贝多芬决不是舒伯特那种意义上有自然灵感的作曲家。他是那类从主题开始的作曲家,使主题成为一个思想的胚胎,然后在其基础上日复一日辛劳地构筑一篇音乐作品。自贝多芬时代以来,大多数作曲家属于这第二类。

第三类作曲家由于缺乏更好的名称,姑且称之为传统型。像帕勒斯特雷纳和巴赫这样的人就属于这一类型。他们俩所代表的这一类作曲家都是在音乐史上某种音乐风格即将达到最高点的某个特殊时期出生的。问题是要在这样的时候用众所周知的被大家公认的方式来创造音乐,并且做得比前人更好。

③ 我吃过的苹果饼中也许数外婆做的最好。还是小姑娘的时候,我就常常看外婆做苹果饼,我对她稳健迅速的动作惊羡不已。外婆不需要食谱,而她的饼总是做得又甜又香,充满慈爱。我对做饼的外壳从来不太感兴趣,但当外婆拿出八个又大又红的苹果时,我的全部注意力都被她吸引住了。

削苹果是我的活,每个又圆又硬苹果的脆嫩的皮都被削成一个螺旋形的长条。同时外婆将我削好的苹果切成四瓣,挖去果心,开始切成薄片放进铺好饼的底壳的平底锅里。我常常偷一厚片好滋味的苹果塞进嘴里,而她装着未看见。

当两只平底锅都堆满苹果时,外婆就洒上许多桂皮末,再在上面撒一勺糖。然后在每块饼上点上一些小方块状的奶油,洒一、两撮磨碎的豆蔻和丁香,再滴上半个柠檬的果汁。

最后,外婆准备好,要把饼的面壳盖上去。她将擀好的面皮折成两半,轻轻放在饼上,再将折上的那一半摊开。然后我仔细地把多出的壳边修齐,在每块饼面上戳六个出汽孔。这时我总觉得很能干,很会做事。当我得意地把做好的饼交给外婆时,她笑容满面,把饼送进了375°的烤炉里。

廿分钟后,热腾腾的香味飘进了起居室,把我们都引向厨房。扑鼻的香味使我相信饼已烤好了,但外婆却说还要再等廿分钟。该是把这冒着热气的佳肴从烤炉里拿出来的时候了。我几乎等不及让饼凉下来。一口咬下去,我就像在天堂里一样,在那厨房里又甜又刺鼻的温暖气味中吃着,置身于幸福温馨之中。

④　也许你奇怪:为什么蜘蛛该是我们的朋友?因为蜘蛛消灭了大量昆虫,而昆虫里有一些是人类最大的敌人。昆虫会使我们无法在世上生活。如果不是有食虫动物的保护,昆虫会吞食掉我们所有的庄稼,杀死家禽和牲畜。我们大大受惠于吃虫的鸟类和兽类,然而他们加在一起杀死昆虫的数目只不过是蜘蛛消灭的一个零头。此外,与有些食虫动物不同,蜘蛛对我们人和财物毫无害处。

不像许多人所想的那样,蜘蛛并不是昆虫,甚至和昆虫一点关系也没有。其差别几乎一眼就可以看出,因为蜘蛛总有八只腿,而昆虫决不超过六只腿。

有多少蜘蛛替我们从事这项工作呢?一位研究蜘蛛的权威人士对英格兰南部草地上的蜘蛛作了一个统计。他估计每英亩超过2,250,000只。在一个足球场上不同种类的蜘蛛大约就有6,000,000只。蜘蛛至少有半年的时间忙于捕杀昆虫。无论作多高的估计,也无法猜到蜘蛛消灭掉多少昆虫。蜘蛛是一种饥饿型的动物,不满足于一天只吃三顿。据估计在英国,蜘蛛一年消灭昆虫的总重量超过了英国全体人口的总重量。

⑤　在当今世界上,为什么有关进步的观念显得如此重要呢？这当然是因为在我们周围实际上正在出现某种进步,而且变得越来越明显。虽然人类在智力与道德方面尚无总的改进,但在知识积累上却取得了惊人的进展。从个人的思想能通过言语传递给别人的时候起,知识就开始增长。随着书写的发明,更有长足的进步,因为这时知识不仅可以传递而且可以贮存。书库使得教育成为可能,反过来教育又扩大了书库:知识的增长在遵循着一种复利法则,并

由于印刷术的发明而大大提高了一步。但这一切都比较缓慢,直到科学的出现,速度才突然加快。知识开始按系统的计划进行积累。滴水变成小溪,小溪现在又变成巨流。此外,现在一获得新的知识,立刻就转入实用。所谓"现代文明",并不是人性各方面均衡发展的结果,而是应用于实际生活的知识积累而成。目前人类面临的问题是:该如何利用这一切知识?正如人们常常指出的那样,知识是一种既可用于善又可用于恶的双刃武器。现在它正被毫不在意地运用于这两个方面。例如还有什么景象比枪炮手们用科学来炸毁人体而另一方面近在咫尺的外科医生又用科学来治愈人体显得更严酷、更奇怪呢? 我们必须十分严肃地扪心自问:随着知识力量的不断增强,如果继续这样双重性地利用科学,会产生什么样的结果呢?

四、议论文

① 今天父母需为孩子们做的事比以往要少得多,家也更不大像一个作坊了。衣服可买现成的,洗涤可上洗衣店,食物可买熟食、罐头食品或腌渍制品,面包由面包店烤好送来,牛奶放在家门口台阶上,三餐可以上饭馆、工厂食堂或学校餐厅。

现在父亲在家里做手艺或其他活计已很罕见。孩子们即使有机会,也十分难得在工作地点看到他。因此男孩子已很少被培养来继承父业。在许多城镇里他们有相当广泛的择业余地,女孩子也一样。拿工资的年轻人往往挣到不少钱,很快就有了一种经济上的独立感。在纺织业地区,母亲外出做工早已成为习惯。这种做法已非常普遍,现在有工作的母亲在孩子的家庭生活中已成为并不罕见的因素。在近 25 年中已婚妇女的就业人数已翻了一倍以上。由于母亲赚钱和较大的孩子拿到相当多的工资的缘故,在本世纪初父亲还是一家之主,现在已很少这样。母亲有了工作,经济收入增加。但是如果母亲因工作在孩子们放学时不能在家里迎接他们,孩子们就失去了十分宝贵的东西。

② 几乎所有好莱坞影片都有一个特征,那就是内容空洞无物。这一点却被表面的感染力所弥补。这种感染力往往采取一种真正壮观的现实主义形式表现出来:在布景、服装、和一切表面的细节方面都不遗余力地使其正确无误。这些努力有助于掩盖人物塑造上空洞的实质以及情节上的荒唐浅薄。房子看起来像房子,街道看起来像街道,人看上去和讲起话来也像人。但他们缺乏人

性、可信性和行为动机。不消说,不光彩的审查法规是预先决定这些影片内容的重要因素。但这种审查法规并不妨碍利润,也不妨碍影片的娱乐价值。它起的作用只不过是使影片变得令人难以置信。这对电影业来说并不是一个承受不了的太重的负担。除了布景的感染力之外,还使用有时似乎具有魔力的摄影技巧。但是如果故事情节、对生活的描绘是空洞、愚蠢、陈腐和幼稚的,那末产生效果的所有这些技巧、努力、劲头对人又有什么意义呢。

③ 在工业化生活的组织过程中,工厂对工人的生理和心理状况的影响完全被忽视了。现代工业建立在以最低成本获得最高产量这一观念的基础之上,以便使个人或一群人尽可能多地赚钱。现代工业的发展完全不顾操纵机器的人的本性,也不考虑工厂强加于人的那种人为的生活方式对个人及其子孙后代的影响。大城市建立起来丝毫不管我们的利益。摩天大楼的形状和大小完全取决于每平方英尺地皮获得最大收入的需要和向房客提供他们喜爱的办公室和公寓房的需要。这就使高楼大厦总建在巨大人群拥挤不堪的地方。文明人喜欢这样一种生活方式。在他们享受住宅的舒适和庸俗的奢侈的时候,却未认识到他们已被剥夺了生活中不可缺少的东西。现代城市由庞然大物的高楼和黑暗狭窄的街道构成。街道上充满汽油的烟雾、煤灰和有毒的气体。出租车、卡车和公共汽车的噪声震耳欲聋,川流不息的巨大人群挤来挤去。显然现代城市的规划并非为了居民的利益。

④ 人们说体育运动在国家之间产生友善,还说如果全世界各国民众能在足球场或板球场上交锋,就会不愿在战场上兵戎相见了。每当我听见这种议论时,我总感到惊诧。即使没有具体例证(如1936年的奥林匹克运动会)说明国际体育比赛导致了深仇大恨,人们也可以从常理推断出这一点。

当今人们从事的所有运动几乎都是竞争性的。参加比赛就是为了取胜。除非全力以赴去争取胜利,否则比赛就没有意义。在乡村的草地上,你随便选择哪一边,不夹杂地方主义的情绪,才有可能仅仅为娱乐和锻炼来打球。但一旦牵涉到声誉问题,一旦你感到输了后你和某个稍大一点的单位就会蒙羞时,就会激起最野蛮的好斗的本能。参加过哪怕是学校足球赛的人都知道这一点。国际级的比赛简直就是一场模拟战争。但重要的不是运动员的行为,而是观众的态度和其背后的国家的态度。他们为这些荒唐的比赛激动得发狂,并认真地相信——至少在短期内如此——跑、跳、踢球是对国民优秀品质的考验。

⑤ 为散步而散步也许正像那些付诸实行的人所认为的那样是一件值得高度赞扬和应该效法的事。我反对的理由是它阻碍了大脑的活动。许多人对我声称当他沿着公路漫步或翻山越岭时,头脑从来没有这样灵活过。在我的记忆中任何一个星期天早晨非要我和他一起散步的人都未能证实过这种大话。经验告诉我,一个同伴无论他坐在椅子上或站在壁炉前的地毯上多么能说会道,领人一起出去散步时,这种本事就马上消失殆尽。在房间里快如云涌的思绪现在哪里去了?他那轻松自在的满腹经纶哪里去了?他那对任何开始讨论的问题快如夏日闪电一样点燃的想象力又到哪里去了?他表情丰富的脸现在变得木然呆板,明亮的眼睛也失去了光泽。他说甲(我们的东道主)是个十足的大好人。往前走50码,他又说甲是他见过的最好人中的一个。再走约200米,他说甲太太是个可爱的女人。一会儿他又说她是他认识的最可爱的女人中的一个。我们走过一个小酒馆,他无精打采地向我大声念道:"王徽酒馆。特许卖酒。"我料到再往前走他看见什么字牌就会念什么。我们走过一个里程碑,他用手杖指着说:"厄克斯明斯特,11英里。"我们在山脚下拐了个急弯。他指着墙说:"车辆慢行。"我远远看见公路边对面树篱上有一小块布告牌。他也看见了。他两眼盯着看,接着读道:"闲人莫入,违者必究。"可怜的人——神经都出毛病了。

第三节 小 说

① 在我的记忆里,安妮·曼斯菲尔德·沙利文老师来的那一天,是我一生中最重要的日子。从这一天开始,我的生活和以前迥然不同,一想到这一点,我就感到非常兴奋。这个重要的日子是1887年3月3日,我差三个月满七周岁。

那天下午,我一声不响,怀着期待的心情站在门廊里。母亲给我打着手势,人们在屋里匆匆地走来走去,我模模糊糊地预感到一件不寻常的事就要发生了。于是我就走到门口,站在台阶上等着。午后的阳光透过门廊上覆盖着的厚厚的一层忍冬,照在我微微仰着的脸上。我几乎是无意识地用手抚摸着我所熟悉的叶片和花朵,这新长的叶片和刚开的花朵在南方迎来了芬芳的春天。但不知今后等待着我是什么,会使我欣喜,还是惊骇。几个星期以来,我又气又恨,感到非常苦恼,这种感情上的激烈斗争过去之后,我感到浑身无力。

(吕叔湘　译)

② 　有一次,他们寂静无声地在炉前坐了很长时间。董贝先生偶尔看了看孩子的眼睛,看到熊熊火光在孩子眼里闪耀,犹如珍珠玛瑙一样,这才知道孩子并没有睡去。这时,孩子用这样的话打破沉默:

"爸爸,钱是什么东西?"

董贝先生感到左右为难。他本想对他解释一下什么是流通媒介、通货、通货贬值、纸币、金条、兑换率,贵重金属的市场价值等等;但是,他向小椅望去,知道其间有十万八千里的距离,这才说:"钱就是金币、银币、铜币、机尼、先令、半便士。这些东西你都见过。"

"嗨、这些东西我都见过,"保罗说:"我不是说这个,爸爸。我是说钱到底是什么?"

……

"钱到底是什么!"董贝先生一面说,一面把椅子向后移动一下,这样,他就可以更加仔细地打量一下这个傲气十足的芝麻大的小人。他感到十分惊奇。这个小人竟然向他提出这样一个问题。

③ 　这些狗、马和他哥儿俩之间,仿佛存在着一种血统关系,比他们的交情还要来得深。它们同样是身体健康、无思无虑的年轻动物,也同样的飞龙活跳,兴高采烈。他哥儿俩跟他们所骑的马同样的玩皮,不但玩皮而且恶作剧,可是谁要摸着他们的顺毛,他们却又脾气好得很。

(傅东华　译)

④ 　到了演出那个晚上,当我登上后台,心里还感到紧张。距离演出还有几分钟时,老师朝我走了过来。"你母亲让我把这个交给你,"说着话她递过来一朵蒲公英。那花儿四周已开始打蔫,花瓣儿从梗上向下有气无力地耷拉着。可是,只要看一眼,知道母亲就在外面呆着,回想起和母亲午饭时说的那些话,我就感到胸有成竹。

演出结束后,我把塞在演出服围裙里的那朵蒲公英拿回了家。母亲把花接了过去,用两张纸巾将它压平,夹在了一本字典里。她一边忙碌着,一边笑,想到也许只有我们俩会珍藏这么一朵打了蔫的野草花。

(姜建华 译)

第四节 戏 剧

①

鲍西娅扮律师上。

公爵: 把你的手给我。足下是从培拉里奥老前辈那儿来的吗?

鲍西娅:正是,殿下。

公爵:欢迎欢迎;请上坐。您有没有明了今天我们在这儿审理的这件案子的两方面的争点?

鲍西娅:我对于这件案子的详细情形已经完全知道了。这儿哪一个是那商人,哪一个是犹太人?

公爵:安东尼奥,夏洛克,你们两人都上来。

鲍西娅:你的名字就叫夏洛克吗?

夏洛克:夏洛克是我的名字。

鲍西娅:你这场官司打得倒也奇怪,可是按照威尼斯的法律,你的控诉是可以成立的。(向安东尼奥)你的生死现在操在他的手里,是不是?

安东尼奥:他是这样说的。

鲍西娅:你承认这借约吗?

安东尼奥:我承认

鲍西娅:那么犹太人应该慈悲一点。

夏洛克:为什么我应该慈悲一点?把您的理由告诉我。

鲍西娅:慈悲不是出于勉强,它是像甘霖一样从天上降下尘世;它不但给幸福予受施的人,也同样给幸福予施与的人;它有超乎一切的无上威力,比皇冠更足以显出一个帝王的高贵:御杖不过象征着俗世的威权,使人民对于君上的尊严凛然生畏;慈悲的力量却高出于权力之上,它深藏在帝王的内心,是一种属于上帝的德性,执法的人倘能把慈悲调剂着公道,人间的权力就和上帝的神力没有差别。所以,犹太人,虽然你所要求的是公道,可是请你想一想,要是真的按照公道执行起赏罚来,谁也没有死后得救的希望;我们既然祈祷着上帝的慈悲,就应该按照祈祷的指点,自己做一些慈悲的事。我说了这一番话,为的是希望你能够从你的法律的立场作几分让步;可是如果你坚持着原来的要求,那么威尼斯的法庭是执法无私的,只好把那商人宣判定罪了。

夏洛克:我自己做的事,我自己当!我只要求法律允许我照约执行处罚。

鲍西娅:他是不是无力偿还这笔借款?

巴萨尼奥:不,我愿意替他当庭还清;照原数加倍也可以;要是这样他还不满足,那么我愿意签署契约,还他十倍的数目,拿我的手、我的头、我的心做抵押;要是这样还不能使他满足,那就是存心害人,不顾天理了。请堂上运用权力,把法律稍为变通一下,犯一次小小的错误,干一件大大的功德,别让这个残忍的恶魔逞他杀人的兽欲。

鲍西娅:那可不行,在威尼斯谁也没有权力变更既成的法律;要是开了这一个恶例,以后谁都可以借口有例可援,什么坏事情都可以干了。这是不行的。

夏洛克:一个但尼尔来做法官了!真的是但尼尔再世!聪明的青年法官啊,我真佩服你!

鲍西娅:请你让我瞧一瞧那借约!

夏洛克:在这儿,可尊敬的博士;请看吧。

鲍西娅:夏洛克,他们愿意出三倍的钱还你呢。

夏洛克:不行,不行,我已经对天发过誓啦,难道我可以让我的灵魂背上毁誓的罪名?不,把整个儿的威尼斯给我,我都不能答应。

鲍西娅:好,那么就应该照约处罚;根据法律,这犹太人有权要求从这商人的胸口割下一磅肉来。还是慈悲一点,把三倍原数的钱拿去,让我撕了这张约吧。

夏洛克:等他按照约中所载条款受罚以后,再撕不迟。你瞧上去像是一个很好的法官;您懂得法律,您讲的话也很有道理,不愧是法律界的中流砥柱,所以现在我就用法律的名义,请您立刻进行宣判,凭着我的灵魂起誓,谁也不能用他的口舌改变我的决心。我现在但等着执行原约。

(朱生豪 译)

②

杰克:费尔法克斯小姐,今天天气真好。

格温多琳：人们一和我谈天气，我总是感到他们一定有别的什么意思，这让我很紧张。

杰克：我的确有别的意思。

格温多琳：我想是这样。事实上我从不会弄错的。

杰克：请让我趁布雷克耐尔夫人暂时不在场……

格温多琳：我当然劝你这样做。妈妈一向有突然回到房间里来的毛病，我常常不得不说她。

杰克（紧张地）：费尔法克斯小姐，自从我遇见您以来，我对您的爱慕……自从我遇见您以来……胜过我所遇见过的任何姑娘。

格温多琳：是的，我很了解这一点。我常常希望无论如何你能更公开地表白出来就好了。你对我一直都有一种无法抗拒的吸引力。甚至在我遇见你以前，我对你就相当关注了。（杰克惊奇地望着她。）我希望你知道，沃辛先生，我们生活在一个理想的时代。这一点在比较昂贵的月刊上经常提到，而且据我所知，连乡村教堂的布道中也说到它。我的理想一直是去爱一个名叫埃尼斯特的人。在这个名字里有一种激起人绝对信任的东西。从第一次阿尔杰农向我提起他有一个叫埃尼斯特的朋友那一刻起，我就知道命中注定我要爱你

杰克：你真的爱我，格温多琳？

格温多琳：热烈极了！

杰克：亲爱的！你不知道你让我多么快乐。

格温多琳：我的亲埃尼斯特！

杰克：不过你该不是真地想说如果我的名字不叫埃尼斯特，你就不可能爱我吧？

格温多琳：但你的名字就叫埃尼斯特。

杰克：对，我知道是这样。不过假设是叫别的什么名字呢？那么你是不是说就不可能爱我？

格温多琳（油滑地）：嗳！这明明是一种玄而又玄的空想，就像大多数玄而又玄的空想一样，和我们所知道的现实生活的实际毫不相干。

杰克：亲爱的，坦白地说，我个人并不太在乎埃尼斯特这个名字……我觉得这个名字根本不适合我。

格温多琳：适合极了。这是个绝妙的名字。它有自己的音乐感。它产生强烈

节奏。
杰克：噢,真的,格温多琳,我得说我想还有许多别的好得多的名字。例如我以为杰克就是个动人的名字。
格温多琳：杰克?……不,杰克这个名字要是真地还有点音乐感的话,那也是微乎其微的。它不令人激动。它绝对产生不出节奏感。……我认识好几个杰克,而他们毫无例外往往全都很平常。此外,杰克是一个大家都知道在家里叫的名字,用来代替约翰。任何女人嫁给一个名叫约翰的男人,我就可怜她。她可能再也领略不到哪怕是一会功夫清静的迷人乐趣了。唯一真正保险的名字还是埃尼斯特。

③
希金斯：回到正题上来。你打算付给我多少学费?
莉莎：啊,我知道该给多少。我的一个朋友是位小姐,跟一位真正的法国先生学法语,一个钟头十八便士。喂,你总不好意思教我本国语也要像教法语一样多的钱吧。所以我给你最多一先令。要就要,不要就拉倒。
希金斯：(在房间里走来走去,一边手在口袋里把钥匙和钱弄得哗哗直响)皮克林,你知道,如果不把一个先令只简单地看成一先令,而是按这位姑娘收入的百分比来算,那就完全等于一个百万富翁的六十或七十个金币。
皮克林：怎么会呢?
希金斯：算一下。百万富翁一天赚一百五十镑。她只赚半个克朗。
莉莎：(骄傲地)谁告诉你我只赚——
希金斯：(接着说)她交给我每天收入的五分之二作学费。百万富翁一天收入的五分之二大约是六十镑。真不错,的确是一大笔钱!这是我有生以来向我出价最高的一次。
莉莎：(吓得站了起来)六十镑!你在说什么?我根本没有出六十镑。我哪儿去弄——
希金斯：住口。
莉莎：(哭出来)可我没有六十镑。啊——
珀尔丝太太：别哭,你这个傻姑娘。坐下来。没有人碰你的钱。
希金斯：要是你再哭的话,倒是有人要用扫帚棍来碰你了。坐下。
莉莎：(慢慢坐了下来)哎—哎—哎—啊—呜—呜。人家会以为你是我的老子呢。

希金斯：如果我决定教你，我比你两个老子都更厉害。拿去！（他递给她自己的丝手帕。）

莉莎：做什么？

希金斯：揩眼睛。把你脸上潮的地方都揩干。记住：那是你的袖子。要是你想在店里当小姐的话，就不要把袖子当手帕用。（莉莎完全迷糊了，不知所措地望着他。）

珀尔丝太太：对她说这种话没有用，希金斯先生，她不懂你的意思。而且，你错了，她根本不会那样做。（她把手帕拿过来。）

莉莎：（夺过手帕）喂！你把那块手帕给我。他是给我的，又不是给你。

④

（探长望着伯林，伯林现在注意到他。）

探长：我想您现在记起伊娃·史密斯了。对吗，伯林先生？

伯林：对，我记起来了。她是我的一个雇工，后来我把她解雇了。

埃里克：这是不是她自杀的缘故？什么时候解雇的，爸爸？

伯林：别说话，埃里克，别激动。这位姑娘离开已快两年了。让我想想——一定是在1910年初秋的时候。

探长：对。1910年9月底。

伯林：那就对了。

杰拉尔德：喂，先生。你不想让我走开吗？

伯林：杰拉尔德，你留在这里我不介意。我相信你也不会反对，是吗，探长？也许我应该先介绍一下，这是杰拉尔德·克罗夫特先生——乔治·克罗夫特先生的儿子——你知道，克罗夫特有限公司。

探长：杰拉尔德·克罗夫特先生，呃？

伯林：是的。碰巧我们在小小地庆祝他和我女儿希拉的订婚。

探长：我明白了。克罗夫特先生要和希拉·伯林小姐结婚？

杰拉尔德（微笑着）：我希望如此。

探长（严肃地）：那末我希望你留下。

杰拉尔德（惊奇地）：啊——好吧。

伯从（有些不耐烦）：喂——这件事没有什么神秘——或者可耻的——至少

我这样看。这是一件完全明明白白的事,发生在超过一年半以前——快两年以前——显然和这位可怜姑娘的自杀毫无关系。对吗,探长?

探长:不对,先生。我不能同意你的看法。

伯林:为什么不同意?

探长:因为她那时出的事也许会决定她后来出的事,而后来出的事也许会逼她自杀。事情是有关联的。

伯大:啊,这样说很妙,你说得有点道理。但仍然我不负任何责任。如果我们对每个和我们有关的人出的每件事全负责任,那就很难办了,不是吗?

探长:很难办。

伯林:我们大家都会处于不可想象的境地,不是吗?

埃里克:天哪,是这样。正像你说的,爸爸,人要照顾好自己——

伯林:对,不过我们不必再说这些。

探长:说什么?

伯林:啊——就在你来之前——我在给这些年轻人一点小小的忠告。现在——还是谈这位伊娃·史密斯姑娘。现在我很清楚地记得她了。她是一个活泼漂亮的姑娘——我猜在乡下长大的——她曾在我们的一个金工车间干了一年多的活。是个好工人。事实上车间的工头告诉我他准备提升她当一个我们叫作领班工——一小组女工的头头。但是那年八月他们放假回来以后,大家都有些不安稳,他们突然决定要求加工资。他们的平均工资是二十二先令六便士,不多不少,恰好是我们这一行的一般工资。他们想提高工资率,拿到平均每周二十五先令。我当然拒绝了。

探长:为什么?

伯林(吃惊地):你是说"为什么"吗?

探长:是的。你为什么拒绝?

伯从:好吧,探长,我看不出我怎样管我的事与你有什么关系。有关系吗?

探长:你知道也许有。

伯林:我不喜欢这种调门。

探长:很抱歉。不过你向我提了个问题。

伯林:在这之前你也问我一个问题,也是一个完全多余的问题。

探长:提问题是我的职责。

伯林：好吧，压低劳动成本也是我的职责。如果我同意这种新工资率的要求，我们就得增加大约百分之十二的劳动成本。这你满意了吗？所以我拒绝了。我说我无法考虑。我们按通常的工资率付钱，如果他们不喜欢这种工资率，他们可以离开，到别的地方去干活。我对他们说这是一个自由的国家。

埃里克：如果你无法离开到别的地方去干活，它就不自由了。

探长：是这样。

伯林（对埃里克说）：喂——你别插嘴。出这件事的时候你还未在工厂里工作。于是他们罢工了。当然时间不长。

杰拉尔德：如果刚好是在放假以后，时间长不了。他们连一分钱也都剩不下——我了解他们。

伯林：对，杰拉尔德。他们大多是这样。一、两个星期后罢工也完了。真可怜。好吧，我们让他们全回来了——仍旧是原来工资——领头罢工的四、五个头头除外。我亲自去了，叫他们离开。这位姑娘，伊娃·史密斯也是其中的一个。她话说得不少——太多了——所以她得走。

⑤

艾莉森：你干得不错吧？

海伦娜：当然。你知道上星期大多数顿饭都是我做的。

艾莉森：对，是你做的。有个人帮忙真不错。我指有另外一个女人。

海伦娜：（穿过左侧）我喜欢做饭。不过每次要用水的时候都要到浴室去打，我再也不会习惯的。

艾莉森：原始，对不对？

海伦娜：对，是有些原始。（她开始把碧绿的生菜撕开放在她从碗橱里拿出的四个盘子上）照顾一个人就真够忙了，照顾两个人可是件大事。

艾莉森：啊，克里弗多少会照顾他自己。其实他帮我不少忙。

海伦娜：我可没看见。

艾莉森：我猜你反倒自己在干。

海伦娜：我知道。

艾莉森：不过你很容易就适应了。

海伦娜：为什么我不该这样呢？

艾莉森：这可不完全是你所习惯的一套，对吗？

海伦娜:你习惯吗?

艾莉森:现在这里一切似乎都很不同了——有你在这里。

海伦娜:是吗?

艾莉森:是的,以前我靠自己——

海伦娜:现在你有了我。你叫我留下不后悔吧?

艾莉森:当然不。你已经告诉他茶好了吗?

海伦娜:我用劲敲克里弗的房门,又大声喊叫。他不回答,但他一定听见了。我不知道克里弗在哪里。

艾莉森:(向后靠在椅子上)我以为洗过澡后会凉爽一些,可我又已经感到热了。上帝啊,我希望他丢失掉那个讨厌的喇叭就好了。

海伦娜:我猜那是吹给我听的。

艾莉森:德拉蕾小姐很快会要我们走的,我知道这一点。谢天谢地,她不在家。你听他吹的。

海伦娜:他喝酒吗?

艾莉森:喝酒?(有些吃惊)如果你是说他是个酒鬼,那倒不是。(她们俩都停下来听喇叭声)马上他会让全街其余的人都来使劲敲门的。

海伦娜:(沉思着)几乎就像他想用它来杀人一样。特别是杀我。我以前从来未看见过在人的眼睛里有这样的仇恨。真有点可怕。可怕,(走到碗橱去拿西红柿、甜菜根和黄瓜)又奇怪地让人激动。

第五节　　诗　歌

① 　　　　榜　样

这儿是一只蝴蝶
做出的榜样;
它栖息在岩石上
仍快乐如常——
岩石上缺香少蜜,
它一任清寂。

任凭我的床坚硬,
我不再关切;

我要让我的欢乐,
像这小蝴蝶;
它快乐的心能把
石头变成花。

(黄杲 译)

② 安 魂 曲

轻轻地走,她就在近旁,
在雪的下面;
轻轻地说,雏菊的生长,
她能够听见。

她的头发虽一片金黄,
已变得黯淡;
她呀,虽然年轻又漂亮,
却一去不返。

她像洁白如雪的百合,
甜美地成长;
她还不清楚她已是个
成年好姑娘。

石板沉重地压在她身上——
还有那棺板;
我独自感到心里哀伤,
她已经长眠。

她已经安息,已听不到
竖琴和诗句;
我的一生已在此埋掉——
请把土堆起。

(黄杲 译)

③ **挽　　歌**

在宽广高朗的星空下，
挖一个墓坑让我躺下。
我生也欢乐死也欢洽，
　　躺下的时候有个遗愿。

几行诗句请替我刻上：
他躺在他想望的地方——
出海的水手已返故乡，
　　上山的猎人已回家园。

④　　这是一年的春季

　　这是一年的春季，
　　　这是一天的早上；
　　　　这是早晨七点钟；
　　　　　山坡上缀满露珠；

云雀在振翅扑翼；
　蜗牛爬到荆棘上；
　　上帝在他的天庭——
　　　多好哇世上万物！
　　　　　　　（黄杲 译）

⑤　失伴鸟伤其偶

失伴鸟伤其偶，
愁栖寒冬枝头；
头上夹雪风吹，
脚下带冰溪流。

空林黄叶飘尽，
大地百花都休；
周天寂静一片，

唯有水轮啁啾。

（黄杲 译）

⑥ 　　　爱情的奥秘
千万别想把爱情倾诉，
　　爱情只能深藏在心里；
因为，那柔风的吹拂
　　无声无息，无形无迹。

我把我的爱告诉了她，
　　把整个心迹向她表白；
我颤抖、冰冷、害怕，
　　可她呀，她竟然走开！

她刚刚从我这儿离去，
　　一位过路人经过身旁；
无声无息又无形无迹——
　　他一声叹息把她带上。

（黄杲 译）

⑦ 　　　箭与歌

射箭入云空，
落地无处寻；
转眼即飞逝，
目力难随行。

高歌入云空，
落地无处寻
目力再敏锐，
焉能追歌影？

后见橡树上，

箭身完无损；
歌声始至终，
永驻友心中。

⑧　　　　　雪夜驻步林边

我想我认识这是谁家的树林。
他的房屋却坐落在远村，
他不会看见我在此处停下，
欣赏他那片银装素裹的树林。

我的小马一定感到十分惊异，
为何停留在树林和结冰的湖间，
左近并没有一座农家的房舍，
在这一年中最黑暗的深夜。

小马摇动了一下套上的铜铃，
询问我是否弄错了地点和时间，
周围再没有别的声息和响动，
只有微风吹拂和雪花飘飞。

树林显得美丽、阴暗而深沉，
但我却有许多约会要履行，
安息之前还要走长长的路程，
安息之前还要走长长的路程。

英语教材系列

新世纪博士生综合英语	19.00元
新世纪英语专业听力教程 1	17.00元
新世纪英语专业听力教程 2	16.00元
新世纪英语专业听力教程 3	13.00元
新世纪英语专业听力教程 4	（估）15.00元
英语学习背景知识：美国加拿大	17.00元
英语学习背景知识：英国澳大利亚	10.00元
英语学习背景知识：欧洲国家	（估）15.00元
高级英文写作教程：实用写作	13.00元
高级英文写作教程：论文写作	17.00元
英汉文体翻译教程	26.00元
美国法治面面观	20.00元
美国重要历史文献导读	18.00元
电影视听英语教程	15.00元
英语专业八级阅读与词汇教程	25.00元